Quaid-e-Azam Muhammad Ali Jinnah

The man behind the curtain

Quaid-e-Azam Muhammad Ali Jinnah

The man behind the curtain

A biographical novel based on life of the man who reshaped the map of the India

Dinkar Joshi

Author of a trend setting novel "Mahatma Vs Gandhi"

PENTAGON PRESS

Quaid-e-Azam Muhammad Ali Jinnah: The man behind the curtain / **Dinkar Joshi**

First Published in 2012

Translated from original Gujrati to English by Dr G Ramachandram

Published by
PENTAGON PRESS
206, Peacock Lane, Shahpur Jat, New Delhi-110049
Phones: 011-64706243, 26491568
Telefax: 011-26490600
email: rajan@pentagonpress.in
website: www.pentagonpress.in

Cataloging in Publication Data—DK
Courtesy: D.K. Agencies (P) Ltd. <docinfo@dkagencies.com>

Joshī, Dinakara.
Quaid-e-Azam Muhammad Ali Jinnah : the man behind the curtain : a biographical novel based on life of the man who reshaped the map of the India / Dinkar Joshi ; [translated from original Gujarati to English by G. Ramachandram].
p. cm.
Translated from Gujarati.
Includes bibliographical references (p.).
ISBN 9788182745926

1. Jinnah, Mahomed Ali, 1876-1948—Fiction. 2. Biographical fiction. 3. Historical fiction, Gujarati—Translations into English. 4. India—History—Fiction. I. Ramachandram, G. II. Title.

DDC 891.473 23

Typeset in Garamond 11pt by The Laser Printers

Printed at Aegean Offset Printers, Greater Noida.

Dedication

In memory of those hundreds of unknown
Innocent, restless souls who were the victims
of riots during the painful partition

Preface
From Facts to Truth

Story Behind

My novel *Prakashno Padchhayo* (in Gujarati) was first published in 1988 (English version 'Mahatma Vs Gandhi'). In the preface to the Novel, I said as a matter of fact that "Gandhi in his life, could never make two persons understand him—his eldest son Harilal and Quaid-e-Azam Muhammad Ali Jinnha." Subsequently, when the novel generated a serious debate, a well meaning friend said to me, "You told us in your novel why Gandhiji could not make to understand Harilal. Now you write why Gandhiji could not make Muhammad Ali Jinnah to understand him." That was an interesting propostion, but I could not give it a serious thought at that time. I retired from the service in 1996. At the farewell function, the same friend again reminded, "When are you presenting us the real picture of Jinnah?"

We will not find any other person as controversial as Jinnah. In India, Jinnah is regarded as a villain and looked down upon with utter contempt and rejection. But in neighbouring Pakistan, which was a part of India, he is the father of the nation–*Baba-e-Millat.*

[Inititially, for a few years, Jinnah's sister Fatima was regarded as the *Mother-e-Millat* in Pakistan. There was a tradition in India, for some years, of regarding Kasturba as the mother of the nation, but there was no such tradition in Pakistan of regarding Jinnah's sister as the mother of the nation. Yet, Pakistan accepted Jinnah as the father of the nation and his sister as the mother of the nation. However, as a quirk of fate, Fatima, treated with respect as the mother of Pakistan, had contested the elections in 1966 against Ayub Khan and suffered a humiliating defeat.]

In the history of the Indian subcontinent, the place occupied by Emperor Ashoka, Chandragupta Maurya, Prithviraj Chauhan, Babar, Akbar, Robert Clive and Warren Hastings is what occupied by Mahatma Gandhi and Muhammad Ali Jinnah in 20th century. India's last Viceroy Lord Mountbatten called Mahatma Gandhi 'one man army' of the subcontinent. In the same way, we can call Jinnah 'one man army' responsible for the creation of Pakistan and for the massacre of lakhs of innocent people consequently. Historically, Jinnah can never be called a visionary of Pakistan, though he had created it. None of his Muslim colleagues could come anywhere close to his stature. Very few of his followers could even understand what Pakistan meant. Jinnah boasted, "I gained Pakistan with the help of only one clerk and one typewriter." Nevertheless, the historians think that Jinnah is the most accepted name after Aurangzeb among the Muslims of the Indian subcontinent.

Life Story

Gandhi and Jinnah belonged to the same region. Their hometowns in the Saurashtra region of Gujarat were close to each other. Though Gandhiji was born in Porbandar, he was brought up and educated in Rajkot. Jinnah's father lived in Paneli, 120 km from Rajkot, till his teenage. Jinnah's grandfather Punjabhai Thakkar, a Lohana of the Vaishanav sect, had converted to Islam and became an Ismaili Khoja. His youngest son Zinia migrated to Karachi to make a living. Zinia became Zinabhai who had seven children—Muhammad Ali alias Maamad being the eldest son.

Muhammad Ali Jinnah's life and work are not a distant history. For writing this novel, I had met the people who had personally interacted with Jinnah. I have more often felt, while checking the references on Jinnah's life and works that we all look at history and events from our own perspectives. Jinnah's ancestral home was at Paneli. People in this village saw Jinnah visiting this village school. Jinnah wrote in the school register, "I am very happy to come to my ancestors' village."

Stanley Wolpert, whose biography *Jinnah of Pakistan* is considered an authentic work on Jinnah, says that Jinnah's ancestors had come to India from Iran. They were among those thousands of Khojas who migrated to India between 10th and 16th centuries due to the atrocities unleashed by the Shah of Iran. According to Wolpert, the word 'jina' is derived from an Arabic word which means the 'wing of a bird'. But in Gujarati 'jina' means 'thin'. When the teenage Zinia went to Karachi, he was so slim that everybody used to call him 'Zinabhai' which gradually became Jinnah. Perhaps Wolpert was either not aware of this background of Jinnah or deliberately wanted to project him as a Muslim whose origin was in Iran. The people who read his biography would never come to know that Jinnah ails from the village Paneli and that his father was a convert. It is even claimed that Jinnah hailed from Bharapar village in Kutch and not of

Paneli. The plaque on Jinnah's tomb in Karachi written in Urdu and English says that Jinnah was the inhabitant of Bharapar in Kutch (*Kutchmitra Asmita 1996, page 273*).

Stanley Wolpert also wrote that, according to Jinnah's sister Fatima, Jiinnah at the time of his first marriage to a fourteen year old girl Amibai, was sixteen and how the groom and the bride looked like in marriage costumes. But the fact is that immediately after the marriage, Jinnah went to London. He went to London in January, 1893, whereas Fatima was born in July,1893. So how could she have witnessed Jinnah's wedding?

Hector Bolitho in his book *Jinnah: Creator of Pakistan* said that Jinnah's family was poor and eked out a living with great difficulty. Stanley Wolpert presents altogether a different picture. He says that Zinabhai owned numerous horses, had a flourishing business, besides being a money lender.

Fatima wrote that Jinnah had not even passed the matriculation. This is confirmed by Jinnah's Private Secretary K.H. Khurshid—who was subsequently Pakistan's High Commissioner to India—in his book *Memoires of Jinnah*. Walport wrote that Jinnah went to London from Karachi to work in a foreign firm. According to Hector Bolitho and Matlubul Saiyad, Jinnah went to London to study law after completing his education in Karachi.

There are many such contradictions in the writings of Jinnah's biographers. I do not wish to narrate all of them here. I chose to narrate only a few instances to show that not only the past events that we call history, but even the contemporary events are doctored according to our prejudices and likes and dislikes to write history. In reality, how the historical events are narrated depends upon the writer's knowledge and his understanding. That is why; the people find it difficult to digest distorted history. Keeping this in mind, I have raised the objections in detail. While writing this novel, I have accepted what I considered to be genuine, considering the overall personality of Muhammad Ali Jinnah—the hero of the novel.

This is a novel. Unfortunately, there is not much about family or personal life of the hero of the novel to draw from. In Jinnah's life only professional and political activities were important. Even in this, he gave more prominence to his political activity. When this novel is written based on the life of Jinnah, it is but natural that his personal life overshadows the contemporary politics and history. That is why, the events between 1857 and 1948 were considered. To avoid imaginary narration of events, it is important to rely only on historical events. Therefore, it has become inevitable to give this novel a shape of history as well. If anyone tries to evaluate this work purely from the yardstick of a novel, he will find a lot of discrepancies.

It is a terrible tragedy of history that Jinnah, a staunch nationalist, had become instrumental for creating bitter feelings of animosity, hatred and enmity between the Hindus and the Muslims during the last phase of his political innings. It is ironical that when he succeeded in securing Pakistan for the Muslims, he proclaimed that Pakistan would remain a secular state, that people professing different faiths—Hinduism, Islam, Sikhism or Christianity—would be equal citizens of Pakistan. Jinnah's struggle for Pakistan lasted just seven years—1940 to 1947. In the world history, there is no parallel of any single individual achieving so much in such a short span. Jinnah, who once dismissed the very thought of creation of Pakistan as a 'joke of a student' and a figment of 'imagination of a poet', became its first Governor-General and Pakistan emerged as the most populous Muslim nation in the world.

It is unfortunate that such a big event is not viewed from a historical perspective. Whatever suits us we accept as reality and try to prove it right. The rulers, the historians and those who call themselves intellectuals camouflage history to serve their own purpose. Aurangzeb, who was regarded until recently as an extremely intolerant, harsh ruler, adversary of the non-Muslims and destroyer of the Hindu temples, who suppressed all forms of arts, is now being described in many books and articles as a very good-natured and pious person, who lived a life of austerity by making copies of the Quran and was benefactor to Hindu temples as well. All this is true but along with all these they write nothing about his religious intolerance and remain absolutely silent about the many acts of cruelty committed by him and then they ask as to how the factuality Aurangzeb's life is historically wrong. The only possible answer to this query could be that the fact is not wrong but the aim is. The intention is not noble and the target is elsewhere.

It is natural that when we write about Jinnah and the most crucial chapter in history, it is important to understand the Hindu-Muslim problem which is the base of the creation of Pakistan. Many have tried to analyse this problem as per their own opinions. Communalism is not a chapter to be buried in the annals of history. By turning a blind eye, we cannot solve the problem. Once a nationalist Jinnah turned into a staunch communalist and even after 60 years of independence this chapter is not closed. When this novel was published as a serial, some of my well wishers wanted to know why I am burying the ghost of communalism. It is necessary to recognise the real picture of this ghost and finish it once and for all. Restraining does not help. The forces that contributed to the creation of this ghost wittingly or unwittingly must be identified. Jinnah's claim that the partition of India is a permanent solution to communalism has proved wrong. The same way, Gandhiji's claim that Hindus and Muslims are like two eyes of a nation is also not proved right. This million-dollar question is still staring at us in our face for an answer. If this novel can find an answer to this question, my efforts would succeed.

To understand the Hindu-Muslim communal problem, it is important to understand the mindset of the people. Once the mind sets of both these communities are clear, it becomes easy to understand this chapter of history.

Political Background

The religious head of the Ismaili Khojas, Aga Khan, lived in Iran for forty five generations. In the middle of 19th century, due to some family problems arisen out of matrimonial differences with the royalty, he left Iran along with his army, servants and horses and thousands of people. After leaving Iran, they did not settle in the neighbouring Muslim countries like Turkey, Iraq or Afganistan and instead migrated to India which in their parlance was *Dar-ul-Harb*. They made Bombay the main centre, participated in the local social and educational matters and took interest in politics and conversion. Aga Khan wrote in his Memoirs that, during his lifetime, he had converted some forty thousand Hindus into Muslims. And he was very happy about it. He mentioned the reasons for leaving Iran; but did not specify why he chose to settle in India. After him, his heir also remained active in Muslim politics and exploited his position as the religious head and succeeded in making the Muslims a distinct community and securing them a separate electorate; he established the Muslim League and kept the Muslims away from the Congress' fight for independence. The selection of this subcontinent as his new habitation can be judged, though not clearly expressed anywhere, from these events and also from the satisfaction he has expressed over the conversion he has effected. As a novelist, I have tried to reason out all this in this novel.

If we examine these chapters of history from 1857, particularly the period between 1915 and 1947, many questions would arise. There are many events which both the sides could argue endlessly on the lines that if this would have happened, that would not have happened and the like. In 1917 or 1918, if Gandhiji had not supported the extremist *Mullahs* and *Maulvis* on the Khilafat issue and not presented them before the Muslim community, the communalism would not have taken such an aggressive turn. In 1928, had the Congress accepted the Muslim League demand for the proportional representation for the Muslims and not insisted on the common electorate, perhaps Pakistan would not have been created. Had the Congress shared power with the Muslim League, as demanded by Jinnah, especially in the United Province and the Bombay Province after 1937 elections which saw the Congress forming Governments in eight provinces, history would not have taken such an ugly turn. In 1939, when the British Government was engaged in World War II, had the Congress governments in the provinces not resigned, Jinnah would never have attained such eminence. At one stage during the partition, Jinnah proposed the safe migration of Muslims in India to Pakistan and Hindus in Pakistan to India which the Congress rejected on the plea that it was a very difficult and destructive proposal. However, the subsequent events proved that the voluntary migration of people on both the sides resulted in the death of lakhs of people.

Today, only four million Hindus live in Pakistan, whereas the number of Muslims in India is larger than that of the entire population of Pakistan.

Jinnah made the Muslims believe that they were not a religious minority, but a separate nation and that their peaceful co-existence with the Hindus in independent India was impossible. He himself did not believe in what he was saying. This is evident from the first speech he delivered after the partition and also from the message he gave on the occasion of the first anniversary of Pakistan's independence. The belief of Gandhiji and the Congress that the Muslims were not a separate nation but shared the common cultural and historical background with the Indian people proved wrong, while Jinnah succeeded in realising his demand. Here the question arises. Can we say that had the Congress acknowledged its failure and accepted the Muslims as a separate nation, there would have been no Hindu-Muslim problem in India today? The Congress continues to oppose the two-nation theory; but could this make India one nation even after 60 years of independence? On the other hand, Pakistan which believed in a separate nation on the basis of religion also failed. The breaking away of East Pakistan and the creation of Bangladesh is an example. If Jinnah's two-nation theory failed, Ganhiji's theory of one nation also did not stand the test of time.

All this will have to be kept in mind for an academic exercise of a free, frank and transparent narration of Jinnah's life. The narration in this novel is, in the language of chemistry, a compound and not a mixture. Whenever I encountered a problem of choosing between truth and fact, I chose the truth as supreme and left the fact behind. When this novel was published as a serial, an elderly scholarly friend warned that the history is likely to overshadow the novel. How can history be disregarded when it forms the basis and background for writing this novel? For history, facts are important, for art, especially novel, it is the truth. When it comes to history, importance is given to facts. But, when it comes to writing about individuals, it is necessary to give importance to truth. The readers must understand this thin line of distinction. I accept this that as a novelist, I have taken the bare minimum liberty as and when this form of literature compelled me to do so. If any historian says, with documentary evidence, that a particular event took place in a particular month of a year, but this novel has not followed the chronology, he is right and I have no dispute with him. If someone says that a particular dialogue took place not in this particular place but elsewhere, I would appreciate his commitment to fact. I have taken care of not distorting events and truth, while keeping in mind the artistic form of the novel.

Gandhiji was a great man. No one, not even his staunch enemies, could raise any doubt about his sincerity and adherence to truth. Yet, he was a mortal, after all. Even in case of the divine incarnations like Ram and Krishna, questions are raised about their life and deeds. The background of such doubts is the prevailing level of understanding. No doubts would have been raised if these two factors are ignored and only the feeling of devotion was to become prominent. A sympathetic reader should constantly remember that since this is a novel the element of devotion has been kept at the subsidiary level. One can not create a novel—to the extent of a piece of art—with prejudices and similarly the feeling of devotion becomes an obstacle to the pure worship of art.

The Hero

Jinnah never wrote anything about his life, likes and dislikes, people and events that influenced and shaped his life. He made no such mention in his personal letters and diaries. His sister Fatima was in possession of some of his personal letters after his death, but they were reported stolen (*Lok Satta 24.12.1976*). In case these personal letters are recovered, it would be possible to think afresh about his life. In contrast, we have lot of materials on Gandhiji—written by himself and by others about him. Mahadevbhai, Pyarelal and Kishorilal have written a lot about him and how the personal and public events influenced his thoughts and behaviour. We can understand the mind of Gandhiji through these writings. But no such material is available on Jinnah to understand his mind. Considering the personality of Jinnah, I have tried, through this novel, to the best of my knowledge, to make justice to the events that happened in his life, from a psychological point of view. Hardly any one has written why the communication between him and his wife Ruttie was snapped and why she left him. There was a big age difference between them. Even their close friend Kanji Dwarkadas evaded writing on this issue in his book on biography of Ruttie. Under such circumstances, it became inevitable to add psychological process and events in order to make the manifested happenings meaningful. Despite this, this is not fiction. I have used fiction only to serve as an interpolation to the found fact and that too whenever it was absolutely unavoidable.

But truth cannot be always comprehended from a static position. To have a vision of truth and to give a glimpse of it to people is a task that only literature can accomplish.

Could we have the Mahabharat[1] today, had the Maharshi Ved Vyas not given to us the history of the Pandavas and Kauravas with absolute neutrality and human approach? This story of the Son of Dharma Yudhishthir and the son of Manyu Duryodhan is neither history nor a novel, neither a religion nor politics nor psychology. In paraphrase we can say *Vyasotchhistam Jagatsarvam*[2].

Though Jinnah may be regarded a villain in India and a hero in Pakistan, the truth lies somewhere between these two extreme view points. The historical scholars know that there are times when nations and people forget their common sense and understanding. Sometimes, even an ordinary matter suddenly becomes a question of pride and existence for people. Then every body forgets the common sense and becomes insane. A moment comes when people look back at history, they realise how insane their forefathers and ancestors have been. Even then, they too slip into some newer depths of madness of their own. If anybody observes the Indian history without bias, after two or five hundred years, he would understand this.

Jinnah never had a personality that makes a hero. We cannot find any traits of a hero in him. Even then, we cannot call him a villain. The villain is one who always harbours animosity towards the hero and creates every possible obstacle to prevent him from succeeding in his aim. He wants the hero never to succeed in his aim.

He knows that he himself can never be successful. Knowing his own limitations, he realises that, in denying the hero, the success he seeks lies in his own achievement. In the Mahabharat, Shishupal is one such villain. But, Krishna is not the hero of the Mahabharat. In the battle field of Kurukshetra, Duryodhan had eleven divisions of army and Yudhishthir had seven divisions. Duryodhan was no less competent than Yudhishthir to rule the kingdom of Hastinapur.

Though justice, truth and righteousness were on the side of Yudhishthir, he did not fully follow the principles of righteousness in conducting the Great War. At the time of his death Duryodhan said, "I have performed *Yagnas*[3], given alms, practiced penance and ruled the kingdom of Hastinapur." He acquired these qualities as a king. In a nutshell, though Yudhishthir, was regarded an embodiment of virtues, he did not achieve everything only through just and fair means. And, although Duryodhan was regarded un-virtuous, he was not inferior to Yudhishthir.

What we see is the striking difference between these two warring cousins—Yudhishthir and Duryodhan. We can see the same difference between the two giant personalities of modern India—Gandhi and Jinnah. If we call Gandhi as Yudhishthir, then we should call Jinnah as Duryodhan. If Gandhi is a hero, Jinnah is not a villain, but a p*ratinayak.*[4] Had Duryodhan not developed deep rooted hatred towards Yudhishthir and not become egoistic, then, perhaps, the lives of the eighteen divisions of army of Aryavart could have been saved. Perhaps, this is what had repeated in 1947, after thousands of years.

The moment Gandhiji entered the Indian political scene, he became supreme. By then, Jinnah had already been associated with the Congress for a decade and working along with the stalwarts like Gokhale, Tilak, Pherozshah Mehta, and Dadabhai Navroji. We must not hesitate to say that the Congress did not accord him a high status. Perhaps because of this Jinnah may have developed an intense jealousy and on account of this his ambitions and arrogance may have turned him against Gandhi, the Congress and at last against the whole nation. Duryodhan in his bid to prove himself superior to Yudhishthir, invited all round destruction and one can not help feeling that something similar to that may have happened in the case of Jinnah.

Jinnah was a staunch nationlist in his early years in the Congress. If Gandhiji deprived him the high status in the Congress, he should have left the Congress, but how could he abandon the nationalist in him? Subash Chandra Bose and Rajgopalachari left the Congress, due to their differences with Gandhiji, but they did not become anti-national. Keeping this in view, one can doubt whether Jinnah was a nationalist at all in his early years. If a person does not get what he thinks is his legitimate right, should he abandon the nationalist in him and work for dividing the country? This is a million dollar question.

In Jain scriptures, there are concepts of *Vasudev*[5] and *Prativasudev*[6]. In two time—cycles, sixty three noble men were born, and from this nine Vasudevs and nine Prativasudevs. Pundarik, Datta, Laxman and Krishna were counted among Vasudevs and Bali, Prahlad, Ravana, and Jarasandha were counted among Prativasudevs—their counterparts. Both these Vasudevs and their counterparts, Prativasudevs, have equal right to go to heaven and attain salvation. Vasudevs emerge victorious by killing Prativasudevs, but they had no right to attain salvation. Since Vasudevs and Prativasudevs had committed violent acts, they went to hell at the end of their lives, but secured the right to attain salvation after several rebirths and atoning their misdeeds. In Bharat Natyashastra[7], 'prathinayak' (Anti-Hero) is considered equal to the hero. However, due to the negative characteristics, he is accorded a lower status than the hero. He stands far above the villain in some respects and is inferior to the hero to some extent. Jinnah had all these virtues and vices. That is why an attempt is made to see him as 'pratinayak.'

I have tried to be truthful and neutral. Yet if somebody notices any shortcomings, I have nothing to regret. It is my duty to remain truthful and loyal to my work. And I have done my job sincerely to the best of my ability. Just as a reader has lot of expectations from the author, the author also expects little understanding and unbiased mind from the reader.

7th November 2011 **Dinkar Joshi**

NOTES

1. The great Indian epic written by the sage Ved Vyas. It is a story of a great war fought in the battle field of Kurukshetra by the cousins Kaurvas and Pandavas over the Kingdom of Hastinapura. This is also called a Dharmayuddha—the war of righteousness.
2. Sage Ved Vyas covered all forms of worldly subjects in his writings, the rest of the world literatures are only imitations.
3. Rituals offered to appease the Gods.
4. Anti-hero—The original title of this novel in Gujarati.
5. An incarnation of super human elements according to Jain mythology.
6. Ibid.
7. An ancient Indian treatise on drama in Sanskrit written by sage Bharat.

Acknowledgement

For many years, my novels are published in the form of serials in one or another periodical, before they are published as books. I had new experience in publishing this novel. Most of the magazines and newspapers refused to publish this novel when they came to know that it is based on the life of Muhammad Ali Jinnah. There were reasons for this: (a) Since Jinnah is regarded as villain in this country, it is not appropriate to publish the novel based on his life, and (b) If this novel glorifies Jinnah, it would not be acceptable to the Hindu readers and if the novel criticises Jinnah it might incur the wrath of Muslims and lead to communal tension. This second observation of the experienced and responsible men of the media world needs to be noted.

I would like to recall my visit to Jinnah's House in Mumbai, where he lived and from where the history of country changed its course many a time. After 1947, it was taken over by the Indian Government. Public entry to the House was prohibited. For a few years, it was rented by the British Deputy High Commissioner on a monthly rent of *Rs.3000.* For quite some time now, it remains neglected. I understand the Union Government spends about five lakhs a year for its maintenance. I had to make extraordinary efforts to obtain permission to visit this House. The people can visit without any restriction, the birth place of Mahatma Gandhi at Porbandar or Rajkot. No pilgrim is ever stopped from visiting the temples of Dwarikadhish or Kashi Vishwanath. But the visit to the Jinnah House is prohibited. I succeeded in getting the permission to visit the House only after exchanging lot of correspondence and the mediation by the then Union Minister Shri Ram Naik. I was permitted to visit the House only in the presence of the government officials on the condition that no photographs of the place would be taken.

We cannot clap with a single hand. But this novel is not a clap, but a clarion call. To give a clarion call, not only do we need two hands, but also two lips and a tongue. Though the cover page of this book bears only my name, however I must express thanks to all those who helped in writing this novel.

I have collected lots of books from almost all important libraries in Gujarat and Mumbai. For this, credit goes to all these libraries and librarians. I express my special gratitude to the female staff of the Library of '*Janmabhoomi*' in Mumbai (which I jocularly refer to as the 'Vrindavan'), particularly to its Chief Librarian Smt. Neelima Desai.

How can I forget my publisher friends Gopalbhai and Pravinbhai Patel (original Gujarati edition), who have shown active interest in this novel. I appreciate the suggestions they offered from time to time. Respected Shri Takhtasinhji Parmar and my friend Kishore Parekh offered critical comments during the writing of this novel.

When most of the editors of daily newspapers expressed their inability to publish this novel, Mr. Saurabh Shah, the then editor of the Mumbai based Gujrati daily '*Mid-Day*', came forward and published the novel as a serial in his paper. I am grateful to him for this kind gesture. I would like to thank Sanjay Nirupam, Member of the Parliament and the then editor of the Hindi daily '*Saamna*' for publishing the Hindi translation of this novel as a serial in his paper. I am thankful to Bimal Maheshwari and Janak Shah, the then editor of '*Samkaleen*' for publishing a detailed report on the novel for Gujrati readers in Mumbai.

Last, but not the least, I sincerely acknowledge that without the help and co-operation of my Assistant Pallavi, who has been my constant companion, my creative work during the past few years, particularly the writing of this novel would not have been possible.

And how can I forget Dr. G. Ramachandram who has translated this book with passion and dedication. Needless to say that but for the active cooperation of Shri Rajan Arya of Pentagon Press, the English version, would not have been seen in the print. I thank both of them.

Email: dinkarmj@gmail.com **Dinkar Joshi**
Phone: 022-28019795

Contents

	Preface	*vii*
	Acknowledgement	*xvii*
1	Treatment of Quaid-e-Azam in hospital	1
2	Jinnah-Fatima relation: Doctor's vigilance on Quaid-e-Azam, Liaquat Ali Khan's visit to the hospital	6
3	Liaquat-Jinnah dialogue, Liaquat-doctor dialogue	11
4	Incoherent talk of Jinnah, plans of shifting to Karachi	16
5	Serious condition and ambulance, Dr. Illah Baksh-Liaquat dialogue in Karachi	20
6	Education of Maamad, fishing business of Punja Valji, boycott by villagers	25
7	Arrival of Aga Khan in India, Punja's conversion to Islam	30
8	Family's opposition to the conversion, boycott by havelis and temples	36
9	Marriage of Punja's sons, discussion about sending Jinabhai to Karachi	41
10	Birth of Maamad, Douglas Graham's Company	46
11	Marriage of Jinnah, Fredrick's advice, leaving for London, working in Graham's Company, Admission to the Lincoln's Inn, name and date of birth	51
12	Barrister Jinnah, meeting at Hyde Park, meeting Dadabhai in Parliament, acting in theatre	57
13	Death of mother and wife, arrival in Bombay, pursuing legal profession, working as assistant to Pherozeshah	62
14	MacPherson's library, appointment as magistrate, encounter with MacDonald in court, working as a consultant of the Bombay Municipal Corporation	67

15 Father's shift to Bombay, admission of Fatima to school, Hindu-Muslim untouchability incident narrated by Fatima 72

16 1885: Establishing of the Indian National Congress, Aligarh Muslim University, Sir Syed Ahemd-Bacon dialogue, Archibald's suggestion for delegation 77

17 Meeting of Aga Khan's delegation with Minto, Establishing of the Muslim League, Jinnah's refusal to join the League, converting to another sect 84

18 Gokhale-Jinnah meeting, Jinnah as Tilak's defense lawyer, new reforms for Indians' participation in administration (1909) 90

19 Opposition to Jinnah in the meeting of Imperial Legislative Council, The Allahabad resolution, compliments from Gokhale, Gandhi-Jinnah meeting in London, Change in the League's constitution, Jinnah's joining of the League 96

20 Felicitating of Gandhi by Gurjar Sabha, meeting with Dinshaw Petit, vacation in Darjeeling 101

21 Ruttie-Jinnah proximity, Dinshaw-Jinnah confrontation 106

22 Watch on Ruttie, Jinnah's refusal to cooperate in the war efforts (World War I), Muslim League's Lucknow session, Khilafat-Gandhi 111

23 Ruttie-Jinnah marriage, Lord Chelmsford's banquet, Lord Willingdon's banquet 117

24 Jinnah's willingness to cooperate in the war efforts, Jinnah's opposition to Willingdon's farewell function (Town Hall), Fatima-Ruttie differences, end of the war, Dina's birth in London 122

25 Ruttie-Kanji introduction, The Khilafat movement: Gandhi-Jinnah differences 128

26 Jinnah's stand on non-cooperation, Nagpur session of the Congress, Ruttie-Jinnah at Lord Reading's banquet 133

27 Ruttie-Jinnah incident of rain, Kanji-Ruttie dialogue in the 'South Court,' experiments on psychic power 137

28 Ruttie-Fatima confrontation about the pet cats, Jinnah-Ruttie quarrel, Kanji-Jinnah discussion about Dina's education, Ruttie's letter to Kanji on her leaving for London 142

29 Khilafat: Ali brothers' posturing, Gandhi's programme of action against untouchability, Jinnah's efforts to break the Congress and form a new party, Jinnah's communal attitude, Motilal Nehru's introduction of Jinnah to other members of the Central Legislative Assembly 146

30 Ruttie-Adyar Theosophical Society, Rutti-Jinnah confrontation about Dina's education, Ruttie's addiction to drugs, Jinnah's stand on the Simon Commission, Secretary of State for India Birkenhead's proposals on constitutional reforms 152

31 Ruttie in Taj Mahal Hotel, Jamshed meeting with Ruttie, Payment of Hotel bills by Jinnah 158

32 Jinnah's meeting with prominent Muslim leaders in Delhi, Fatima-Jinnah discussion on communalism, Gandhi-Jinnah views on the Shariat, All party meeting in Bombay on the Nehru Report, Jinnah's opposition to the Nehru Report, meeting of the Muslim League, All party meeting in Delhi on the Nehru Report, Jamshed at Delhi station, Hooting of Jinnah in the train 163

33 Ruttie in Paris for treatment, Chamanlal's poetry, Ruttie at Kanji's house, Ruttie's birthday—death 171

34 Ruttie's last rites, removing Ruttie's belongings 176

35 Congress refusal to participate in the First Round Table Conference, Breaking of the Salt Law by Gandhi, partition in the Round Table Conference by other parties, Jinnah in London, Willingdon as the Viceroy of India 180

36 Iqbal's meeting with Jinnah in London, Second Round Table Conference, Gandhi-Jinnah meeting in London 185

37 Third Round Table Conference, Jinnah in London—Privy Council, Jinnah's unsuccessful attempt to enter the British Parliament, Jinnah-Rehmat Ali Choudhari meeting, Muslim League in India without Jinnah, Jinnah-Dina on 'Grey Wolf,' biography of Kemal Ataturk 190

38 Liaquat-Jinnah meeting in London, Jinnah's return to India, Jinnah-Shahidgunj mosque in Lahore 196

39 Jinnah in mosque with shoes, settlement between the two communities in Lahore, political reforms, New Viceroy Linlithgow, Central Assembly in Delhi-Jinnah's views 200

40 Jinnah-Khurshid meeting, face lift to the 'South Court,' Jinnah's conversation with a friend's son throughout the night, Jinnah-Khaliquzzamman-Rafiq Ahmed Kidwai 205

41 Jinnnah-Jawaharlal Nehru correspondence, Jinnah as the permanent President of the League, Muslim League session in Lucknow, change in Jinnah's dressing style, refusal to accept a toy free of charge 210

42 Elections of Provincial Assemblies (1937), Jinnah-Begum Rana meeting in Lucknow, Gandhi-Jinnah meeting postponed 215

43 Hue and cry about alleged injustice to Muslims, Gandhi's letter to Jinnah, Gandhi-Jinnah meeting in the South Court, Jinnah's refusal to accept inquiry into alleged atrocities against Muslims, Pirpur report, Jinnah's press conference 220

44 Beginning of World War II, Viceroy's appeal to Gandhi-Jinnah for cooperation in war efforts, Resignation of Provincial governments, observing the 'Day of Deliverance and thanks giving', Linlithgow-Jinnah parleys, Muslim League session in Patna, Viceroy's rejection of Jinnah's suggestion to form Provincial governments 225

45 Dina-Jinnah conversation about marriage 230

46 Dina's marriage, Jinnah's will, Jinnah-Linlithgow meeting, Muslim League-Jinnah strategy for Pakistan-option 234

47 Lahore session of Muslim League, demand for Pakistan 238

48 Generous donations to Jinnah in Ahemedabad, Jinnah-Tej Bahadur Sapru on Quran in a court in Hyderabad, study of Quran by Jinnah, Ban on Jinnah's entry into Gondal 242

49 Jinnah in Junagadh and Gondal, Jinnah in Karachi, meeting with the students of law 246

50 Madras session of Muslim League, the question of a separate Dravidistan, Jinnah in Ooty, appointment of Muslims as members of the War Council by Linlithgow, Jinnah in Kashmir, Tej Singh: question answer, Gandhi's advice to Hitler 250

51 1942 'Quit India Resolution,' arrest of Gandhi, Jinnah's reaction, Gandhi's letter to Jinnah, Jinnah's refusal to sign appeal demanding Gandhi's release, attack on Jinnah 255

52 Rafiq's arrest, Rafiq-Jinnah dialogue in court, Rajagopalachari's formula 260

53 Gandhi's release from jail, Gandhi's letter to Jinnah, Jinnah's health, Jinnah's instruction to Dr. Jaal Patel to keep his disease a secret 264

54 Fatima's knowledge of Jinnah's disease 269

55 Gandhi-Jinnah parleys, Wavell's reaction to the parleys 273

56 Jinnah in magistrate's court in Agra to fight the case of Shyamlal-recommended by Vasant Kripalani 279

57 Jinnah-Khizar-Hayat Khan of Punjab Unionist Party, Roosevelt's pressure on Churchill, Liaquat-Bhulabhai understanding, Gandhi's stand on the understanding 284

58 Simla Conference, Wavell-Jinnah – June 1945, Prime Minister Attlee's address, elections of 1945, Jinnah-Iskandar Mirza-North West Frontier Province, Nawab of Bhopal 288

59 Election results, the naval mutiny in Bombay, Cabinet Mission, Jinnah-Pethic Lawrence meeting, discussion with Stafford Cripps 293

60 June 1946—Second Simla Conference, Jinnah-Maulana Azad handshake, Pethic Lawrence-Jawaharlal Nehru-Jinnah, Jinnah aborts understanding, Cripps-Jinnah clash, Jinnah's deteriorating health, Cripps-Alexander enquiry about Jinnah's health, Dr. Jaal Patel-Jinnah 298

61 Pethic-Lawrence-Jinnah-Jawahar-Maulana meeting not materialising, Nizam-Jinnah meeting, Cabinet Mission proposals, Jinnah in a dilemma, Mullah-Maulvis, Cabinet Mission's approval for interim government, Congress—interim government, Jinnah's call for 'Direct Action' 303

62 Direct Action: Riots in Calcutta, Muslim League in the interim government, Liaquat-Jawaharlal—Budget 308

63 Failure of Jawaharlal-Jinnah-Attlee parleys in London, Churchill-Jinnah correspondence: pseudo name, Jinnah-Baldev Singh talks, Jinnah-Muslim Conference in Cairo, Mountbatten-Edwina acquaintance, Wavell's welcome to Mountbatten, Mountbatten-George Catleen: perception of Gandhi-Jinnah 313

64 Mountbatten-Gandhi-Jinnah parleys, Edwina-Fatima meeting, Jinnah-Mountbatten talks regarding division of Punjab and Bengal, Jinnah's declaration on the question of majority-minority in Pakistan, Gandhi's reaction 317

65 Noakhali, riots in Bihar, Mountbatten's suggestion for joint appeal for peace, Gandhi's consent, Jinnah in a dilemma, Viceroy-Gandhi on transfer of power, Jinnah's reaction, Churchill's advice to Mountbatten on the partition 321

66 Viceroy's house—partition plan, Mountbatten's advice to Jinnah, Jinnah-Viceroy late night talks, Jinnah's nod for the partition, Jinnah-Nehru-Mountbatten broadcast on All India Radio, Punjab, Bengal, North West Frontier Province on partition, date for independence 326

67 Violence in the Frontier Province, Khurshid in Peshawar, Sikh-Muslim marriage, Viceroy's visit to Peshawar, Selling of Jinnah's bungalow in Delhi 331

68 Meeting of the Partition Council, Jinnah-Radcliffe, Jinnah's attempt to hold the first meeting of the Pakistan Constituent Assembly in Delhi, Jinnah declares himself to be the Governor-General, Jinnah in the 'Jinnah House' 336

69 Remembering Ruttie in the 'Jinnah House,' trunks—Ruttie's possessions, visit to Ruttie's grave 341

70 Muslim League's last meeting in Delhi, question-answer, second meeting of the Partition Council, India-UN-Pakistan, Jinnah's arrival in Karachi, Governor General's residence—sports, library radio etc., refugee camps, First meeting of the Pakistan Constituent Assembly in Karachi 346

71 Plot to murder Jinnah, Jinnah-Mountbatten—14th August parade, bonquet at the Governor-General's residence, Mountbatten-Fatima conversation, Jinnah's plan to visit Kashmir, rejection by King Hari Singh 353

72 Jinnah's plan to take revenge on Kashmir, General Messervy, Autocratic rule of Jinnah in Pakistan, keeping in personal custody files relating to Kashmir, Jamshed Patel-Jinnah dialogue, Jinnah's no to compound wall for his residence 358

73 Jehangir Patel-Jinnah-Gandhi, Gandhi's fast in Delhi, assassination of Gandhi, condolence message from Jinnah, riots in Lahore, massacre in train,—Pakistan's empty treasury—Nizam, Special car and aircraft for Jinnah, Jinnah in Dacca—emphasising on Urdu as the national language of Pakistan 363

74 Jinnah's desire to meet Badshah Khan-Qayyum Khan, denial of permission to Liaquat to meet Jinnah, Jinnah's condition—Dr. Riyaz Ali, Sri Prakash—Jinnah House, Jinnah residence in Ziarat, treatment by Dr. Illah Baksh 369

75 Jinnah in Ziarat, buying of waistcoat, Jinnah's message on the first anniversary of independence of Pakistan, Jinnah's serious condition, return to Karachi, the last breath 374

Bibliography 379

1

Treatment of Quaid-e-Azam in hospital

The sun stood still for a moment in the sky on the Indian subcontinent, in the middle of the 20th century. *Mahakaal* [1] had never seen before anything like this on this earth. He had seen eighteen army battallions destroying each other totally in the battlefield of Kurukshetra. He had seen Changez Khan, Hulalku Khan, Taimur Lang invading and burning one village after another, massacring thousands of innocent people, raping brutally countless women, destroying sacred religious places and ruining cities. But, what he witnessed a while ago, he had never witnessed before on this earth. To *Mahakaal*, death is common, nothing is special about it. For the first time, he witnessed that death could be so gruesome, devoid of human dignity. From time immemorial, we have been habituated to see the bright sun rays in the open sky. But today the same sun rays are soaked in blood.

An independent Pakistan had emerged on the world political map. A scenic hill station called Ziarat is located seventy kilometres north-west of Quetta, the capital of Pakistan's mountainous border province of Baluchistan. An eerie silence prevailed in a house located on the top of the hill. The doctor and the nurse were particular not to disturb the patient, who briefly opened his eyes to stare blankly at the ceiling. The six feet tall patient was so slender and skeletal that one could easily count the bones of his body.

The nurse who came to check the patient's temperature turned back because he was in a deep sleep. He was not sleeping well these days. She postponed the temperature checking. After sometime, the patient opened his eyes, perspiring in the air-conditioned room, staring at the sky in the north-west direction through the glass. This was the same direction where *Takshashila*, a renowned world centre of culture and civilisation flourished in ancient times. This was the route through which the Greeks, Sakas, Muslims and others invaded this land. And thousands of Muslims who accepted this place as *Dar-ul-Harb* had now migrated to the treacherous neighbouring Afghanistan which they regarded as *Dar-ul-Islam*. A few months ago, the patient could see and understand all these. But today there is emptiness in his eyes, devoid of any emotions.

"Sir," a melodious voice broke the silence in the room. It had no impact on the patient staring in that direction.

The nurse came closer to the bed. She put her hand very gently on the patient's forehead. Without looking at her, the patient closed his eyes, his lips trembling.

The nurse removed the hand, took the thermometer in hand and asked, "Sir, how do you feel now? It is time to check the temperature."

He opened his eyes and stared at the nurse without any response.

"Sir, please open your mouth, let me check the temperature. Look, your health has improved today."

"What happened to my health, sister? Nothing happened to me. A little exertion caused this fatigue. Let me sleep peacefully, I want to sleep," said the patient in a faltering voice, with his lips trembling. The self-confidence and the force of authority were missing in his voice.

"Yes Sir, you are absolutely normal. I am here to make you comfortable. After having the temperature checked, you can sleep comfortably," said the nurse.

Like an obedient child, the patient opened his mouth. The nurse placed the thermometer under his tongue carefully. She looked at her wristwatch and removed the thermometer. She noted the temperature in her file kept on a nearby table.

"Sister, tell me, how much fever do I have now?" The nurse heard once again a self-confident and authoritative voice. She approached the patient and smiled with great effort.

"Sir, you don't worry. The doctor will take care of everything."

"Sister, this is not the answer to my question. I want a clear answer. Tell me, how much fever I have now," asked the patient, expressing the displeasure on his face, his jaws taunt and deep sunk eyes turned to slits with anger. The nurse trembled.

"Forgive me, sir. But, I cannot answer your question. The doctor ordered that…"

"Order!" the patient screamed in anger. "Sister, you are forgetting, I give orders. I do not accept any orders."

The nurse was in a dilemma. The doctor had clearly instructed her not to discuss with the patient anything about his health, diagnosis and treatment. In order to pacify the patient, she once again put her right hand on his forehead.

"Sir, calm down. Whatever you want to say, please say to the doctor."

He grew impatient and suddenly pushed his blanket and grabbed the wrist of the nurse.

"Sister, I won't tolerate all this. What do you mean…?"

The nurse tried to loosen her wrist from his grip, but the fingers of a seemingly fragile patient held her wrist in a firm grip. She saw much exertion and strain on his face. She was afraid that something might happen to him. She put her other hand on his shoulder and tried to loosen the wrist from his grip.

"No, you cannot go this way. Until I get what I want, I cannot rest. I will not let you go this way. This is my order," thundered the patient, and tried to sit. The nurse was shaken. She knew that it could be fatal for the patient. Something might happen...

She tried to put him back to bed. In the meantime, the grip of the patient loosened. All this happened so suddenly that the nurse was stunned.

At that very moment, the doctor pushed the door and entered the room, his face showing the mark of an army disciplinarian. He took the file from the table without uttering a single word. He glanced at the file for a while and then turned his gaze towards the patient.

The patient's anger subsided. He closed his eyes. The doctor looked at the nurse. Her eyes showed her predicament—how will she control the patient, if he behaves again the same way he did a short while ago? She told herself...let God bless him! But what if she is unable to control him and something unpleasant happens!

This thought made her worry all the more. She summoned some courage, went close to the doctor and said slowly,

"Doctor, I have a request!"

The doctor looked at her inquisitively.

"It would be better, if you could get a suitable male attendant to look after the patient instead of me," said the nurse at last.

Before the doctor could understand and say something, the patient opened his eyes.

"No. Sister, you cannot go! I do not need a male attendant. No one can take care of me better than you. You are the most suitable."

The doctor went close to the patient immediately and said, "You don't worry, Sir. As per your wish, this nurse will remain here to look after you," and glanced at the nurse.

The nurse understood the doctor's intention. It was better to close the matter there. She took the comb from the dressing table and began combing the tousled hair of the patient.

"Do you want to cover the bald patches or show them?" chuckled the patient.

The nurse did not say anything. The temperature was receding. The patient again closed his eyes.

The doctor took the stethoscope hanging around the neck in his hand, held the patient's hand and checked the pulse.

"You are making an unnecessary fuss. I do not have any major ailment. Because I have been working fourteen hours a day for the past fifty years, now I am suffering from some exhaustion and cold. After resting for a few days, everything will be alright," said the patient without noticing the presence of the doctor.

"Yes, Sir." The doctor nodded in agreement. "There is nothing seriously wrong with you."

"You are telling a lie, doctor or you don't know how to diagnose a patient." The patient suddenly retorted in an authoritative voice. "If you cannot diagnose my disease, then let me tell you..."

The doctor and the nurse glanced at each other for a moment.

"Do you know that Sir?"

"Yes, three and a half years ago, my doctor friend in Bombay had clearly told me..."

"What did he tell, Sir?"

"You have seen all these files, doctor. Do not pretend... the doctor had told me that my lungs were damaged and the TB was in the last stage. Not only was that but blood also infected with the germs of cancer." The patient said in a matter of fact manner. The next moment, his face turned pale, and he had difficulty in breathing.

"You knew everything, Sir. We are trying. We are praying to Allah for mercy."

"Look, doctor," said the patient in a serious tone. "I instructed my Bombay doctor that he should never spread the news of my illness. Till date, he followed my instruction very faithfully. Pakistan was within my grasp. It was like a ripe fruit falling into my hands from the tree. I was afraid that, at such a time, if the news of my illness spreads, the ripe fruit, instead of falling down, could disappear from the tree itself," said the patient with a smile on his lips. "And I wanted that nothing like that should happen."

The doctor and the nurse were listening to the patient quietly.

"And listen, doctor," said the patient in a commanding tone. The doctor was surprised. From where did the patient in such a fragile condition get such strength to speak so forcefully?

"You should also follow the footsteps of the Bombay doctor. No one should know the real condition of my health."

"Sir, the Prime Minister's Secretary instructed me to give all the details of your health to the Prime Minister's Office."

"Prime Minister! Who? The Prime Minister whom I have positioned on the throne of Pakistan has no right to enquire of my health. This is my clear order that there is no need for any one to know the real news about my health. No one. I know the Prime Minister is waiting for my death..." As he said this, he started coughing. The nurse immediately offered a glass of water...the patient sipped two drops.

"Calm down, Sir. As per your order, the secret of your disease shall not be disclosed. But I have told Madam Fatima earlier about it."

"You have not done the right thing, doctor. You should not have told even Fatima about it"

The doctor's faced looked forlorn, like a guilty criminal.

"But...it's alright," said the patient. "In a way, it is alright that Fatima knows about it. But now follow my order strictly."

"Yes, Sir," said the doctor, like an obedient child and added, "If you permit, the Prime Minister would like to see you."

The patient seriously contemplated for a moment.

"Prime Minister!" said the patient in a choked voice. "I know why he wants to see me."

"Sir, the Prime Minister wants to come and enquire about your health," said the doctor slowly.

"Not health, say illness, doctor. You do not understand anything doctor," said the patient raising his right hand fingers, "Your Prime Minister wants to see how long would I survive. But I am not going to die so soon."

The doctor said nothing. After an uneasy silence for some time, the patient said.

"Well, doctor, give the Prime Minister time to visit me after checking with Fatima."

"Thank you, Sir," said the doctor, concluding the conversation.

The nurse was a French woman named Sister Dunham.

The doctor was an eminent physician from the Pakistan Army named Illah Baksh.

And the patient fighting a losing battle against death was the Quaid-e-Azam Muhammad Ali Jinnah—Punja Valji Thakkar, Native-Post Paneli, District Rajkot, Kathiawad.

NOTE

1. Shiva, the destroyer in the Divine Trinity, according to the Hindu mythology. (The Eternal and infinite time—the Supreme Being).

2

Jinnah-Fatima relation: Doctor's vigilance on Quaid-e-Azam, Liaquat Ali Khan's visit to the hospital

When Dr. Illah Baksh asked Fatima for fixing the time for the Prime Minister's visit, she said somewhat discerningly, "Doctor, you know *Bhaijaan*'s[1] condition. In this situation, there should not be any stress on his mind. If the Prime Minister comes here, my brother will not restrain himself from discussing politics."

"I know that. If we say no to this meeting, the political situation will get more complicated. Not only will there be a suspicion regarding the Quaid-e-Azam's health, but also accusations. It is good, if the Prime Minister visits him," said the doctor candidly.

"Do as you think right. But, be sure about what you want to discuss about brother's health with the Prime Minister."

"I know that. You don't worry. The Quaid-e-Azam already instructed me about it." Fatima did not argue any further. The doctor knew that Fatima was more concerned about her brother's health than the doctor and the nurse. It was natural. Fatima has been taking care of everything about her brother, his likes and dislikes, food, clothes and the house which is a public place.

Fatima became the shadow of her brother, ever since Zinabhai left Karachi along with his six children and started living in a two-room apartment in Bombay's Khoja Mohalla. Her mother Mithibai died on her birth. Her father Zinabhai, who was seriously in debts and harassed by creditors, wound up the business in Karachi and shifted to Bombay. He hoped that, with the help of his eldest son Maamad, who went to London and returned as barrister, he would be able to restart his company M/S Punja Valji Thakkar in Bombay and that the prospect of education and marriage of Mammad's six younger brothers and sisters would improve. Zinabhai harboured a superstition that the family's misfortune began with the birth of his youngest daughter Fatima. Because of this, he disliked and neglected her. As she grew up, she realised how her father neglected her. That is why, though she lived with her siblings in the Khoja Mohalla, she used to slip away to her brother Maamad's residence, whenever she got a chance, and spend hours with him. Even when her brother was not at home, she would spend hours in cleaning and decorating the residence.

Fatima used to spend most of her time at her brother's place—be it the single room in Railway Hotel at Charni Road or the well-furnished elegant house at Apollo Fort area. Her brother got her admitted to a Christian Missionary School in Bandra and she stayed in the school hostel. Her brother would visit her every Sunday morning, riding a horse. She used to be excited at the sound of the galloping horse in that locality of scattered dwellings. She heard from her father and siblings that Maamadbhai had a liking for horse riding since his childhood. In those days, when M/S. Punja Valji Thakkar Company had a flourishing business, the family owned several horses. Maamad, a teenager then, used to ride horses fearlessly. Maamad's body was not strong. Yet the lean boy was so strong-willed that he would not be afraid to ride even wild horses. On returning home, tired Maamad would be pleased to see the house neat and well arranged. Her father and siblings rarely came to see him, and even when they did, they came with some problem or the other, particularly financial. Fatima was the only one who would quietly do whatever was necessary with her tender hands, without expecting anything in return. Whenever any delicacy was prepared at home in the Khoja Mohalla, she would invariably bring it for her brother. She would feel happy seeing her brother's radiant face as he ate it. Fatima saw in her brother a fearless, ideal man.

But a strange habit of this ideal man amused Fatima. Whenever she entered the house in his presence, he would become serious and first ask her, "Fati, have you washed your hands with soap?" Fatima would not understand why her brother was so obsessed with the washing of hands. She would wash her hands quietly. Whenever her brother returned home, he himself would first wash his hands thoroughly with soap. Once, when she could not resist the curiosity, Fatima asked him, "Bhaijaan, why do you wash hands again and again?"

"Fati, you don't know, the black fever bacteria has spread in Bombay. They are present in the air and spread the deadly fever through the fingertips. This is the only way to prevent it. You too, should develop the habit of washing hands."

Fatima never saw any bacteria on her hands or fingertips. She was amused that her brother, who dressed in a fashionable style wearing a coat and trousers, spoke English and looked like an English gentleman from the city should entertain such fear of imaginary bacteria. Nobody in her family at the Khoja Mohalla washed hands like this again and again, and yet none of them ever had any black-fever. She was amused at her brother's behaviour.

Doctor Illah Baksh, after receiving approval from Fatima, fixed the time for the Prime Minister's visit. The medicines required for the treatment of patient were not available in Ziarat. That is why; most of the medicines were being procured from Quetta, the capital of Baluchistan, seventy kilometres away. But, some medicines were not available even in Quetta. The portable x-ray machine that the doctor brought with him from Karachi became outdated. Modern machines were available in America. The doctor requested the Prime Minister's office to procure one such portable x-ray machine from America for monitoring the treatment of Quaid-e-Azam. Now, while fixing the time with the Prime Minister's Principal Secretary, the doctor again reiterated the importance of procuring the machine and the essential medicines and sending them to Ziarat with the Prime Minister's entourage.

The doctor was greatly surprised by the lack of a satisfactory response from the Prime Minister's Office regarding the machine. He could not understand why he did not receive any satisfactory response regarding the machine, in spite of sending a detailed telegraph, a week ago. By this time, the machine should have come from America. The doctor was lost in deep thought.

"Sister," the doctor called nurse Dunham softly and instructed, "Keep a copy of the telegram that we sent for the machine. Now onwards, whatever correspondence we may have with Karachi, make a file and keep it with you."

"Yes, doctor," responded the nurse immediately. She could not understand the meaning behind the doctor's instruction, but she did not question him.

"And, remember sister, whatever correspondence or talk we may have with the Governor of Quetta or with the Prime Minister's Office regarding the treatment of the Quaid-e-Azam, now onwards, keep a record of all that and show it to me everyday."

Sister Dunham narrowed her eyes questioningly, and her forehead was marked with lines of consternation. But she did not think it wise to ask him anything, for the doctor was from the army and that she was attending to no less a person than the Governor-General of Pakistan, the Quaid-e-Azam Muhammad Ali Jinnah. She quietly accepted the doctor's instruction. Dr. Illah Baksh, for a while, looked at the low-lying buildings of Ziarat and the people moving around in the verandah. The armed security guards stood in attention at the main gate of the bungalow.

The Prime Minister Liaqat Ali Khan and his entourage arrived at the appointed time. The security vehicle had reached earlier giving a prior notice of the Prime Minister's arrival. A group of local Pathans of Ziarat, standing a little distance away from the main gate, were watching with curiosity the arrival of vehicles. If any one from the crowd tried to come forward to have a glance at the vehicles or the persons sitting inside the vehicles, they were forcefully pushed back, if required with the riffle butts, by the security men. No celebrated person like the Governor-General had ever come to stay in the small town of Ziarat before. That the Governor, the Governor-General and even the District Collector had to be an English man was so fixed in the people's mind. But seeing some one belonging to their own religion, holding such an important position was a very fascinating experience for the simple and illiterate people.

The Prime Minister Liaqat Ali Khan, wearing the smile of a cunning seasoned politician on his face, stepped out of the car, opened by an Army Officer. Dr. Illah

Baksh and other officers greeted him. Behind that smiling face of Liaqat Ali Khan laid the deceit and cunning diplomacy which Dr. Illah Baksh could immediately discern, because of his vast experience in the Army. The Prime Minister led by Dr. Illah Baksh reached the verandah of the bungalow. They stopped for a while in the drawing room. After completion of all the formalities of welcoming him, the Prime Minister ordered that they should meet the Quaid-e-Azam in his room and enquire about his health.

"Sir," the doctor addressed the Prime Minister in a hushed tone. "I would like to draw your attention to something."

The Prime Minister looked inquisitively at the doctor.

"The Quaid-e-Azam's health is delicate. There is no immediate danger, but it is important to remember that any talk does not cause him mental strain. It is my request that this medical advice be kept in mind."

"You don't worry, doctor. I understand the meaning of your advice." said the Prime Minister, wearing the same cunning smile on his face.

"And one more thing," said the doctor enthusiastically, "The portable x-ray machine and the medicines, about which I spoke to your Office, are required urgently. I trust your staff must have brought the machine and the medicines."

Liaqat Ali Khan stared at him for a while and then looking at his private secretary said, "You talk to him about this matter; he will give all the information."

Dr. Illah Baksh could not understand what the Prime Minister meant. He does not want any information. He wanted the machine and the medicines urgently. The doctor could not understand why the Prime Minister, instead of telling him clearly whether these are bought or not, directed his private secretary to reply. But, he did not say anything further.

Before the doctor could say anything or talk to his private secretary, the Prime Minister started walking.

"Come, doctor. Let us meet the Quaid-e-Azam. It is my first duty to enquire about his health, the rest of the business you can attend later."

The doctor had no other option. It was not possible to talk to the Prime Minister's private secretary about the machine and the medicines. An unpleasant thought came to his mind for a moment. Does not the Prime Minister want me to talk to his private secretary about this in his presence?

When Liaqat Ali Khan entered the Quaid-e-Azam's room, he was asleep with the blanket pulled till his neck. His eyes were closed, Fatima sitting beside his head, was reading something from the Holy Quran. Nurse Dunham sat on the opposite of the bed. As soon as the Prime Minister stepped into the room, she stood up and came forward with a faint smile.

"Welcome, Sir," she said softly, bowing her head slightly.

Fatima turning her neck looked at Liaqat Ali Khan. She put a finger between the pages of the book held in her hand and without getting up she murmured something to the Prime Minister. He greeted her and then standing by the bedside of the Quaid-e-Azam said very humbly,

"*Aadab arz*[2] Quaid-e-Azam." Then he held his right hand to his forehead, closed his eyes and chanted *Bismillah Hirrahma Nirrahim*[3].

The sound broke the silence of the room and Quaid-e-Azam opened his eyes. His dimmed eyes flashed on seeing the Prime Minister. His face remained expressionless, but his dimmed eyes glanced at all those standing in the room.

"How are you now?, Quaid-e-Azam," enquired Liaqat Ali Khan in a soft tone.

The Quaid-e-Azam shook his head and then looking directly into the eyes of the Prime Minister asked, "Begaum Rana has not come with you, Liaqat?"

The query was unexpected by everybody else, except the Prime Minister. A few taut lines creased Fatima's face.

NOTES

1. Brother (used to address elder brother).
2. The Islamic way of greeting.
3. In the name of Allah—the merciful.

3

Liaquat-Jinnah dialogue, Liaquat-doctor dialogue

"Begum Rana is not keeping good health these days. There is nothing to worry, but the doctor advised her to take rest. She too is praying to Allah for your recovery. Otherwise, she would not have agreed to stay back," Liaqat Ali Khan said very gently bowing his head slightly.

The Quaid-e-Azam nodded and raised his hand pointing to the sofas and chairs near the bed. All those standing by the bedside now sat down.

"The entire country is worried about your health, Quaid-e-Azam. I hope you will recover soon."

"We are making the efforts in that direction, Sir. Your good wishes and the country's prayers shall succeed," said the doctor extending the conversation.

"The government is also worried that…"

"There are many other problems for the government to worry, Liaqat. All those problems should be resolved soon," Said the Quaid-e-Azam cutting short the Prime Minister's talk in a faint but firm voice.

"As you know, Quaid-e-Azam, the country is facing many difficult problems and all of us are trying to overcome them. Yet, as the Prime Minister of this country, my foremost concern is your health. It is in the interest of the country that the Council of Ministers should know the real condition and full details of your health," said Liaqat Ali Khan emphasising on each and every word like a cunning politician.

"Liaqat, you do not have to remind me that you are the Prime Minister. I have only made you the Prime Minister to sit on the throne," said the Quaid-e-Azam in distaste.

"I am thankful to you, Quaid-e-Azam," said Liaqat Ali Khan without hesitation.

"After accepting the position of the Prime Minister, it is my duty to take my Ministerial colleagues and the people of the country into confidence."

"Your duty is simply to follow my order. You can accept whatever information Dr. Illah Baksh gives to you about my health and act accordingly. I do understand why you are so concerned about my health."

"You are misunderstanding, Quaid-e-Azam,"said Liaqat in a soft voice.

"Perhaps, I have misunderstood until now, but now I understand the truth. I am not ignorant of your intention."

"You are unnecessarily getting annoyed, Quaid-e-Azam. Serving the country and its people is my noble intention, *Insha Allah*[1]."

"The manner in which you are working, surrounded by *Mullahs* and *Maulvis*[2], the Pakistan of my dreams cannot be created. My Pakistan can only be modern, not medieval. I have made you the Prime Minister for making Pakistan a modern nation. I feel, my decision was wrong," said the Quaid-e-Azam in a loud and angry voice.

Dr. Illah Baksh, who sat in front, noticed the excitement in Quaid-e-Azam's eyes.

He stood up, came close to the bed and said, "Sir, now you must take rest. We will take care of the rest."

"Mr. Prime Minister. You understand what I am saying," said the Quaid-e-Azam disregarding the doctor's advice. "I demanded Pakistan in the interest of Hindus and Muslims—living for centuries in this subcontinent. But, the events of the past one year will lead to permanent suffering of both these communities. You are not moving in the right direction; you are taking Pakistan towards the medieval age to be ruled by the *Mullahs* and the *Maulvis.* This is not acceptable to me. Now, enough! I feel like going to Delhi and meeting Jawaharlal to tell that..."

"Bhaijaan,"Fatima put her palm on the quivering lips and interrupted," Now, you do not say anything...Your health does not permit you to exert so much." And then turning to Liaqat Ali Khan she said, "Prime Minister, I think it would be better if we sit in another room to talk further on this."

Liaqat looked at Fatima curiously. Nobody could understand what was happening between the two. Liaqat got up with a faint smile and said.

"Fatimaji, I can see, how delicate the Quaid-e-Azam's health is. You are right. It is better; we do not talk any more here." Turning his eyes to the Governor-General and putting his right hand on his forehead and bowing slightly, Liaqat Ali Khan said, "May God show mercy on you, Quaid-e-Azam! *Khuda Haafiz*[3]."

All left the room one by one, like tutored puppets. Fatima and nurse Dunham only sat down there.

Outside, in the Guest Room, high tea was arranged. All were sitting around the table. Dr. Illah Baksh ending the silence in the room said,

"Prime Minister, you can understand the condition of the Quaid-e-Azam. Whatever he said in anger could be due to his ill-health. I request you, not to pay attention to all that."

Suddenly, Liaqat Ali Khan had a hearty laugh. Dr. Illah Baksh could not understand his unrestrained laughter.

"Doctor, this old man at last understood his mistake," said Liaqat laughing again.

The doctor looked surprised. He did not expect this from the Prime Minister.

"I have not understood, Sir? What do you mean…?"

The meaning is clear, doctor. It seems the old man has regained his brain on his death bed.

Whether the creation of Pakistan was his mistake or there was something else on his mind, only God knows," said Liaqat, after a pause. "You heard, doctor. The old man now wants to meet Jawaharlal Nehru in Delhi and create turmoil. Had Fatima not put her hand on his lips, we could have come to know something new."

The doctor kept quiet.

The few minutes he had to spend with the Quaid-e-Azam and the Prime Minister had embarrassed and deeply saddened him. It is true such things were heard through the news papers and the gossips. But, that even the big people could be so petty minded, now for the first time he experienced it personally. The Governor-General and the Prime Minister do not see eye-to-eye on the newly created state of Pakistan—that has unnerved the doctor. He did not think that he would have such a distressing experience.

The doctor was more worried about the medicines and the portable x-ray machine. They were absolutely necessary for the treatment. The doctor had expressed his concern to the Prime Minister on his arrival. But he was not sure about whether the Prime Minister was serious about them or avoiding them. The doctor was restless. He tried to enquire about them at the first opportunity. As per the information he received, the medicines procured were inadequate and the x-ray machine had not yet arrived from America.

"Sir," the doctor expressed his concern to the Prime Minister's private secretary. "The medicines and the machine are absolutely essential. The machine that we are using now is outdated. New machine will help us to understand much better the actual condition of the patient."

"What you are saying must be true from the point of treatment but, you know, such machines are not made in Pakistan."

The doctor was flabbergasted for a moment. What is the sense in reminding that these machines are made in America and not in Pakistan? If any body has the right to say any thing about the machine, it is the doctor. What does the Prime Minister's private secretary know about it?

"Sir, I have sent all the details regarding the machine and its utility to the Prime Minister's Office. In this age of telephone and aeroplane, considering the status of the patient and the condition of his health, I should have got all these things by now," said Dr. Illah Baksh expressing his displeasure.

"The Government will remember your competence and concern. But treating the patient is one thing, and running the government is another thing. We are making all possible efforts and we will keep you informed of the further developments. *Khuda Haafiz*!"

It was evident that the matter was closed.

But where the matter ended with the Prime Minister's private secretary, it began in the mind of Dr. Illah Baksh. He had more serious doubt in his mind. The doctor had earlier instructed nurse Dunham to get a file from the temporary Office of the Governor-General functioning from this bungalow and keep it in her custody. The Quaid-e-Azam was battling with death. As a doctor he did not expect him to survive.

Treating the Governor-General was his responsibility. But in the absence of the proper equipment, it was not possible to shoulder the responsibility. If the government could be so callous in procuring the essential medicines, tomorrow the doctor alone would be held responsible for neglecting the treatment. He pondered for a long time over the various aspects of these issues. The doctor himself has been a witness to the distrust and the strained relation between the Prime Minister and the Quaid-e-Azam.

After some time, he called nurse Dunhum.

"Sister, the file I asked you to bring from the superintendent of the Governor-General's Office..."

"That file is with me, Sir," said the nurse. "As per your instruction, I have made some notes. Please put your signature on the notes."

The doctor glanced through the file. It contained the copies of the correspondence relating to the procurement of the medicines and the x-ray machine. The doctor noted in his own handwriting the inadequate supply of the medicines by the Prime Minister's convoy today. He also noted the talk he had with the Prime Minister's private secretary regarding the machine.

The doctor was lost in deep thought for a while. The Prime Minister's convoy is about to leave in a short time. He decided on something in his mind and then called a stenographer from the Governor-General's Office and prepared a note immediately.

In this note, he demanded that, considering the deteriorating condition of the Quaid-e-Azam, two more doctors be assigned to assist him. He specified the qualifications required of them and recommended that this work be entrusted to some doctors, if possible. He signed the note and was ready to leave. After completing all other procedural formalities, he handed over the note to the Prime Minister's private secretary.

"Sir," said the doctor, "there is no possibility of getting any medical assistance here. If some thing untoward happens when I am not here, there would be chaos. To avert any situation like this, I have requested in this note for two more doctors to assist me."

"Your caution is commendable. Immediately on reaching Karachi, suitable arrangements shall be made to meet your demand," said the private secretary.

The doctor doubted the reliability of the assurance. The doctor felt that if some senior and trustworthy doctors are with him, they can also be a witness to the treatment. Dr. Illah Baksh's efficiency and reputation were unmatched. He did not need any assistance or guidance.

However, the doctor was not fully satisfied even after handing over the note to the private secretary. He drew the attention of the Prime Minister to this as well. "Mr. Prime Minister, we are fighting a difficult battle here. We expect your help in winning this battle. You could see I do not receive any assistance in this hill station."

"The government knows that you are the most efficient and reputed doctor in this country. That is why, we have entrusted the life as important as the Quaid-e-Azam's to you,"said Liaqat Ali Khan in a sweet voice.

"Thank you, Sir. But if the essential medicines, the x-ray machine and other medical assistance required for the treatment are not provided..." the doctor gulped the rest of words.

"Then, what will happen, doctor?" asked Liaqat Ali Khan, climbing down the stairs.

"Only God knows the answer to that question, Sir," said the doctor in a soft voice.

"What God knows we should not bother but don't you think, doctor, we should be more alert about what we know."

"You mean?" the doctor tumbled a step. His footstep faltered.

"You must remember that the well being of the Governor-General is a national concern. If the Government does not get the real information about the condition of his health and if, tomorrow, something untoward happens, who will be responsible for that?" Liaqat Ali Khan passed by the ADC, who stood with the car door open, put the one foot inside the car and turning on the other foot asked pointedly,

"I hope you understand your interest properly and remember that it is not different from the interest of the country. *Khuda Haafiz.*" Having said that, Liaqat Ali Khan turned his back and sat inside the car.

The doctor began sweating, in trying to make out what all that meant. He himself was an Army man. By the time he understood what Liaqat Ali Khan had meant, the Prime Minister's motorcade had descended the hills of Ziarat and sped up on its way to Quetta.

NOTES

1. God Willing.
2. Muslim clergymen.
3. May God keep you safe (used customarily to say goodbye).

4

Incoherent talk of Jinnah, plans of shifting to Karachi

Even after using the latest instruments, based on modern science, Dr. Illah Baksh's patient has not shown any improvement. In fact, he was moving every day closer to his ultimate end. His health had deteriorated so much, during the past few days that the doctor began doubting the success of any further treatment. The official government bulletins on the health of the Governor-General, the father of the nation, the Quaid-e-Azam were published daily in Pakistan newspapers; but how much of this news was true or manipulated only three persons knew—Dr. Illah Baksh, nurse Dunham and Madam Fatima Jinnah. In such a situation, there was no meaning in staying at Ziarat in the isolated residence. Ziarat was chosen because of its dry and pure air, besides being convenient to regulate strictly the visitors.

For the past few days, the Quaid-e-Azam was lapsing into a semi-conscious state and even talking irrelevant things. He had become unmindful of the place and time. Staying here further does not serve any purpose when considering that something untoward might happen. After having secret parleys with Fatima, the doctor decided to convey this in an unequivocal note to the Prime Minister's Office at Karachi and wind up the camp at Ziarat immediately.

"Good morning, Sir," the doctor greeted the Quaid-e-Azam, while conducting the routine morning check.

"Yesterday's reports were all very good, Sir. Your face is also fresh, today. It looks you had a good sleep last night."

The Quaid-e-Azam fixed his unemotional deeply sunk eyes on the doctor's face.

As usual, Fatima stood beside her brother. Nurse Dunham stood behind the doctor, going through the case file held in her hand. The doctor put the stethoscope on the patient's chest.

"Doctor, why don't you understand?" Every one heard the Quaid-e-Azam's frail, quivering voice. "How many times have I told you that I am not sick? Simply, some exhaustion. Let me sleep. In a day or two, I will be all right. I do not need your medicine. You go away from here," said the patient stretching out his skinny and bony hand. The nurse took his hand into hers and said in a gentle voice,

"Sir, you sleep peacefully. You are right, nothing happened to you." The Quaid-e-

Azam, taking his gaze away from the doctor looked at the nurse. His sunken eyes flashed the strain showing on his face. He closed his eyes for a moment and then said,

"Oh! Forgive me. I have become old now. You do not feel bad, if my behaviour is harsh sometimes…", then immediately added, "But, remember I am not sick."

Thereafter, he did not argue further. The doctor quietly completed his job, checked the blood pressure, pulse and temperature. He dictated his observation to the nurse in a slow voice.

"I have a meeting on Kashmir today. Why the papers have not yet reached me?" The Quaid-e-Azam suddenly banged both his fisted hands in the air in a great rage and pointing his index finger towards the ceiling and opening his eyes unusually wide said loudly, "My hands are clean. I told Mountbatten too…" Fatima, quiet but worried, while watching all this, put her hand on the patient's eyes. Dr. Illah Baksh became alert. He could see the patient slipping into delirium.

"Pakistan is incomplete without Kashmir. Liaqat is making a Pakistan of Mullahs. I will not allow this to happen…" and then suddenly his voice trembled. "Oh! This massacre… very terrible… But the left out Muslims in India and the Hindus in Pakistan… Pakistan is incomplete without Kashmir." He had trouble in breathing and started trembling.

The nurse came running. She handed over an injection to the doctor. The doctor closed his lips forcefully and gave the injection to the patient. He did not resist at all; accepted it quietly. In a few minutes, the injection had the expected effect. The Quaid-e-Azam fell into a deep slumber.

11th September, 1948

Rain clouds hovered over the mountainous skyline of Baluchistan. Amidst the gloomy stillness on earth, a group of shabby but stout, six feet tall pathans were looking at the hillock of Ziarat. The armed guards were guarding the main gate of the residence of the Quaid-e-Azam. Very few people knew that the Governor-General's entourage was about to leave the place.

An ambulance vehicle and two other cars were ready on the ground. As per protocol, considering the security and the status of the Governor-General, a military van was stationed at the gate. The whole programme was planned. The distance of seventy kilometres between Ziarat and Quetta would be covered in about two and a half to three hours and the Army aircraft kept at the airport would take another two hours to reach Karachi. If everything goes as per the plan, the Quaid-e-Azam can reach his residence at Karachi before evening.

Dr. Illah Baksh, after checking all the primary preparations, called the two attendants standing at a little distance. Both of them, carrying a stretcher, bowed their head, entered the Quaid-e-Azam's room.

"Sir, now we are returning to Karachi. The stretcher is ready to take you to the ambulance," said Dr. Illah Baksh to the Quaid-e-Azam politely.

"What did you say?" asked the Quaid-e-Azam in a semi-conscious state of mind.

"You do not understand anything, doctor. Do you understand any etiquette or not?"

The doctor, the Governor-General's ADC, Fatima and nurse Dunham—all standing in the room—were stunned.

"You are taking me to Karachi. Karachi! Pakistan's capital Karachi! Why, are you forgetting that I have made Karachi the capital of Pakistan? How can the Governor-General of Pakistan go to Karachi without being attired properly? Take away this *pyjama* and *kurta*[1]," said the Quaid-e-Azam in a frail, authoritative and harsh voice.

Illah Baksh looked at Fatima. Even she did not expect this reaction from her brother. The Quaid-e-Azam believed in etiquette and never made any compromise on that. Fatima knew it very well. But she was astonished at his anger in such condition.

"Fati, you know that my wardrobe always contained about two hundred suits. Go and get me a new suit with a matching tie. And, you remember I do not wear the same tie the second time."

Fatima nodded in agreement. In a moment, all left the room, except the doctor and the nurse. Fatima brought the new suit with the help of an attendant. The Quaid-e-Azam looked at it and shook his head in satisfaction. A brand new, stylish suit was draped on the lean body that was almost a skeleton. The Governor-General was not in a condition to button the coat himself.

"Fati, why have you not brought white silk handkerchief along with the suit? The handkerchief that you brought does not match with this." The Quaid-e-Azam refused to accept the handkerchief brought by the attendant.

Fatima turned back to bring a matching handkerchief.

"And Fati, I want to wear my pump shoes with this suit…And do not forget to bring my monocle."

All of them were stunned by this strange behaviour of the Quaid-e-Azam.

Fatima brought another handkerchief. Quaid-e-Azam insisted on opening and checking its folds. Nurse Dunham helped him to wear the shining pump shoes. The shoes looked too large on the shrunken feet. For a moment, the nurse wondered what if the Governor-General orders to bring new shoes that suit him!

But, Quaid-e-Azam gave no such order. Yet, the nurse's apprehension turned right in another way—

"Nurse," the Quaid-e-Azam drew her attention by shaking his head. "You have not put the monocle on my eyes as yet."

"Yes Sir. I am sorry." The nurse took the monocle specs from the accessory tray in her hand and put it on the right eye of the Quaid-e-Azam—a strange happiness spread on his face, the lines on his cheeks more pronounced, lips tightened. The nurse avoided looking at him and turned her face, lest others might notice what she was observing.

In a few minutes, the full entourage sat in the vehicle waiting outside and it speeded up in the direction of Quetta airport.

There was considerable delay in reaching the Quetta airport due to the drizzling, the mountainous slopes and the foggy atmosphere. The vehicle reached the Quetta airport after a tiring four-hours journey. The army aircraft guarded by the security men was waiting for the arrival of the Governor-General. None, including pilot knew who the travellers were. All the guards on duty stood on alert as they saw the Governor-General's vehicle enter the airport. As per the plan, the Governor-General was shifted to the waiting aircraft, without even a moment's delay. Dr. Illah Baksh, nurse Dunham and Fatima joined the crew members in the aircraft. When the aircraft took off from the Quetta airport, it was half past two in the afternoon.

"Doctor," said the Quaid-e-Azam slowly when the plane ascended to the desired height, "Where are you taking me, without my permission? I have just got a slight fever. This fever will go away in a day or two. You cannot take me like this."

"Sir, we are going to your house in Karachi. Your health is absolutely normal. No need to worry," the doctor said softly.

"Karachi! There! Very good. I like going to Karachi. I was fed up of that isolated room in Ziarat. But...but..." the Quaid-e-Azam stopped suddenly as he remembered something. Quiet for a moment. The aircraft jerked.

"But, you cannot take me to Karachi in this condition. I do not wish to go to the Governor-General's palace in Karachi in this helpless condition. As you know, on the way to my room from the main gate of the building, there are my ADC's room, the army advisor and other officials' rooms. I cannot bear the humiliation of being taken to my room in a stretcher right in front of them. Doctor, this is my order. Turn back the aircraft."

Fatima started gently soothing her brother's forehead and cheeks. Suddenly, the Quaid-e-Azam's eyes filled with tears.

"I know, Fati. Now, I am not going to live long. The sooner I die, it's better."

Fatima sobbed, covering her mouth with her *dupatta*[2].

The aircraft was flying in the sky over the land now carved out and called Pakistan. A lot more remained hidden in the realm of unknown than what the people in the aircraft knew. The journey of four hundred kilometres from Quetta to Karachi passed off without any inconvenience. In between, Fatima was looking out without blinking through the windows of the aircraft. Dr. Illah Baksh's mind was troubled with various thoughts. More than the patient's treatment, he was thinking about himself that how he was drawn into politics. He could not forget what transpired when he met the Prime Minister last. The doctor knew only that during the past twenty years the Governor-General and the Prime Minister had fought arm-in-arm for the community's interest. He had never imagined that they distrusted each other so deeply. He could not fathom where this distrust would ultimately lead to. But he understood now that there is no question of saving the life of the patient.

When the aircraft landed on the Mauripur airport of Karachi, the sun was setting and the sky was clearly visible.

NOTES

1. An Indian attire.
2. A piece of cloth worn by women across the chest.

5

Serious condition and ambulance, Dr. Illah Baksh-Liaquat dialogue in Karachi

Most of the employees at the Mauripur airport, making arrangements for emplaning the aircrafts, knew only that some very important person is arriving escorted by the entourage. They could identify the person only when they saw the aircraft in the sky. What a few selected high officials, sitting in the control room at the airport, knew so far has now become the subject of hush-hush talk. Almost every one was familiar with the Quaid-e-Azam's Viking aircraft. The British Viceroy used to keep a special private aircraft before 15th August 1947. The Quaid-e-Azam too followed the same practice after the creation of Pakistan. This private aircraft was hardly used in the past six months because he instructed his army officers that nobody, except the Governor-General, the Quaid-e-Azam, should use it. Even the last year, when the government utilized all its resources and infrastructure to bring the Muslims to Pakistan from India and the situation was very bad, the Quaid-e-Azam did not permit any one to use the Viking aircraft.

As per the instructions issued earlier, the ambulance reached the aircraft as soon as its door opened. The army men emplaned from the Dakota aircraft immediately put the stretcher carrying the Governor General in the ambulance. The vehicles were ready to take the passengers of other three aircrafts to the Governor's House. There was no national emblem or flag on any of the vehicles, so that the pedestrians do not get any idea of the important occupants. Only Fatima and nurse Dunham sat with the Governor General in the ambulance. Dr. Illah Baksh and others sat in another government vehicle. The entire process was completed speedily and the convoy of vehicles sped towards the south direction. The rays of the setting sun on the west fell on the glittering surface of the vehicles.

All the people were quiet. Fatima, sitting in the ambulance, was looking out through the closed glass windows. There was hardly any traffic on the road. On both sides of the road, in the open grounds, the houses were scattered here and there. Nurse Dunham was checking the pulse of the patient lying on the stretcher now and then and her face turned grim after every check.

The driver of the ambulance put the brake suddenly. The speeding ambulance stopped near a corner on the left side of the road. Other vehicles following the ambulance also stopped, like disciplined soldiers. The drivers of the vehicles in front of the ambulance saw this through the mirror, took a sharp U turn and stopped in front of the ambulance. The driver of the ambulance jumped out. Fatima was scared. She peeped out of the window and enquired,

"What is the matter? Why has the ambulance stopped?"

"Madam, I will look into it. Perhaps there is no petrol in the vehicle... You don't worry," said the driver and started checking the engine.

Fatima looked around. The road was deserted. This part of north Karachi was sparsely populated. The refugee camps opened for the Muslims who came to Karachi from India were a few steps away. Owing to the fresh rain, puddles and potholes filled with dirty water were seen everywhere on the uneven ground. Some dirty children, almost naked, were jumping and playing in the water. Some dull people moving helplessly around the refugee camps were seen. When Fatima opened the ambulance window, mosquitoes and flies entered inside. Sister Dunham unsuccessfully tried to drive them out with her two hands.

Dr. Illah Baksh who was in the vehicle behind got down, with anxiety writ large on his face. It looks the unexpected sudden stoppage in the half way raised his blood pressure. He came running to the ambulance and shouted at the driver,

"What is happening? What is the meaning of stopping the ambulance half way?"

"Sir, you don't worry. This is a vehicle. Sometimes it breaks down suddenly. It seems the engine has some problem. Like I say, everything will be all right."

In the meantime, the drivers and the passengers of other vehicles came out and stood worried. The drivers consulted each other, took out the instruments from the deck behind the vehicles and started checking the engines. Dr. Illah Baksh's graph of anxiety was rising rapidly. His assistant Dr. Mistry also got down from the vehicle along with him. He asked in a low voice,

"Doctor, I think this is an emergency. I will get into the ambulance and check the condition of the Quaid-e-Azam."

"You are doing the right thing, doctor. I agree with you." said Illah Baksh.

Dr. Mistry went into the ambulance. The Quaid-e-Azam had already lapsed into unconsciousness. A cluster of mosquitoes forced inside behind Dr, Mistry. The doctor checked the patient's pulse and heart beat. He opened the Quaid-e-Azam eyelids with his fingers. His face showed he was not only worried, but also despondent. He came out quietly. The mosquitoes, liking the atmosphere inside, preferred to stay there, buzzing over the Quaid-e-Azam's uncovered face and flying around.

Fatima, understanding the expression on the face of Dr. Mistry, came out along with him, worried and furious. Nurse Dunham, trying to drive out the mosquitoes with her two hands inside the ambulance, put her hand on the Quaid-e-Azam's forehead. He just opened the eyes, closed till then, and then raised his skeletal weak hand and put the fingers on the nurse's wrist. She looked at the deep sunken eyes of the Quaid-e-Azam with great pity. She read many a time the story of Jesus' last meal with his disciples. The priests often recited this story in the church premises at Sunday services. Nurse Dunham suddenly remembered the betrayal of Jesus by his disciple Judas and the agony of the crucification of Jesus by his enemies. In two thousand years, Judas must have been reborn many times. Jesus was not reborn even once. She looked outside.

The refugee camps were lit here and there. As if waiting for the darkness to fall, the refugee men and women were looking for some cover to attend to the nature's calls. No one among them, who came here considering Pakistan a heaven, knew that the person who created Pakistan was breathing his last a few steps away. The principle of natural justice came face-to-face with the blind scale of justice. A few vehicles were passing on both sides of the road. But none of them were aware that the creator of this infant independent country was nearby lying helplessly in the last stages of his life.

Dr. Mistry whispered in Dr. Illah Baksh's ear, "Sir, the condition is very critical. There is no hope. I could not even count the pulse."

Dr. Illah Baksh nodded.

"What are you people doing here? At such a critical time, was not there any better vehicle with the government to take the Governor General? Somebody run and tell Liaqat Ali Khan that..." Fatima screamed in a fit of rage.

The driver of ambulance, checking the vehicle, lying on the ground, put his neck out and said trembling,

"Forgive me, Madam. Now the engine is all right. We are leaving."

All of them got back into their respective vehicles. Nurse Dunham drove away as many mosquitoes and flies as she could and then closed the glass. The convoy was heading in the direction of Karachi. But at such a critical time, one important hour was wasted. The houses of Karachi could be seen from a distance. But it would take still another half an hour to reach the Governor's House. Fatima, furious, lips quivering, looked at her wristwatch. It took four hours from Quetta to reach Karachi airport. And now, in reaching the Governor's House from the airport, two hours were wasted.

When the convoy entered the Governor's House, the Prime Minister and the other politicians were present there. The Quaid-e-Azam was in a semi conscious state throughout the journey. A curious doubt arose in Dr. Illah Baksh's mind. The Quaid-e-Azam himself knew that he was breathing his last, yet he insisted on putting on his formal dress at Ziarat, despite lying on the stretcher. It is a blessing in disguise that he was not conscious now. He would not have tolerated his being carried on a stretcher past the lobby and the steps of the Governor's House. Had he been conscious, perhaps he would have insisted on being properly attired and even wearing the monocle. He would have adamantly insisted on walking. And if that happened...

Illah Baksh could not imagine its consequences.

Liaqat Ali Khan came forward and greeted the Quaid-e-Azam, *Aadab Arz* slightly bending. Fatima, who was standing close to him, did not look at him. Liaqat Ali Khan ignored Fatima and did not ask anything about the condition of Quaid-e-Azam. But he took Dr. Illah Baksh aside and started telling him,

"Doctor, the entire country is waiting to know the actual condition of your patient. The cabinet is prepared for any eventuality, even emergency, but all this depends upon you."

"Sir, I am unable to understand what you are saying. I would be obliged if you could tell me clearly."

"Doctor, we do not have much time to argue. God forbid, if something untoward happens to the Governor General, the news should not go out without my permission, you remember that. This you can take not as my request, but the order of the Prime Minister. I do not want you to be held responsible for any national crisis," said Liaqat Ali Khan in a firm voice and keeping a firm hand on the doctor's shoulder looked at him.

Dr. Illah Baksh did not expect all this. He never thought that the Prime Minister would be so discourteous and firm with him. His face betrayed confusion. This was what Liaqat Ali Khan wanted. Sensing the doctor's feelings, he asked him gently, "doctor, could you tell me why we partitioned India and got this independent country?"

For the doctor, this question too was unexpected. Yet, he replied in a clear voice.

"The answer is obvious, Sir. We secured Pakistan for the welfare of the Muslims."

"Good, doctor. You have real foresight. What do you have to say if the same community for whom we endured so much suffering are relegated to the background?" asked Liaqat Ali Khan.

"'How can that happen, Sir?"

"You are right. That should not happen. Our first duty is to ensure that the Muslims enjoy more privileges than other communities. We have to ensure that Pakistan remains *Dar-ul-Islam*[1] in future and there should be no fear of it becoming *Dar-ul-Harb*[2]. And if there is any hurdle in having this, it is our prime duty to find a way out."

"Yes, Sir. I agree with you."

"But just agreeing won't do, doctor. The Quaid-e-Azam got us Pakistan, but we cannot allow Pakistan to be destroyed by the vision of the Quid-e-Azam. He wants once again to make this country equal for the Hindus and the Muslims. He wants to build this country defying the orders of the *Imams*[3] and the *Maulvis.* But we will not allow that to happen." The Prime Minister, while concluding the conversation said, "Doctor, the Quaid-e-Azam is the past and Pakistan is the future. We cannot allow the past to determine the future. Just keep all this in mind and then make the next move, *Khuda Haafiz*!"

Liaqat Ali Khan ended his conversation. Dr. Illah Baksh was stunned by the last sentence of the Prime Minister. The Prime Minister's order was clear that, God forbid, if the Quaid-e-Azam died, the news should be kept a secret for the time being.

When the Governor General was laid on the bed in his air conditioned room, he opened his eyes slightly, indicating his regaining of consciousness. The doctor looked at the patient with great hope. The patient looked around. It was difficult to understand his emotions. He closed his lips tightly. Dr. Illah Baksh said something to Dr. Mistry, standing by his side. Dr Mistry very politely requested the persons present in the room to leave.

Fatima, the two doctors, nurse Dunhan and the Prime Minister Liaqat Ali Khan were present in the room. The doctor feared that, if the Quaid-e-Azam becomes conscious he would not like the Prime Minister's presence in the room and might even strain his mind. But Dr. Illah Baksh did not have the courage to tell the Prime Minister to leave the room. The Quaid-e-Azam's end was inevitable. Liaqat Ali Khan leaving the room may give some relief, but only for a short while. The doctor knew this unambiguously. In such a situation, telling the Prime Minister to leave the room would not only be an affront, but futile.

In the meantime, Dr. Mistry asked the nurse for some medicine. Dr. Illah Baksh checked the Governor General's blood pressure. He also checked the heartbeat and the pulse. The result was not encouraging. The Governor General was breathing heavily.

"Fati..." the Quaid-e-Azam feebly called out.

Fati bent, put her ear close to his lips. She waited for sometime, but did not hear anything again. A strange eerie silence prevailed in the room.

Dr. Illah Baksh was holding the injection prepared by Dr. Mistry. Fatima moved away her face from the Quaid-e-Azam. The doctor said in a very soft voice,

"Sir, this is a very strong injection. God willing, you will get a new life."

The Quaid-e-Azam's eye lashes fluttered. His lips quivered. Every one in the room was eager to hear.

"I knew, doctor. Now, I am not going to live," said the Quaid-e-Azam, as he held the lips tightly and closed his eyes again.

Dr. Illah Baksh was stunned. That the patient, whose heartbeat and pulse had sunk so deep and the blood pressure disappointingly low, could speak so clearly and firmly at that moment was amazing indeed.

NOTES

1. Land which is ruled by Islamic principles.
2. Land where Islam does not rule.
3. A Muslim clergymen.

6

Education of Maamad, fishing business of Punja Valji, boycott by villagers

"Maamad," the forty year old Zinabhai called out to his eldest son Muhammad who was sixteen or seventeen years old. His name was spelt as Muhammad in *Jamaatkhana*[1] and the school register, but among the six children of Zinabhai and his acquaintances, he was known as Maamad.

Since this afternoon, Zinabhai has been anxious about his son's activities. Maamad was admitted to a *Jamaatkhana* to get some religious education, but two years later a *Maulvi* complained that he was not good in studies. Then, Zinabhai was involved neck-deep in his business. He reprimanded his son, and then got involved in his business. But the *Maulvi* advised him that instead of sending Maamad to the *Jamaatkhana*, he should send him elsewhere. Zinabhai's import and export business was flourishing, owing to the good equation he had with the British Douglas Graham & Company. The Manager of the Company, Sir Frederick Croft was very efficient in his job. By looking at him, Zinabhai more often felt that learning the language of the *Saheb*[2] would be advantageous in getting more work, and knowing the rules and regulations would help in understanding their style of functioning. Zinabhai himself did not know any other language, except Gujararti and Sindhi. He spoke broken Hindi, but that too with a mix of Gujarati and Sindhi. Sometimes, he would utter a sentence in English by mixing few words, that too applying the ancient Gujarati grammar rules.

Therefore, if Maamad was not getting religious education, unable to recite Quran or *Al Fatiha*[3], Zinabhai did not regret. He admitted Maamad to a *Jamaatkhana* at the insistence of his wife Mithibai. Zinabhai, right from the beginning, wanted Maamad to study in an English school, not in a *Jamaatkhana*, so that he could become clever and efficient, like Frederick Croft, and look after his business. Now, he removed Maamad from the *Jamaatkhana* and admitted him to a Christian Missionary School.

Zinabhai's business was flourishing. His business involved travelling not only to Karachi, but also to other neighbouring regions. The Punja Valji Thakkar Company was dealing with cotton, fur, leather and food grains. The centres for purchase of these goods were located at distant regions, away from Karachi. In the absence of the proper transport facilities, Zinabhai had a few thoroughbred horses. He travelled to distant places riding on these horses, to carry out the day-to-day business. The other trusted *Kathiawari* colleagues too made use of the horses. Maamad liked horse riding more than his studies. This afternoon, Zinabhai came to know that Maamad was not going to school since the last two days. In the morning he went on a ride on his Arabian horse to roam around. Maamad was a good horse rider. Zinabhai knew this. Maamad was very skinny and tall for his age. But the way he used to mount the horses, hold on to the reins and tame even the wild horses by holding on to their manes, made Zinabhai confident that he would not fall off the horse or meet with any accident. But Zinabhai's main worry was how to manage the family business in these fast changing times if Maamad did not study even in the English school.

As soon as Mammad reached home in the evening, Zinabhai called him. Zinabhai's attention was drawn to the sound of the galloping horse. Maamad's sharp eyes could see his father noticing him coming home, from the second floor of an old three-storeyed Vazir Mansion on Newnham Road. The road was always buzzing with loaded camels and camel carts. The road was so narrow that sometime camels could peep inside through the open windows on the first floor. But, today, being both Friday and *Amavasya*[4], the Muslim traders had gone to the Mosque to offer prayers, while the Hindus observed a holiday. Zinabhai had nothing to do with Friday and *Amavasya.* He would have a holiday, only on the day when Douglas Graham & Company observed the holiday.

"Yes, *Abbajaan*!" Maamad greeted his father with a very innocent face.

"Maamad, is it true that you did not go to the school for the last two days?" Zinabhai asked his son.

Maamad did not give any answer. He was looking out of the window, as if he had not heard his father.

"Why are you silent? Haven't you heard me?" said Zinabhai raising his voice.

Maamad realised that now he could not escape without answering, so he said, "*Abbajaan*, I have no interest in studying in this English School. Whatever the Christian teachers and the priests teach is all confusing."

"Look Maamad, if you are not interested in learning from the *Maulvis* of the *Jamaatkhana* or from the priests of the Christian School, then help me in my work. You will become a good businessman in a year or two."

Maamad neither rejected nor accepted his father's suggestion. He started looking after the day-to-day working of the Company, but in that too, he did not show much interest. It would be catastrophic, if he was taken out from the school and asked to assist in the business.

He knew his father's nature. Zinabhai was a mild natured man, but if any idea comes to his mind, he would pursue until it is realised. Maamad, understanding the situation, said gently,

"*Abbajaan*, I will now focus on my studies. Let me pass the matriculation, at least." Zinabhai felt happy.

"Good! If you pass the matriculation nothing could be better than that. You have my blessings. But remember that you are the eldest of your siblings, and you have to shoulder the responsibility of the family. Never forget, that it is your duty to look after your younger brothers and sisters."

Yes, "*Abbajaan!*"Maamad felt the issue was settled at least this way.

*

In the middle of the nineteenth century, some two hundred royal families carved out their kingdom in a famous region called Kathiawar, situated on the west coast of India. The British Agency did not give them any work, except leaving them to enjoy drinking opium, hunting rabbits and deer and partaking in traditional meals in the markets. Rajkot was a central place in Kathiawar. The British Agency had established its Headquarters there to keep a watch on the royal families. Besides the upper caste families of the Brahmins and the Vaishyas, the Rajputs, the Patels and the other communities had also lived there. Among them, the Lohana community was the most prominent. A few families who were converted to Islam and became Khojas also lived in Paneli. They earned a living by doing some small business, besides farming. The minor skirmishes that used to take place among the small fiefdoms had now come down. And due to the British Rule, the peace loving people found it easy to earn their livelihood.

Punja Valji Thakkar's family was not very large, but Punja had a business acumen. Rajkot, after becoming the Headquarters of the Agency, had progressed and its business developed very rapidly. The Kathiawar region had a significant number of Muslims. And now it had become a dominant place for the white people. The Memon, the Vora, the Vagher and the Khoja Muslims preferred eating fish. Punja observed that the Lohana community had good business in all the trades in Paneli and its surroundings. But no one had any trading in fish till now. Punja Thakkar had seen how in Veraval and Porbandar, the fishing business flourished. He studied the market price of the dry fish in Veraval and Porbandar and estimated the price at which the dry fish could be sold in Rajkot and other places.

Punja's family, as per the Lohana tradition, followed the *Vaishnav*[5] sect of Hinduism, but was not particular in observing the rituals at home. The idol of *Shrinathji*[6] was kept in one corner and Punja Thakkar's wife used to chant *Shri Krishna sarnam mam*[7] every morning and, after the bath, prayed and offered, among others things, sweet milk to *Shrinathji*. Punja's father was a staunch Vaishnavite throughout his life and his mother observed all the rituals till her last breath. But, after her death, Punja deposited the idol in a local *Haveli*[8].

As Punja started trading in dry fish, the *Vaishnav* community and all other upper caste Hindus felt offended. The Lohana community in Paneli felt restless as to how a son like Punja Thakkar was born in the family of Valji Thakkar, who was a staunch Vaishnavite. Some elderly people in the village rebuked Punja.

"Punja, if you cannot feed your stomach, slit the stomach, but are you not ashamed of forgetting the Vaishnavite traditions of your forefathers and doing this dirty business? This is the business of the Muslims."

Punja got used to such remarks every day. The dry fish used to be brought from Veraval and Porbandar to Paneli on bullock carts. But, it was difficult to hire any bullock cart from Paneli to transport the material to Rajkot and other markets. It was not that there were no low caste bullock cart owners in Paneli, but because of the stinking smell of the fish, no one wanted to come closer. Punja was willing to offer a high rent, but no bullock cart owner in the village and in Rajkot was prepared to associate with this business.

Punja was very stubborn. It was not in his blood to give up any thing once he had decided. The fishing business was profitable. Why should the Lohana community and the other upper caste Hindus be jealous of him, if he earned money in his business? The bullock cart owners kept a distance from him. Had he committed such a serious crime that he deserved such a severe punishment, in spite of living in the village for many generations?

There was a possibility of incurring loss, as the fish from Veraval and Porbandar was not reaching Paneli on time. The fish had to be stored in godowns. Even at this, the people opposed vehemently and screamed and shouted,

"Punja, this is a Brahmins' locality, not of the butchers." Stop storing this stinking fish here. In this locality, your Muslim life style is not acceptable."

Punja was enraged. This is my village. This is my house. Those objecting to my business were not angels themselves. Punja too was aware of their many wrong doings. If these sinners believed that by putting *tilak*[9] on their forehead and chanting *Shri Krishna sharnam mam* they became pure, let them do so. Punja had to worry feeding five mouths every day—three sons and his wife and himself. No Brahmin or Vaishya in the village would satisfy his hunger. Why should these people insult him, if he was making money from his business without harassing or causing any inconvenience to any one?

At that time, some thing unexpected happened.

Adamji Khoja had good friendship with Punja. Adamji Khoja's forefathers were Lohanas converted to Islam and then became Khojas. Adamji was not a native of Paneli, but lived in Salaya near Halvad. After becoming Khojas, his family did not like living in ancestral village. They left the village and settled in Paneli. Adamji had mingled with the people so well that he was now considered a native of Paneli. Ever since Punja's relations with the villagers were strained, he used to spend most of his time with Adamji. He felt relieved by pouring out his woes to him. Adamji tried to boost his confidence. Adamji was a well respected person in the village. He used to get involved in all the events of the village, besides spending money.

During one of his meetings, Adamji gave the news to Punja.

"Punja, His Majesty Aga Khan is coming to Rajkot next month."

NOTES

1. A Muslim school which imparts religious education in Islam.
2. An address for Britishers used by Indians before Independence i.e. Sir.
3. The fist *Sura* or chapter of the Quran. It is the prayer, which a Muslim performs at the time of Namaaz.
4. The last day of the new moon phase, according to the Hindu calendar.
5. A devotee of Lord Vishnu.
6. An incarnation of Lord Krishna worshiped by the Vaishnavites.
7. A hymn in praise of Lord Krishna.
8. A Vaishnav Temple.
9. A red mark (vermilion) or a mark made by sandalwood paste applied by the Hindus on the forehead.

7

Arrival of Aga Khan in India, Punja's conversion to Islam

At the beginning of the nineteenth century, Aga Hasan Ali Shah, the religious head of the entire Ismailian Muslim world, had received the title of 'Aga Khan' from the Emperor of Iran.

Aga Hasan Ali was the forty-fifth Imam, since the Islam began its victorious march at the beginning of the seventh century. He was revered, throughout the Islamic world, as the direct descendant of Prophet Muhammad's daughter Fatima.

The title 'Aga Khan' added to his glory. This religious head, worshipped by the millions of Muslims, made India his home around 1840 AD.

When Aga Hasan Ali Shah put his foot in Sindh, he had about a thousand people consisting of family members, the servants and the army soldiers. It is almost a millennium since the Islamic invasion had forced the Zoroastrians to flee their homeland. Aga Hasan Ali Shah, whose ancestors made Iran their homeland, had not only exercised the religious authority as the Chief of the millions of the Ismailian Muslims, but also had an absolute control over the Iranian city of Karman. In Karman, he had his own palace, forts and an independent army. But an event had forced him to leave all that in search of a shelter, like a refugee.

Aga Hasan Ali Shah was the son-in-law of the emperor Fateh Ali. After Fateh Ali's death, his son Mohammed Shah ascended the throne. Mirza Ahasi was Mohammed Shah's teacher in his teenage. Mohammed Shah revered him as his ideal teacher. And when Mohammed Shah became the King, he appointed Mirza Ahasi as the Prime Minister. The Prime Minister became all powerful. Aga Khan had a very beautiful and intelligent daughter. The Prime Minister Mirza Ahasi wanted that Aga Khan's daughter should marry his son. He mooted the proposal. It was a difficult problem for Hasan Ali Shah Aga Khan. His daughter was also the grand daughter of the late Emperor of Iran. Iran's royal blood and the holy blood of Aga Khan… how could such blood be merged with that of an ordinary Muslim family like that of Mirza Ahasi? Before Aga Khan could find any solution to the problem, Mohammed Shah brought on him pressure and supported Mirza's proposal. Now that Mirza was not alone, but had the King's support, Aga Khan faced a predicament.

Aga Khan confronted Mirza a few days later by closing the Karman fort, but he knew that he could not sustain this for long. It was easy to get money from the devotees across the world, but this was like a sword play. Aga Khan had no option. He should either leave Iran immediately or accept the blood relation with Mirza's family, as per the King's wish. Aga Khan, the religious head of the millions of the Ismailian Muslims, left the city of Karman one midnight along with his entire entourage and escaped safely into the mountainous region of Afghanistan. But this mountainous region was not suitable for living. Even in the midst of the nineteenth century, this region and its people were still living in the medieval age. Hasan Ali Shah was an astute person. Kabul or Kandhar could not be any special place for functioning. Afghanistan and its eastern neighbour India had fought many a time. In its eastern neighbourhood, the British rule was being established. It is possible that the Britishers might conquer Afghanistan in future and if that happened, they too would have to suffer.

India was *Dar-ul-Islam* until now. In spite of eight hundred years of the Muslim rule, India had not become an Islamic country. When this had not happened under the Muslin rule and now when the Muslim rule ended and the British rule being established, it was a good opportunity to promote Islam. What was not achieved by the sword may be achieved by establishing the headquarters of Islamic religion in India. The Muslims ruled India by defeating the Hindus, who lived there since the dawn of civilisation. Now the Christians defeated the Muslims and established their rule in India. India known as *Dar-ul-Islam* until now, had now become *Dar-ul-Harb*.

He was the first Aga Khan who came to India in 1848 A.D. and established his headquarters in Bombay. He gradually started utilising his vast treasury for the benefit of the Ismailian Muslims in India. Various educational, medical and financial trusts were established for the welfare of the Muslims. For the Muslims in India, Aga Khan was an idol until now, but now he presented himself in person before them. The Ismailian Muslim community was eager to meet their idol, offer him gifts and even lay down their lives for him. After spending some time in Bombay, he set off on a countrywide tour to meet the other Muslims. As a part of this tour, he was arriving in Rajkot.

To Adamji, Aga Khan was an idol. He was thrilled, when he came to know that he could see him in person. Adamji often used to visit Rajkot for the purchase and sale of goods. Just as he maintained the business contacts, he also maintained the religious contacts with the *Mullahs* and the *Maulvis.* Sometimes, he would offer a *chadar*[1] at the shrine of a Muslim saint and go to the mosque to offer prayers. On one such occasion, he came to know that the Muslims of Rajkot sent an invitation to Aga Khan on behalf of their entire fellow-religionists of Kathiawar. And a programme to offer special gifts at the feet of Aga Khan was also planned.

As a part of this programme, it was decided that each Ismaili Khoja, who received the message of God from the Prophet Muhammad, should pass it on to at least one more *kafir*[2]. Adamji did not know much about it. But, from the Imam's talk he registered in his mind that if a good Muslim could convert a person into Islam on that day, God would not only be pleased with him, but that a helpless *kafir* would walk on the path to heaven.

Adamji had a lot of sympathy for Punja. He was a witness to the sufferings of Punja in his life. Adamji felt that his community was, without any reason, accusing him for no fault of his. Ever since the *Maulvi* in the mosque impressed upon him to bring a *kafir* to the court of God, the first thing that came to his mind was Punja. His community ostracised him. He had financial problems. He had the responsibility of educating, marrying and settling his three sons. In such a situation, if Punja is ready, he would get satisfaction of having done some good thing and Punja would be free of the sufferings. With the blessings of Aga Khan, his children would get education and also a livelihood.

Punja did not know anything about Aga Khan. When Adamji told him about the arrival of Aga Khan, he listened without any excitement.

"Punja, I have an idea that would put an end to your difficulties, if you do not mind,"Adamji began talking slowly.

"My goodness, if you had any such idea, why did you wait till now? Now even I want to show these rascals that I am no less." Punja said in anger.

"Look, even my forefathers belonged to your community. When your community ostracised us, we had received the divine blessings of the Prophet Mohammed. Now, if you too take to the path shown by the Prophet Mohammed, you will also receive the blessings of Allah." Adamji uttered each word cautiously.

"I do not understand anything. Tell me clearly what you want to say." Punja straightened his neck, and looked at Adamji with his eyes wide open.

And Punja began pondering over what Adamji had said. What he said was clear. Adamji also said that others, like him, would also get converted to Islam on the occasion of welcoming Aga Khan. Some people would get from them scholarships for their children's education and some others would get medical expenses for their family members at Bombay. Those also included, the people who lived for generations in the village, but not allowed to take water from the village wells and barred from entering the temple to pray to Lord Rama. If all these people receive the blessings of Aga Khan, as suggested by Adamji, they would lead a very happy life.

Punja knew that ever since he started the fishing business, his village Brahmins and Vaishyas, Rajputs, Kolis and even his own Lohana community had turned against him. He also knew that some times, they used to call him a 'converted turk' behind his back. He was storing the dry fish in his own godown, yet the people in the neighbourhood used to abuse and insult him day in, day out. How long this would go on! For quite some time, he was thinking of giving them a befitting reply, but he did not get any idea until now. If he accepted Adamji's idea...

That way, Punja was not a man of religious beliefs and practices. He deposited the *Shrinathji's* idol that his mother used to worship in the *Haveli*, after her death. His wife performed some trituals at home, but he never took any interest in them. If he converted to Islam, as per Adamji's suggestion, there would neither be any change in his mentality nor his way of life. It would be a befitting reply to the people who are bad to him. That he should ask his wife and children about this never occurred to him. And he was not aware of the legal implications either.

Gangji, his eldest son, was now of marriageable age. He would not be able to bear, if his community refused to give a girl in marriage because of his business. His second son Nathu, after completing the schooling in Paneli, started assisting the father in his business. But if the business continues like this, he would have to take also the responsibility of feeding his daughters-in-law, after the marriage of their sons. All this was very difficult for Punja Thakkar. The youngest son, Zinia, was still a minor, but he would become an adult in a couple of years. Punja Thakkar was most worried about his youngest son. Gangji and Nathu were healthy and robust. They had the physical strength to beat others and bear the beating from others, if necessary. But, Zinia was very weak and thin. At the time of his naming ceremony his sister, called him "Brother, your son is very thin and delicate. He is so small that Zinia (meaning equivalent to small in Gujarati) would be befitting name for him."

Thus, Punja's youngest son was named going by his physical appearance, not by his zodiac sign. Because of the weakness, Zinia used to fall sick too often. Punja Thakkar sometimes used to worry about him and at other time pity him. He felt that if Zinia remained like this, he would find life difficult. Both Gangji and Nathu adjusted to the fishing business once it started and never complained. But Zinia had complained to his father many a time.

"Father, all the boys in the village tease me by labelling me as a fish eater. None of us eat the fish at home, yet the boys spit on me,"Zinia looked at his father with a pathetic face.

Punja felt that when he was doing the business, how his innocent son was at fault. He could understand if the village heads rejected him, but there was a limit. How these rich children can harass his innocent son Zinia. He became so furious for a moment that he felt like slaughtering the children who insulted Zinia, unmindful of the consequences.

But Punja knew his limits. If he did something in anger, he would have to face the consequences. The villagers would join hands and ask him to leave the village. The Brahmins and the Vaishyas were all right, but the Rajputs and the Patels would make his life miserable.

When Punja was lost in deep thought, Adamji suddenly made the proposal. Punja felt that Adamji alone could save his sinking boat. He thought over the

Adamji's proposal. What difference does it make if he became a Muslim? As per Adamji's assurance, nothing could be better than Gangji and Nathu settling in some business in Bombay or Rajkot. Zinia had completed his primary education in Paneli school. Punja was not financially sound to put him in a boarding school at Rajkot, nor Zinia's health was good enough. In such a situation, if Gangji and Nathu could do some business in Bombay with the blessings of Aga Khan and earn money, Zinia could also be sent there to study at least till matriculation. If Zinia passed the matriculation, he would be able to get some government job. His frail son would not be able to bear the strain of running a business. In a government job, he would earn a living without ever going hungry.

Punja made up his mind. Adamji was overjoyed when he told him about his decision. He hugged Punja. Adamji jubiliantly regaled and narrated to Punja many stories of how Allah had shown mercy on those hapless souls who returned to His fold.

To Punja, this was the best way to take vengeance against the people of Paneli. Not only would he be able to avenge and silence the people, but his sons' future would also be secure.

But no one should know about his decision till Punja Valji Thakkar Raghuvanshi Lohana atoned for the misdeeds of his past life at the feet of the Almighty Allah. Punja did not want his wife and children to obstruct him. Once he was converted, they would have no option.

Adamji reassured Punja in every possible way. It may take Punja an eternity to reach heaven, but Adamji felt he had done a good thing and was sure of receiving the Divine blessings of Allah. He was pleased by the offering he would make to Aga Khan. Fearing Punja might reconsider his decision, he said cautiously to him,

"Punja, His Highness Aga Khan will seek Allah's blessings on your behalf at the time of *Magrib* during the *Namaaz*[3] on Friday. The Imam will perform the necessary ceremony. We have still two days. If you agree, we can go to Rajkot right now and make all the arrangements. We can give the excuse of taking the goods to Rajkot. The *Imamkhana*[4] over there will provide us accommodation and meals."

Punja felt that there was some sense in what Adamji said. His weariness was growing day-by-day. He thought, it would be better to unburden as soon as possible. Once he became a Muslim, he would scorn the village and say,

"You scoundrels, you used to call me Turk and Muslim. See, now, I have actually become a Muslim and standing on your chest. Go and do whatever you can!"

His heart stopped for a moment whenever he said this to himself. He stopped looking at the picture of *Shrinathji* since the last two days. He did not step into the prayer room for the past two days.

He immediately accepted Adamji's suggestion. Both the friends left for Rajkot the next morning.

Adamji and Punja returned to Paneli from Rajkot on Saturday morning. Punja hardly spoke during the journey, in spite of Adamji trying to talk to him now and then. Adamji's joy knew no bounds. As he held Punja responsible for bringing him so much joy, he indulged with Punja.

When Punja stepped on the threshold of his home, he was no longer a Raghuvanshi Lohana, but an Ismaili Khoja blessed by Aga Khan in the service of Allah.

He suddenly stopped on listening to his wife singing the hymn *Manglashtak*[5] behind the closed door.

NOTES

1. A quilt of cloth offered on a grave.
2. Infidel, non-believer in Islam.
3. Islamic way of prayer.
4. A shelter offered to the pilgrims in a mosque.
5. A Hindu Prayer.

8

Family's opposition to the conversion, boycott by *havelis* and temples

Punja had doubted, right from the beginning, that his wife and children would not accept this change of religion. The reason behind his conversion was to take revenge against the Paneli villagers, particularly the Lohana community and his relatives. Unlike him, his wife and his children were not consumed by the flames of vengeance. Though the youngest son was ostracised by his peers, he did not have any enmity with them. But Zinia was still a child. He had not seen the world as yet. But Punja had seen the world and experienced its ways quite well. The people were against his business as they did not want him to prosper. Because of their wickedness, it was natural for Punja to develop the feeling of vengeance against them. Even then, he feared that his wife and his children would oppose his decision. But he was also confident that they would accept it.

But his confidence was misplaced. His wife was dumbstruck when she came to know that her husband was no longer a Raghuvanshi Vaishnav Lohana, but an Ismaili Khoja, who prayed twice a day. This change of religion was unbearable and unimaginable for the woman who remained resolute in most trying times. She lost her appetite. She was afraid to move out of the house. She was horrified at the thought of her neigbours and the villagers pooh-poohing her. She chanted hundreds of times '*Shri Krishna sharnam mam*' and '*Om, namo Bhagvate Vasudevay*'[1] from this house. She knew the *Manglashtak* and many other hymns by heart. Punja's mother, her mother-in-law, thrust into her hands a copy of the holy book *Shrimad Bhagvad Gita*[2] at the time of breathing her last. She had preserved the holy book for years in her prayer room. The house was no longer celebrating the birthdays of Lord *Rama, Krishna, Narasimha or Vamana*[3]. When Punja's father Valji Thakkar was alive, they used to celebrate these occasions in a grand way. Punja's wife had seen them right from the beginning of her marital life. Though these festivals were no longer celebrated in the house they still used to fast on those days. Punja becoming a Khoja meant that now all these rituals had to be abandoned. Punja's wife was shattered. She cried incessantly.

Gangji and Nathu apart, even Zinia, whose complaints traumatised him so much, forgot his grievances, and was shocked by the conduct of his father. All of them imagined in their mind that becoming a Muslim meant, wearing a bright checked *lungi*[4], sporting a beard, moving around with a half naked body and holding a sickle in the hand ready to slaughter a cow or a goat. Adamji was a Muslim, but he had no such attributes. In spite of knowing and understanding this, they would not change their stereotyped mindset about the Muslims. When the cow is worshipped her body was touched with the right hand, then the hand was put on the eyelids and then they bowed before her in reverence. All this was so inherent, to imagine that Punja and his family would be ready to slaughter the very cow tomorrow, made them shudder.

Punja's wife prepared the food and served him alone, not to others. His wife and three sons refused to eat the food. He was stunned to know that his family gave up the food. He loved his wife and children so much. He changed the religion, of course, out of vengeance, but also due to the concern for a better future for his children. If, now, his children and his wife were grieved so much about his decision, how would he keep them happy? He did not touch the food. The culture that he inherited over the generations had not deserted him; as per the culture, he bowed before the food and stood up.

Just what had happened at home, had also happened outside. The elderly people of the village, who had ostracised him for his dry fish business, turned away from him, as if he was a leper. They scorned him,

"Punja, if you could not feed the stomach, slit it. But, are you not ashamed to do the thing that would condemn your forefathers to hell? Would you plant the wormwood in the very courtyard where you used to worship the holy basil? Instead of worshipping the cow, would you now slaughter her? Shame on you, Punja."

Punja never thought of these consequences. Even he liked the basil plant.

When he was young, his father had a cow in the courtyard. Punja used to feed her fodder. The cow would feed herself, while her calf suckled. Punja loved the cow. The very thought of slaughtering a cow was unbearable to him. On the *Makarsankranti* day his mother used to worship the cow, bring the millet cakes from the market and feed her with a lot of care and love. The thought of slaughtering such a cow, Punja was shaken up.

When he returned home, he found his wife and his children sitting huddled in a daze. The four pairs of eyes looked at him with an emptiness, as if they had lost every thing in life. There was no expression on their face, except a pall of gloom. All of them turned away their faces on noticing the arrival of Punja.

Punja stood still on the threshold quite for some time, staring at the basil plant.

He took a deep breath of the air coming from its direction, filled his lungs, then realised for the first time the aroma of its blossom.

The second day also passed almost in the same manner. Every thing stood still. In his childhood, he heard in a fairytale and folklore of a cursed city. In the cursed city, rivers, creeks, trees, animals, birds, air and even human beings turned motionless for a moment because of the curse. Punja now felt the same way.

He went to Adamji. He alone could guide him. He poured out his woes to Adamji.

"Punja, my brother, be a man, do not lose your spirit. The people, who tread on the path of truth and righteousness, experience such difficulties at the beginning. This is a testing time for you. If you sincerely seek the blessings of Allah, He would certainly rescue you from this situation. Have patience and courage. Try again and again to make your wife and children to understand the mercy of Allah. And, you will succeed."

As per the advice of Adamji, he repeatedly tried, but now suddenly he could not understand why, unlike earlier, there was no vengeance in his mind. Even he told his family that what was destined had happened. Whether it was good or bad, his wife and children should cooperate and stand by him. If they did not stand by him, there was no meaning in his living.

"Bapu," the eldest son Gangji said slowly, "There is no doubt that you love all of us so much. If you also respect our feelings then…"

"Then, what?"Punja asked curiously.

"Then you become what you were earlier,"added his second son Nathu. Punja was taken aback. He looked at his wife.

"Yes, you correct your mistake for the sake of all of us. If you say, we will leave this village and go elsewhere. Children have grown up now. They will soon start earning and the house will be filled with grand children. All of us will forget this nightmare."

Punja felt agonised.

"What mother is saying is right, Bapu! You accept what we are saying, respect our feelings. Then we will do whatever you say for the rest of our lives. We swear by *Shrinathji*." Tears flew from Zinia's eyes and he slumped on to the floor.

Punja lost his composure. His tongue totally dried up. His throat parched. Suddenly, like it happens in an earthquake, everything around crumbled. He pressed his palms on his temples, sat for a long time and then ran to his room on the first floor.

Punja could not sleep the whole night. His wife did not light the fire in the kitchen at all. However, as per the tradition of Valji Thakkar's family, the *diya*[5] in the courtyard near the basil plant was lit—its rays brightening the courtyard and the passage. Once it was burnt out, the house again plunged into darkness. After that, no body in the house, lit even a lamp.

Punja remained awake the whole night. He could not hear any traces of movement downstairs. Throughout the night, he kept looking, without blinking, at the stars on the sky through the open window. He went on looking at the stars including the star, Venus through the window. As the light of the Venus faded, he made a decision in his mind. He got up slowly. He washed the face, and gulped down two glasses of water. The stream of water jabbed in his empty stomach like a sharp weapon. He climbed down without creating any noise. He saw his wife and children fast asleep on the floor in the passage in a huddle. He stepped out of the house slowly and then started taking long strides on the road leading to Rajkot.

*

Whenever Punja came to Rajkot earlier, he made it a point to vist the *Haveli*. But this time when he was entering the *Haveli,* his feet stopped for a moment.

It was a shrine of the *Vaishnav*. He was now a Ismaili Khoja. His steps would pollute the sanctity of the *Haveli*. He himself guarded its sanctity until yesterday. But today he had no right to step into it. He entered inside feeling guilty, like an offender, and started looking all around, fearing that someone might notice him.

There were a few devotees in the courtyard. There was still time for the next glimpse of *Shrinathji.* A few *Vaishnav* friends were offering the services. Punja walked towards the chief priest's room.

"Whom do you want to meet?"Luckily, the chief priest was standing near the door.

"Jai Shri Krishna," Punja greeted the priest, as per the tradition, by folding his hands and bowing, but experienced a different feeling this time. He never had such an experience before, though he had greeted in the same fashion several times in the past.

He said consciously, "I want to meet *Maharajshri*.[6] I shall be obliged if he could spare a minute for me."

Luckily for Punja, the priest did not ask many questions. He simply asked him,

"What is your name? Where have you come from? The *Maharajshri* has gone upstairs."

Punja gave his name and address.

The priest went upstairs. Punja started looking at his back, with his heart beating fast, as if he was awaiting for the result of a test.

Punja was lucky. He immediately received an audience with the *Maharajshri*. The priest gesturing him to go upstairs said,

"You are fortunate. Had the *Maharajshri* sat down for the worship you would have to wait for two hours."

Punja went upstairs.

The *Maharajshri* sat on a swing in a big room. A silk rug adorned his seat. At his feet also, a silk cloth was laid. Punja bowed to him, as per the *Vaishnav* tradition. Had it been some other time, he would have touched his feet, but today he thought if he touched his feet he would be polluting him and committing a sin. Even then, he did offer a rupee coin at the feet of *Maharajshri*. The bulky *Maharajshri* did not notice the offering of Punja.

"Maharajshri,"Punja said with folded hands standing at a distance of five feet. "I am in a difficulty."

The Maharajshri without saying anything looked at him inquisitively.

"If any Vaishnav converts to become a Khoja and again wants to become a Vaishnav from a Khoja, will he receive the blessings of *Mahaprabhuji*[7] or not?" Punja asked in a timid voice as he was gasping for breath.

"No, this can never happen. A Hindu who converts once, can never again convert back to Hinduism. The Hindus are not converted, they are born. For the Hindus, conversion is a grave sin,"said *Maharajshri* firmly as a matter of faith.

Punja was stunned. His face turned pale. He said with great difficulty, "*Maharajshri*, please tell me, if *Shrimad Bhagvat*[8]or *Mahaprabhuji's Subhodhini*[9] had shown any way for a Muslim to become a Hindu."

"If a Mulsim or a Christian wants to enter a Hindu temple, he will have to take another birth, brother. The Hinduism is not something available on any roadside." The *Maharajshri* said with self-esteem, straightening his neck and then asked,

"But why are you asking all this? By the grace of *Shrinathji*, you were born in a *Vaishnav* family."

Punja's heart forgot to beat for a moment. He had fallen from the grace of *Shrinathji*. Like a naïve child, he had turned down his good luck. He was not a *Vaishnav* any more. Now he was a Khoja.

And now to be a Vaishnav again, he would have to take another birth.

NOTES

1. A hymn in praise of Lord Krishna.
2. A sacred book of Hindus.
3. They are among the ten incarnations or avatars of Lord Vishnu, the protector in the Divine Trinity.
4. A loose flowing garment wrapped around the waist by men.
5. A small earthen bowl with a cotton wick lit on auspicious occasions.
6. The direct descendant of Shri Vallabhacharya.
7. Shri Vallabhacharya, the founder of the Pushti margiya Vaishnav sect of Hinduism.
8. A religious book of Hindus.
9. A holy text of Vaishnavism.

9

Marriage of Punja's sons, discussion about sending Jinabhai to Karachi

It could not be said that Punja was devasted by what *Maharajshri* said. Though the door to return was closed, he made every possible effort to return to Hinduism. In Rajkot, he kept on meeting the priests of many temples, the heads of Ashrams and sects and the ascetics and saints. He received the same answer from every one.

"Once a person converts, he cannot be accepted back into Hinduism. The converts from other religions cannot become Hindus. To become a Hindu, one has to take another birth."

A dejected Punja returned to Paneli. Now, he did not have any other way out. He candidly poured out his woes to his wife and sons. Whatever he had done—be it a mistake, a crime or a sin—the wife and the children should accept it large heartedly, as there was no other way out. If they did not do so, it would not only be diffcult, but impossible for him to live. If his wife and children did not stand by him by converting, he would either be forced to renounce the house and go to a far away place or commit suicide.

In Paneli, along with Adam Khoja's family, one more Muslim family, that is, Punja Khoja's family was added.

The Lohana community in Paneli and its neighbourhood discussed the incident for a few days with astonishment and hatred. But in the Lohana community, Punja's family was not the first to convert. In Kathiawar, there were many Lohana families who converted to Khojas. Similarly, there were many business people who became Memons. People witnessed in this land that even the Brahmins converted to Muslim Voras to derive the benefits of the Muslim rule. This sort of conversion did add to the prestige, but it was not treated so contemptuously either. This was what had gradually happened to Punja. Now, the dry fish business did not look so despicable to the people.

Adamji, as a true friend, had supported and helped Punja. He did whatever possible to help Punja's sons Gangji and Nathu to get some business. Punja hoped that his sons would go to Bombay and do some business and that Zinia would study there and become something—nothing of the sort had happened. However, his two sons managed to get some small business to eke out a living.

Punja's big worry was about his sons' marriage. Adamji had a solution for this too. The people who became Muslims, three or four generations ago, considered themselves as true Muslims. And the people who became Khojas or others during the past ten, twenty and thirty years were considered *muhajirs*[1] by the true Muslims. Though the true Muslims accepted them into their religion, they were reluctant to give their daughters in marriage into such families. Punja could not dream of having any matrimonial alliance for his sons with the Lohana community. Those who became Khojas recently were actually Lohanas. Therefore, these new Khoja families had cultural similarities. Thus, Adamji tried to solve Punja's problem.

And actually, Adamji found a solution to the most difficult problem of Punja. Adamji contacted the families of similar background as that of Punja in Rajkot, Jamnagar and Dwarka and found some suitable girls for Punja's sons. Punja felt a heavy burden had been lifted off his shoulders.

Punja initially wanted only the marriage of Gangji and Nathu. But when the search for girls proved time consuming, he felt that even Zinia[2] had grown up. Not only that, but now he and Adamaji were growing old. If Zinia's marriage was postponed to the future and if, God forbid, something happened to him or Adamji, it would be very difficult to find a match for Zinia. His wife hardly took any interest in such matters. He knew that she could no longer visit the Ram or Shiv temple in the village.

After a lot of thought, Punja realised that if Zinia also got married along with his two elder brothers it would be a great relief for him—like the one feels after taking a dip in the Ganges. Gangji and Nathu had established themselves quite well in their business. They were capable of eking out a livelihood. Zinia had not reached that stage as yet. But Punja had faith that Zinia would also find a suitable job for himself.

And so, one after another, three brides arrived in the house and became daughters-in-law as part of the family.

But their arrival in the family was not that smooth as Punja thought. Gangji and Nathus used to earn and give some money in the house, but Zinia was not able to do that. Punja noticed that his two elder dauthers-in-law did not like Zinia and his wife. It was not that Punja did not earn any income, but Zinia not earning mattered the most. Zinia was helping in the fishing business, but even that was not lucrative any longer. In Rajkot, many big traders entered the market. Hence Punja's chances of succeeding in his business and earning proft were very bleak. Before the marriage of his three sons, Punja thought getting girls for them was the most difficult problem. But, now he realised that the problem would not end with the arrival of the daughters-in-law. There was a huge age difference between his second son and the younger one Zinia. Similarly, Zinia's wife Mithibai was quite young and innocent.

As the time passed, the daughters-in-law drifted, so also their husbands. In the meantime, the two elder daughters-in-law had gifted grand children to Punja. After becoming mothers, they became more aggressive. Zinia and his wife Mithibai were treated as if they were useless and were pushed to a corner in the house. Punja was deeply grieved by all this, but he was unable to find a way out.

He told Adamji about his difficulties. Adamji heard him out patiently with compassion and then said,

"Punja, Allah has the keys for every lock. We don't know, which key to be used for which lock and hence we get confused. But if you listen to me..."

Punja's eyes brightened.

"Tell me, brother. Zinia is married, but now if you could give me an idea regarding how he can stand on his own feet, I would be greatly obliged," Punja said with hopeful eyes.

"There is an idea, Punja. Many families of Paneli went to Rajkot and Bombay and settled. Instead of living in this village, if the youngsters migrated they would be happy."

"You mean, Zinia should be sent to a far–off land!" Punja asked as well as gave the answer himself.

"I am ready to send Zinia to Bombay, but who will keep him there?"

"Not Bombay, if you are ready to send Zinia to Karachi, there is an idea which can secure his future."

"Then tell me, brother. Why should we delay in good work?"

Adamji's two uncles had business in Karachi. About three decades ago they left Kathiawar and settled in Karachi. Their sons were taking care of their business. But their business had expanded manifold. Adamji met them, a month ago when they came to Kathiawar. The uncles had not forgotten their nephew. They stayed one day in Adamji's house at Paneli and recalled their past intimacy. While talking they just happened to say,

"Adam, with the grace of Allah, our business went on expanding. We do not find trustworthy people here. We never know the Sindhis, we employed, could cheat. If we can find some suitable boys from our own community, our work would be done and the boys also would secure their future. There is no dearth of business in Karachi and there won't be any difficulty in making money, honestly by the grace of God."

For Punja, there was no difference between Bombay and Karachi. To him, both were alien. There can be no better news than Zinia going to Karachi and doing some job. He felt the godess of wealth came knocking the door of Zinia.

Punja returned home and indulged in daydreaming. Punja himself had never travelled beyond Ahmedabad. Whatever little knowledge he had about Bombay was based on what he heard here and there. He knew some families who were staying in Bombay. But about Karachi he did not know anything. He just knew that Karachi was a port located somewhere in the upper region of the Kutch. If Zinia could work with Adamji's uncles in their business, all his troubles would be over.

He made up his mind and called Zinia. He looked at Zinia and then realised how weak he was as compared to Gangji and Nithu. Like him, his wife Mithibai was also of small frame. Would not these naïve children be troubled in an unknown land?

"Zinia,"Punja said to his son, with a firm resolve. "No matter how sweet the water in the father's well, it gets dried up one day and we cannot sit waiting for the water."

"I do not understand, Bapu."

"I will make you understand, my son. I think the doors of your destiny are now open. Adamji's uncle has made some arrangement for you."

Zinia was listening attentively to what his father was saying.

"Son, we are among those people who knew no one, nor are we educated. The time is changing now. The people say that now there are engine cars which run by the steam. What these cars are, only those who sit in them can know, but I hear that the people who used to take fifteen days from Ahmedabad to reach Bombay now take only one day to reach. You have got such an opportunity that all roads are now open to you."

Zinia looked at his father with his eyes wide open. The words that he was hearing were coming as images before his eyes.

"I mean, I want my son, you go to Karachi. You work in Adamji's uncles' business for two years and then learn the tricks of the trade. And if you do not feel like staying in that alien land, you can come to our home in Paneli. By the grace of God, you will be able to eke out a living here too."

Zinia's knowledge of Karachi was not even as much as that of his father Punja. But the idea of venturing out to a new and unknown land appealed to his young mind. He was excited about the prospect.

"Bapu, you don't worry at all. Adamji uncle never says anything half-heartedly. He does every work perfectly," Zinia said very confidently.

"I know this. Because of this trust only, I am venturing to send you to such a far off and unknown land."

Adamji wrote a letter to Karachi informing his uncles about the arrival of Zinia and his wife Mithibai in Karachi and asked for their consent. He also informed them about the day and time of Zinia leaving the ship at Okha Port and reaching Karachi and explained how Zinia and his bride were complete strangers to Karachi and that they knew nothing about the world around. The arrangements were made to receive Zinia at the Karachi harbour.

Though Punja was not supposed to believe in the auspicious and inauspicious days for starting the journey any more, but knowing his mind, Adamji said,

"Punja... we will leave for Okha on the first day of the next lunar month. The ship will leave on the fifth day."

Punja, Adamji,Gangji, Nathu and a couple of Zinia's friends came to see him off at the Okha port. Some of them never travelled beyond Rajkot. When Punja started the dry-fish business he had gone to Veraval and saw the ships moving here and there in the sea. Adamji also had seen the sea and the ships. For all others, this was an exciting experience. Zinia and his wife were told again and again to protect themselves from the sea winds. They were told not to be frightened if the ship shakes. And if they get sea sickness they should keep cloves in their mouth and close their eyes..

Zinabhai Punjabhai Valji Thakkar stepped into the ship anchored at the shore, as if he was entering into a curious world.

Then who could have known that in the history of the subcontinent, a breathtaking but horrifying chapter of Paneli would be written in the name of Zinia.

NOTES

1. A refugee.
2. A Gujarati word equivalent for a 'small structured'person.

10

Birth of Maamad, Douglas Graham's Company

When Zina and his wife set foot on the Karachi harbour, whether the day was auspicious or not one would never know, but Punja must have definitely ensured that he left Paneli on a very auspicious day. Admaji's uncle already made provision for his stay. Khardar Street was located at the end of Newnham Road in Karachi. Zinia's residence was on the second floor of an old spacious three-storied building called Vazir Mansion in this narrow street. Karachi, spread far and wide, had plenty of uninhabited open space. Hardly a population of fifty thousand people resided in the widely spread out bungalows and houses. Because of the businessmen and the working people, the Newnham Road remained busy and congested. But the picture was totally different with Khardar Street. This narrow street was mainly occupied by the business godowns and the offices. Bullock-carts, handcarts pulled by the labourers, camel carts and donkeys laden with goods were seen everywhere. Some of the houses were so low, that when the camels were being loaded with goods they could crane their necks into the houses on the first floor as if to enquire about the well-being of the people inside. The question of pollution by petrol or steam was still a distant reality. The bicycles were the only mode of transport.

What Adamji's uncle had said was true. The business was brisk, but there were few people to manage it. It was only a few years since the mutiny of 1857 occured. But its flames of revolt had not reached to that extent to the coast of Sindh. The British firms in Karachi were safe. The Queen's rule was firmly established. And therefore, now there was no fear of skirmishes among the Kings and the Sultans or of the dreaded thugs. Zinia understood, in a very short time, the nuances of the business. In two or three years, he became so proficient that he started his own business. He had no inclination for a particular business or commodity. He was ready to take up any business of buying and selling that could fetch him good money. He had seen in the Karachi markets, the buying and selling of goods like cotton, wool, leather, foodgrains, cloth, metal and sugar on profit. He started his business in all these goods.

Zinia was very fortunate. Who knows whether Punja Thakkar got his horoscope read. His horoscope must have shown him as a successful business man. Now Zinia was no longer Zinia, he became Zinabhai.

Zinabhai's success was credited to the good deeds of his forefathers. And that is why, he gave his Company the same name as that of Punja's Company in Paneli, M/S Punja Valji Thakkar Company. Intially he rented the vehicles for transporting the purchased goods and managed the business, but in a short time he bought his own vehicles along with two to three horses. It was necessary to travel to the nearby places for purchasing the goods and now it became easy to cover three or four places in one trip due to the horses.

In the meantime, his wife Mithibai gifted him the first child. When Mithibai was pregnant, they had a discussion about selecting the name of the child.

"Son or daughter," Zinabhai said to wife, "We will give a customary name to the child, like our forefathers. We had given up the religion, but now if you retain our identity, we can be somewhat happy."

"Would you accept my suggestion." said Mithibai blushing. "We left Paneli and came to Karachi. By coming to Karachi, have we become happy or sad?"

"Why are you asking this? We have become happy. Had we stayed in Paneli, we would have hardly earned a morsel."

"If that is so, tell me on whose mercy have we come here?"

"You know this, we have come here due to the mercy of Adamji uncle."

"Yes, but don't you think for sending us here by Adamji uncle, the real credit should go to the Prophet Mohammed? Would he have sent us here if we did not become Khojas?" Mithibhai asked staring at her husband.

Zinabhai felt that he never thought the way his illiterate wife had. Mithibai was right. Had Punja Thakkar not converted from a Lohana to a Ismaili Khoja, he would himself never have come to Karachi. He knew the words like *Namaaz*, the holy Quran and the *Hadith*[1], *Al Fatiha*[2] and *roza*[3], but he never had an opportunity to delve deeply into them. Sometimes, he used to go to the Jamaatkhana to pray. He would open the Quran and try to read and understand its verses by using whatever reading ability he had. Sometimes, he would attend the Friday sermons to listen to the *Mullah—Maulvi* or *Vaiz.* Yet he had never felt grateful to the Prophet Mohammed as Mithibai had. She was right in saying that if the Prophet Mohammed had not brought light into his life, he would have been nowhere.

"What are you thinking?"asked Mithibai.

"You are right. But what has that to do with the name of our child?"

"It has, that is why I am saying. If we get a son let us name him Muhammad, so that the name lingering with us throughout our life would be an expression of our gratitude."

"But what if it is a girl?" asked Zinabhai.

"Then we will name her Fatima. Because Fatima is the name of the Prophet Mohammed's daughter."

Zinabhai was lost in thought. His wife was absolutely right. He felt deeply indebted to Islam, the Prophet Mohammed, Aga Khan and Uncle Adamji. As an expression of gratitude, he would, hereinafter, offer regular *namaaz*, observe fasting on *Ramzaan*[4] and study the holy Quran. Islam had suddenly cast its spell over him.

Be it a son or a daughter, the husband and the wife were to welcome the child as God's gift. God gifted a son to Mithibai. As decided earlier, Zinabhai named the child Muhammad. Both the husband and the wife called him affectionately Maamad. On seeing Maamad, Zinabhai would remember what he heard on his birth. He would tell his wife laughingly, how thin and small he was. Zinabhai was short, not tall enough even now. Maamad was like his grandfather—thin and tall. He was tall like his grandfather. Punja Thakkar was six feet tall. When Mithibai took the infant Maamad in her lap, his legs would stretch out. Maamad had to keep friends with doctor and hakims in his childhood. Though he had no serious ailment, his thin frame would fall prey more often to cold, fever and cough. Right from his birth, he was very thin. He was so thin that any bout of illness would make him almost skeletal in frame. If Zinabhai or Mithibai tried to make him stand on his wobbly feet, he would plant his feet firmly on the floor. Sometimes, in a fit of anger, he would pull Mithibai's hair, making his parents to wonder from where he got that strength. At times, if some thought came to his mind and his parents did not understand him, he would throw a fit. He would cry, scream and shout till his throat got dry, yet would not give up once he registered something in his mind. To pacify Maamad, his parents would show him the moon, the flying birds, give him the toys and even sweets, but of no avail. That his parents did not understand him was something he could not bear and, therefore, he would continue to cry incessantly.

When Maamad reached the age for admission to *school*, Mithibai already gave birth to two more children—Rehmat and Mariam—and with the blessing of God, the third son Ahmed was about to be born.

For two years, Maamad studied the Islamic religion through a Maulvi. But he could not learn reciting. The *Maulvi* taught the first verse of *Al Fatiha Bismilla Hirruraham Nirruhim*. When the *Mauvli* taught the *Al Fatiha* and the entire class recited the verse, Maamad would simply move his lips. The Mauvli believed that, like other children, Maamad also memorised the *Al Fatiha*. For a long time he did not realise that Maamad was only moving the lips. One day, when the examination was conducted all the other children recited the verse correctly but Maamad could not say even the first word *Bismilla* correctly. Then the *Mauvli* understood the cleverness of Maamad.

When the *Maulvi* told Zinabhai that Maamad was not showing any interest in his studies, he thought over it from a different perspective. His company business flourished quite well. Now in doing the business in the Karachi market, he also learnt the tricks of another business. There was a huge demand in foreign countries for cloth and metals like copper and brass. A British firm called Douglas Graham & Company used to purchase all these goods from the local markets and export them. Zinabhai had good business contacts with the firm. The manager of the firm Frederick was a robust young man of thirty five years. He used to dress smartly and in order to ensure that there is not a single fold on his cloth, he would wear new clothes every day. Besides English, he managed to speak a smattering of Sindhi or Hindi and could understand both the languages.

Initially, Zinabhai did not know any language other than Gujarati, that too a rustic Kathiawari Lohanha dialect. But with the time he learnt a few Sindhi and Hindi words and managed to run the business by mixing the language disregarding the rules of grammar. But ever since he started working with Frederick he faced difficulty. To listen and understand the conversation between Frederick and Zinabhai was a matter of amusement. Fortunately for both Frederick and Zinabhai, they had employees who could understand both English and Hindi and managed the business with the help of interpreters.

When Zinabhai learnt that Maamad was not studying the religious lessons, first he thought that Maamad should study English. If that happens it would be easy to do the business with the Douglas Graham & Company. All the business correspondence was in English. Whatever papers Frederick prepared, Zinabhai would simply put his signature in Gujarati. If Maamad studied English, he would be useful. Considering all these, Zinabhai withdrew Maamad from Jamaatkhana. The Christian Missionary High School on Lawrence Road was well reputed for the English education it imparted. The educated upper class people in Karachi sent their children to this school to ensure that they were on par with the English children. The parents used to feel proud when their children, instead of praying to Goddess Amba[5], crossed their heart and bowed before Mother Mary. Whenever they listenend to the children speaking English fluently, they would stare at them with wide open eyes.

Zinabhai admitted Maamad to the school run by the Christian Missionaries.

But Maamad did not take interest in studies in this school either. Just as he did not have any interest in *Al Fatiha* at Jamaatkhana, he did not show any interest in the school's daily morning prayers. Maamad could not make out anything from the stories of the Bible or those of Jesus narrated by the Fathers in the name of the Gospel. He would yawn when the subjects like Maths and Science were taught by the Fathers. Many a time he would bunk the school and ride the horses.

Horse riding was dear to him. His father's stable had two to three horses. A *syce*[6] was appointed to look after the horses. Most of the time, the horses were used by the Company. Sometimes when a horse was in the stable, Maamad would befriend the *syce* and take the horse. Within the wink of an eye he would mount the horse and hold its reins firmly. He would dig in his heels into the horse's back and hold on tightly. Even the *syce* would be amazed. He could not understand, how this lanky boy got such courage and strength. The manner in which Maamad mounted the horse and controlled, it would even rouse envy in a skilled horse rider.

The sharp eyes of the Father in the Christian Missionary School caught Maamaad's irregularity in attendance. Unlike the *Mauvli* at the Jamaatkhana, he did not wait for long.

He summoned Zinabhai and told him, "Maamad did not take part in any activities of the school, except the Christmas celebration." The Father was right. Why did he like the Christmas celebration? He found the Christmas celebration quite dazzling and attractive as compared to the *Eid*[7]. He was specially attracted to the pomp and show displayed by the representatives of the British Officers moving around at the Christmas celebration.

Even then, Zinabhai continued his efforts to educate Maamad. But when he was convinced his efforts would not succeed, he started thinking from a different perspective. If Maamad could assist him in the business, he would learn the nuances of the business in two years.

But Maamad was not destined to excel in his father's business either.

One day Zinabhai said casually while talking to Frederick, "Now, I am not able to manage the business all alone. I am thinking of withdrawing Maamad from the school and put him in my business."

"What are you saying, Zinabhai?"Frederick said expressing surprise. He was looking quite handsome in a spotless white crisp suit. "This is the time for Maamad to study. Let him study further."

"That is the difficulty, he does not want to study. He studied neither at the Jamaatkhana nor at the Christian school." Zinabhai said candidly what was in his mind. "To tell you the truth, I want to make him a *Sahib* like you."

"Then I will help you in this." said Frederick. "Our Company's Headquarter is in London. I will make Maamad join there. You send him to London. If he stays for two years he would move ahead of me and then become a big *Sahib* in India."

Zinabhai's eyes gleamed for a moment. His mouth watered. He reminisced for a moment how he came to Karachi from Paneli and became prosperous and happy.

Douglas Graham & Company was a big business firm. If Frederick sent Maamad through the company then…

Zinia Punja's entire family would prosper. Zinabhai had never seen His Excellency Aga Khan or the Prophet Muhammed, but he felt Frederick was no less.

NOTES

1. Prayer offered by the Muslims during the fasting.
2. A prayer offered by a Muslim at the time of Namaaz.
3. Fasting during the month of Ramzaan.
4. A holy month of fasting and prayers of Muslims.
5. A Hindu Goddess.
6. A stable keeper.
7. A Muslim festival.

11

Marriage of Jinnah, Fredrick's advice, leaving for London, working in Graham's Company, Admission to the Lincoln's Inn, name and date of birth

Zinabhai was quite excited on hearing Frederick's proposal. For a moment, he felt that he should accept Federick's proposal immediately and ask Maamad to join the Douglas Graham & Company's Headquarters in London. At present Frederick had some influence at the Headquarters and whatever he said there carried some weightage. The business relations between Zinabhai and Frederick had benefited the Company. Today's situation is opportune, it is possible that tomorrow the Headquarters might recall Federick to London or he might leave the company for better prospects elsewhere. It is also possible that due to the fluctuating market prices, his business with this British company might come down. In such an eventuality, certainly Federick would not be so excited about Maamad.

Zinabhai had looked at the matter from another angle. Maamad, right from the beginning, had never been bright in his studies. In case he was unable to stay in London for long and had to return to India, if he passed at least the matriculation examination he would do something on his return although Zinabhai did not have full confidence that Maamad would pass the matriculation examination. However, when Maamad himself had shown interest in passing the examination, which was not far away, he felt, waiting for a few days would not make much difference.

When Mithibai came to know that the arrangements were being made to send Maamad across the seven seas to the white people's country, initially, she outrightly opposed the idea. She had no idea how big the world was beyond Kathiawar and Karachi. She had seen many a time the white officers' wives. She had also seen their haughtiness and arrogannce. They did not hesitate even beating up the native people, on the slightest pretext. When she compared the Kathiawari veils and the muslim *burqas* to the revealing outfits of these damsels moving freely, leaving their arms and knees exposed, she felt they were utterly shameless. If the young Maamad joined such people, with no one to keep a watch on him, he might go in the wrong direction. If the white *sahib* beat him, there would be no one in the unknown country to lend him a shoulder to cry. How long would an inexperienced innocent young man resist the temptation of such pretty looking women?

Mithibai thought at length on all these matters. However, she felt that if Maamad was getting an opportunity to go to London, she should not be an obstacle. Just as they came to Karachi from Paneli and prospered, the same way if Maamad went to London and became more happy and prosperous, it would be a windfall. But what would happen to his image and reputation, if he strayed? There was only one solution to all this. Maamad should be married off. After the marriage, he could go to London and call his wife there once he settled himself in the business. Once a young son was tied down to the marital vows, he would think a hundred times before straying.

"Listen," she said slowly to her husband. "If we want to send Maamad to London, let him get married first before he goes."

Zinabhai did not think of that. He admired his wife for having such a foresight for the future.

"Times are changing very rapidly. There is a world of difference between our tradition and lifestyle in Paneli and that of Karachi. We cannot imagine from here how the country of these white people could be. It should not happen that we send our son there and then we lose him. That is why, you must get him married before he goes," Mithibai placed before her husband her thoughts. Zinabhai immediately understood. He started making efforts in that direction.

Maamad took the matriculation examination but as Zinabhai doubted, he did not pass the examination.

Still the time was passing and Zinabhai wanted to utilise it meaningfully in two ways. First, searching for a suitable girl for Maamad and second making a provision for meeting the expenses of Maamad's stay in London for two to three years. Frederick made it clear to Zinabhai that getting an opportunity to work as an apprentice in such a big company itself is a big thing. Frederick also had told him that if Maamad went to London he would recommend to his senior officers to give him some stipend. But as of now, Zinabhai should be mentally prepared to bear the entire expenses of Maamad.

Zinabhai started working to meet these goals. There was no difficulty in making the provision for meeting the expenses of Maamad stay in London. He was able to bear the expenses. But for Maamad's marriage, going to his native village Paneli became unavoidable. It was ages since he left Paneli. The weakling Jiria of Paneli had now become Seth Zinabhai. Both his elder brothers Gangji and Nathu were still staying in Paneli. He wanted to derive the happiness of performing the wedding on a grand scale in his native village. When he wrote to his elder brother about Maamad's marriage before going to London, his brother was excited. His brother wrote to him that Maamad's maternal uncle in Beraja village of Jamnagar district had a marriageable daughter and her parents were looking for a boy. They were worried about the daughter's marriage. The Beraja village was at a distance of a night's journey on a bullock cart. If, Zinabhai reached Paneli immediately along with Maamad all the things could be arranged.

Zinabhai did not want to miss this opportunity. What could be a better news than his own brother-in-law's daughter coming to his house as the daughter-in-law? Hence, there was no need for much enquiry. His married life with his wife Mithibhai had been blissful. If Mithibhai's niece became Maamad's wife, they too similarly would have a happy married life.

Zinabhai took the first ship together with his entire family and arrived at the Okha harbour. From Okha, they rented two bullock carts and, after a day's journey, reached Paneli. When the luggage was being unloaded from the carts in the courtyard of the house, the two brothers' families along with neighbours kept on staring with their eyes wide open. The elder brother Gangji could not restrain from saying, "Ah Zinia! You have completely changed. Now you cannot be recognised."

Zinabhai fixed the marriage of Maamad with his maternal uncle's daughter Amibai. Paneli had never seen before such a lavish wedding procession. Zinabhai had arranged a banquet for the entire village. When the procession reached the village square, the band stopped to play the rich variety of musical notes. Some ten vehicles, a number of horse riders, the band, the escorts—forming a huge formidable wedding procession—and the sixteen to seventeen-years-old groom Maamad had reached the decked up spot for wedding. The bride was the fourteen year old Amibai. The groom was adorned with flowers from head to toe and the bride was wearing glitzy clothes and sparkling ornaments. The groom and the bride were bathed in perfumes. Maamad returned to his home Vazir Mansion with the girl, whom he had never seen and accepted as his life partner.

Now, all the roads going to London were open. It was sheduled to leave for London by the ship of the Pacific and Orient Steamship Company. The ticket was purchased. The woollen clothers for wearing in London and other necessary things were also bought. Zinabhai remained calm, but Mithibai was a mother, after all. Maamad was actually leaving for London and that he would not return for two-three years made her worried. The distance between Karachi and London was beyond her comprehension. She was all along worried that the ship from Okha took two days to reach the Karachi harbour and that the ship fom Karachi would take a month to reach London.

On a cold winter morning in 1893, the ship of the Pacific and Orient Steamship Company took off from the Karachi harbour. Then the sky, from Karachi to Kandahar and from Kashmir to Kanyamukari, was looking at a blank sheet of history—not the history of the past but the history to be created by the coming future.

*

When exactly after a month the ship reached the Southampton harbour, the weather was foggy and very cold. Maamad had no idea that it could be so intensely cold. He was wearing a sweater, a coat and a hat. Yet the breeze was so intense and cold that he started shivering. For a moment, he felt he forgot his way and by mistake landed in the midst of unfamiliar faces and hostile environment. After disembarking at the Southampton harbour, he stood wondering how to reach the hotel that Frederick had suggested. During the course of the journey, he acquainted himself with an old English gentleman. That way, Maamad was habituated to listening and talking in English. In the Christian Missionary School at Karachi, the teachers and the fathers used to converse only in English. Therefore, he did not have much difficulty in conversing in the language.

In the ship, while conversing with the old gentleman, he collected the necessary information. The old gentleman helped him sit in a train at Southampton that would take him to Victoria.

Maamad reached the hotel recommended by Frederick. He did not have much luggage. Hence he did not take much time to settle down. All facilities were available in the hotel. Maamad felt relieved. For a long time, he stood looking at the streets of London through the glass window.

Maamad had never seen before the vehicles running on the road without the help of any animal. He knew the vehicles had two wheels, but the vehicles could have four wheels as well was a revelation to him. He was not that surprised to see the horse-drawn carriages and the horse riders. But he was too surprised to see the motorcars speeding up in their midst. The motorcars were not yet seen in India.

The next day morning, Maamad wearing the necessary warm clothes had set off for the Douglas Graham & Company's Headquarters. As per the information received from the hotel, he reached the bridge of the river Thames, after a ten minutes' walk. In his mind, he began comparing the flow of the river Thames with that of the Indus.

Maamad, with his hands thrust in his pockets to warm up, was walking along. His eyes flashed when he saw the sign board of Liden Hall Street at a corner. The Douglas Graham & Company should be somewhere nearby. He stood on the footpath and read one sign board after another. Suddenly, his eyes were brightened. He was excited to read a familiar word—INDIA. He felt, though he was far away from his motherland, it was close to him. He began reading the prefix and the suffix of that word. He was quite familiar with the name. He secured pass marks in one or two subjects at the matriculation examination. One of these subjects was history. He heard the name of the East India Company. About three hundred years ago, this Company, which had come with very little capital to trade in India, enslaved India. That much history Maamad was aware of. Though the Company was wound up about thirty five years ago, he knew how the Company won the mammoth country India during its three hundred years of existence. Maamad pursed his lips and looked at the office of the Company. He was thinking that though the Company that enslaved India was dismantled, India was still forced to tolerate the bondage. "How long will this vast country continue to be the slave of the British empire?" Maamad wondered.

He could locate the Douglas Graham & Company immediately. As per the recommendation of Frederick, he got the job in the Company. The Company had a large staff. Maamad was allotted a separate table and chair for doing his work. Around him, the cupboards, the wooden racks, the records and the books of accounts were spread out. To Maamad, the work and the environment were unfamiliar. But he was not the one to be intimidated. In fact, he was thrilled at the challenge thrown at him in a new world and the daunting task of standing on his own feet. He was brimming with self confidence to understand the work assigned to him.

But he got bored within a few days. He felt suffocated working within the four walls of the office. He was not interested in taking down copies, posting figuers and keeping books and arranging files. He got more disappointed when he talked to his seniors who had been working there for so many years. They had been doing the same work for years. Buying and selling the goods, depositing the cheques in banks, tallying the accounts every day, making bills—all this was monotonous. However, what he found fascinating was tallying at the end of the day the goods purchased and sold and recording of receipts and expenditure meticulously. Thousands of employees performed different types of work and yet everything was tallied and accounted for that was something which impressed him immensely.

Soon Maamad realised that the clothes he wore were old-fashioned. What he considered modern in his country looked old fashioned here. He had only two or three suits. People wearing the modern clothes there looked quite handsome. He used to remember Frederick. Frederick was wearing a new suit every day. And sometimes, he even changed the suit twice a day. His ties were elegant which he used to change daily. If he could buy new suits and ties like Frederick, he too would look no less than Frederick in the midst of these foreigners.

He bought new very stylish suits and ties from the London stores. Now, he would change the suit daily and knot the tie very carefully. He would keep the handkerchief in his suit pocket in such a way that its well crisped and folded edge would be seen stretched out. And in his thoughts he would often compare himself with Frederick.

Maamad felt quite lonely in the mornings and the evenings and on the holidays. He had neither acquaintances nor friends. Therefore, he would roam around here and there in the streets of London. He realised that he would not benefit much from the job with the Douglas Graham and Company. If he had come to stay in London for two or three years, the job that he was doing would have no meaning and he would learn nothing from it. But he did not find any clear way out to leave the job and go elsewhere. Fortuntely, his father Zinabhai had deposited enough money in the bank account.

At this time, his attention was suddenly drawn to a Company called Lincoln Inn. It was an educational institution teaching law. He thought, if he studied the law and returned to India, he would lead a peaceful life. He had no interest in his father's business. Even if he learnt something in the Douglas Graham & Company, it would be relating to his business in which he had no interest. Instead of getting into his father's business, if he studied the law he could earn money, name and fame. His father was earning good money, but the white people never respected him. If he studied the law, he would receive the respect from the white people.

He went to the office of the Lincoln Inn and made enquiries. Anyone could get admission to study the law if he passed a test in basic knowledge. He carefully read the form for the test. The candidate had to write his name in the first column of the application form. Maamad stopped at the column thoughtfully. Maamad did not like the name Muhammad Ali Zinabhai Thakkar as it was too long and the English people might also find it difficult to pronounce the name. He made up his mind to change the name to make it on par with the English people. Maamad Z. Thakkar or M.Z. Thakkar...No! The Z was not proper. Thakkar also was not proper. After thinking a lot, he felt that his father's name could be spelt Jinnah instead of Zina, it would sound better. But he did not like Muhammad Ali Jinnabhai either. At last he wrote his name as M.A. Jinnah.

The second column in the form was about the candidate's date of birth. Maamad was lost in thought again. His date of birth in the Sindh Madressa-Tul-Islam in Karachi was 20 October, 1875. He thought that was his father's guess because according to him and as per his knowledge he was born in 1876. His father was not educated enough and initially he knew only the Hindu calender. The Muslim calender was unfamiliar to him and the Christian calendar was used only for transacting the business with the Douglas Graham & Company.

Maamad thought that this was the opportunity to rectify the mistake. He had no doubt that he was born in the year 1876, but he was indecisive on how to determine the date and the month.

Suddenly, an idea flashed in his mind. The Christian Missionary School at Karachi used to celebrate the Christmas on a grand scale on the twenty fifth of December. This Christmas festival would be celebrated on a grander scale in London. If he had to guess and give some date of birth, what was wrong in writing 25th December. It was a golden opportunity to fix the date so that the entire Christian world would always celebrate his date of birth. He smiled. That he was going to make fool of the entire Christian world, made him feel triumphat and self-confident with his clever eyes gleaming. He wrote in the form—Date of birth—25th December, 1876.

12

Barrister Jinnah, meeting at Hyde Park, meeting Dadabhai in Parliament, acting in theatre

The persons who became barristers after studying the law for three years at the Lincoln's Inn were called "dinner barristers"in those days. More than the lectures and the notes, the importance was given for arranging twenty four parties in a semester. The students were required to attend at least six parties in a semester. The eminent jurists and the University legal experts were invited to those parties. The students would dine with them and listen to their lectures in those get-togethers. At the parties arranged in a jolly atmosphere the port wine and the champagne were served. For the students, the attendance at the parties was more important than the attendance in the class. In a year, some four examinations were conducted and a student could take the examinations as per his convenience. The examination results were very liberal. And the number of students failing at the examination was minimal.

The eighteen year old Maamad had now become Mr. Jinnah. His British colleagues identified him as Mr. Jinnah because of the way he spelt his name. Instead of the native name Jina, he liked Jinnah as it sounded new and modern. Jinnah had learnt to stay in rented rooms and sometimes staying as a paying guest. He had left the Douglas Graham & Company. He wrote a letter to his father at Karachi informing him that he had chosen a new course of life other than what his father had decided for him.

Frederick had also learnt in Karachi from his London office that Jinnah had left the Company's job. When he came to know about this, he became furious. All these years he was earning profits for the Company. Now he had to lose his face at the Head Office. He had summoned Zinabhai and vented his anger. Zinabhai too was disappointed at his son's hasty decision. He was distressed and worried fearing that he might become a victim of Frederick's anger. Punja Valji's Company had prospered because of him. Frederick's displeasure might affect his business. Zinabhai had pacified Federick with great difficulty and assured him that he would write to his son asking him to rejoin the Douglas Graham & Company.

Zinabhai wrote a letter to his son. He wrote that Frederick and he himself were very annoyed about his decision. If his son had returned to Karachi, after gaining necessary experience from the Douglas Graham Company, it would benefit his business. There was every possibility of Punja Valji Company making brisk business with the Douglas Graham & Company in near future. If his son could understand the situation at home, he would be helpful in taking care of his young brothers and sisters and the ageing parents. To become a barrister is to move into an uncertain and unknown future. Zinabhai was also worried about the future of his daughter-in-law Amibai.

The reply that he received from from his son was very disappointing. He did not accept any of his father's contentions. His father even threatened saying that if he did not return to the Douglas Graham & Company, he would not send him money any more. He also wrote that if he was not interested in the Douglas Graham & Company, he should give up the pretence of studying the law and return to Karachi. Jinnah did not listen to his father. He was not worried much about the money because his father already had deposited money in a London bank. However, the money would not be enough to meet the expenses of his legal education for three years. Therefore, it became imperative to take up some job, otherwise it would be difficult to manage the things.

The education system at the Lincoln's Inn had provided ample free time to the students. Jinnah made full use of the free time. He used to spend hours in reading the law books at the British Museum. When the Museum was closed on Sundays and public holidays, he would go to the Hyde Park to attend the public meetings and listen to the speakers. Many speakers used to speak on politics and current political problems at these meetings. Jinnah was deeply influenced by these public speeches. At one such meeting, the speech of Alfred Webb, the leader of the Irish Parliamentary Party, on the problem Ireland had with England had a deep impact on Jinnah. Although the Irish people were a minority in Britain, they were capable of paralysing the entire British administration if they were denied justice. When Jinnah heard such threatening speech from Alfred Webb he admired him.

As a result of reading the law books and listening to such public speeches, Jinnah developed a keen interest in current politics. At that time, Dadabhai Navroji, known as the grand old man of Indian politics, was elected to the British Parliament by a margin of three votes. He had fought the election as a Liberal Party candidate and won. Yet the opposition leaders used to call Dadabhai Navroji 'blackman' and publicly insulted him. The young Jinnah would become furious by this racist attitude.

He gradually began to realise that if the British people harboured such prejudices, they would never do justice to India. Dadabhai had a fair complexion. Jinnah had seen him. If the English people called such a handsome person 'black' what about him, who was actually dark skinned? Jinnah was so happy about

Dadabhai's victory that he made special efforts to secure an entry to the visitors'gallery to listen to his speech in the British Parliament, the following week. He was thrilled on listening to Dadabhai's speech. He felt that he was an able person to fight for the rights of the Indians. He was eager to meet him and felicitate him.

During the break of the Parliamentary session, many Indians sitting in the visitors' gallery had surrounded Dadabhai. One of them was Jinnah. They had a frank discussion on the Indian political problems and the policies of the British government. The Indians had poured out their doubts, anger and grievances to Dadabhai. Jinnah was very much impressed by the manner and the patience with which Dadabhai heard them all. When the people talked about the racial prejudices of the British and their derogatory behaviour towards the Indians, Jinnah could not check himself. He said angrily, "the people who insult a leader of Dadabhai's stature, cannot be expected to do any justice and we cannot expect the government of such people to show us any social concern. The Indians will have to fight this injustice and insult."

Dadabhai looked at Jinnah after listening to his anguished voice. Jinnah looking into his eyes continued, "if English people could call a fair complexioned Dadabhai black, we are shades darker than him. They will not take us into account at all."

Dadabhai listened to Jinnah carefully and said putting his hand on his shoulder,

"Young man, your anger is justified, but haste is not good." And while taking a walk he asked, "What is your name? What are you doing here?"

Jinnah introduced himself in brief.

"If young people like you start working in India, it won't be difficult to open the eyes of the British," said Dadabhai and moved, "When you return to India, do meet me." Jinnah was delighted.

Thereafter Jinnah had visited the visitors' gallery more often and observed the Parliamentry proceedings. He developed a keen interest in the speeches and the proceedings of the Parliament. He had observed the speeches made by every speaker. He was very much impressed by the speech made by Joseph Chamberlain—a senior British leader—wearing a monocle and the sheer force of the speech and the impact it had on others swept him off his feet. Jinnah had never heard before this such a magical speech that left the parliamentarians spell bound. Jinnah felt the personality of Chamberlain was enhanced due to the monocle he wore. Suddenly he had an idea. Like Chamberlain, he too was tall and lean. And if he also wore the monocle like Chamberlain his personality would be enhanced.

The next day he bought the same kind of monocle and went on looking at his changed face in the mirror for hours. He felt that the modern clothes like those of Frederick and the monocle like that of Chamberlain had added an aura to his looks. He was making efforts to improve his looks and at the same realised the need to earn a few pounds.

In his free time, besides reading the law books and listening to the speeches at the Hyde Park and at the British Parliament, sometimes he also went to the various theatres to watch dramas. Once when he watched Shakespeare's play "Romeo and Juliet," he took the fancy to be an actor. When he saw the actors on the stage receiving a huge applause from the audience, he too felt like receiving such an applause. He felt that if he could work in a theatre, in his free time, he would not only be able to dazzle the packed audience, but also could earn a few pounds. When the actors acted on the stage, the hundreds of people in the auditorium watched them with their eyes glued to the performance. Jinnah used to imagine that he was acting on the stage. He would imagine that if he had played the role of Romeo on the stage, the entire audience would have watched him with similar intensity and applauded him.

Jinnah had neither acted on the stage nor given any speech before. Yet he was confident that he would not be found wanting if he did either of the two. He did proper homework before approaching the manager of a drama company. He went to the library and read the play 'Romeo and Juliet' with full concentration. To impress the manager, he had also read other plays of Shakespeare. Then he met the manager beaming with confidence and courage.

After listening to the young attractive man, wearing the latest fashionable clothes, the shining shoes and the monocle, the manager asked him, "Which plays of Shakespeare have you studied?"

Jinnah narrated the names of all the plays of Shakespeare, the characteristics and the themes with remarkable ease. The manager impressed by Jinnah asked him to speak a dialogue from any of the plays he liked. Jinnah like an experienced actor said the dialogue from the play 'Romeo and Juliet' as if he was playing the role of Romeo on the stage. The manager of the dance company was delighted. The young man's acting skills had impressed him. He realised that if he was given an opportunity he would become a good actor. He immediately took Jinnah into his company. Jinnah's joy knew no bounds. He started dreaming of playing the role of Romeo on the stage. He informed his father in Karachi about his success.

This had incensed Zinabhai all the more. If a scion of a business family got involved in acting in this way, it would not augur well for the family and for his business. In the childhood he had seen the dance troupes enacting plays in Paneli. The people used to like the plays, but the minstrels acting in the plays were looked down upon. The minstrels did not command any high respect in the society. Zinabhai was unable to accept that his son could choose the profession of acting like those minstrels. No one could earn by acting. In reply he shot an angry letter to his son. He wrote, "Son, you have a very big family responsibility. To enable you to discharge the responsibility and achieve success, I had sent you to a far off place to learn the nuances of the business. You have not learnt how to run the business and now you are acting and roaming around!"

When Jinnah received this letter in London he pondered over the feelings of his father. He felt that making his father angry over a small matter like acting in a drama was not right. He was clearing each semester of the legal studies successfully. It would not take much time to register his name with the Bar Council. After all, acting was only an interim measure to support himself. In fact, his aim was to return to India and practise as a Barrister and earn money, name and fame. Then why should he displease his father further?

Jinnah gave up the idea of becoming an actor.

But Jinnah did know the trials and tribulations that the Punja Valji Company was facing each passing day at Karachi. The main reason for this was the decision of the Douglas Graham & Company to stop the business with Punja Valji Company. Jinnah was responsible for the destruction of the company. When Frederick came to know that Jinnah had defied his father's advice and stuck to his stand he became furious. All these years he helped the Punja Valji Company to earn a lot of profit, made arrangement for this Sindhi to gain rare work experience in the London Office, yet he was ungrateful! Frederick was grinding his teeth in anger. All Indians living in Karachi were Sindhis for Frederick. Karachi was the capital of Sindh. Because Zinabhai had been doing business in Karachi for so many years, Frederick thought he was also a Sindhi. He had manipulated and used all his influence to employ this Sindhi boy in the Head Office with great difficulty. All that had come to a nought. His position had become awkward before his superiors. He banged the table with his fist and screamed,"I made a big mistake by helping this rascal, ungrateful Sindhi. Now I would teach him a lesson."

Frederick had decided not to do any business with the Punja Valji Company any more. Most of Zinabhai's business was transacted through the Douglas Graham & Company. The decision of Frederick would destroy Zinabhai's Company. For some time now, Zinabhai had been doing his business only through this Company. It was a very competent and prestigious company. A business company spurned by Frederick had no place in the market of Karachi.

13

Death of mother and wife, arrival in Bombay, pursuing legal profession, working as assistant to Pherozeshah

Before Jinnah appeared for the final semester at the law examination, he received the news from Karachi that his mother Mithibai and wife Amibai had died suddenly within a short span. Jinnah could not get any special occasion to live with Amibai. He had just seen her moving in the house after the marriage for a few days. Immediately after the marriage he left for London. They were separated for a long time. Nevertheless, there had been no communication between the teenage couple during this long separation. Jinnah had never mentioned about Amibai in his letters to his father. And the question of his writing separate letters to Amibai did not arise. He would get some news about Amibai from his father's letters. As a matter of fact, Jinnah was neither excited nor interested in getting the news about his wife. He believed that bringing Amibai to his house was a mere excuse to get his mother's permission to go to London.

It was different in case of Mithibai. In their house at Vazir Mansion, among a half dozen siblings only two were the objects of his affection. One was his mother Mithibai for whom he had a soft corner in his heart and the other was the horse in the stable. The joy and thrill that he had found in riding the horse, he did not get in doing anything else. His father was involved neck-deep in the business and always wanted his children to grow as per the norms of discipline that he had set. Jinnah did not like the kind of discipline his father wanted to impose. Jinnah had heard about the birth of one more child in the family. After Jinnah left Karachi, Mithibai gave birth to a baby girl and she was named Fatima. Jinnah had no knowledge that the pious names of Muhammad and Fatima were connected to the founding of Islam.

Jinnah's returning home in the absence of his mother at Karachi, after the examination, meant living with the youger brothers and sisters devoid of modern life style and mannerism. After staying three years in London, the English mannerism and life systle became an integral part of his life. The life style, the mannerism, the eating habits and the freedom that he was accustomed to in London could not be replicated at home in Karachi. His father Zinabhai was eagerly waiting for him to return to entrust him with the entire responsibility of running the business. He had informed him through his letters from time to time how the family business had suffered during the past three years. He also told him that the reason for the loss of business was Federick's annoyance with them. It meant that as soon as he returned to Karachi, his father would hold him responsible for the loss of the family business and he would again start telling him that Frederick would not have been so displeased had he not left the Douglas Graham & Company.

Jinnah was troubled by all these thoughts. In the meantime, Jinnah passed the last semester examination. Maamad of Karachi had now become Barrister M.A. Jinnah.

Jinnah decided that if he had to return to India and practice law and earn name and money, his father's home at Karachi would not be an ideal place. Jinnah was attracted to Bombay. He knew that Bombay was a home for most of the intellectuals. Though Dadabhai Navroji was a member of the British Parliament, his main working place was Bombay. Jinnah also knew that the important persons like Lokmanya Tilak, Gopal Krishna Gokhale, Annie Besant and Pherozeshah Mehta had successful careers in Bombay. If he had to work in the company of these leaders and earn money Bombay would be the right place. He did not know anybody in Bombay except one or two distant relatives. Yet Jinnah had decided to go to Bombay instead of returning to Karachi from London. He was very confident that in a place like Bombay which was known to him, he would make a successful career. If he could find his way in an unfamiliar and strange place like London three years ago, Bombay, in comparison, would be much easier to settle down.

After completing the formalities of registering his name as a barrister, he took the ship to Bombay. When the ship reached the Bombay harbour, it was a hot summer day in May. The most important work for Jinnah, returning with the bank balance of London, was to search for a suitable accommodation in Bombay. Though Jinnah was holding an important position of a barrister, he was not in a position to afford a residence or a hotel commensurate with his position. Yet he did not want to compromise on his lifestyle. On landing in Bombay, he had collected the necessary information and took a Victoria and reached the Appollo Hotel near the Charni Road Railway Station. The hotel was comparatively cheap and since it was located in the heart of the city, it was also convenient from the angle of business.

The nineteenth century was coming to an end. Among the few barristers in Bombay one or two barristers were Muslims. Therefore, in the beginning of his career, Jinnah being ambitious was not happy about the few cases he was getting. At that stage, he got a case which had brought him name and fame and professional success as a barrister. An appellant wanted to entrust a case which was in its final stage to Jinnah. When the case was in its final stage, his advocate declined to fight the case on his behalf, due to some reason. For the appellant, it was a very difficult situation. If the case was given to a new advocate, he feared that the case might be dragged for long unnecessarily. And if he engaged an experienced and reputed advocate, knowing his condition and the final stage of the case, he might ask for some exhorbitant amount as his fees. The appellant's financial condition was not good. In such a condition, he was not in a position to pay very high fees. The young Barrister Jinnah, due to his modern way of dressing and smart appearance, used to attract people. That was how, the appellant met Jinnah. After studying the case in detail, Jinnah told the appellant that he would charge a fee of hundred rupees per day to argue his case.

It was not possible to guess how many days the case would take. Jinnah's charge was too high. But the appellant had no other option. If he accepted the fees charged by Jinnah, he would not know for how many more days the case would go on and how much more money he would have to pay. He requested Jinnah, "Sir, it is difficult to say for how many days the case would go on. I would request you to accept rupees two thousand as a fee for the case, instead of charging on daily basis." Jinnah refused to accept the offer flatly and said in a harsh tone, "I cannot work this way. You look for another advocate."

The poor chap was cornered from all sides. There was very little time. He did not want to drag the case further. The possibility of another advocate studying the case was remote due to the shortage of time. Having no other option, he had accepted Jinnah's condition.

Jinnah argued the case extremely well in three days in the Court. The case was decided promptly and he won the case. The grateful client wanted to offer Jinnah the fees of rupees two thousand that he had volunteered earlier.

"Sir, I won the case because of you. Not only that, the case was decided so soon. I was mentally prepared to pay you the fee of rupees two thousand, please accept it."

Jinnah refused to accept the additional amount. He told him firmly that since he had agreed to charge a fee of rupees hundred a day, he had no right to accept any amount more than rupees three hundred. The client was impressed by Jinnah's principled stand and his professional ethics and the honesty in the financial matter became a subject of discussion in the Court premises.

Jinnah was not to be satisfied with such little success or fame. He was looking for some big opportunity. He was looking for such an opportunity that would enable him to prove his professional competence and legal knowledge so that he could become the centre of attention for all. Fortunately, one day he read in a newspaper that Dadabhai Navroji was in Bombay. Jinnah used to read every newspaper he could get hold of very carefully. Perhaps, he never read anything else, except the daily newspapers and the law books. On learning that Dadabhai was in Bombay, he had remembered the conversation that he had with him at the British Parliament. Dadabhai himself had told Jinnah to meet him in Bombay.

Presently, Dadabhai's status in the political and social life was very high. If he could take advantage of his acquaintance with Dadabhai...

Jinnah met Dadabhai. He did not forget the young man who drew his attention with his excitement and anger in the British Parliament House. Knowing that now Jinnah was a barrister and wanted to settle in Bombay, he said, "Young man, a bright barrister like you should get training as an assistant under a reputed barrister like Pherozeshah Mehta."

"I agree with you, Sir," Jinnah said politely, "But I do not have any intimate acquaintance with any such top ranking barrister."

"You go and meet Pherozeshah Mehta tomorrow. I will talk to him about you. You will understand in future the value of learning from him," Dadabahi said warmly.

"I am very thankful to you, Sir," Jinnah said expressing his gratitude.

When Jinnah went to meet Pherozeshah Mehta the next day, he was called inside his chamber immediately, though a large number of people were already waiting to meet him. It was evident that he got a message from Dadabhai. Jinnah had entered the chamber of Pherozeshah Mehata with an inner satisfaction that he had enjoyed a special position vis-à-vis the visitors waiting to meet him. The lean and tall Jinnah, wearing a monocle and dressed meticulously in a suit with a crisp handkerchief peering from his coat pocket caught the attention of Pherozeshah Mehta.

At the first meeting, Pherozeshah Mehta had realised that Jinnah was well versed with the law as well as the current affairs. And since a senior political leader like Dadabhai Navroji had recommended him, Pherozeshah Mehta immediately asked him to join his Chamber as an assistant.

This was a golden opportunity to Jinnah. Jinnah knew that as an assistant to Pherozeshah Mehta he had enjoyed a special position among his fellow advocates. He was waiting for such an opportunity to project his own personality by taking advantage of the special position. He got the opportunity so soon!

Pherozeshah Mehta was considered the uncrowned king of Bombay and had exercised an absolute authority over the Bombay Municipal Corporation. The English people envied his position. They did not like the prospect of his being elected as the representative of the Corporation in the Governor's Council. The Britishers had conspired against him, manipulated the election and prevented him from becoming a member of the Governor's Council. Pherozeshah Mehta's friends and supporters were outraged at the manipulation of the election. Taking advantage of the situation, Jinnah had encouraged them to challenge the conspiracy in the Court. Jinnah himself had acted as the counsel for the appellant, and argued the case, citing the various sections of the laws and quoting from the past cases and even taking the examples from the international cases.

The case had received wide coverage in the newspapers not only in Bombay but across the country. The case received wide publicity because it was connected with a high profile citizen. Naturally, Jinnah was also benefited by the publicity. Because the case was discussed widely. Jinnah's name became quite well known. He did not win the case, but the case brought him good reputation.

At this time, MacPherson, the British Advocate General of the Bombay Province, had noticed Jinnah. He read in the newspapers that Jinnah had quoted extensively in the Court from the prestigious international law books. MacPherson was present in the Court in connection with some other matter when he heard Jinnah arguing the case. The way he argued the case forcefully and effectively had impressed him very much. Jinnah had seen MacPherson before, but did not have the opportunity to meet him. When the Court was adjourned after the hearing, Jinnah greeted MacPherson who said to him pleasantly, "Barrister Jinnah, the way you have studied the legal books is admirable. In case you need to look for any reference, you can make use of my government library."

Jinnah's joy knew no bounds. Jinnah was the first Indian advocate to have made use of MacPherson's government library.

14

MacPherson's library, appointment as magistrate, encounter with MacDonald in court, working as a consultant of the Bombay Municipal Corporation

The Advocate General of Bombay Province, MacPherson, had enjoyed a high reputation in the government and the social circles. His government library had a good collection of rare books on national and international law. The library had a lot of books on the world history related to the political revolutions and the political systems of various countries. Ordinarily, the library was not open to anyone. Jinnah's profession did not yet expand so much as to keep him occupied all the time. He would spend his leisure time, after attending to the court matters, in MacPherson's library. He had a keen interest in the law, the world history of political revolutions and the political changes.

At that time, the country's political history was taking a different shape. The Indian National Congress was established in 1885. The aim of the organisation was to enable the Indians to assist the British administration, to provide a link with Her Majesty's government and to keep the British government well acquianted with India. However, the Indian National Congress had gradually moved away from its original aim and soon emerged as a political organisation. Around this time, the Mohammedan Anglo Oriental College, established for the study of the Islamic politics and religion, transformed into the Aligarh Muslim University. These two developments did not escape Jinnah's attention. However, presently Jinnah was more worried about his financial condition. He did not yet acquire the financial status that he was aspiring to.

One afternoon when Jinnah was carefully going through the newspapers and the official gazette in MacPherson's library, his attention was drawn to a news item. Jinnah knew that the Bombay court had four magistrates. One of the magistrates was retiring soon. The government was looking for a suitable person to fill the post. Sir Charles, a member of the Law Department in the Bombay Province, wanted to appoint a young barrister well versed in the international law to the post. Jinnah was so deeply lost in thought on reading the news that the cigarette in his hand burnt the fingertips. It was not a bad idea to take up the job for some time to get relief from the financial burden. Jinnah looked outside, through the library window, saw a Victoria and stopped it and ran across and jumped into it. In a few minutes, the Victoria took him to the premises of Sir Charles' Office.

When Sir Charles had learnt that Jinnah was the first Indian to have used the MacPherson's library, his attitude towards him changed completely. And further, when he came to know that this bright young man was working as an assistant to Pherozeshah Mehta he thought Jinnah was the most suitable person to be appointed to the post of magistrate. After making some preliminary enquiry with MacPherson, he had immediately appointed Jinnah to the post of magistrate. Jinnah had accepted the appointment with a monthly salary of fifteen hundred rupees. However, he was unhappy about the fact that this position would never make him realise his ambition of acquiring a high financial status; yet considering the present financial condition, this job would give him some relief for some time.

In the meantime, the influence of the nationalist leaders like Gopal Krishna Gokhale and Lokmanya Tilak on the Indian National Congress was growing. Jinnah had observed their style of working very closely. These leaders often used to have meetings near the Shantaram Chawl in the vicinity of C. P. Tank where Jinnah would listen to their speeches. The Chowpaty and the Azad Maidan were not yet that popular for such public meetings. There was a marked difference in the approach of Tilak and that of Gokhale to politics. Their political thinking was also different. Jinnah had unwittingly noticed the difference in their approach and the impact that it had on the national issues and the Indian National Congress. In his free time, Jinnah used to discuss the current political issues with Pherozeshah Mehta. Jinnah's political acumen and his legal approach to every issue had impressed Pherozeshah Mehta.

In a few months, Jinnah got bored with the job of the magistrate. Jinnah had realised that this job would be a permanent hurdle in securing the financial status and the security for the future which he was aspiring for. Jinnah was looking for an independent and challenging task. As luck would have it, he got such an opportunity due to an incident.

The hearing of a very controversial and exciting case was proceeding in the main room of the Bombay High Court. The arguments of the advocates of both the sides, the statements of the witnesses and the cross examinations relating to this case were reported in details in the newspapers. The Court room used to be packed with the public. It had a separate enclosure for the advocates. As per the tradition of the Court, nobody—not even a member of the public or a government officer or even a journalist—could sit in the reserved seats.

That day Jinnah was present in the Court room to observe the proceedings and listen to the arguments in the case. As usual, the Court room was jampacked with public that day. There was no vacant seat anywhere. Even at the entrance, people were standing due to lack of seats. On entering the court, Jinnah looked at the enclosure reserved for the advocates. There all the seats were occupied too. He glanced at all those sitting in the enclosure. His eyes stopped on noticing a person whom he knew, though not personally. Every citizen of Bombay knew him. He was James MacDonald, the chairman of the Bombay Municipal Corporation. Jinnah had seen this Scotish gentleman two or three times in connection with his government duties. Though Jinnah had not met him, he could recognise him. Although he had the right to be the first citizen of Bombay, by virtue of being the Chairman of the Bombay Municipal Corporation, he had no right to sit in the enclosure meant for the advocates. It could be said that when a reputed advocate like Jinnah was standing, MacDonald had usurped the seat. The Court is meant for protecting the law, and not for breaking the law. Moreover, as the first citizen of Bombay, the Chairman of the Corporation ought to protect the law. Jinnah slowly approached MacDonald with a serious look and said sternly, "Gentleman, you have occupied the wrong seat. This enclosure is reserved for the advocates of the court only."

MacDonald got very annoyed, looked at Jinnah and said contemptuously, "You do not have to teach me the law. I don't know, who you are. Please do not disturb me."

"If you don't know who I am, you will come to know soon," said Jinnah and walked away angrily.

Jinnah approached official of the court responsible for the court proceedings and drew his attention.

"That gentleman has occupied the seat meant for the advocate which is wrong. You know I am a barrister. There is no vacant seat. Now, it is your duty to make him vacate the seat and give it to me as per my right."

The official knew Jinnah, but when he came to know that he was complaining against the Chairman of the Municipal Corporation MacDonald, he said to Jinnah, "Sir, it is very difficult to tell the Chairman of the Corporation to vacate the seat."

"Whether it is difficult or easy, it is not my concern. It is your duty. If you do not perform your duty, I will file a case in the court against you for not performing your duty," Jinnah said in a very firm tone.

For a moment, the official was in a dilemma. He felt that instead of annoying Jinnah, it would be appropriate, as a part of his duty, to draw the attention of MacDonald. If MacDoland did not vacate the seat, at least he would be able to say that he had performed his duty. Then the issue would be between MacDonald and Jinnah. If Jinnah wanted he could lodge a police complaint. He approached MacDonald along with Jinnah.

"Sir," he whispered very politely in MacDonald's ear, "excuse me, you are sitting in a wrong place. As per the court order, this place is reserved only for the advocates." And then he added in a very soft voice, "I will arrange another chair for you on the other side."

MacDonald raised his face. Jinnah stood firmly. MacDonald looked at Jinnah. He felt that the young man was indeed very courageous. He changed his opinion about the young man who had questioned the first citizen of the city to defend the law.

He stood up from the seat, demonstrating the Scottish mannerism and putting his hand on Jinnah's shoulder said, "I am sorry, brother. You have the right to sit here." And then he left the place along with the court officail. Subsequently he enquired with him about Jinnah.

A sudden and surprising thing had happened to Jinnah the next day. He received a special invitation for tea from the Chairman of the Bombay Municipal Corporation MacDonald. Jinnah was surprised. He was unable to understand how MacDonald whom he had forced to vacate the seat as per the law the previous day could invite him for tea. Even then, he had no fear of MacDonald in his mind. He would not be intimidated, however powerful and influential the British official MacDonald might be. Jinnah had accepted the invitation and confidently reached the Office of MacDonald on time for tea.

When Jinnah reached MacDonald's Office, another surprise awaited for him. MacDonald extended him a very warm welcome. Jinnah thought MacDonald would receive him with utter disregard and contempt. But whatever happened was totally different. Nevertheless, he shook hand with MacDonald very cautiously.

MacDonald, in keeping with the English mannerism, started talking about weather and such other matters, as if nothing had happened the previous day. Jinnah was anxious. He knew that MacDonald had not called him to discuss these matters. But he did not want to show his anxiety before MacDonald.

Jinnah's anxiety ended after a while.

"Mr. Jinnah," MacDonald now came to the main issue, "I want the Bombay Municipal Corporation to avail of your services as a Legal Adviser. After seeing your firmness yesterday, I feel you are the most suitable person to defend the law. Your courage to defend the law, without fear or favour, is highly appreciable. I saw your fearlessness in yesterday's incident. I appreciate such fearlessness. I am pleased to appoint you as a legal adviser to the Corporation with a monthly honorarium of rupees one thousand."

Jinnah was speechless. For a moment he calculated the likely advantage of this income in comparison to the fifteen hundred rupees that he was getting as a magistrate. As a magistrate he was not able to do any other job and earn additional income. Now in addition to being an honorary adviser to the Corporation he would be free to pursue his independent career as an advocate.

Jinnah immediately accepted MacDonald's offer and thanked him.

When Jinnah had resigned from the post of magistrate, Sir Charles, a member of the Legal Department, pleaded with him, "Mr. Jinnah, you are in haste. I wish to see you as a High Court Judge holding a highly responsible position. In the present situation, it is not prudent to lose a monthly income of fifteen hundred rupees."

"I am thankful to you Sir," pointing out the index finger of his right hand towards the wall, Jinnah said, "But I wish to do such kind of work so that I can earn fifteen hundred rupees a day. I am confident that I will be able to realise this wish very soon."

Charles was stunned. He was surprised by the self-confidence of Jinnah. Stretching out his right hand towards Jinnah, he said, "Mr. Jinnah, your ambition is pretty high, even then my good wishes are with you. I wish you success." Jinnah shook hand very warmly with Charles.

*

It was not that the time was writing a strange chapter rapidly for Jinnah alone, but was also writing new chapters for his father Zinabhai in Karachi rapidly. From the point of business, the Punja Valji Company was totally bankrupt. Zinabhai could not afford the lifestyle of the family at Vazir Mansion. Deprived of his wife, Zinabhai not only had aged physically but also had become weak mentally. He was grieved at his son Mamaad's neglecting not only his business but also the manner in which he neglected the family. In addition to getting jobs for his children, he also had the responsibility of arranging their marriages and helping them to settle down. Though Mamaad had ignored the family relations and neglected his responsibility, Zinabhai knew that now he was having good income. Zinabhai felt that in such a situation it was not possible in his old age to live in Karachi and earn the income the way he used do. Then he decided to settle in Bombay and take the help of his son. Zinabhai had two or three close relatives residing in Bombay. Hoping to rely on all these people, Zinabhai had closed the business in Karachi and came to Bombay with his six children, staying in a two-room apartment located on the third floor in a house on the Khoja street.

15

Father's shift to Bombay, admission of Fatima to school, Hindu-Muslim untouchability incident narrated by Fatima

When Zinabhai had left Karachi and came to setlle permanently in Bombay with his children, Barrister Jinnah saw for the first time his youngest sister Fatima. He did not like his father coming to Bombay. By that time, Jinnah had created a niche for himself in the legal profession. Within a few days, he had shifted from a rented room in Charni Road to a spacious flat in Appollo Bunder. He was fashionable and attracted to a lavish lifestyle. He had a liking for the foreign branded cigarettes and high quality wine. He enjoyed going to the high society gymkhanas and clubs. All these habits were quite expensive, but he was earning enough to meet the expenses. When Jinnah was rising rapidly in his social status, his father and his family did not fit into his scheme of things. The thought of his staying with his father and family and taking care of them was unbearable.

However, initially when his father and family was bankrupt, Jinnah had rendered them some financial assistance. But he never went to meet the family living at Khoja Street. Fatima was an exception. His mother died at her birth. She had no recollection of her mother. In the motherless family which was going through a serious financial crisis, she had grown up as a neglected child. Her father had never paid any attention to her upbringing or education. After coming to Bombay, she met her elder brother Jinnah for the first time. She heard so much about him from her father, brothers and sisters. But when she saw her elder brother's English lifestyle and mannerism, she was shocked. With great difficulty, she had managed to get a little education in Karachi.

When Barrister Jinnah saw his younger sister for the first time, he was astonished. Fatima looked exactly like his mother. Jinnah grew fond of her because she had a striking resemblance with his mother. Because he was the eldest among the seven children, he had received a lot of love from his mother. He could not see his mother again and she had died before he returned to India after becoming a barrister. Although, his life took altogether a different turn, he remembered this now and then. He could not forget it. That is why, Fatima's coming home brought him some relief. When he learnt that Fatima could not study, he decided to get her admitted to a good Christian school.

If Fatima was admitted to a school centrally located in the city, she could remain in touch with the family at Khoja Street daily. But Jinnah wished that if Fatima had stayed away from the family, her personality could take a different dimension. Therefore, he got her admitted to a school having the hostel in Bandra, far away from the heart of the city.

Bombay was a city of seven islands and Bandra was one of them. Since Bandra was located at a distance of about fifteen to twenty miles, it was not possible to develop it. Between the city and Bandra, there existed an unoccupied forest land, surrounded by sea water and the tides made the commuting difficult. When Jinnah proposed to his father about admitting Fatima to the school, he did not oppose it. In fact, to his father, Fatima was unwanted. Zinabhai had considered Fatima responsible for the death of his wife Mithibai and for the ruining of his business. He felt that, with no earning in a city like Bombay, he would be relieved of the burden and the responsibility of looking after her. Considering this, he immediately agreed to his son Mammad's proposal. This was what Fatima wanted. She was excited at the prospect of leading a comfortable life in a new environment, free from her father and the family. She felt indebted to her brother for the rest of her life. In spite of the busy schedule, Jinnah would make it a point to spare some time and visit Fatima at her hostel in Bandra every Sunday to enquire about the progress of her studies. Cars were still a rare sight on the roads of Bombay. Whenever the British officials were seen travelling in the cars, the pedestrians would stop and look at the vehicles with great surprise. The Victoria carriages were seen everywhere. The steam engine trains were running from Colaba. People used to travel on these trams without any fear. It was possible to reach Bandra by these trains. But Jinnah considered it beneath his dignity to travel in these trains with the crowd. He was so well off financially that he could afford to travel in a Victoria from his residence in Appollo Bunder to Bandra. However, the Victoria would not go beyond Dadar, due to the dense forest and the water puddles. To overcome these difficulties, Jinnah had found a unique way. He had a liking for horse riding right from his childhood. He was a skilled rider too. The Victoria carriages used to get a very few passengers on Sundays. Jinnah had made an arrangement with the owner of one such Victoria carriage of hiring a horse every Sunday. He would purchase a gear of his choice for the ride to pop up his image. And Jinnah would ride the horse every Sunday to Bandra and meet Fatima. In the hostel, Jinnah became popular as a famous advocate who visited his sister every Sunday at a particular time without fail. Fatima would look forward the remaining six days to her elder brother to come and spend some time with her.

Majority of the girls in the hostel were Christians. In the school also, the Christian girls and the daughters of the British officials used to study. Fatima used to feel very lonely among them. All Christian girls would go to the church every Sunday without fail and pray and listen to the sermons of the Fathers.

Attending the prayer was compulsory for all the girls staying in the hostel. Fatima knew how to offer *Namaaz.* She had memorised all the seven verses of *Al Fatiha.* She used to respect the Holy Quran. But here nothing was practised from it. She was annoyed that she had to go to the church and kneel down along with these Christian girls. Once when she had expressed her displeasure about all this to her elder brother, he laughingly told her, "Fati, religion, faith, prayer, Quran, Bible—all these are only for consoling the weak. There is no truth in them. Whether you pray or offer *Namaaz,* it makes no difference. What is important is how you reach your goal. Man had discovered the faith as a means to attain success."

Fatima could not understand what her brother was saying. She could not accept that the faith is only a means to attain success. She was unable to forget the incident that had occurred in her childhood in Karachi.

Fatima was not that naïve at that time. One Friday when her father Zinabhai returned after offering the *Namaaz,* three of his business friends were waiting for him at home. Fatima knew quiet well one of them who was Rehman uncle. He came to the house more often. She had not seen the other two guests before. Being hospitable, Fatima's elder sister offered the guests glasses of water, while Rehman uncle quenched his thirst, the other two guests had politely declined to have the water. Fatima would not have paid any attention to this, but for the introduction of the guests to her father by Rehman uncle. The two guests were Brahmin priests from a small village near Rajkot. Since Rehman uncle was also from the same village, the three of them knew each other pretty well. These priests had come to Karachi to collect donations for a temple. They had some patrons in Karachi. Because of their good acquaintance, they came to meet Rehman uncle and after receiving the hospitality from him, they were brought here to meet Zinabhai. Zinabhai's father Punja Thakkar was also a resident of the village Paneli near Rajkot. These Brahmins also had some partrons in Paneli. And they used to visit Paneli frequently. When Rehman uncle had told them that Zinabhai was also from Paneli they expressed a desire to meet him, developing a sudden liking for the man whom they had shunned.

Zinabhai had almost cut-off his link with Paneli. His father had died. He remained occupied with his business and the big family. Yet, he had some emotional attachment to Paneli. He warmly welcomed the guests and they recalled the days gone by with nostalgia. Fatima, sitting in a corner, was listening to the conversation with keen interest. Prior to this, she knew nothing about Paneli or the religious conversion of her grandfather. Some of the families residing around the Vazir Mansion were Hindus. Fatima had seen some of the Brahmins applied the three-pronged *tilak* on their foreheads and wear threads on their bare chests and chant prayers on festival days. Fatima knew that she was living in a different community than that of the Hindus. Yet this difference did not matter much to her.

Her father had offered the guests some snacks and glasses of butter milk.

Rehman uncle enjoyed the offer. But the other two guests, folding their hands, very politely declined the offer. Fatima was very surprised about the attitude of the guests. When the guests came from outside, they were sweating profusely and yet they did not drink the water. And now after sitting for so long, they neither ate the snacks nor drank the butter milk. Her father Zinabhai did not say anything. Nor did Rehman uncle say anything to them either. And yet these four grown up men went on discussing with great warmth everything under the sun for hours.

When the guests left after a very long time, Fatima put the question which was in her mind for quite some time to her father. She said "*Abbajan*, why did not the guests eat or drink any thing? Rehman uncle was enjoying the food, but they did not even touch any thing!"

"Because they are Hindus, my child, and that too Brahmins. They do not eat and drink in our home." The father explained to the daughter in brief.

"But why like that, *Abbajaan*[1]? When Rehman uncle and you could talk with them about your childhood, then why is it a crime for them to eat or drink in our home?" Fatima asked innocently.

"My child, the Hindus consider themselves superior. Their faith tells them that if they eat or drink with us they would become impure. Everyone has to live as per the diktat of his faith," as Zinabhai said he remembered something and his eyes brightened. He said something, as if he was talking to himself,

"My child, we were also Hindus in Paneli. We used to pray to *Shrinathji* at home and observe the festivals and I along with my siblings would push each other for the *Prasad*[1]."

Fatima could only understand that her family was Hindu in the past. It was beyond her comprehension as to how a Hindu family got converted into Islam. But out of her curiosity, she continued with her query and asked Zinabhai,

"*Abbajan*[1], if Hindus become impure by eating at Muslim homes, why did we who were Hindus earlier got converted into Muslims? Now, can't we become Hindus again?"

Zinabhai listened to his daughter and stared at her. He remembered how his father Punja Thakkar had made unsuccessful efforts to reconvert to Hinduism. Every one from the *Maharajshree* in the *haveli to* the priests in Shiv and Hanuman temples had said the same thing—"Hindus are not made, they are born. Those who renounce Hinduism once will have to take another birth if they want to become Hindus again." Zinabhai felt mentally anguished. He did not know how to explain the whole thing to his daughter. She would not understand. Yet he said, "My father became a Mulsim, but he wanted to become a Hindu again. Once you renoucce Hinduism, the doors of Hinduism are closed. Hinduism does not welcome the converts from other religions." And to end the conversation he said, "my child, every one has his own faith. It is better to live as per that faith. One should not enter into argument and should be content with the life that

God has given." Zinabhai had tried to explain in the most simple way the philosophy of his life.

At that age, Fatima could not understand fully all that. But her mind was bogged down for long with the thought, how the Hindus were different from the Muslims? She felt very angry that the *Maharajshree* and the priests did not accept her grandfather into Hinduism. However, gradually these thoughts got relegated to the background with the passage of time.

But, now in the context of what her brother had said, she recollected the Christian girls' prayers, the sermons of the Fathers and the long forgotten incident of Karachi. Her brother might say that the faith is a means to attain success, but the behaviour of the Christian girls and the attitude of the Hindu Brahmins who considered themselves superior and refused to drink even a drop of water from a Muslim home had left a deep impact on her tender mind. Fatima, who used to trust her elder brother instinctively for every thing had realised for the first time that in the matter of Faith she herself had to make her brother understand. He did not understand the truth in this matter. The teenage Fatima had registered this in her mind.

NOTES

1. Father as addressed by the Muslims.
2. An eatable item offered to the God and then accepted as His blessings.

16

1885: Establishing of the Indian National Congress, Aligarh Muslim University, Sir Syed Ahemd-Bacon dialogue, Archibald's suggestion for delegation

The whole country had experienced a great shock by the revolt in 1857 against the rule of the Brtitish East India Company. It was called the Sepoy Mutiny or the First War of Indian independence. The emperor Bahadur Shah Zafar of the Mughal Empire which was almost nearing its end was forced to be happy in ruling over a few regions around the capital Delhi. The chieftains of Avadh, Bengal and Gujarat had broken away from the Mughal Empire and proclaimed independence. In the Southern India, except for the kingdoms of Tipu Sultan and the Nizam, the Hindu rulers were asserting themselves. The Marathas of Shivneri who had extended their rule upto Delhi and the Rajput kingdoms of Rajasthan were liberated much earlier from the Mughal rule.

The revolt was intensified. One of the soldiers Syed Ahmed had fought on behalf of the company. The revolt was crushed and the Company emerged victorious. But this had resulted in the Queen of England taking over the reins of India from the East India Company. Now the Indians were ruled from London. This was an extraordinary development. The Indians had witnessed the change of rulers many a time, but they could never imagine that one day they would be ruled from a centre of power located thousands of miles away across the seven seas. In the revolt of 1857, the Maratha leader Tatya Tope, Queen Laxmibai of Jhansi and Bahadur Shah Zafar had fought jointly against the Company, but they were defeated due to the latter's military might. Syed Ahmed took to arms against his own Hindu and Mulsim colleagues.

On the occasion of the coronation of the Queen, the loyal Indians were rewarded, one of them being the Muslim soldier Syed Ahmed. After the revolt, Syed Ahmed was made an officer in the British army. His experience in the British army made him realise that the British East India Company could crush the revolt not because of its military might but due to its manoeuvring. The valour with which Tatya Tope, Peshwa Nanasaheb and Queen Laxmibai had fought and the manner in which the Indian soldiers had lost, made Syed Ahmed sympathetic.

He felt sad that the Muslim rule of many generations had ended. Though the Muslims had come as conquerors to India from outside, there was no denying the fact that they had become an integral part of this country. The British East India Company which had come to India for trade and commerce now became the ruler of such a big country. It was obvious that, unlike the Muslims, the Britishers never wanted to become a part of India. For them, India was a cash cow. The Britishers were businessmen and they had developed various kinds of business in India during the past hundred and fifty years. The majority of the Muslims were employed in the government offices. And the Hindus were involved in the business. The Britishers, therefore, had developled close ties with the Hindus. The benefits of the English education also had gone to the Hindus. Syed Ahmed thought that if the Muslims also had received the modern education, both the Hindu and the Muslim communities could unite once again against the British rule, in near future. He realised that the Muslims should leave behind the *Madrassas* of the *Mullahs* and *Maulvis.*

Syed Ahmed was well acquainted with the British government. Because of his service in the army, he had good contacts with the British officials. He started exploring his contacts to introduce the new education for the Muslims. This exercise continued nearly for a decade and a half. And then in 1875, Sir Syed Ahmed had established the Mohammadan Anglo Oriental College in a village called Aligarh in the United Province. He had succeeded in getting Sir Bacon, a senior British gazetted officer, appointed as the first Principal of the College by the government. The aim of the college was to provide the new English education to the Muslim youth.

During this period, the political awareness in the country was scaling new heights and taking unexpected turns. Sir A.O. Hume, a British gazetted officer, due to his huge experience in the government service, realised that if the British administration in India had to succeed and become popular, some link between the British government and the people was necessary. A section of the Indian people had received the English education. And if this section of the people could be used as a link the British government would be able to understand the needs and aspirations of the majority of the illiterate people living in rural India. And the success of any government depended on the happiness of these people. The British government was not able to reach out to them because of the cultural and educational barriers. If the English educated Indians were involved it would be beneficial in the long run. Sir Hume mooted the idea with Lord Dufferin, the Governor General. Lord Dufferin liked the idea and gave him the permission to go ahead.

Consequently, one fine morning in December 1885, an organisation called the Indian National Congress was founded at Sir Gokuldas Tejpal Auditorium in Bombay. At the first meeting of this organisation, seventy two representatives were present and all of them, the English educated upper class, represented the high society. It was natural that most of them had represented the Hindus, a few represented the Christians and the Parsees and hardly one person represented the Muslims.

The daily English newspaper, *The Times of India* was owned by the British. In fact, the Britishers had started this paper with a view to make the English educated people happy and to create a conducive atmosphere for the British administration. After the Congress was established, this daily newspaper in its edition of 5 February 1886 had reported that this organisation could not be called an all India organisation as there was no Muslim representative in it. If the Muslims did not join the Organisation or did not associate themselves with it, any demand made by the Congress could not be construed as the demand of all India, because it did not represent the entire population. Though the historians had not made any special mention of this, on close scrunity, an inference could be drawn that this had sowed the seeds for the partion of the country almost a little more than a half a century later. The Muslims had constituted twenty per cent of the country's population. Yet for the first time, the correspondent of *The Times of India* had come out with the bizarre idea that even if the remaining eighty per cent people had made any demand in one voice, it could not be construed as the demand of the whole country.

For the past one decade, Sir Bacon was the first Principal of the Mohammadan Anglo Oriental College established to impart new English education to the Muslims. Bacon's powerful personality, his oratory skills, knowledge of history and politics and amiable manners had deeply impressed Sir Syed Ahmed. The rules and regulations of the College were framed as per Bacon's wish. Bacon also read the scorching report in *The Times of India*. Then he got an idea. The political awareness was spreading rapidly among the Hindu and the Parsee leaders. He doubted whether the Queen in London from a distance of five thousand miles would be able to administer such a vast country, if awareness continued to spread like this. He felt the report in *The Times of India* had some hidden solution to this.

Principal Bacon had remembered an incident that occurred two days ago. A business organisation of the Hindus had organised a felicitation function for Sir Syed Ahmed. Principal Bacon was also present at the function. The organisation had comprised of the educated and rich Hindus. Some Muslim professors of Sir Syed Ahmed's colleges were also present at the function. The speakers at the function, while praising Sir Syed Ahmed's interest in education and his political awareness, had repeatedly said,"We the Hindus appreciate Sir Syed Ahmed's awareness and patriotism. Though he is a Muslim, he is one among the Hindus."

In reply to the felicitation, Sir Syed Ahmed said, "There is no relation between nationality and religion. Whether we are Hindus or Muslims, all of us are destined to be together. We all inherited the common culture. I am saddened to know that by addressing yourselves as Hindus, you have deprived me of a common identity."

Principal Bacon would have forgotten the incident, but the report in *The Times of India* had made him think. If the eighty per cent non-Muslims could be considered incomplete without the twenty per cent Muslims, then... Bacon had decided. Now his only job was somehow to erase from Sir Syed Ahmed's mind the thought of a nationalist and instead convince him that all those living in India were not Hindus and that the twenty per cent Muslims were a different people. These people instead of merging with the eighty per cent people of the population should maintain their special religious and cultural identity. Then only the Muslims would survive and for that they must cooperate with the British government. Such thoughts should be injected into the mind of Sir Syed Ahmed. Principal Bacon had put his new doctrine into practice immediately.

One day Bacon got an opportunity and said to Syed, "Mr. Syed, the Muslims were ruling India for hundreds of years. Now that their rule has ended, what are you thinking of their future?"

"Keeping their future in mind only, as you know, the Mohammedan Anglo Oriental College was established," said Syed.

"That is all right, but this one College cannot educate crores of Muslims. There is a lot of poverty in the Muslim community," Bacon said to extend the conversation.

"That I knew and for that the Muslims will have to unite to demand some special facilities from the government," said Syed.

"Mr. Syed, you have ignored one very big truth. Why are you forgetting that in India the Hindus are either kings or landlords or quite prosperous as businessmen?"Bacon said cleverly.

"This is natural, Sir. When the Muslims were looking after the administration, the Hindus were involved in trade and commerce."

"But, now the mere awareness of this reality will not improve the future of the Muslims. That is why the people of your vision will have to think differently," Bacon said looking straight into the eyes of Sir Syed Ahmed.

"Means? I have not understood..." countered Syed.

"The people of this country consider the British rule as alien. The British rule somehow had survived the revolt of 1857. Had the East India Company been defeated then, Bahadur Shah Zafar would have sat on the Indian throne as the Emperor. But the Mughal dynasty had now ended. God forbid, if 1857 is repeated who will rule the country, have you ever thought of it?" Bacon was very cleverly opening his cards one by one.

To Sir Syed Ahmed this was totally unimaginable. He never thought of it. Though he might have fought for the Britishers in 1857, after all, he was an Indian. He had a deep desire that there ought to be a native Indian rule of any sort in India rather than the foreign rule. What will happen tomorrow? no one can predict, but if 1857 is repeated then...

"In which thoughts are you lost, Mr. Syed? You have not given any answer to my question. The day when the British rule ends in this country, the rulers of this country will be Hindus and not Muslims. Why can't you understand such a simple thing? The Muslims had ruled the Hindus for hundreds of years. If ever the power falls into the hands of the Hindus, they will not rest without taking revenge against the Muslims for the atrocities committed against them under the Muslim rule. These majestic mosques, tombs, minarets and forts are connected to the Islamic religion. All these will be destroyed under the Hindu rule," Bacon painted a very gloomy picture by giving the colours of reality.

Sir Syed Ahmed, for the first time in his life, could not sleep that night. He was thinking about what Bacon had said. Principal Bacon had spent that whole night planning his next move. He had succeeded in his first attempt in stirring up the mind of Sir Syed Ahmed. Being satisfied that his effort had borne the fruit, he was now trying to ensure that the seed that he had sowed blossomed. The Mohammedan Anglo Oriental College used to publish a journal regularly. Sir Syed Ahmed was the editor of the journal until then. Bacon very cleverly had now taken in his hands the responsibility of the editor of the journal. The journal was widely read and quite popular among the educated Muslims. Bacon used the journal to publish his thoughts in print which had resulted in causing uneasiness among the educated Muslims.

But the term of Bacon now ended. Bacon thought that after him if another gazetted officer of his kind was appointed as the Principal, he would be able to carry forward the work started by him. This foresight made him to ask the Executive Council of the College to write a letter to the government recommending a name. He created such an atmosphere in the college that if the person called Archibald was appointed as the Principal, the English education among the Muslims would progress very rapidly. Bacon knew Archibald quite well. He was confident that Archibald would execute his ideas. The government had accepted the demand of the College Executive Council and appointed Archibald as the Principal.

At that time, Lord Minto was the Viceroy of India. Colonel Dunlop Smith was his private secretary. Archibald was a close fiend of Smith. Both of them were friends right from their college days, before they joined the government service. The seed sowed by Bacon blossomed under Archibald. In this, Smith's contribution was also very significant. If the Muslims had to be kept away permanently from the Hindu main stream, they must be offered something tempting, like a sweet lollipop that could water their mouth. Archibald had discussed this plan with Smith who decided to take Lord Minto's opinion on this.

Smith realised that Lady Minto, rather than Lord Minto, was more enthusiastic about the gameplan that Archibald and he had worked out. Lady Minto was excited to visualise that if the Viceroy had consented to their gameplan, the Indian history would take a new turn and the twenty per cent people would be in a permanent conflict with the country's eighty per cent people. The Viceroy Lord Minto had quietly listened to the plan of Smith, without betraying any emotion befitting of an eminent British officer. He did not react immediately. But the clever Smith, owing to his experience in the government service, could understand that the silence of the boss meant consent. Moreover, the way Lady Minto responded enthusiastically, he was confident that whatever had to be done she would support to execute that. Thus, being assured, Archibald had explained his plan to Nawab Mohsin-Ul-Haq, Chairman of the College Executive Council.

Following the path of his predecessor Bacon successfully Archibald said, "Nawab Sahib, there is a golden opportunity for you. Everything is arranged with His Excellency the Viceroy. If you along with a special delegation meet His Excellency the Viceroy, on behalf of the sixty million Muslims and demand political rights for the community, the Viceroy would certainly accept the demand."

Nawab Mohsin-Ul-Haq, who could not imagine such a thing, got excited. In the capital Calcutta, he had seen the Viceregal grandeur. He had been to the court of the Viceroy once or twice. He was in a dilemma as to what he should do if he were to present himself before the Viceroy.

"Sir, what you have said is all right. But I am in a dilemma, how do I put the demand on behalf of the community before His Excellency the Viceroy? I don't know what to do,"the Nawab expressed his helplessness.

"Don't worry about that, Nawab Sahib. The Viceroy's private secretary Smith had arranged everything. You have to just submit a written appeal to the Viceroy and take tea with him at his Simla palace," Archibald clarified to the Nawab.

"But how to prepare this appeal?"

This was what Archibald wanted. He said sympathetically, "You don't worry about this at all. I will prepare the appeal keeping in mind the legitimate demands of the Muslim community."

"That would be very nice, Sir. We would be grateful to you," said the Nawab expressing the gratitude in advance.

"But for that I have a condition. The understanding we reached and the talk we had, no one else should come to know."

Nawab Mohsin-Ul-Haq had no difficulty in accepting the condition. He accepted the condition.

"And you have to search for an eminent person, whose presence can have an impact, to lead the Muslim delegation," Principal Archibald said.

The Nawab pondered over the matter for a while and then said, "Sir, you please suggest someone's name."

Archibald had already planned the whole thing. He said, "If you accept, it would be most appropriate for His Highness Aga Khan, the religious head of the Ismaili Khojas, to be the leader of the delegation. If Aga Khan accepts this, not only the Viceroy, but also the entire Muslim community of the country would be with you.

And your demands would reach the Muslims of Baghdad, Damascus, Mecca and Medina."

Nawab Mohsin-Ul-Haq had accepted the proposal of Principal Alchibald with great excitement. He told Archibald that he would discuss with His Highness Aga Khan the formation of the delegation of the Muslims immediately. If Aga Khan joined the delegation, the worked out plan for the Indian Muslims would have an impetus. Archibald was excited.

17

Meeting of Aga Khan's delegation with Minto, Establishing of the Muslim League, Jinnah's refusal to join the League, converting to another sect

Aga Khan's position among the millions of Ismaili Khojas spread over twenty countries was similar to that of Goswami, the heir to Vallabhacharya among the followers of *Pushti Margiya Vaishnavs*[1]. The title Aga Khan was conferred on him by the Shah of Iran in the 19th century, but prior to that his ancesters, considered to be the heirs to Prophet Muhammad, were the Imams for a millennium. After the death of Prophet Muhammad the founder of Islam, all his three heirs, who succeeded to the throne of the Kalifa one after another, were murdered. Hazrat Ali was the husband of Prophet Muhammad's only surviving child daughter Fatima. He was the son-in-law and nephew of the Prophet. He became the fourth Caliph. His supporters claimed that the three Caliphs before him had usurped the throne without any right. Ali's supporters came to be known as Shia Muslims in history. These Shia Muslims considered the children of Fatima and Ali as the holy religious heads.

This tradition had lasted only for a few years. Thereafter, Musa and Ismail, the sons of an Imam called Jafar Sadiq, fought for inheriting the position of the Imam. The Shias who supported Ismail came to be called Ismaili Khojas. The children of the Ismailis had succeeded as Imams one after another and had exercised the power over the millions of Khojas, who revered them. The forty-fifth Imam Aga Hasan Ali Shah was conferred a special title of 'Aga Khan' by the Emperor of Iran. But unfortunately Aga Khan could not stay for long in Iran to avail the benefits of the honour. The power proved to be mightier than the religion. Aga Khan had to flee Iran one midnight along with his family and the army. He made India his headquarters.

Although the *Dar-Ul-Islam* had continued for seven or eight hundred years, India could not be converted to Islam fully. And now the Christian rule had begun.

Now a military victory over India to prevent it from becoming Christian and to make it Islamic was not possible. The forceful conversion to Islam had succeeded the world over. Now the forceful conversion of Indians to Islam was impossible. And wherever the Muslim rule was established, force had succeded in converting the people to Islam. If the mission of converting the Indians to Islam had to succeed, it was necessary to befriend the British instead of fighting with them. It was important to win the trust and friendship of the British. Fortunately, Aga Khan got such an opportunity so soon.

The Emirs of Sindh were an obstacle to the expansion of the British Empire. They were like helpless princes, but great nuisance. They were the Sunni Muslims. They were not very influential or powerful, but they became a nightmare to the British who wanted to extend their Empire to the Sindh. Aga Khan, the chief of the Shia Muslims, had realised the importance of supporting the British against the minority Sunni Muslims. The Emirs of Sindh would be eliminated under the British rule. It would be a wise thing to support the British against these Emirs to win their trust. Aga Khan had made a very calculated decision.

Aga Khan had succeeded in his plan. The Shia Muslims, particularly the Ismailis, in the British army were enthusiastic about it. Until now, these Muslim soldiers in the British army were not deployed to fight the Emirs of Sindh in the battlefield. However, after receiving the support from Aga Khan these Muslim soliders had joined the Britishers in their fight against the Emirs. The Emirs' rule could not last long. After destroying them, the British rewarded its newly trusted ally, Aga Khan. He was conferred the title of "His Highness"which the Britishers gave to the Indian Kings. And then he was honoured and given the pension for life.

In the meantime, Principal Archibald of Aligarh College was making preparations for the delegation of Muslims who were about to meet His Excellency, the Viceroy, with an appeal. Two generations passed since Aga Khan had fled Iran. The present Aga Khan was the forty-eighth head of the Ismailis. He was just twenty nine year old. The trust of the Britishers that his grandfather had earned remained intact. Hence, he continued to enjoy the respect of the Britishers and the adulation from the millions of his followers.

Nawab Mohsin-Ul-Haq had brought together about seventy persons, comprising of Nawabs, Imams and Maulvis, representing the country's sixty million Muslims, under the leadership of Aga Khan. Most of them did not have the English education. These people were used to leading a luxurious and lavish lifestyle under the garb of religious sanctity. Meeting the Viceroy and having tea with him was a very big thing for them. Hardly a few of them could understand the demands of the Muslims that Arlchibald had included in the appeal.

After establishing the Congress in 1885 and with the spread of the new English education, an elite class of educated Hindus, Parsees and Christians had emerged on the political scene and they started demanding more and more representation in the various government bodies. The Congress Party was emerging as the voice of every Indian. Until the emergence of a fiery leader like

Lokmanya Tilak, the Congress leaders were submitting the Memorandums of Appeal or making speeches in polite tone. Now they adopted an aggressive posture. At the same time, they began to realise that without the Muslims' active support, the Congress would not become a representative organisation of the whole country. A few leaders like Badruddin Taiyabji had joined the Congress due to its growing influence, but their primary objective was to promote their community interest. Meanwhile, the Queen of England had conferred the title "Sir"on Syed Ahmed, the founder of Aligarh Muslim College. After receiving the title, what Bacon said in connection with the Hindu-Muslim politics had become sacred like the Bible to Syed Ahmed. When Badruddin Taiyabji was elected as the President of the Congress, in its session in Madras, he had sent a message congratulating Sir Syed Ahmed for receiving the title from the Queen. In reply, Sir Syed Ahmed wrote, "Your accepting the Presidentship of the Hindu Congress had deeply hurt the Muslims. The words Indian National Congress sound as if all the sections of people have joined it. There are many religions in India and the Muslims form the main group. Are they all equal? It is wrong to think so. The Congress is not only hurting the interest of the Muslims, but in the long run it will also hurt the interest of the country."

The Congress President Badruddin Taiyabji, in reply to Sir Syed Ahmed's letter, had said,"I accept your contention that India is not one nation because the different communities in India have unique problems of their own. But all of them also have common problems. I think if all of us come together on one platform, the Muslim community stands to benefit more. There is no question of difference between the communities in the Congress. If the Muslims are united, they can attain their goal by remaining with the Congress. We can work together with the Hindus as far as the common issues are concerned and whenever our interest is hurt we can oppose tooth-and-nail."

In such a background, the Muslim delegation, under the leadership of the Aga Khan, met the Viceroy Lord Minto. Aga Khan presented two main demands on behalf of the Muslims which were included in the appeal drafted by Archibald. Firstly, Her Majesty the Queen must not treat all Indians as one people. The Hindus were a majority in the country, hence they secured the positions in the government and the representative bodies due to their sheer number. This was unfair to the Muslims. Therefore, there must be some reservation of seats for the Muslims. And only the Muslims should elect the Muslims to fill these seats. Thus the poisonous seed of religious bigotry was sowed to create two nations out of one country. The Indians were not one people, but a collection of different religious groups. Secondly, the Muslims must get the government jobs not on the basis of population, but on the basis of their loyalty. The British government must take into consideration the service, the loyalty and the support of the Muslims and give them greater representation than their proportion in the population. If this was not done, the Muslims would feel dejected and their loyalty would be impeded.

The appeal was already given to the Viceroy by his private secretary Dunlop Smith. Therefore, there was no discussion on it. Lord Minto gave them a warm welcome. He praised the contribution made by the Aligarh Muslim College and thanked the Muslims for their cooperation and loyalty. At the end, he read out to the delegates a reply, prepared beforehand, assuring the protection of special rights of the Muslims. The loyalty of the Muslim community would be taken into account. Then the delegates bowed before the Viceroy and expressed their gratitude and satisfaction. Before leaving, some of them said to Lady Minto, "Now we are convinced that you are our friend."

Around this time, Barrister Jinnah had acquired a good reputation as an able educated Muslim in Bombay. Some delegates had insisted and even tried to include him in the delegation. Jinnah did not agree with Aga Khan's move to present the Muslims as a separate religious group. He did not like the personal leadership of a religious head. Jinnah was annoyed the manner in which Aga Khan interfered in the individual and the family affairs of the Ismaili Khojas. He feared that if he remained an Ismaili Khoja, Aga Khan might exercise legal and moral authority over him. In fact, Jinnah had no attachment to the religion. He had nothing to do either with the Quran or the *Namaaz*. Smoking and drinking were his companions. He liked non-vegetarian food. He did not accept any religious restrictions. When he learnt that the delegation demanded a separate identity for the Muslims, he opposed it and said that in the country all people were the Indians first, then the Hindus or the Muslims.

After receiving the unexpected success at the very first meeting with the Viceroy, Aga Khan and his colleagues decided to establish an organisation of the Muslims as a rival to the Indian National Congress. Salimullah Khan, a wealthy landlord from Dacca in Bengal could not join the Aga Khan delegation due to illness. He had invited the prominent Muslim representatives to a convention organised in Dacca. Some fifty eight delegates representing the Muslims across the country, met at Dacca in December, 1906 and formed the 'Muslim League' to give a definite direction to the Muslim politics. Everyone wanted Jinnah to join the League. But he had bluntly refused.

Salimullah Khan, being very disappointed by Jinnah's refusal, had tried to use the influence of Aga Khan to prevail upon him. Jinnah was an Ismaili Khoja and from the point of religion, Aga Khan had the authority over him. And therefore, if Aga Khan had invited Jinnah to join the Muslim League it would be difficult for him to reject the invitation. Aga Khan was aware of the fame and reputation of Jinnah. He also knew that Jinnah had refused to be part of the delegation that met the Viceroy. The success of the delegation had excited the Muslims and heated up the political atmosphere. Aga Khan thought that if he invited Jinnah to join the new organisation of the Muslims, as suggested by Salimullah Khan, he would certainly reconsider his decision and from the religious point of view, being his disciple, it would be impossible for him to reject the invitation. Taking all these into consideration and confident of being successful, Aga Khan had accepted the suggestion of Salimullah Khan and wrote a letter to Jinnah inviting him to join the new organisation.

But Jinnah turned out to be a person altogether different from what Aga Khan had thought of. Accidentally he happened to be a Khoja. His professional success and his relation with the country's elite class, made Jinnah consider himself a different and unique person. Jinnah had realised that millions of people in the country were illiterate or semi-literate and living in abject poverty unaffected by the modern standards and values. He felt the letter of Aga Khan was more a religious decree than an invitation. Aga Khan was exercising his religious authority. Jinnah was furious. He was upset at the thought of someone exercising authority over him. Even if Aga Khan's authority was for namesake, Jinnah did not like its shadow falling on him.

He made a decision.

Though Aga Khan had a sway over the Ismaili sect, he had no influence over its sub-sect Ishna-Ashri of Iran. Both the Ismailis and Ishna-Ashris were Khojas. Jinnah wanted to know the legal route for joining this sub-sect. There was no question of religious conversion. It was just a matter of signing an affidavit and declaring the change before an Imam. Jinnah had rejected the invitation of Aga Khan. And the very next day he changed from being an Ismaili Khoja to an *Ishna-Ashri* Khoja.

Aga Khan was disappointed to receive the letter from Jinnah. More than the rejection, it was the reason given for the rejection that Aga Khan had found difficult to digest. He wondered how could any sensible Muslim think like that. Jinnah had written that he would not join any organisation which raised the communal demands rather than the demand for the independence of India. He feared that such demands could divide the country. A dejected Aga Khan admitted at the convention of the Muslim League, "I have tried a lot to bring the Muslim barrister from Bombay into our fold, but he continues to oppose us bitterly. He wants to distance himslef from us as he thinks that the communal demands of the Muslims could divide the country."

Nawab Mustak Hussain of Hyderabad was the President of the first convention of the Muslim League. He had declared in his speech that the Muslims constituted one-fifth of the population and that if the British leave the country, the Muslims would be crushed by the majority Hindus. The Muslims were living in fear in spite of the protection from the British. If the British leave the country, the Hindus would destroy both their religion and the community. To prevent that from happening, the Muslims must strengthen the British rule at any cost.

A declaration *Lal Ishtihar* was released at the convention and all the Muslims were advised to honour the declaration. It called upon the Muslims to beware of the Hindus, to boycott the Hindu schools and shops, to refuse to employ the Hindus, to refuse to work under them, to realise the strength of the Muslims, to make miserable the lives of Hindus who became rich by robbing the Muslims and force them to come to the holy path of Allah and so on and so forth.

Jinnah who read all this in the *Amrit Bazaar Patrika*, a daily published from Calcutta, had become so furious that he slammed the newspaper on the table. While trying to control his anger he was lost in his thoughts for a long time. He was unable to understand how anyone could mix nationalism with religion. He realised that the people who bring religion into politics were doing a great disservice to the country.

NOTE

1. A Hindu Sect.

18

Gokhale-Jinnah meeting, Jinnah as Tilak's defense lawyer, new reforms for Indians' participation in administration (1909)

Two decades had passed since the establishment of the Indian National Congress. It had not only grown in stature in these two decades, but its nature of functioning also changed. After the defeat in the 1857 revolt, the feeling of dejection that the intellectuals had on the issue of political freedom was now ventilated through the Congress. As per the tradition of the Congress of holding a session every year, its twentieth session was organised in 1904 in Bombay. Pherozeshah Mehta was the Chairman of the Reception Committee. His office worked till late in the night to make arrangements for the Session. Jinnah, in his capacity as an assistant to Pherozeshah Mehta, took a lot of interest in making the arrangements. Pherozeshah Mehta was very much impressed by Jinnah's organisational skills, his political acumen and balanced stand on the national issues and the contemporary problems.

When the session started one morning in December, Pherozeshah Mehta introduced Jinnah to a mild-mannered Maratha leader wearing a turban. Jinnah knew this Maratha leader quite well as he had seen his photo many a time in the newspapers.

"Mr. Jinnah, Gopal Krishna Gokhale and Bal Gangadhar Tilak are the two pillars of political aspirations." And then Pherozeshah Mehta turned to Gokhale and said, "Mr. Gokhale, I think you will be able to utilise this young barrister properly in the Congress agitation."

Jinnah was very much impressed by Gokhale at this first meeting. Gokhale was considered a moderate political leader of the Congress. His apparent mild-manners, along with his firmness and principles had a deep impact on Jinnah's mind.

As per the suggestion of Pherozeshah Mehta, Jinnah was entrusted with the work of giving final touches to the draft resolution before it was taken up for discussion in the Congress Working Committee and adopted at the session. Gokhale was satisfied with the way Jinnah worked in drafting the resolution. If

Jinnah felt that words used in the resolution were ambiguous or mild he replaced them with words having the dual meaning. And whenever he noticed the language used was firm and clear or felt it would not serve the interest of the country in future, he argued that the words having the dual meaning should be used so that they could be interpreted differently depending on the situation. This aspect of Jinnah's personality had impressed the mild mannered Gokhale and the fearless Pherozeshah Mehta.

A demand was made at the Congress session that two representatives be sent to London to present the demands and the aspirations of the Indians so that the members of various political parties in the British Parliament could consider them sympathetically. After all, any political reform had to be endorsed by the British Parliament. Most of the British Parliamentarians accepted whatever the Secretary of State for India had presented as the gospel truth. These Parliamentarians were only interested in ensuring that the Queen's Empire remained safe in India.

They were accepting the half-truths and the distorted facts presented to the Parliament by the Viceroy and the Secretary of State for India. It was possible for these Parliamentarians to adopt a liberal approach towards India, if they were presented the correct picture about India and her problems. Considering all this, a resolution was adopted at the Congress session to send two representatives to London. The names of Pherozeshah Mehta and Gokhale were suggested and they were accepted unanimously.

At that time, Pherozeshah Mehta was not keeping good health. He was not in a position to travel such a long distance, taking the sea route. When the question of choosing a substitute for him came up, Pherozeshah Mehta had himself suggested the name of Jinnah. His understanding of the political problems, the ability to present them in historical and international perspective and his acquaintance with the British system—all these would be very useful. Gokhale had accepted the suggestion. Thus, Jinnah suddently became a part of the country's political movement.

Jinnah left for London with Gokhale. During this travel by the sea route, Jinnah came closer to Gokhale. Jinnah thought that he could learn a lot from Gokhale about the country's political problems. The clarity with which Gokhale presented before the British Parliament had a deep impact on Jinnah's mind. In spite of a huge difference in age and experience, Gokhale had consulted Jinnah on every issue. He gave him the opportunity to express his views freely. During this period suddenly the Viceroy Lord Curzon had announced the partition of Bengal into Hindu and Muslim provinces. Bengal was partitioned by the British government on the basis of the Muslims' demand, under the leadership of Aga Khan. Bengal was in the forefront in the political agitation. It was mainly confined to the Hindus. If Bengal was partitioned on the basis of religion, it would lead to many communal problems. The Congress was against the partition. It supported the agitation against the partition. The reason given for the partition was that, due to the huge size and population, it was very difficult to administer. It was more convenient to administer the two units. Whatever might be the official reason for the partition, the way it was done on the basis of religion, people felt that it was a conspiracy by the British government to divide the Indian people. Gokhale had reacted angrily. He said the conspiracy of the British to divide the India people on the basis of religion should not be allowed to succeed. Jinnah was so impressed by Gokhale's political vision that on his return to India he publicly declared that his ambition was to become a Muslim Gokhale.

The nationwide agitation against the partition of Bengal was inspired by the song "*Vande Mataram.*" The song, written in the context of Bengal and its pride, had soon crossed the Bengal border and become a national spell. The poet Rabindranath Tagore had sung this song at the session of the Congress held in Calcutta. The song had an emotional appeal and spread the political awareness, forcing the Governor General of Bengal to ban it. This had fanned the national sentiments all the more.

Jinnah was present at the Calcutta session of the Congress. The President Dadabhai Navroji was to deliver his presidential speech, but was unable to do so due to his advanced age and poor health. He asked Gokhale and Pherozeshah Mehta to prepare his speech and read it out on his behalf. Both of them in turn asked Jinnah to assist Dadabhai. Dadabhai knew Jinnah. Jinnah had accepted the assignment. Jinnah had thus reached a stage where he could play an important role in the Congress politics.

At this time, the news of the South African government's atrocities on the Indians and of the battle of life and death under the leadership of an Indian barrister called Mohandas Karamchand Gandhi had generated a political temperature in the country. Most of the Indians in South Africa were Gujaratis, mainly Khojas. An organisation called Anjuman Islam in Bombay had taken up the problems of the Indians in South Africa with the government in England. It was looking for an able person who could understand the problems of these hapless countrymen settled in such a far away land and secure justice to them. Barrister Jinnah was chosen for the job. It was a challenging task. Jinnah accepted the job. In a short time, he studied the problems of the Indians in South Africa and travelled to England once again. He did not succeed in his mission. However, the report that he had presented incited angry feelings among the people against the British govrnment.

At this time, an unexpected incident occurred.

Lokmanya Tilak had exerted great influence on the Congress and the country. Tilak due to his radical views had become a model for the extremists in the Congress. Tilak's extremist views and Gokhale's moderate views had divided the Congress into two groups—the extremists and the moderates. Tilak was publishing a Marathi newspaper called *Kesari* from his home town Poona. His paper was very critical of the British government. He had criticised the government actions in a very harsh language. He wrote fiery articles in his paper. He was arrested on the charge of sedition for writing one such an article.

The Governor of Bombay had sought the legal opinion from a British solicitor called Sir George on the trial to be conducted against Tilak. Sir George knew Jinnah. He called Jinnah to his chamber and asked,

"Mr. Jinnah, the Governor of Bombay had sought the legal opinion regarding the trial of Lokmanya Tilak. You must have read the article which created such a furore."

"Excuse me, Sir," Jinnah said in a firm voice, "I have not read the article and do not wish to read."

"Why? Why so?" asked surprised Sir George.

"The reason is simple," Jinnah said without hesitation, "If a national leader like Tilak writes something, it must be in the interest of the country and if such a patriot is charged with sedition I keep myself free to fight against the charge."

Sir George did not expect this from Jinnah. He was amused. But he learnt a few days later that in fact Jinnah was fighting on behalf of Tilak in the Court of Justice Davar. He was very surprised to know this. Barrister Jinnah argued, quoting the numerous instances from the international law, that the act of patriotism was not a sedition. He quoted many examples to show how partriotism was important for alert citizens in a civilised society. The other advocates in Bombay were not interested in fighting Tilak's case. Gurudev Rabindranath Tagore had organised a meeting on this in Calcutta and collected a fund of seventeen thousand rupees for fighting the case. He had sent three advocates to Bombay with the fund. In spite of all these efforts, Tilak was sentenced to six years rigorous imprisonment on the charge of sedition.

After this judgment, the British government had felicitated Justice Davar by conferring the title of "Sir." Shortly after that, the Bombay High Court Bar Council had decided to felicitate Justice Davar. The Bar Council had sent a circular to that effect to all its members. When Jinnah received the Circular, he wrote a note on it and returned it with the peon. His note read, "The government had rewarded the Justice who pronounced such a barbaric sentence on a patriot like Tilak to appease the government. We should be ashamed to celebrate such an occasion."

Justice Davar was upset when he came to know about the angry note of Jinnah. He observed Jinnah always following the court proceedings in a very disciplined manner. He liked Jinnah's disciplined behaviour. He called Jinnah to his chamber. After exchanging greetings, Justice Davar asked Jinnah, "Mr, Jinnah, as a High Court Judge, have I ever misbehaved with you that you could complain about?"

"Not at all Sir. I never experienced anything like that about you. Nor have I any complaint against you." Jinnah replied politely.

"Then, why did you write such a scathing note against me on the Bar Council Circular?"

"The reason for that is clear, Sir. I do not agree with the sentence given to a patriot like Tilak for his patriotism. I believe that you have conducted the trial not on the basis of truth, but with prejudice. I am grateful to you for your goodwill towards me as an advocate, but I have no hesitation in expressing what I consider is the truth,"Jinnah said fearlessly stressing each and every word.

Justice Davar was stunned and had nothing to say.

The words *Vande Mataram* and *Swaraj* had created a new patriotic fervour among the millions of people in the country. For the first time, Dadabhai Navroji had used the word *Swaraj* in his presidential speech at the Calcutta Congress session. Jinnah had only read out his speech. It would not be wrong to say that Jinnah was instrumental in giving the word to the country. As a protest against the partition of the Bengal, the agitation to boycott the British goods was intensified. The British government was startled by the word *Swaraj* that became part of the agitation. The growing influence of the Congreess and the large number of people joining it had shaken the British. The British were looking for a smooth way out from this. The Muslim League had distanced itself from the agitation. The League supported the partition. This had deepened the difference between the Hindus and the Muslims. The Hindu elements opposing the Muslims had become more active. This was a natural reaction.

In such a surcharged atmosphere, the British government had announced certain reforms to ensure greater participation of the Indians in the administration. The Central and the Provincial Assemblies would have more Indian representatives. But it was not democratic election. A small number of Indians would elect or nominate the representatives. A certain number of seats were allotted to the Muslims, the Sikhs and the Christians in order to separate them from the rest of the Indian people. They were allotted more seats than proportionate to the population. The Muslims who constituted twenty per cent of the population were allotted 8 out of 28 seats in the Provincial Assemblies. The Muslim League had accepted the reforms with great enthusiasm, but the Congress was disappointed. The Congress did not accept the principle that only the Muslim electorate would elect the Muslim representatives and that the Sikhs and Christians would elect or nominate their community representatives alone. The Congress believed that it was an organisation representing all the people of the country. But the British ploy was to ensure that it remained an organisation of the Hindus only. Hence, the Congress made a lot of efforts to attract the Muslims to its fold. In order to ensure greater participation of the Muslims in its sessions, the Congress provided special facilities to the Muslims. Some nationalist Muslims who were unhappy with the Muslim League's divisive politics, had supported the Congress. But their number was very small. And a majority of the Muslims was anti-Congress and pro-British.

The government started implementing the reforms. The government nominated Barrister Jinnah as the representative of the Muslims of Bombay. The issue of nominating a Muslim representative from Bombay in the Viceroy's Imperial Legislative Council had become a bone of contention. The pro and anti-government Muslims, the Shias and the Sunnis, the Mullahs, the Maulvis and the Imams and the educated Muslims—all of them had fought bitterly over the issue. Jinnah was against the representation based on religion and, therefore, had distanced himself from it. But those who could not agree on a common candidate had proposed Jinnah's name as a compromise. The moment Jinnah's name was announced, every one had accepted his name with a hidden message, "It does not matter, if I am not elected, but you should not get elected." Jinnah was opposed to the communal representation. However, the moment he was nominated as the representative of the Muslims he accepted without any hesitation. At 35, Jinnah became the youngest member of the Viceroy's Imperial Legislative Council. He was not so naïve not to have understood how important this opportunity was for fulfilling his political aspirations. The Muslim League was jubiliant about Jinnah's nomination. The League was hoping that now that Jinnah had become a representative of the Muslims he could be trooped into the League.

But the manner in which Jinnah had conducted himself in the very first meeting of the Imperial Legislative Council, all the calculations of the Muslim League went for a toss.

19

Opposition to Jinnah in the meeting of Imperial Legislative Council, The Allahabad resolution, compliments from Gokhale, Gandhi-Jinnah meeting in London, Change in the League's constitution, Jinnah's joining of the League

As per the political reforms of 1909, a sixty member Imperial Legislative Council was constituted. Barrister Jinnah, as one of its members, was in the company of the illustrious personalities of India such as Gopal Krishna Gokhale, Pandit Motilal Nehru and Surendranath Banerjee. At the very first meeting of the Council on 25 February, 1910, Jinnah and the Viceroy had a heated argument. A very insulting and humiliating treatment was meted out to Indians by the racist government of South Africa. Barrister Mohandas Karamchand Gandhi had been carrying out a new non-violent protest movement called *Satyagraha* against it for more than a decade. The news of this protest was reported not only in the daily newspapers of South Africa, but also in the Indian and the British newspapers. Gopal Krishna Gokhale had moved a resolution in the Council. It urged His Majesty's government in England to protect the Indians in South Africa from the suffering due to the policy of apartheid. The Indians living in South Africa were the subjects of the British Empire and, therefore, the British government should do something to mitigate their sufferings. The resolution stated that the protest movement led under the leadership of Mohandas Karamchand Gandhi had the support of the Council. Jinnah supporting the resolution said in his maiden speech, "I want to tell His Excellency Viceroy that on this issue all sections of the Indian people are one. The racist government in South Africa had done great injustice to the Indian community."

The Viceroy Lord Minto was presiding over the Imperial Legislative Council session. More than the resolution, he was annoyed by the harsh tone of Jinnah and then interrupted his speech, "The Hon'ble member must remember that he was talking about South Africa which is a part of the British Empire. He should not use harsh and unpleasant words."

Jinnah was the youngest member in the Council. This was the first meeting of the new Council. Besides the Viceroy, many other members were quite senior in politics. Jinnah without being cowed down responded to the Viceroy fearlessly, "Excuse me, your Excellency. In fact, I should have used more harsh words. But considering the decorum of this House, I did not use the words which I had in my mind. But I would say that the atrocities committed against the Indians by the South African government are cruel and barbaric and on this issue the whole country is one."

The Viceroy was taken aback by this totally fearless conduct of Jinnah. He had encountered the leaders like Tilak and Surendranath and the moderate leaders like Gokhale and Dadabhai. But none of them had spoken so fearlessly and impertinently. After the speech in the Council, Jinnah became famous not only in politics but perhaps in the whole country. Many newspapers had published the photograph of Jinnah exchanging a verbal duel with the Viceroy.

Another move of Jinnah had earned him a good reputation. Jinnah did not support the Muslims' demand for a separate electorate. He refused to join the Muslim League in spite of the concerted efforts made by Aga Khan and other Muslim leaders. Jinnah believed that any division on the basis of religion would ultimately harm the interest of the country. Any Indian living in India was Indian first and then a Hindu or a Muslim or a Parsaee or a Sikh. Yet when His Majesty's government had constituted the Imperial Legislative Council based on the separate electorate for the Muslims, he agreed to represent the Muslims of Bombay. In spite of being a representative of the Muslims' separate electorate, he moved a resolution at the twenty-fifth session of the Congress held in Allahabad. In the resolution, he criticised the system of separate electorate and warned that the attempt of the British government to divide the country on the basis of religion was dangerous. At a time when the majority of the Muslims were supporting the system of separate electorate and were rejoiced at the division, Jinnah's stand was an act of rare courage. A Muslim representative from Bihar supported Jinnah's resolution.

After this resolution was adopted, Gokhale complemented Jinnah saying,

"Mr. Jinnah, I appreciate your sensitivity and courage. The way you are shaping up in politics, you have a very bright future."

"Thank you, Sir. But I consider you as my model. I am new to politics. You are my guide." Jinnah said with modesty which was not his characteristic.

Gokhale had a hearty laugh and patting Jinnah's shoulder said,

"When I had been to South Africa, Mr. Gandhi also said something similar to me. If both Gandhi in South Africa and Jinnah in India consider me as their political guru, there is no doubt that India would gain independence very soon."

In the meantime, the pressure on Jinnah to join the Muslim League was mounting from all sides. A pan-Islamic feeling that all the Muslims cutting across the national borders were one people was growing. The political upheavals in Turkey, Iran and Egypt had resulted in conflict of interest among the Europen countries, particularly between Germany and Britain. In such a situation, considering the interest of the Muslims, Maulvi Muhammad Ali once again tried to persuade Jinnah to join the Muslim League. Jinnah told him bluntly, "The Muslim League works for the welfare of only one community. Even its constitution emphasises on loyalty to the community. I do not accept that loyalty to the community means disloyalty to the country. My loyalty is to the country first and the interest of the country is above that of the community."

This inflexible stand of Jinnah disappointed the Muslim League. There was a political reason for this disappointment. In 1905, Lord Curzon had partitioned the Bengal on the communal lines and in 1911 His Majesty's government revoked the partition. The Muslim League and the Muslims from Bengal and other parts of India had supported the partition. At that time the Muslims' demand for a separate electorate was accepted. The revoking of the partition greatly disappointed the Muslims. The Hindus of Bengal and the nationalist Muslims in the Congress welcomed the revoking of the partition. This made the Muslim League weak. If Jinnah could join the Muslim League he would strengthen its position considerably. There was only one way to attract Jinnah to the League and that was to amend the constitution of the League making its stand clear on the independence of the country. The League leaders had a lot of differences on this issue. A Muslims delegation under the leadership of Aga Khan had met the Viceroy before the League was established when they had pledged their loyalty to the British crown. Some Muslims now felt that since the British government had betrayed their cause by revoking the partition of Bengal, the Muslim League was under no obligation to remain loyal to the British.

However, the Muslims to whom the religion was the supreme looked at the issue differently. The Islamic Empire in Turkey was in shambles. This Ottoman Empire did not serve the British interest. Germany and Turkey had formed an alliance against the British. The Muslims in India were sympathetic to Turkey. The Emperor of Ottoman was also the Caliph. He was the supreme authority both in the state and religious matters. The Muslims in India who believed that the Islam was a universal religion cutting across the national boundaries were partial to Khalifa.

To placate such Muslims, the British government had repeatedly declared that it would not have any enmity with the Caliph and that the Muslims' religious sentiments would not be hurt. Taking this as a solemn assurance, the Muslims in the country wanted to remain loyal to the British government. They were more interested in protecting the institution of Khalifa than the independence of the country.

At this juncture, an important event had occurred that made the Muslim League change its attitude.

India was administered by the British government officials as per the orders issued by the Crown in London. However, in order to keep a check on the administration, a supreme authority called the Secretary of State for India was created. The Secretary of State had a very big secretariat. Huge money was spent in maintaining the secretariat and its staff. A whopping twenty four per cent of the revenue collected in India was spent on the secretariat of the Secretary of State for India. This act of filling the treasury in London with the earnings of the poor Indians was highly deplorable. These expenses were shown as "home charges." Jinnah moved a resolution at the Congress session demanding that these expenses should be borne by the British government from its own treasury. Nobody had thought of raising the voice against this until then. Jinnah said that it was atrocious to collect the charges for administering the country, as if ruling the country was not enough. This stand of Jinnah enhanced his status and position in the Congress. The Congress decided to send a delegation to London to present this resolution to the British government. Jinnah was entrusted with the responsibility of leading the delegation.

On the one hand, the Muslim League as an organisation was weakening and on the other, Jinnah was growing in stature. There were other Muslims in the Congress. But Jinnah stood out from the rest due to his intelligence, logic, punctuality and firmness. Precisely for these qualities, the Muslim League needed Jinnah. If Jinnah had to be brought into the Muslim League, it became inevitable for the League to change its communal approach and join the Congress struggle for independence.

Jinnah was firm on his decision.

When Jinnah reached London as the Congress representative, an unexpected event happened. Mohandas Karamchand Gandhi, the leader of the Indian community who fought successfully against the racist South African regime for two decades, was returning to his homeland. His struggle had now assumed a new name called *Satyagraha*. Until now the world over any struggle had meant killing or dying. But Gandhi changed all that. He now proved that the truth and non-violence were the real means to victory. The people who mocked at him initially, now acknowledged the victory of his struggle. The same Gandhi was returning to his homeland triumphant. However, the ship in which he was travelling could not enter the Indian Ocean. The war between Germany and Britain had broken out and German submarines were not allowing a safe passage of any British ship in the Indian Ocean. Hence, Gandhi's ship had to change its course mid-way and turn towards London.

Jinnah was well acquainted with Gandhi's name and his work. He did not pay much attention to Gandhi's ideas of non-violence and *Satyagraha*. And he never had faith in such metaphysical ideas. Yet, the success that Gandhi achieved in his chosen path attracted Jinnah. The Indians in London organised a felicitation function for Gandhi at the Cecil Hotel. It was a coincidence that Jinnah happened to be in London at the time as the leader of the Congress delegation. The other members of the delegation were Sarojini Naidu and Lala Lajpat Rai. The organisers of the function had also invited the three of them as the main speakers.

Thus, the two distinguished persons, quite contrasting in their approach, who considered Gokhale as their political guru met unexpectedly for the first time. Jinnah was well aware of Gandhi and his struggle. But Gandhi did not know much about Jinnah's work. But he was somewhat familiar with his name. As a main speaker at the felicitation function, Jinnah said, "History will recall the successful struggle carried out by the Indian community in South Africa under the leadership of Mr. Gandhi. I congratulate Mr. Gandhi for carrying out such a unique struggle so successfully. I trust that the people of India would benefit by the experience of his struggle. On behalf of the people of India, I welcome Mr. Gandhi's homecoming."

In his reply, Gandhi said that he would take part in the struggle for the independence of India and that he would be happy to work with colleagues like Jinnah.

In the war that broke out in Europe, Germany and Britain were fighting against each other. In India, the Congress while siding with the British in the war proclaimed that if the Indian people demanded rights from the British Empire as its subjects, it was their duty to side with Britain in the war. Turkey joined hands with Germany and declared war against Britain. With this declaration, the Muslims in India had turned against Britain to protect the Khalifa. The Muslim community, which had assumed that the loyalty to the British government was in their interest, saw this as yet another major blow after revoking the partition of Bengal. In this background, the Muslim League adopted a resolution to oppose the British rule and support the Congress struggle for independence of India. The constitution of the Muslim League was amended accordingly.

Now there was no obstacle for Jinnah joining the Muslim League. Hence, for the next meeting of the Muslim League not only Muhammad Ali Jinnah, but the senior Congress leaders like Sarojini Naidu were also invited. Welcoming Jinnah, Sir Shafi Ahmed, President of the League, said, "We all agree with the ideology of our friend Barrister Jinnah. And the Muslim League supports the Indian National Congress demand for dominion status for India. We hope the interest of the Muslim community is not compromised."

20

Felicitating of Gandhi by Gurjar Sabha, meeting with Dinshaw Petit, vacation in Darjeeling

The delegation led by Jinnah that went to London to persuade the British government returned without success. Gandhi also returned to India almost at the same time. Gandhi's reputation and fame for the success of his struggle in South Africa had spread far and wide in India. The people all over India, particularly the Gujarati community, were eager to accord him a reception.

An organisation of educated Gujaratis in Bombay called *Gurjar Sabha* was quite active. This organisation, besides conducting cultural and educational programmes, was also organising political functions. It decided to accord a special reception for Gandhi for his achievement, particularly as a Gujarati. Muhammad Ali Jinnah was the President of the Gurjar Sabha. Though Jinnah was born in Sindh, the Gurjar Sabha made him the President as he was a Gujarati. Jinnah was taking active interest in the activities of the Sabha. Considering Jinnah's ascendancy in the national scene, the Gurjar Sabha had chosen him as its President. Besides, when Gandhi and Jinnah met in London and greeted each other warmly the members of the Gurjar Sabha were very happy and enthusiastic. Jinnah welcomed Gurjar Sabha's decision to accord Gandhi a reception. On the auspicious day of *Makar Sankranti* [1], the reception was organised at Mangaldas Wadi. Barrister Jinnah had presided over the function.

As was the practice at such functions, the people in their speech heaped praises on the achievement of Gandhi. Gandhi and Kasturba were honoured with garlands of sandalwood. The proceedings of the programme were conducted in Gujarati. Jinnah had delivered his presidential address in English. The people assembled were not surprised at this. They had heard him speak earlier too in English at Gurjar Sabha and other organisations. They all knew that Jinnah never spoke in any language other than English.

But Gandhi was astonished that Jinnah spoke in English to the audience exclusively of the Gujaratis. At the reception in London, Jinnah had spoken in English and he himself replied in English. That was natural because the audience comprised of the Indians with different linguistic background, besides the English speaking Britishers. Jinnah's father might have migrated to Sindh, but his mother tongue was Gujarati. Hence, Gandhi could not imagine that Jinnah did not know the Gujarati language at all. Moreover, Jinnah could have spoken in Hindi if not in Gujarati. He felt, this was enslavement to English. He thought most of the people in the audience must not have understood what Jinnah had said in English.

In reply, expressing his sentiments, Gandhi said, "I am overwhelmed by your goodwill. But whatever work I have done in South Africa was due to the trust God reposed in me. How do I repay your goodwill? To honour the trust God reposed in me, I would like to dedicate the rest of my life to the service of the country."

Then he turned to Jinnah and said, "Barrister Jinnah is an asset in our public life. It is a matter of pride for us Gujaratis that he is also a Gujarati. That is why I am saddened and surprised that being a Gujarati himself, he had made his speech in English when the audience comprised exclusively of Gujaratis. Had he spoken in Gujarati, I would have been very happy. I know it is difficult for him to speak in Gujarati. I hope he will learn Gujarati soon. I am saying this as a friend. I am very happy that, in spite of being a Muslim, he is so enthusiastic about the public life and service to the country."

The audience applauded Gandhi's speech. But Jinnah did not join the applause, his face showing deep resentment. His younger sister Fatima was present in the audience. Reading her brother's face she was looking at him.

After the reception, on the way back, Fatima said to Jinnah, "*Bhaijaan*, it is not possible that you have not understood what Gandhi had said."

"What do you want to say, Fati?"

"What I want to say, I could read on your face," Fatima said, teasingly.

"Fati, I know you are very clever. But why don't you say what you have in mind."

Fatima was quiet for a moment, staring at the sky. She remembered the two Hindus who had visited her father at Vazir Mansion in Karachi. Though they had talked politely and affectionately with her father, they did not take the snacks served and not even the glass of water. Then her father told her that they were Hindus and that too Brahmins. They would be defiled even if they had water from a Muslim. It was true her father was a Muslim. But he had started his life as a Hindu, that too in a Vaishnav family. She did not see her grandfather Punjabhai. After he got converted to Islam he wanted to reconvert to Hinduism. But the Hindus had treated him as an outcaste and turned him away. Her father told her all this.

"*Bhaijaan*, Gandhi said to you…in spite of being a Muslim…"

"I know that Fati. Gandhi's speech is an example of how even the educated Hindus in public life think," said Jinnah interrupting Fatima.

"*Bhaijaan,* I feel what Gandhi had said is what the Hindus think. The Hindus always consider the Muslims inferior to them." Fatima spoke her mind. Jinnah did not say anything. But he was displeased by Gandhi's speech. He also felt that Gandhi's advice to speak in Gujarati was a ploy to please the audience.

*

Jinnah had spent most of his leisure time in reading the newspapers, after giving time to his profession and public life. Besides the newspapers, he read mostly the books relating to law and politics. He had the habit of keeping the newspaper clippings. After shifting to the new flat in Appollo Bunder, he maintained a personal library at home. He spent most of his evenings at the westernised Oriental Club, the membership of which only the affluent could afford. The Club was patronised by the high ranking British officials, the rich Parsee businessmen and the English educated Hindus. The Club had served a variety of high quality drinks, which Jinnah was fond of. Jinnah had loved the non-vegetarian delicacies like the pork and ham made of the pig meat. The contacts the high society people developed here, made them think that they were a distinct class. And that feeling was very satisfying.

Jinnah would play for hours the games like billiards and chess. The members used to gamble by paying twelve *annas*[2] for every hundred points in billiards. At one such game Jinnah met Dinshaw Petit. He was a very reputed industrialist of the Parsee community and his business spread out in various cities in India. Dinshaw Petit had heard Jinnah's name and his professional reputation. Because of their regular meetings and the dinners at the Club, they soon became close friends. Dinshaw thought that if Jinnah became his legal adviser it would benefit him a lot. Keeping this in mind, one day he invited Jinnah to his home.

Dinshaw Petit's bungalow like palace had a separate room for guests, besides a special room for intimate personal friends. Dinshaw and Jinnah would sit in this room and share drinks. Their intimacy grew. Jinnah would spend Saturday evenings at the bungalow of Dinshaw. Both of them used to have highly intellectual debates.

The Bombay weather changed as their friendship grew. The Court had a long summer vacation. Jinnah wanted to study some important volumes during the vacation. In Bombay's hectic public life, it was not possible to get peaceful time for the study. During a conversation, Jinnah shared his dilemma with Dinshaw,

"Mr. Dinshaw, this vacation, I wish to go to some hill station and study some important volumes peacefully. It is difficult to get time in Bombay."

"It is not a big thing," said Dinshaw excited. "This vacation, our family has decided to spend in our bungalow at Darjeeling. If you could accompany us to Darjeeling, I will have good company. This is my invitation to you."

Jinnah accepted his friend Dinshaw's invitation.

Dinshaw's bungalow in Darjeeling was located at a very beautiful place, where the sunlight on the mountain peaks on one side and the valley with water falls on the other side made it wonderfully picturesque. The place was indeed very attractive. Unlike the scorching heat in Bombay, the weather was so cold that they had to wear the warm clothes all the time. Dinshaw's wife Dinabai Petit was a very amiable and hospitable woman. Jinnah's acquaintance with this couple turned out to be very beneficial to him. He spent most of his time reading and playing chess with Dinshaw.

Jinnah was in his forties at that time. When he was seventeen years old and leaving Karachi for London, his father Zinabhai got him married to a girl called Amibai. Immediately after the marriage, he went to London. When he returned from London, after becoming a barrister, his wife had already expired. He was so busy with his profession and public life that he had no time to think of marriage. He had spent nearly twenty five years in building his career. As he had said at the time of quitting the post of the magistrate in Bombay, he was now earning fifteen hundred rupees a day instead of a month. His work had now increased manifold. He had to employ many persons like butler, cook, personal assistant, typist and other employees. He was fortunate that all these years Fatima lived like his shadow. She was looking after his profession and home quite efficiently. The apartment at Appollo Bunder was inadequate. Hence, he had bought an old nineteenth century bungalow, measuring some fifty thousand square feet, in a posh locality called Malbar Hills on the sea shore. Though the bungalow was not constructed keeping in view the modern lifestyle, it had the grandeur of a King or a Nawab. Its verandah and the exquisitely carved wooden architectural designs were very attractive. The single storied bungalow had all the amenities on the ground floor. Jinnah had furnished the bungalow with appropriate furniture and other necessities. The bungalow had separate arrangements for visitors, guests and friends and also space for the office and a study room. More than Jinnah, Fatima had to shoulder more responsibilities after moving into this new residence. Besides taking care of the gardeners, the driver and the servants, she had to take care of the guests who visited now too frequently.

Darjeeling, away from the hustle and bustle, had a serene atmosphere where the only sounds that one could hear were those of the cascading waterfalls in the night, of birds in the morning and evening. The Petits had only a daughter called Ratan. She had turned sixteen years two months ago and looked quite attractive due to her talkative and pleasant disposition and brilliant mind. She took a keen interest in the discussions that her parents and her father's friend, almost of his age, used to have. Sometimes she would go out alone to roam around the romantic mountain peaks. At other times, she would join her parents and Jinnah in their outings.

One day, a close friend of the Petits invited them for tea. Dinshaw asked Jinnah to join them, but it was not in Jinnah's nature to mingle with strangers. He was sitting in the study room turning the pages of his volumes. A beautiful evening was setting. Jinnah felt bored due to long reading and making notes. He slowed down the thermostat in the room and pulled off the curtains hanging on the windows and looked down the mountains. The lush green mountains looked enchanting in the mixed rays of the setting sun and the rising moon. Jinnah had buttoned up his coat as he came out of the bungalow and started walking towards the mountain track taking long strides. The cool breeze invigorated him.

Jinnah had stopped at a slope. The houses below looked like dolls. The snow peaks of the distant mountains had reflected vivid shades of light and colour. Jinnah's eyes flashed suddenly. He saw a girl emerging from the shades of light walking, nay rather gliding, towards him. Jinnah was astonished. Though he did not believe in fairies or angles, he wondered for a moment whether she was a fairy. When she came close to him he stared at her without blinking. The girl, whose beauty matched with the romantic nature of Darjeeling and the Himalayan sky had stirred some incomprehensible emotions in Jinnah's mind. Though she was wearing the woollen clothes from head to toe, her figure was so transparent that ...

"Mr. Jinnah," the girl came close to him and shouted, happy and excited.

Jinnah was startled. He immediately recognised the girl's voice.

Before he could say anything, the girl had jumped and stood beside him, as if she had the wings to fly.

"Come on! Mr. Jinnah, what are you looking at? Haven't you recognised me? I am Miss Ratan, Ratan...Dinshaw Petit," she said and then laughed loudly. Jinnah, who had never been left behind in talking, was for the first time at a loss for words and could not answer her laughter.

NOTES

1. A Hindu festival, symbolising the sun's entry into the northern hemisphere that falls on January 14 every year.
2. The then prevailing coin in currency.

21

Ruttie-Jinnah proximity, Dinshaw-Jinnah confrontation

Barrister Muhammad Ali Jinnah, reputed for speaking for hours with the high ranking British officials, in packed court rooms and in the meetings of the Imperial Council in the presence of the awe-inspiring Viceroy, could not sleep that night till the wee-hours of the morning. He flipped the pages of law books and then the books on politics. He went through the newspapers from Bombay, Delhi, London and New York that were scattered around. He used to read books with keen interest, but nothing could interest him that night. A strange sweet feeling had overtaken which he had never experienced. Jinnah could not understand the reason for this feeling.

His friend Dinshah Petit's daughter Ratan was not a stranger to him. He had met her several times in Dinshaw's bungalow at Bombay and spoken to her. When Jinnah and Dinshaw were lost in the game of chess holding wine glasses in their hands, this only beloved daughter of Dinshaw would say to her father leaning over his shoulder, "Daddy, not this, move that. Checkmate Mr. Jinnah's king."

Jinnah now remembered what Ratan had said then. He felt that this time it was not Dinshaw checkmating him in the game of chess, but Ratan herself. For a moment, he felt embarrassed by the thought, which went against his nature. It was difficult to accept somebody challenging him. He never felt so defensive. In a desperate attempt to conceal his distress, he pulled the blanket from the feet to his shoulder and closed his eyes till he felt asleep.

To the teenage girl Ratan things were different. She would read Jinnah's name now and then in the newspapers with awe. Her father Dinshaw was a powerful man, but he was never in the news. He had no interest in politics. She heard about the eminent persons like Dadabhai Navroji, Pheroze Shah Mehta, Gopal Krishna Gokhale and Lokmanya Tilak, though she never had the chance to meet them. Whenever she read the name of Barrister Jinnah along with these leaders in the newspapers she used to get thrilled. Jinnah rubbed shoulders with them and worked. It was natural for her to meet Jinnah and talk to him. When Jinnah and her father had intellectual debates, she would listen to Jinnah's uninterrupted flow of talk. Nothing had happened in the few minutes that Ratan had spent with Jinnah last evening in the midst of cool breeze and the dark surroundings, except that Jinnah who had always talked non-stop could not utter a word before Ratan and she had the last laugh. In Dinshaw Petit's bungalow at Darjeeling, Jinnah was trying hard to fall asleep in one bed room and the blossoming youthful Ratan was spending a sleepless night with sweet thoughts in another bed room.

The next morning, as usual, when all had assembled at the breakfast table, only Sir Dinshaw Petit and Lady Dinabai made all the talking. But both Jinnah and Ratan were sitting quietly.

"Mr. Jinnah," Noticing Jinnah's unusual silence Dinshaw asked, "Are not you feeling well today?"

"Nothing of the sort," Jinnah said startled. Then for a moment he wondered what was he startled about? Why was he feeling guilty like a criminal caught red handed? He cleared his throat and then said, "I am quite alright."

"Then, why are you so silent today? When we returned home last night, you went out alone for a stroll in the mountains. Sometimes, the joy of strolling alone in the mountains is overwhelming. You must have experienced something similar."

Jinnah became cautious at once. Did Dinshaw say it casually or did it have any other hidden meaning? He glanced at Ratan sitting at the other end of the table. She looked the other way as if she had also become cautious of Dinshaw's remarks.

The days were rolling fast. The vacation was nearing end. The day for returning to Bombay was already decided. These days both Jinnah and Ratan were meeting without any verbal exchange, as if they had some mutual understanding. Considering his age, Ratan's attitude put Jinnah in a dilemma. On the other hand, Jinnah was an enigma to Ratan. Both of them wanted to unburden by venting out their unexpressed feelings.

They got such an opportunity the evening before leaving for Bombay.

A stream was running by the garden of the bungalow. The sun was about to set. Ratan sat with her back on a rock, on the bank of the stream, with the rays of the setting sun falling on her pretty face and body. To feel the warmth of the setting sun, she pulled off the cloth covering her hands and legs. Her fair skin had turned gold under the rays of the setting sun. Jinnah who was standing in the balcony on the first floor of the bungalow looked down and saw Ratan enjoying the sun rays. Ratan who was looking at the stream suddenly looked up, as if some strange warmth had crept in. Jinnah did not divert his glance. Ratan made no effort to cover her hands and legs. Jinnah smiled at her. Ratan bit her lips fluttering the eyelashes. Jinnah waved at her and then climbed down fast.

Jinnah walked towards Ratan who was sitting on a rock on the bank of the stream. He thought that on seeing him she would set her clothes properly. But she did not do that. Instead she shook her legs rhythmically as if she was rocking to a song. Looking at the baffled Jinnah, she had a hearty laugh.

"Welcome, Mr. Jinnah. This evening won't come again. Sit and enjoy the warm sunshine, the cool breeze, the music of the stream and the beauty of the sky."

"That's all?" The fortytwo-year-old Jinnah felt suddenly like a twenty two year old and said in a mischievous voice.

"There is so much more… if you wish…" Ratan said as if she was attacking the very entity of Jinnah.

Jinnah was speechless. The girl whom he had considered naïve seemed altogether a different person today. Ratan was neither naïve nor a child. Jinnah went close to her. She sat still as if she was challenging him. Jinnah sat next to her and held her hand. Her smile on the lips and the rhythmic shaking of legs continued.

"Ratan," Jinnah's lips quivered.

"Ratan," she laughed teasingly. "I hear this from everybody. Do not you want to say something new today?"

Jinnah stood baffled by this mischievous countenance of Ratan.

"If you do not have anything to say except this one word, then let us leave this place," she looked at him with anger without making any effort to get up.

"Ratan," said Jinnah stressing each syllable. "No…No…Darling…Ruttie… You are…you are my sweetheart…Ruttie…Ruttie…"

"Really!" Ratan hugged Jinnah. "If I am your Ruttie, you are my Jin…no more Mr. Jinnah…Oh Jin…Dear Jin… How sweet it is…"

*

After returning to Bombay, Jinnah was busy in clearing his pending work. In between, he would find some time to meet Ruttie regularly. The First World War was in full swing. The Indian Muslims were very restless on the question of the Khalifa. Jinnah, who believed that the Muslims were not a separate section of the country but a part of the Indians fighting against the British rule, saw an opportunity in this growing unrest among the Muslims. Until now, the nationalist sentiments of the Congress and the communal approach of the Muslims were running parallel. In 1913, the Muslim League had amended its constitution and accepted the principle of Home Rule. Since then, Jinnah had participated in the meetings of the Muslim League. By now Jinnah had occupied a unique position in the Indian politics. He was a Congress leader. His voice was heard even by the most senior leaders in the Congress. He was the President of the Muslim League. And as a member of the Central Legislative Council he was in touch with the Viceroy. In the contemporary Indian politics, no other person had occupied such a position at three different levels. Taking advantage of the situation, Jinnah wanted to bring the Muslims into the mainstream of the country. He believed that if both the Congress and the Muslim League had come together on one platform and challenged the British rule, independence could be achieved soon.

Jinnah's residence had now shifted from Appollo Bunder to Malabar Hills near the sea shore. It turned into a very modern house. It was surrounded by a fortress on all sides, like a medieval palace, which came to be known as the South Court. A security guard was posted for twenty four hours at the main entrance.

Since he was meeting Ruttie regularly, Jinnah thought that he should inform Sir Dinshaw Petit about their affair, and discuss freely and frankly his intention to marry his daughter. Dinshaw was a modern minded gentleman. Hence, he would secure his consent to marry his daughter without any difficulty. Yet the lawyer in him suggested that instead of trusting Dinshaw, he should secure his consent through manipulation. The lawyer in him overpowered Jinnah the lover.

Jinnah made up in his mind to discuss the matter in his meeting with Dinshaw next Saturday. The sound of the musical notes coincided with the sound of the wine glasses as they cheered each other. They just finished the game of billiards which Dinshaw had lost that day. At the rate of twelve *annas* per hundred points, Jinnah had earned a lot of money. That was nothing unusual. It had happened many a time.

"Mr. Dinshaw," Jinnah said suddenly, as he sipped the wine.

"In our country national unity had become a problem because we have different communities. What is your opinion?"

"I totally agree with you. Modern educated people like us should take some steps to dissolve the communal differences," said Dinshaw.

"We should think about it seriously," Jinnah responded politely. "A very few marriages take place among the people of different communities, sects and religions."

"This is our misfortune, Mr. Jinnah," said Dinshaw after finishing the first peg and then taking the second peg. Jinnah had already taken the second peg. "To tell you the truth, the root of all religions in the country is the same, the common culture. This cultural unity must not be broken due to religion."

Jinnah felt that Dinshaw was fully entrapped by the verbal net that he had spread out. He had gulped down the second peg in a single sip with a victorious countenance and said, "I feel that if inter-religious marriages take place, it would strengthen the national unity."

"You are absolutely right, Mr. Jinnah," said Dinshaw enthusiastically. "In our country, if the Hindus, the Muslims, the Parsees, the Christians—all these communities—start having inter-religious marriages, we can achieve the unity in the country within a century."

Jinnah felt that Dinshaw was trapped fully by his own words.

"I want to take a step to establish such unity in the country and for that I need your support. Would you support me?"

"Of course! I am always with you in all your public causes. If you have planned any public campaign for inter-religious marriages, I shall always support it."

"That is what I expected from you." Jinnah said in a firm tone. "I want to marry…"

"Oh!" exclaimed Dinshaw spilling out some wine from the glass.

"Really! I congratulate you, Mr. Jinnah. When and how did it happen? Who is the lucky girl?"

"Her name is Ratanbai. And her father is a noted Bombay Parsee industrialist Mr. Dinshaw Petit." Jinnah said taking a deep puff of the cigarette held in his hand.

"What? What did you say?" screamed Dinshaw raising his voice. He banged the glass on the table, with his neck straightened and eyes wide open.

"Are you in your senses, Mr. Jinnah?"

"I am fully in my senses. And I am saying this with full responsibility. I am giving you an opportunity to take the credit for bringing the reform that you consider necessary for the cultural unity of the country," Jinnah said emphasising on every word and looked piercingly at Dinshaw.

22

Watch on Ruttie, Jinnah's refusal to cooperate in the war efforts (World War I), Muslim League's Lucknow session, Khilafat-Gandhi

"Mr. Jinnah," rising from the chair Dinshaw addressed, "You are trying to be too clever today. I feel you drank more and hence the evil thoughts of your mind..."

"No. You are mistaken. I have no evil thoughts in my mind. If a man and a woman want to get married by mutual consent, no wise man can call it an evil thought. We both have discussed and decided. Now only your consent is needed for the marriage."

Jinnah said politely interrupting Dinshaw.

"That can never happen. I have to think about the future of my daughter. At this age, how could you think of it? Please, do not say that again. You are unworthy of my friendship," Dinshaw said in anger.

"The future will decide who is worthy and unworthy. Now..."

"Now, leave this place at once," said Dinshaw shivering in anger. "Never step in here again. Our friendship ends here."

"But a new relationship begins from here and you won't be able to stop that Mr. Dinshaw," said Jinnah standing.

"I hate you for harbouring such thoughts about my tender daughter at your advanced age. I do not want to see my daughter a widow. Please get out." Dinshaw clenched his fists and then turned away.

Jinnah came out of the bungalow, but he was not willing to accept what Dinshaw had said. He had never thought of marriage until now. He never remembered Amibai as his first wife. Now that he had decided to marry, he would not allow anything to come in his way. Jinnah in his life had never believed in family and relations. He had never dreamt of having his own family. Ruttie was a daughter of his good friend Dinshaw. That was how he knew her till yesterday. What had happened in Darjeeling was not an aberration. He never looked upon Ruttie as a daughter. That was not possible for him. These were dictionary words for him. The relations meant nothing to him. However, Fatima was an exception.

But deep down Jinnah knew that Fatima was not just a sister, but a necessity. He knew that without Fatima not only his huge business apparatus would have collapsed, but he himself would have been crippled. Jinnah had measured the relations in terms of their utility.

At any other time, Dinshaw could have delivered a good public speech on issues like individual freedom or upbringing of children. He would have even donated money to encourage such organisations. But he had no doubt in his mind that his daughter Ratanbai needed no such thoughts, but his protection. Dinshaw knew that once Jinnah had registered something in his mind, he would not give it up. He was aware of Jinnah's character that he would go to any extent to achieve his goal. Jinnah was a clever advocate. Dinshaw knew that more than the knowledge of law, an Advocate needs firmness and the skill to juggle with the language.

He made a decision. He had decided what to do next.

Dinshaw had a frank discussion with his daughter on this issue. He made her understand how difficult it would be for a naïve and pampered girl like her to adjust with Jinnah's family which had a different religious and cultural background. He pointed out the difference in age of more than two-and-half decades between Ratan and Jinnah and the physical and mental hazards that come with it. All this had no effect on Ratan. She told her father bluntly that nobody except Jinnah would enter her life.

Dinshaw had no other option. Ratan was sixteen years old. As per the law, she was a minor. As a father, he was responsible for her welfare. He hoped that her infatuation for Jinnah would ebb away with the passage of time. Jinnah would be committing a criminal offence if he married her. Jinnah might be an advocate, but Dinshaw was aware of the law. The first thing that he did was to restrict her movement. Ratan, who used to hop in and out of her father's huge bungalow like a butterfly, was forbidden from moving out of the house. The security guard at the entrance was given strict instruction. Dinshaw hoped that he would weather the storm once she became an adult after two years, when she would turn eighteen.

But Dinshaw knew that this restriction on his daughter would not work. Jinnah would try to establish contact with her through telephone or letter. If this happens the storm would be intensifying instead of weathering. Ratan might even resist vehemently and precipitate something untoward.

Dinshaw decided to take the protection of the law. He filed a writ petition in the Bombay High Court praying the Court to restrain Barrister Jinnah from meeting his minor daughter or establishing any contact with her. The High Court passed the order that Dinshaw wanted.

Jinnah knew that he could do nothing and accepted the Court order.

*

Just as Jinnah was facing the biggest challenge in his personal life, his public life also had reached a very crucial stage. The position of the Indian Muslims had completely changed once Turkey entered the First World War. A large section of the Indian Muslims were worried about the Khalifa. Jinnah wanted to make this a national issue and bring an understanding between the Congress and the Muslim League and establish a friendly relation between the Hindus and the Muslims permanently. The British government had appointed a Parliamentary Committee to consider the question of bringing more political reforms in India. Jinnah deposing before the Committee said that if the separate electorate for religious minorities was unavoidable, it should be only a temporary and not a permanent measure. He also said that he was looking forward to a day when the Hindus and the Muslims would be equal on the political stage. As long as England fought against Germany, the Indian Muslims did not mind supporting Britain. But, when Turkey had joined Germany and declared Britain as its enemy the Indian Muslims attitude towards Britain changed overnight.

Gandhi had now become a dominant force in the Congress and consequently in the Indian politics. He said that if the Congress and the Indian people consider themselves as the British subjects, they should not only demand the rights but also perform the duties. Gandhi said that at a time when Britain was going through a very difficult phase, it was the duty of the Indians to assist Britain in its war efforts rather than creating more problems. If Britain was defeated in the war and Germany emerged victorious, the Indian slavery would be more intensified, because the German militarism would be more dangerous than the British imperialism. If the Indians assisted Britain in its war efforts now, the demand for the local self-governance would be strengthened. Britain would not be able to deny this after the war.

Jinnah could not understand why this type of statement was coming from Gandhi, who had fought successfully in South Africa. Gandhi had assisted the British government in South Africa in the Boer war and in the Zulu mutiny on the pretext that the Indians were the loyal subjects. Jinnah knew this. However, after receiving the assistance the clever British government had given nothing in return. In fact, the government had come out with more severe laws. Jinnah strongly believed that the slaves had no duties. When slavery was imposed from above, it was wrong to expect any reward for loyalty. In the meeting convened by the Viceroy to seek the support of the Indians in the war, Jinnah said raising his voice, "if the Indians had to shed blood, they can do so as free people, not as slaves. If Indians are given rights equal to the British citizens, you can expect loyalty from them. First of all, bring a resolution providing a representative government in India and then present it before the British Parliament for consideration." The Viceroy Lord Chelmsford expressing disgust asked Jinnah, "Mr. Jinnah, it seems you are bargaining at such a difficult situation. Your attitude is very deplorable."

Jinnah, in response, said without any hesitation, "The demand is made to uphold my self-respect; can you call it a bargain? If I demand the right to be a free citizen in my own country from my rulers, is it a bargain? If you call it a bargain, then I accept it."

Jinnah had rejected Gandhi's proposal to assist the government in its war efforts. Nothing could be achieved from such benevolence in politics. In the Congress meeting, Jinnah said that as an organisation it should reject Gandhi's proposal in the interest of the country.

Taking advantage of the anti-British sentiments among the Muslims, Jinnah had made the Muslim League accept certain things. The separate electorate was dividing the country. The interests of the different communities were clashing. Jinnah had succeeded in making the Muslim League accept the abolition of the separate electorate. It was due to the Muslim League's demand that the system of separate electorate was introduced seven years ago. The Muslim League now gave up the demand and instead accepted the common electorate with the Hindus. And the Congress accepted the electoral process that would not only protect the interest of the Muslims, but would also ensure election of adequate Muslim candidates. Thus, Jinnah succeeded in bringing about a compromise between the two communities and unity to fight against the foreign rule.

This success of Jinnah weakened the position of the President of the Muslim League Aga Khan, the religious head of the Ismaili Khojas. Aga Khan had invited Jinnah to join the League at the time of its formation. But Jinnah had not only rejected the invitation, but even changed his sub-sect to avoid the religious control. Aga Khan had not forgotten this. Jinnah had changed from Ismaili Khoja to Ishna-Ashri. This was an insult to Aga Khan. The same Jinnah now making the Muslim League to fall in line with the Congress was something that Aga Khan could not bear. In protest, Aga Khan resigned from the post of the President of the Muslim League.

In his Presidential speech at the Lucknow convention of the Muslim League in 1916 Jinnah emphasised that the interest of the Muslims was not different from the interest of the country. But he also emphasised that the apprehension of the minorities should be removed to make them feel secure. Elaborating his idea of security at the Congress session that immediately followed, Jinnah said, "Only the people who have something can give those who do not have. The majority Hindus should allot seats generously to the Muslims so that they can feel secure. And if that happens, it will be easy for us to overthrow the foreign rule."

The Congress accepted the proposal of Jinnah. In no time, the feeling of Hindu-Muslim unity swept across the country. The Muslim League which until now was fighting only for its community cause has now joined hands with the Congress to fight for the interest of the country. This was the most fulfilling moment in Jinnah's life.

Though the Muslim League had accepted the independence of the country as the ultimate goal, under the influence of Jinnah, for the majority of the Muslims it was a step for achieving a larger objective. They were more interested in pressurising the British government to protect the Caliph of Turkey than the independence of the country. To the Muslims across the country the position of the Caliph as the religious head was more important. To them, a country not having the Islamic rule was *Dar-ul-Harb* and not *Dar-ul-Islam*. India was *Dar-ul-Harb*. Turkey was *Dar-ul-Islam*. Hence, the Muslim League had adopted a resolution demanding that the Caliph should not be punished after the war by the British government. Jinnah had opposed the resolution. He said that constitutionally, the Muslim League had no right to interfere with the foreign policy of the British government. The issue of Khilafat was a part of the government's foreign policy. Moreover, the Khilafat was an institution and not a religious order. The Quran made no mention of it. Considering all this, the demand was not justified.

But Jinnah was in the minority. Jinnah could see the Muslim League was supporting the Congress, but he could not comprehend its intention behind. It was like a game of politics played in the manner you play the game of chess. The future alone would tell who would win and who would lose the support. Being unable to prevail upon the League, Jinnah walked out of the meeting in a huff.

Jinnah, who had reached the peak of his political career, was waiting for an event that jolted him. This was Gandhi's declaration of support to the Muslims on the question of the Khilafat. Gandhi accepted the ultra-orthodox and the conservative Maulana Mohammed Ali and Maulana Shaukat Ali as the representatives of the Muslim community and treated their problem as a national problem. Gandhi declared that the Khilafat was a matter of life-and-death for the Muslims and, therefore, the Hindus should support their Muslim brethren in their hour of difficulty. Further, he volunteered to lead the campaign for protection of the Khilafat. Presiding over the first meeting of the Muslims in this connection, Gandhi said the problem of the Muslims was not their problem alone, but a problem of the whole country. However, he made a condition for leading the campaign that the Muslims should swear to adhere to non-violence. The Maulvis and Maulanas present in the meeting debated on Gandhi's condition. They argued that when a war was just even the Quran had endorsed violence. Since this was a just war there was no need to observe non-violence. Gandhi, a professionally failed lawyer in the court gave a different interpretation of the Quran saying that it did not make the violence obligatory. Even the Muslims settle the disputes among themselves not through violence but through the courts of law. The Ali brothers accepted Gandhi's interpretation and so also all the others.

As a reciprocal gesture to the Hindus for supporting the issue of the Khilafat, the Ali brothers asked the Muslims to give up the cow-slaughter. The Muslims supported the suggestion. Gandhi opposed it. He said that both the issues of the Khilafat and the cow-slaughter should not be mixed to bargain. If the Hindus think that the Khilafat was a just issue, they should support the Muslims without any expectation in return. And similarly, if the Muslims think that the Hindus' sentiment on the cow-slaughter was just, they should give up the cow-slaughter, even if the Hindus did not support them on the issue of the Khilafat.

Jinnah was distressed when he learnt about all this. He spoke out in a very angry tone, "Khilafat? What is this Khilafat? Whether the Khalifa is saved or thrown out what do the Indians have to do with it? Let the sages and the sadhus debate endlessly the issue of cow-slaughter, but Gandhi's policy of dragging the Mullahs and the Sadhus into politics is very dangerous. This sentimental nonsense will never be accepted."

23

Ruttie-Jinnah marriage, Lord Chelmsford's banquet, Lord Willingdon's banquet

It was not possible to establish communication with Ruttie, due to the Court order. Jinnah had, therefore, no other option, but to wait for Ruttie to complete eighteen years. He knew that, in the meantime, if he had tried to communicate to Ruttie and Dinshaw Petit found any evidence to that effect, he would be in a very awkward position. Yet he clandestinely managed to establish the contact with Ruttie. She was equally clever in this matter. She assured Jinnah that once she completed eighteen years on 20 February, 1918 she would leave her father's house and that he should make whatever arrangements were required by the law for their marriage.

Jinnah had already made all the arrangements. On completing eighteen years, one morning in April, Ruttie left her father's palatial bungalow. She was fond of English literature, specially poetry. While leaving the house, she had collected some of her favourite books. She had the liking for the fashionable and skin tight transparent clothes. A variey of perfumes, flowers and jewels were also part of her persona. Whenever she had a ride in her father's horse-drives carriage, she used to carry two cats and a pedigree dog with her. She considered all these as her primary needs. Now when she left her father's bungalow, besides carrying all her personal belongings she also took a cat with her.

On the morning of 18 April, 1918, forty four-year-old Muhammad Ali Jinnah, ignorant about Islam, and eighteen years old Ratanbai Dinshaw Petit, more ignorant about Islam than Jinnah, solemnised their marriage before an Imam in a mosque. Ratanbai Petit had given up her Parsee religion and got converted to Islam. She was renamed as Mariambai.

As a matter of fact, the change of religion or name had mattered little to both of them. However, Ruttie did not expect this religious conversion. She had expected Jinnah to give a notice under the Civil Marriages Act and register their marriage in a court of law. Therefore, the conversion surprised her.

But Jinnah was well versed with the law. Ruttie was an innocent girl. Jinnah was aware of all aspects of the marriage. Personally, he had no attachment to either Islam or The Quran. However, when he realised that his paternal Ismaili tradition became an obstacle in his way, he did not hesitate for a moment in renouncing the Ismaili religion headed by Aga Khan and changing himself into an Ishna-Ashri. His sister Fatima had remained an Ismaili Khoja. His father Zinabhai had expired long ago. He had cut off all relations with his siblings living in abject poverty at Khoja Mohalla.

Yet, Jinnah had ensured that his marriage was performed by an Imam in a mosque instead of registering before the Registrar of Marriages, under the Civil Marriages Act. He understood its importance. The marriage under the Civil Marriages Act required both the parties to file an affidavit consenting to the marriage and declaring that they were secular, not attached to any particular religion and free from any religious bindings. Such an affidavit had no importance to Ruttie. As per the Parsee religious tradition, she had ceased to be a Parsee the moment she married a non-Parsee. She had forfeited the right to be present at the Parsee religious ceremonies or pray to the Holy Fire at the *Agiari*[1]. But Jinnah's position was different. Personally Jinnah might have nothing to do with the Islamic religion. But in 1910, he was nominated to the Imperial Council as a member from the Bombay Muslims Constituency. If Jinnah had filed such an affidavit, it would have meant that he had renounced Islam. He would have ceased to be a Muslim. Thus he would have been disqualified from the membership of the Council. How could a non-Mulsim represent a Muslim Constituency? If that happened, Jinnah would have lost everything. Jinnah did not want to place himself in such a predicament. Though always contemptuous of Mullahs, Maulvis and Imams, he now found them very useful and did not mind using them.

On the very evening of the marriage, the newly-wed couple instead of heading to Ooty, Shimla, Kodaikanal, Mahabaleshwar, or Kulu-Manali for honeymoon had set-off to the capital Delhi. The meeting of the Council was scheduled. And it was very important for Jinnah to attend the meeting. When Ruttie came to know that her husband chose a bustling and crowded city like Delhi for the honeymoon she was disappointed.

"Darling Jin," she said to her husband, "In Delhi, you will be busy with politics. We will have no privacy. I hoped that for the honeymoon, we would go to some hill station or to a Caribbean island or Switzerland. I cannot understand, how we can enjoy in Delhi."

"I am helpless, Ruttie," said Jinnah. "I have to attend the meeting of the Council. We will certainly go to some hill station some other time. I have booked a special suite meant for the honeymoon couple in Delhi's Hotel Maiden. You will not feel missing a hill station."

The honeymoon suite at the Hotel Maiden was indeed regal and very attractive. At the very first sight, Ruttie liked it. When she heard and saw Jinnah arguing with the Viceroy in the Central Hall, she felt very happy and satisfied that she had married such a distinguished person.

At the end of the Council session, a dinner banquet was arranged at the

Viceregal lodge in Shimla. Mr. and Mrs. Jinnah were invited to the banquet. Ruttie was enthralled to learn that they were invited to Shimla as the guests of the Viceroy. She felt very lonely. Therefore, she was very excited about this opportunity of dining with the Viceroy.

At the Viceregal lodge, the Viceroy Lord Chelmsford and Lady Chelmsford had accorded a warm welcome to the guests. All of them were wearing woolen clothes due to the cold weather. But Ruttie was an exception. She was looking very pretty in a tight pink dress. The diamonds in her jewels were dazzling under the lights. The most important thing was that she was the youngest among them. And yet all of them were attracted to her, mainly because she was Jinnah's new bride but also due to her youthfulness and beauty. Everybody knew of her love affair with Jinnah and their subsequent marriage. The newspapers across the country had covered the news of their marriage.

Jinnah introduced Ruttie to the Viceroy. The Viceroy acknowledged the attractive bride and stretched out his right hand to shake hands with her.

But as the Viceroy stretched out his hand, Ruttie had joined her two hands and said *namaste*[2] to him slightly bowing her head. He did not expect this. He was aware that the Hindu women greeted this way. But he was amazed that the girl who had a love marriage with Jinnah, a national leader and modern man, and herself coming from an ultra-rich high society could behave this way. He knew that even the women from the conservative background would look to an opportunity to shake hand with the Viceroy. Therefore, he not only felt Ruttie's behaviour strange and astonishing, but also insulting. He quietly withdrew his hand as if nothing had happened.

After the dinner when all the guests had gone, the Viceroy said casually to Ruttie,

"Mrs. Jinnah, your husband has a very bright future. You must support him to ensure success in his political career."

"Your Excellency, I am thankful to you for the suggestion. And I do support my husband in his career," Ruttie said smiling.

"I am afraid, Madam, you are not fully supporting him. You must observe the western etiquette in socializing. If you do not observe that, I am afraid, Mr. Jinnah's political life may be jeopardized. It is wise to live like a Roman when you are in Rome," the Viceroy said at last what he had in his mind.

Ruttie had the inkling of the Viceroy's exasperation. Yet she could not imagine that a man of Viceroy's stature could taunt her this way. She became cautious and said without any hesitation, "Your Excellency, what you said is right. When you are in Rome, behave like a Roman, it is worth remembering. Therefore, the people living in India must accept the Indian way of life. You must have noticed that I have greeted you in the Indian tradition."

The Viceroy Chelmsford was more hurt by Ruttie's reply than her greeting him with a *namaste*.

It was a new experience for him that the young girl, who looks like a child, could talk so fearlessly and logically. He had no other option, but to end the conversation.

Thereafter the newly wed couple returned to Bombay. Lord Willingdon was the Governor of Bombay. Jinnah held the Governor in high esteem. He had a very cordial relation with him. Lord Willingdon too was considerate of Jinnah's standing. After their return from Shimla, he invited Jinnah and Ruttie for dinner at his official residence.

Ruttie had seen the Governor's house many a time. She had seen the splendour of the house from outside. She was once again delighted to receive the invitation for dinner in the midst of such grandeur. The experience with the Viceroy Chelmsford was still fresh in her mind. The way she silenced the Viceroy by the jugglery of words had boosted her self-confidence and pride. She felt that her fearlessness was making her a worthy wife.

When the Jinnah couple reached the Governor's house, it was late evening. The hot day had ended, but there was no relief from the heat. Ruttie was wearing summer clothes. She loved light and tight fitting clothes. And such clothes suited her fair complexion and youthful body. That day she was wearing an open-neck blouse, exposing, neck body and fair hands. Her blouse was so tight that it almost looked like her skin. She looked very pretty with the modern jewels and the flowers in her hair.

The Lord and Lady Willingdon took the Jinnah couple to the drawing room. The air-conditioners made the room very cool. The outside heat and humidity had vanished at once. The decoration of the drawing room was very aesthetic. Jinnah had introduced Ruttie to the Governor and his wife. For Lady Willingdon, wearing tight clothes was not something new. In the western society, she had seen women wearing such clothes. She herself wore such clothes quite often without any hesitation. And yet, Lady Willingdon was amazed and annoyed that Ruttie was wearing such revealing clothes. The fifty year old Lady Willingdon saw the reflection of Ruttie and herself in the mirror fixed on a wall in the drawing room. She reminiscenced her past for a moment. She had never looked so beautiful even in her youth. Then she looked at her husband who was talking to Jinnah. Lady Willingdon had suddenly noticed that, while engaging in a polite conversation with the guest, Lord Willingdon was glacing at Ruttie now and then.

Lady Willingdon talked for quite some time, but all the time she was watching Lord Willingdon. The husband was totally unaware that his wife was watching him. He was engrossed in his conversation with Jinnah, while throwing frequent glances at Ruttie.

The coolness of the air-conditioned room felt like winter.

The Governor's ADC and other attendants were standing at the door. Lady

Willingdon suddenly called the ADC by a gesture with her hand. The ADC walked upto her and stood.

"The room is too cold and I think Mrs. Jinnah might catch cold. Go and get a shawl for Mrs. Jinnah to cover herself," Lady Willingdon said and then held her lips tightly.

Jinnah heard Lady Willingdon's instruction. He had noticed her sealed lips that conveyed her feelings. Jinnah did not take much time to understand what Lady Willingdon had wanted to say. He flared up to see his wife being insulted. He could not bear Lady Willingdon censuring his wife's clothes.

"Her Excellency is unnecessarily worried. Mrs. Jinnah knows quite well how to take care of her health. You do not have to worry," having said so, Jinnah stood up.

There was stunned silence in the room.

The ADC who was going to fetch the shawl stopped as if someone had put brakes on his legs. Lord Willingdon himself was stunned by Jinnah's harsh voice. Jinnah held Ruttie's hand and then said, "Darling, it is not possible to dine here after such an insult. Come! Let's go."

Before anybody could say or comprehend anything, Jinnah had left the house with his wife.

NOTES

1. The Fire Temple of Parsees.
2. The Indian way of greeting.

24

Jinnah's willingness to cooperate in the war efforts, Jinnah's opposition to Willingdon's farewell function (Town Hall), Fatima-Ruttie differences, end of the war, Dina's birth in London

Jinnah feeling insulted had left the Governor's house in a huff. Lord Willingdon's term as the Governor was to end six months after the incident. In the meantime, Jinnah and Lord Willingdon had another verbal duel. Jinnah had publicly declared time and again that if Britain wanted any support from India for the First World War, the Indian people should be granted the same rights as the British citizens. But Gandhi, as opposed to this, was of the view that at a time when Britain was deep in trouble, it was the duty of the Indian people, as the loyal subjects of the British, to assist the government in its war efforts. Governor Willingdon convened a meeting of the prominent citizens of Bombay to seek their support for the war. Jinnah was also present at the meeting. Presiding over the meeting, Willingdon said that, at a difficult situation like this, a gentleman, influential in the public life, was behaving in a manner hardly commendable and that his attitude had raised doubt about his intention in public life.

It was very obvious that Willingdon was referring to Jinnah. Jinnah did not forget how Lady Willingdon had insulted Ruttie. The rude manner in which Jinnah boycotted the dinner was an insult to Governor Willingdon. Jinnah realised that, keeping the incident in mind, the Governor was doubting his intention. He responded immediately, "The Governor should understand that if our assistance and support is required, the educated citizens of this country should feel that they are equal to the British citizens. If that is not possible, all these efforts are futile. You will get nothing from this meeting."

In these six months nothing else happened except this minor friction.

Jinnah's attention was drawn to the advertisement released by the Sheriff of Bombay in the month of December. A farewell function was organised by the citizens of Bombay at the Town Hall to express gratitude to Willindon for the service rendered by him. On reading this, Jinnah became furious. He became more furious when he learnt that this function was organised at the behest of Sir Stanley Reid, the editor of *The Times of India*. It was very absurd on the part of an English journalist to decide what service Governor Willingdon had rendered. Jinnah thought that this was a golden opportunity to avenge publicly the insult he had suffered at the hands of Willingdon. He would not have objected to the function, had it been organised by the well wishers and the friends of Willingdon. But this function was being organised on behalf of the citizens of Bombay. And Jinnah was one of the citizens. It meant that he would be a party to the function. Jinnah wrote a letter to the Sheriff on behalf of the citizens objecting to the function.

Jinnah was the President of the Bombay branch of the Home Rule League. Many prominent citizens were associated with this organisation established by Annie Besant. All of them supported Jinnah's objection to the function organised by the Sheriff. The prominent intellectuals who supported Jinnah included Omar Shobani, Kanaiyalal Munshi, Chimanlal Setalvad, Shankarlal Banker, B.G. Horniman and Kanji Dwarkadas.

However, the Sheriff ingnored the objection. Jinnah's supporters met Gandhi at his Ashram in Ahmedabad to seek his support. He heard them patiently and then said, "Both the sides are free to think from their points of view. You are opposing the function as the citizens. And the Sheriff and his friends are organising the function as the citizens of Bombay. Unfortunately, I am not a citizen of Bombay. Had it been the issue of the whole country, the situation would have been different. This is an issue pertaining to the citizens of a particular city. I cannot say anything on behalf of the citizens of Bombay."

The function was to start at 5 p.m. on 10 December, 1918. About three hundred friends and fans of Jinnah had assembled at the steps of the Town Hall the previous night. All of them had waited on the long steps of the Town Hall till 8 o'clock in the morning. As soon as the door was opened, they rushed into the hall and occupied the chairs. Both Jinnah and Ruttie had reached the Town Hall in the afternoon at 3 p.m. They were greeted with loud cheers. The police stood guard on the steps outside. The Sheriff and his supporters arrived on time. Jinnah's supporters had jeered at them. Jinnah stood stiffly by the side of the stage. The police was regulating the crowd gathered at the door. Ruttie was seen leading the crowd.

The Sheriff inaugurated the function and Jamshedji Jijibhoy, a prominent Parsee leader, presided over the function. Jinnah, Ruttie and their friends stepped on to the stage and started shouting, "No! No! No!" The police rushed inside the hall and tried to evict them. Amidst all this chaos, a resolution praising the service of Governor Willingdon was presented on behalf of the citizens of Bombay. There was a lot of commotion in the hall. In the midst of jostling and the din, nobody could make out who said what. The Sheriff declared that the resolution was passed and concluded the function.

Feeling triumphant the people surrounded Jinnah and Ruttie. Hundreds of people had gathered outside the Town Hall on the Apollo Street. Everything came to a stand still for sometime. Jinnah climbed on the portico of a bank on the street and addressed the crowd, "This is the victory of the citizens of Bombay. This is the victory of democracy. Let both the bureaucracy and the autocracy do what they want, but they cannot stop people's uprising. You have proved this today. Come! Let us all celebrate this victory."

The crowd had listened to Jinnah's speech with rapt attention. Then they congratulated and showered him with flowers. Jinnah's friend Omar Shobani suddenly came out with a proposal at the gathering,

"A public hall be built to mark this victory against the British rule. And that hall be named after Barrister Jinnah."

The crowd clapped demonstrating their support to the proposal. Even Jinnah had never dreamt of this. His lean body turned more stiff. He was happy that he had avenged the insult. He took pride that he suddenly became a hero. His lips were sealed even more tightly.

Omar Shobani then said, "Let us all the citizens of Bombay celebrate this victory by contributing a rupee each for the construction of the hall."

The crowd was excited even more. In no time, the huge collection of the silver coins having the imprint of King George VI piled up.

An amount of sixty five thousand rupees was collected. The Hall was constructed very soon near the Kennedy Bridge at Grant Road and the hall named 'Jinnah Hall' was dedicated to the citizens of Bombay by the Irish lady Madam Annie Besant, a leading advocate of India's freedom and a well-known theosophist and the President of the Home Rule League.

*

Fatima was quite unhappy about the changes brought in the family matters after her elder brother's marriage. She was unable to give vent to her unhappiness. She was not happy about the behaviour of Ruttie. She was the shadow of her brother for the past one decade. It was natural that Ruttie had now taken her place. Fatima always felt that she was ignored because of Ruttie. Until now, it had been a practice that whenever Jinnah had returned home in the evening or late in the night, he would discuss the political situation with Fatima. She did not like Jinnah's marriage with a Parsee girl. She had admiration for Islam and the Muslim community. She had no interest in any other religion, except Islam. Since her childhood, she had harboured hatred towards the Hindus which now developed into a feeling of revenge. Fatima was also unhappy about Jinnah's liberal attitude and his opposition to the Muslim fundamentalists on the issue of the Khilafat. She felt Jinnah had made a mistake in attempting to bring the Hindu-Muslim unity by projecting himself as a nationalist. During the discussions she would always express her views. Sometimes Jinnah would accept her views. But immediately he would argue brilliantely and demolish her defence. At such time,

Fatima would say, "Bhaijaan, whatever you may say, the muslims are the Muslims, they can never live together with the Hindus. The Hindus will never accept the Muslims as their equals. There is no other option, but to conquer the Hindus and make India *Dar-ul-Islam*."

Jinnah would always laugh at Fatima and dismiss her argument. But sometime he would ponder over the logic of her arguments. And whenever he was unable to refute her argument with conviction, instead of being apologetic, he would say to her,

"Fati, all these things happen that way. You won't understand it. In politics there is no Hindu or Muslim. A true politician is concerned only about his goal."

And then the argument between the brother and the sister would end.

All this had stopped after the arrival of Ruttie. Although Ruttie had been converted to Islam and adopted a Muslim name Mariambai, after all she had belonged to a different religion. Because of this, Fatima would become very cautious of talking about Islam and other religions, particularly Hinduism, whenever three of them sat together for tea or dinner. Ruttie's conversion to Islam was just a matter of convenience. It was not due to any belief in Islam. Therefore, Fatima felt that if she expressed her communal feeling, Ruttie would oppose and she might even spread that outside damaging the repution of Jinnah. After the arrival of Ruttie, Fatima was not getting time to talk to her brother. She considered Ruttie a big obstacle in her way.

Apart from all this, Fatima, being a Muslim woman, was irritated about Ruttie's lifestyle, her manner of dressing and hobbies. Fatima herself led a very simple life in the midst of prosperity. In managing the huge household she had accounted for each and every paise. She would not pay anything extra to the servants. Nor would she allow them to take leave. Most of the people who visited Jinnah were served with only glass of water and rarely offered tea or coffee. Ruttie was totally different. She squandered her money. Ruttie had pet dogs and cats and played with them for hours together. She had trained persons to look after them and a veterinary doctor would visit regularly for their health check-up. Fatima would become furious whenever a cat or a dog was found wandering outside Ruttie's bedroom or in the guest room. She would become acrimonious with Ruttie. Whenever Jinnah was busy in the court or in his study room, these pets were the only companions for Ruttie in the huge palatial bungalow. She was mad about her pets. She had given special names to all of them. She knew Fatima hated all this, but she did not care. She ridiculed Fatima's stinginess. Fatima hardly talked to Ruttie. To escape the loneliness, Ruttie would spend all her time with the pets or sometime read the literature books, particularly poetry.

Dinshaw Petit's bungalow was at a mile's distance from Ruttie's bungalow. The doors of her father's home were closed to her forever. The doors were closed the day she had left the house. When Dinshaw Petit learnt that Miss Ratanbai Dinshaw Petit had become Mrs. Mariambai Muhammad Ali Jinnah, he publicly disowned her. He cut off all relations with his daughter. The daughter was fully aware that her father's anger would not subside. She knew quite well that the road to her father's house was closed to her forever. She had lost her parents' affection. She felt emptiness within.

One morning Ruttie told Jinnah that she had planned some special programme for the evening. She wanted to drive Jinnah in her new car to the place behind the big rocks on the Harkness Road to take a dip in the sea water. Jinnah, seeing the excitement of his wife, promised to return home on time.

Ruttie sitting in her balcony was looking at the sea. She could see the movement of vehicles on the Mount Pleasant Road from the other end of the balcony. The drivers of the horse driven carriages, popularly known as *Victorias,* cracking the whips in the air, were shouting in their typical base language at the pedestrians to make way for them. There were few motorcars those days, hence there was no nuisance of horns. Ruttie was looking in that direction. The time had passed, but Jinnah did not come yet. When she dialled his office phone, out of anxiety, she was told that he had left his chamber an hour ago.

A disappointed Ruttie had no option except patting the furry cat in her lap.

Her wait had ended at last. As soon as Jinnah arrived, Ruttie holding his shoulder in the courtyard near the steps said angrily, "I had a programme to go to the Harkness Road today. Yet you did not come on time. I was calling your office for a long time," and she grabbed his tie.

"I am sorry, darling. I did not forget, but I had to stay back due to some case," Jinnah said affectionately putting his hand around her.

"OK! I forgive you today. If the crime is committed again, the criminal shall be punished." Ruttie said with a hearty laugh. Then she said, "But we must go to the Harkness Road tonight and dip our feet in the sea. Look at the sky, how pleasant is the moon. Let's go and feel the touch of the sea water."

"Sorry, darling. We cannot go anywhere tonight! I have to prepare the case and I have brought all the files home. Hence, I cannot wait even for a minute. I had the dinner outside. Please send a bottle of champagne to my study room." Jinnah said and started walking towards the steps.

To Ruttie, this reply of Jinnah was not only unexpected but very hurting too. She looked as if someone had clipped her wings when she was about to fly. She turned her face and looked back. She saw Fatima standing on the first step of the door. She could see a sense of triumph on Fatima's face. She wondered why Fatima was smiling. They glanced at each other and then looked away.

*

The country's politics saw a new change. The war had ended. The British Parliament had proposed some political reforms for India. A Parliamentary Committee appointed to study the proposals was seeking the opinions of the prominent Indians. Among the prominent Indians invited by the Committee to London to discuss the draft proposals, Jinnah was there. It was about two-and-a-half decades since Jinnah had studied the law and settled in Bombay. He travelled to London quite often. Jinnah loved going to London.

This time, Ruttie accompanied him to London. The trip was meant for making a presentation before the Parliamentary Committee on the proposed reforms on behalf of the Indian people. But Jinnah had something in mind. The Indian Muslims had accepted his leadership. However, he visualised the possibility of a clash with Gandhi in future.

The Congress had accorded a special position to Gandhi due to his achievement in South Africa. He was the most popular person among the British politicians. Jinnah also was well acquainted with the British political leaders. If Jinnah was given the right to speak on behalf of the Indians at the international level, he would not only become equal to Gandhi, but rise above him in stature.

After the defeat of Turkey in the war, the allied powers were meeting in Paris to decide about its future. Britain was leading a delegation on behalf of the allied powers. Jinnah wanted India to be represented in the delegation as a British colony. He was acquainted with Montagu, the Secretary of State for India. He thought that if he could take the advantage of this and get nominated as the representative of India at the Paris meeting, he would get international recognition as the voice of the Indian Muslims. But unfortunately, this wish of Jinnah could not be realised for Lord Willingdon had sent a detailed report to the Secretary of State for India on Jinnah. Montagu, therefore, did not give any importance to Jinnah.

The report had cautioned the Secretary of State for India pointing out that Jinnah was the most untrustworthy among the Indian politicians. He was very clever in talking and his intentions were malicious. He was one of the leaders who did not practice what he said. Thus, Jinnah's dream of proving himself superior to Gandhi remained unfulfilled. He was greatly disappointed.

However, the London trip provided some consolation. As if it was an indication of the future, Ruttie had given birth in London to a baby girl between the midnight of 14th and the dawn of 15thAugust. The dates that were to become unforgettable in future for both India and Pakistan had become memorable in Jinnah's personal life as well. After spending a couple of months in London, the Jinnahs returned to India with their daughter Dina.

25

Ruttie-Kanji introduction, The Khilafat movement: Gandhi-Jinnah differences

The English writers Wordsworth, Tennyson, Byron and Oscar Wilde were Ruttie's favourities. She had special fondness for Oscar Wilde. She had a collection of all their works. In her lonely moments, she found solace in their poems. Ruttie wanted Jinnah also to take interest in these poems. But Jinnah was not interested in them. Sometimes she would get ecstatic while reading the poems and walk into Jinnah's office or study room. And Jinnah would get immersed in his law books or in files or in discussisng politics with his friends. Ruttie lost in her own world of poetry would rush into his room unmindful of the people sitting and sit on the arm of his easy chair or push the files aside and sit on the table. Then dangling her legs, she would give the poetry book to Jinnah and say excitedly, "Oh! Jin. This is wonderful. Read this. You will forget everything."

Jinnah would take the book in hand and without reading anything would say to her laughingly, "If something in this can make me forget everything, then I should not read it."

Ruttie would feel disappointed, but then argue, "Oh! Jin darling. You do not understand anything. What we forget in reading a poem is in reality worth forgetting. A drop of nectar can render a bottle of champagne useless."

"Ok…Ok… even what you say is right, the nectar or the champagne is of no use to me right now. The burning problem before the country at the moment is what we do with the Mullahs, Maulvis, priests and Mahatmas," Jinnah would say and then read the newspaper clippings or continue the discussion with the people sitting. After a while, Ruttie would leave the room, hoping Jinnah might stop her. But Jinnah would say to his wife on entering the bedroom at night, "Oh! I did not know when you left my study room. When I looked up suddenly, you were not there."

Ruttie had mingled freely with Jinnah's friends and sometimes even discussed the issues relating to public life. Kanji had a special place among Jinnah's friends. Every Saturday or during the holidays he would join Jinnah for lunch. He respected Jinnah's views and held him in high esteem. He was born in a Kapol business family of Saurashtra. Besides taking interest in the business, he had also developed interest in politics. He was actively involved with Annie Besant's Home Rule League. There was a huge age difference between Kanji and Jinnah. Kanji was almost twenty years younger to Jinnah. Yet, Jinnah liked his companionship. He continued to visit Jinnah at the South Court even after the marriage. Gradually, Kanji became very close to Ruttie. Among the close friends of Jinnah, he was the only companion to Ruttie in her loneliness.

Kanji was interested in the study of extra-sensory powers of human beings. He often claimed that he had mastered the art of communicating with the spirits. His close associates believed that he had mastered the mystical power whereby a person could make his near and dear ones feel his presence, even when he was not physically present. Kanji believed that there was a force beyond the five senses which could be mastered with practice. He had had such an experience.

Jinnah did not believe in all this. However, Kanji remained a loyal associate of Jinnah in his activities in the Home Rule League and the Congress. Ruttie was interested in the mystical power. Kanji told her that with willpower and practice one could master it.

*

Under Gandhi's leadership, the Muslims throughout the country were agitating on the issue of the Khilafat. And at the behest of Gandhi, the Indian National Congress had passed a resolution supporting the Khilafat movement. Jinnah had opposed the resolution. He said the issue of the Khilafa had to be decided by his followers and it had nothing to with the national politics. If religion was mixed with politics, it would pose a big problem. The people who surrounded Gandhi in the name of Islam had nothing to do with the religion. Jinnah had made his stand clear. The Congress rejected Jinnah's arguments. Not only the common people, but even the intellectuals like Pandit Motitlal Nehru and Chittaranjan Das, whom Jinnah held in high esteem, sided Gandhi. Besides, Pandit Madanmohan Malaviya, Swami Shradhanand and other Hindu leaders also sided Gandhi and supported the Muslims on the issue of the Khilafat. Gandhi and the Congress leaders believed that this was a good opportunity to bring the Muslims into the freedom movement. If this opportunity was missed, the Hindu-Muslim unity would break. These leaders also believed that without the Muslims, the freedom movement launched by the Congress would not be called a national movement. The British government had always harped on the thing that the Hindus and the Muslims as the two different communities. Until now, due to the patronage of the British, the Muslims were insisting that they were not only a separate community, but also a separate cultural national entity. Gandhi thought that the isssue of the Khilafat was a God-sent opportunity to bring about the Hindu-Muslim unity.

Jinnah was the President of the Muslim League. Yet, in spite of understanding the feelings of the majority of the Indian Muslims, he was unwilling to compromise on the issue of the Khilafat. And in his presidential speech at the convention of the League in Calcutta, instead of taking a firm stand on the issue of the Khilafat, he cleverly left ambiguity on the issue and misled the people.

He said, "Today, as a community we are attacked from the two fronts. The British government had attacked both our freedom and religion. Unfortunatley, we are not independent. Our voice at the international level is heard through our British masters. If our voice is to be heard internationally, the independence is the only option. The British government had promised us to protect the Khilafat. The promise is broken. Now we must ask ourselves how long we should remain loyal to the government which had broken the promise. The Congress and Gandhi had chalked out a programme on the issue of the Khilafat. Now you have to decide whether you want to accept the programme or not. Remember that once you decide there is no going back."

Thus, Jinnah had cleverly circumvented the whole issue of the Khilafat by his double talk. This was not possible with the Congress. Those days the different political organisations like the Congress, the Muslim League, the Home Rule League and the Hindu Mahasabha were working together. When the Congress held its session in Calcutta to discuss the issue of the Khilafat, Jinnah opposed Gandhi. He hoped that the leaders like Motilal Nehru and Chittaranjan Das would support him. Lala Lajpatrai was the President of the Congress. Jinnah hoped that a conservative Hindu like Lala Lajpatrai would never support Gandhi on the issue of the Khilafat. But he was stunned by the turn of events. Gandhi had entered the country's politics, particularly the Congress, hardly two years ago, while he had worked with the Congress leaders hand-in-hand since 1906. He was outraged that these leaders had ignored him and instead accepted Gandhi's pre-eminence in the Congress. He wondered, for the first time, how he could work in the Congress if the leaders had accepted the dominance of Gandhi this way.

Jinnah still remembered what Gandhi had said at the function organised in his honour by the Bombay Gurjar Sabha. Gandhi then had said, "Mr. Jinnah, in spite of being a Muslim, is enthusiastic about the public life and service to the country."

Jinnah did not pay much attention then to what Gandhi had said. Yet, he remembered how bitter Fatima was about Gandhi's remarks. He had laughed at her. He was born in a Muslim family, but how could that change his nationality? He was an Indian and looking at the issues only from the perspective of an Indian. He felt that according to Gandhi, a Muslim could not take part in the public life or serve the country. If a great leader like Gandhi harboured such prejudice against the Muslims then…

Jinnah was of the firm view that in the name of the Khalifa, who had nothing to do with the country, Gandhi was taking the freedom struggle on a different course. He feared that this would make the Muslim fundamentalists like the

Mullahs and the Maulvis more influential and powerful. This would polarise the country on communal lines. Jinnah's resentment to Gandhi's ideas had gradually transformed into personal animosity against Gandhi.

Gandhi had declared a non-cooperation movement against the British government, as a part of struggle for freedom. Until now, the Congress struggle was confined to making speeches, holding sessions, sending delegations, contesting elections, etc. Among the country's three hundred million people, only a small fraction could take part in the struggle. Gandhi had the experience of involving the common people in such a struggle successfully as he had done in South Africa. Gandhi felt that the struggle for freedom would not yield any result by giving mere speeches and memoranda. Therefore, if the common people join the struggle and organise strikes, public rallies and boycott the government offices, the schools and the courts, it would be difficult for the Englishmen to rule the country. Hence he had declared non-cooperation movement. A special session of the Congress was convened at Nagpur to chalk out a programme of action.

Jinnah was still livid about the Congress leaders supporting Gandhi on the issue of the Khilafat the previous year. Gandhi, the Congress and the fundamentalist Mullahs and Maulvis could not do anything on the issue. The British government had destroyed the Ottoman Empire of Turkey. Yet the religious bigots like the Mullahs and the Mauvlis were trying haplessly to save the Khilafat. The Congress and Gandhi were proved wrong. However, they were not willing to give up the issue. Jinnah felt that Gandhi was yet taking the country on a wrong path. Jinnah now remembered what Annie Besant had said in a meeting of the Home Rule League. She had said, "In a way, Gandhi is an extremist. He is interested in rupturing the social fabric. Inflicting pain on the self ... is his interest. Inflicting pain on the self is more important to him than freedom."

Jinnah believed that if the common people took to streets without understanding the politics, it would seriously harm the freedom struggle. Fortunately for him, Pandit Motilal Nehru and Chittaranjan Das did not agree with Gandhi on this. After discussing with them, Jinnah decided to oppose Gandhi's proposal for non-cooperation at the Congress session in Nagpur.

Lokmanya Tilak and Gopal Krishna Gokhale were no more. Had they been alive, they could have easily prevailed on Gandhi to abandon such a course of action. Jinnah had always thought so.

Prior to this, Gandhi and Jinnah had an altercation. Annie Besant had desired that Gandhi lead the Home Rule movement. She had resigned from the Presidentship of the Home Rule League. Jinnah had proposed in the meeting of the League that Gandhi should succeed Annie Besant as the President. The proposal was accepted. After becoming the President, Gandhi had proposed that the name of the Home Rule League be changed to Swaraj Sabha. Jinnah had opposed it. The members like Jaykar, Mangaldas Pakwasa and Kanaiyalal Munshi sided with Jinnah. Yet, the majority had accepted Gandhi's proposal. Gandhi declared that those who did not wish to associate with the new name of the organisation were free to leave.

This was a challenge to Jinnah. Annie Besant had resigned from the Presidentship to pave the way for Gandhi. And Jinnah had himself proposed his name for the Presidentship. Jinnah was associated with the Home Rule League for so many years. Gandhi, who had just arrived on the scene, could sway the majority in his favour and capture the organisation was something unbearable to Jinnah. Until now, Jinnah's career in the public life had shaped up with ease, without any struggle. He had never tasted defeat so far. Jinaah had always considered success as his privilege. The success that he had achieved so far had made him believe that he would never be defeated and if ever anybody defeated him, what would happen? how he would face it?—Jinnah very seriously thought about it. With this in mind, Jinnah opposed Gandhi's proposal for non-cooperation at the Congress session in Nagpur.

26

Jinnah's stand on non-cooperation, Nagpur session of the Congress, Ruttie-Jinnah at Lord Reading's banquet

Fatima had played a very important role in Jinnah opposing Gandhi's non-cooperation movement. This had happened rather unwittingly without Fatima and Jinnah realising it. As soon as the programme for the non-cooperation was announced, Fatima told her brother, "*Bhaijaan*, now the Congress leaders will be arrested and the government will confiscate their property. I do not understand Gandhi at all. Are you also going to join the Congress in this programme?"

"Fati," said Jinnah, "South Africa and India are two different countries. Gandhi has no experience of the people and the government here. Unfortunately, there is no one in the Congress to check Gandhi. Gokhale and Tilak are no more."

"So what! The Congress has big leaders like Pandit Motilal Nehru and Chittaranjan Das. You too, can show Gandhi his place," Fatima said teasingly.

"That's the problem," Jinnah said dejected. Suddenly it flashed to his mind that Motitlal Nehru and Chittaranjan Das had opposed Jinnah and sided Gandhi on the question of the Khilafat.

"Now all these leaders will go to prison and wear the clothes of convicts. They will wear shorts and vests and dig the ground or grind the flour on the grindstone. And when they are in prison, the government will harass their families and confiscate their property in order to recover fine. The people who can endure all this suffering alone will be called patriots," Fatima said jokingly.

But Jinnah could not laugh. He thought Fatima had presented a realistic picture of those people joining the non-cooperation movement. If the Congress accepted Gandhi's programme all the leaders will have to bear the consequences. Gandhi had experienced such eccentricities in South Africa. If the people supported Gandhi, they should be prepared to lead a rigorous prison life.

Jinnah glanced at his palatial bungalow. He looked at the carpets, the architectural designs and the magnificent furniture. He wondered how long he could endure the hard life in prison. Jinnah had opposed Gandhi's non-cooperation movement for political reason. It was due to the ideological differences. But now it was getting personal. If Gandhi became prominent on the national political stage, in this way, all that he dreamt about would be shattered. Gandhi was playing with fire. And he must be stopped by hook or crook.

Jinnah was in a predicament. His experience of working with the Muslim League had made him realise that none of its leaders could come close to him in stature. They could not think beyond the community, the Quran and the Islam. Jinnah was disillusioned that even after the great War, when the course of the world history was changing rapidly, the people were still thinking in the old fashion. However, he was happy that the Muslim League and Aga Khan, had accepted his leadership. He liked the nationalistic idelogy of the Congress and hoped to become a leader like Gokhale within the Congress. The Congress leaders and even the British government had recognised his eminence. Jinnah realised that if Gandhi was not stopped in his tracks, all that he had achieved would be ruined. His dislike for Gandhi intensified.

A large number of delegates had turned up at the Nagpur session of the Congress. This had baffled even the political observers. When the Congress was established in 1885, there were only seventy two delegates. This went upto five thousand in 1916 and upto seven thousand in the following year. The Nagpur session had more than fourteen thousand delegates. A large number of delegates were Muslims. This was an unusual situation. Gandhi's call for non-cooperation had created a patriotic fervour among the people. And when Gandhi made the speech moving the resolution for non-cooperation, he was applauded and cheered. He said, "Our non-cooperation is not against the British people. It is against the British government and our slavery. I know this non-cooperation means sacrifice. We may have to shed our blood. But at least the future generation would not accuse us of betraying the cause of independence of the country. Whether we shed blood or get killed, how does it matter?"

Jinnah was sharing the dias with Gandhi. Maulana Muhammad Ali, whom Jinnah disliked, was also present. Jinnah knew that Chitranjan Das and Lala Lajpatrai were opposed to Gandhi's non-cooperation. He was under the notion that they would oppose the resolution. In fact, Chittaranjan Das had brought about two hundred fifty delegates along with him to oppose Gandhi. However, Gandhi had pacified and won over them. Jinnah was not aware of this development. Both of them spoke in support of Gandhi's resolution. Jinnah could not tolerate this. If Gandhi could discuss and pacify them before the start of the session, why did not he discuss with him? Gandhi knew that he had also opposed him. Jinnah's position in the Congress was no less important than that of Chittaranjan Das, Motilal Nehru or Lala Lajpatrai. Did Gandhi consider him inferior to others?

Jinnah remembered what Gandhi had said at the function in Mangaldas Wadi. His echo was reverberating at this Nagpur session of the Congress. Though he was a Muslim, he was a patriot. Gandhi still considered him a Muslim and not a nationlist Congress leader. Jinnah's lean frame suddenly became stiff. Chittaranjan Das and Lajpatrai might have backed out, but Gandhi's resolution was not in the country's interest. How could the people call him *Mahatma?*[1]

A poised Jinnah, with an inexplicable smile, rose to address the delegates. He said, "This resolution of Mr. Gandhi..."

Before he could say anything, a chorus from the audience- "Not Mr. Gandhi, say Mahatma, say Mahatma."

Jinnah stopped for a while and then said firmly, "I oppose this resolution of Mr. Gandhi."

The chorus from the audience continued, "Not Mister, say Mahatma." Pretending as if he had not heard the audience, he said firmly again, "I would say with goodwill and respect to Mr. Gandhi,"the chorus again rose from the audience, "Not Mister, say Mahatma."

This time the President appealed to the audience to keep quiet and allow Jinnah to address. He said the dissent should be tolerated. Thereafter the delegates kept quiet. Then Jinnah addressed:

"The non-cooperation demands determination and will power. The limitations of human nature and the peoples' emotions are not taken into consideration. The basis on which Mr. Gandhi wants to launch this movement is completely at odds with the nature of the masses. It is unrealistic to assume that the collective endurance will bring the desired result. If the students boycott the schools and the colleges and spin the wheel, it will not pose any challenge to the British government. On the contrary, the youth would be misguided and their energy wasted. Their non-cooperation will have meaning only when we make alternative arrangement and provide them national schools and colleges on a large scale. We must remember that most of the children do not go to schools. Practising non-violence on a mass scale is itself against the human nature. If we teach the masses to boycott the government and break the law, they will not remain peaceful after independence and that can pose a serious problem to us. Creating this sort of mass hysteria will prove disasterous."

The speech of Jinnah sought to be disrupted by the audience. But undaunted by the disruption, Jinnah continued, "I do not agree with Mr. Gandhi's views on *Khaadi*[2] and *Swadesh*[3]. I want to ask the delegates present here—Have you accepted *Khaadi* completely? Have you boycotted the foreign goods completely? If we have not done this, why should we have this superficial programme?"

The delegates did not have the patience to listen to Jinnah's speech peacefully. They were influenced so much by Gandhi that they were not willing to listen any more. They had already made up their mind. Jinnah's speech did not have any impact on them.

Jinnah managed to complete his speech. But the delegates rejected his arguments. The Congress adopted Gandhi's resolution to launch the non-cooperation movement. Jinnah felt that the country's freedom struggle was going in a wrong direction. Gandhi, due to his fixed ideas, was playing a dangerous game with the country's history.

*

Lord Chelmsford's term as the Viceroy had come to an end. Lord Reading took over as the new Viceroy. The new Viceroy arranged a dinner party in order to gauge the political situation in the country. After a careful consideration, only a few selected guests were invited to the dinner party. It was arranged at the Viceroy's house in New Delhi. Mr. and Mrs. Jinnah were invited. As usual, Mrs. Jinnah, dressed in an ultra-modern style, attracted the attention of everyone present. When Ruttie was introduced to the Viceroy, as etiquette demanded, he accorded her a warm welcome. He hardly spoke for a minute with the other guests, but he spent more than ten minutes talking to Ruttie. While the other guests waited for introduction, the Viceroy was engrossed in talking to her even on personal matters.

At the banquet, Ruttie sat to the right side of the Viceroy. He engaged her in conversation enquiring about Jinnah, the politics, the weather and many other matters. Ruttie was astonished that the Viceroy was talking to her so much in the very first meeting, ingorning other prominent leaders. But she was enjoying the attention. It seemed as if he wanted to know every thing from the history, the geography and the social life in one go from her. In the midst of the conversation, the Viceroy said, "Mrs. Jinnah, I did not have the inclination to come to India."

"Really!,"said Ruttie surprised with eyes wide open, "Why, you do not like India?"

"Nothing like that. But I liked Germany more. I wanted to work in Germany for the British government."

"Then, why did not you go to Germany?" asked Ruttie.

"There is a reason," the Viceroy said quietly to her, as if he was sharing a secret with her, "The Germans reject the British. After the war, the Germans have begun hating the British. That is why I had to give up the idea of going to Germany." "Really!" Ruttie's eyes twinkled with mischief. She forgot that the person she was talking was the Viceroy and that she was his guest. She completely forgot the advice that Lord Chelmsford had given to her at Shimla a few years ago. She could not restrain. With a mischievous smile she asked innocently, "Really! Then, how can your Excellency stay in India?"

Lord Reading had no answer to this blunt question. He could not imagine that Ruttie would respond in this way. He felt hurt for a while. Then he turned to the other guests and started talking to them, as if he had not heard what Ruttie had said.

NOTES

1. A great soul.
2. A hand woven cotton cloth.
3. One's own country.

27

Ruttie-Jinnah incident of rain, Kanji-Ruttie dialogue in the 'South Court,' experiments on psychic power

Ruttie had another hobby, besides being crazy about the pets. The common people in Bombay were weary of the heavy rains. Ruttie had enjoyed the torrential rains right from her childhood. She would get drenched in the pouring rains and watch the raising tides in the sea. Her parents would rebuke her. She would get excited with the touch of rain drops.

After the birth of Dina, Ruttie had become a loving mother and a dutiful wife. She was no longer accompanying her husband on his travels across the country, like she had done in the past. She had to stay back at home to look after her daughter. Besides Dina, she had to take care of the pets. In addition to reading poetry, she also liked listening to Kanji's stories of experiences with the spirits. She would develop an urge to master the art. Sometime she would ask Kanji,"Why cannot you teach me this art?"

Then Kanji would reply, "This art is like mercury. It is very difficult to learn and use it in a proper way."

"However difficult it might be, I am interested in learning it. I am willing to do whatever you say," Ruttie said enthusiastically. Sometime when Jinnah heard them talking he would dismiss it with a cynical smile. Kanji used to discuss many things with Jinnah, but he never discussed this topic with him.

That day the dark clouds had hovered over the Bombay skyline. The daily life had come to a standstill due to heavy rains. The low lying areas were submerged with water. Ruttie, holding her pet cat in her arms, was watching the incessant downpour from her balcony. It created a rhythmic sound. It sounded like a melodious music to the ear. At a little distance, the roaring of the sea tides could be heard at the queen's necklace—the place that resembled Queen Victoria's necklace. Ruttie suddenly remembered that she did not have the opportunity to get drenched at the sea beach after she had left her father's house. She was excited. She thought how wonderful it would be to take Jinnah and run to the beach.

Fortunately, Jinnah was at home that day. He was preparing a case in his study room. To protect himself from the wet weather, he had closed all the windows. Ruttie unable to control her excitement ran to Jinnah. The way she had banged the door startled Jinnah. He asked her, "Hey! What happened! Why are you panting? Are you all right?"

"I am all right. Nothing happened to me. But if you do not come out with me right now, then something might happen," Ruttie said, playfully as she took away the papers from his hand and made him get up by holding his hand.

Jinnah could not understand Ruttie's behaviour. He thought that it was a prank.

"Ruttie darling, I have a very intricate case to argue tomorrow. Perhaps, I may have to sit very late."

Ruttie without heeding to his pleas, dragged him out of his chair.

"Look outside, how enchanting is the weather! And you are sitting inside with all the windows closed."

Jinnah came out, with his coat buttoned and the hands slipped into the pockets.

"Look how wonderful is the rain,"Ruttie said pointing towards the sea. "The sea is stormy. Come on! Let's go to the beach and get drenched"

"Get drenched!" Jinnah screamed as if he heard something terrible.

"Have you any idea, if you get drenched in this rain you might catch cold, even get pneumonia in no time."

Ruttie stood still. She had been getting drenched in the rain since her childhood. She had never caught a cold, leave alone pneumonia. In fact, the rain water had rejuvenated her body and mind.

"Please darling, come on! Do not say no," Ruttie said rather unexcitedly.

"Ruttie, the monsoon is the season of epidemics. It does not take time for the viruses to spread. The water is too dirty. These days, we should be more cautious. Even little carelessness can lead to sickness in no time," Jinnah said in all earnestness.

Ruttie had studied all this in her school days. But they were meant only for writing in the answersheets at the examinations. She had never experienced any such disease so far. She was surprised to know how frightened Jinnah was about the diseases. She gazed at her husband.

"However, if you want to go out in the rain, take the driver, close the windows of the car and take a round on the queen's necklace," Jinnah said putting his hand on her shoulder. And then turning towards his study room, he said, "Go and enjoy yourself, we will have coffee when you return."

Ruttie did not stop Jinnah. She looked at him as he entered the study room and closed the door behind. Then slowly she walked to her room, picked a book from the shelf and lay on the bed.

Two days later, on an evening as Ruttie lay on the sofa in a verandah watching the cats play, one of the cats sat near her rubbing her head against Ruttie's legs. Since the morning, she was not keeping well. She developed a headache in the afternoon. She told the servant that she would not entertain any visitors. Because of the electric work was in progress in the verandah, the electric wires and other equipments lay scattered here and there. And the workers having finished the day's work had just left.

A servant entered the verandah and handed over a visitor's card to Ruttie. It was Kanji's card. He visited them quite often, but only after taking prior appointment. There was no need for him to send the card. The security guards and the servants knew him pretty well. Today, his visiting without prior appointment and sending the card was unusual.

"Send him here," Ruttie instructed the servant.

Kanji entered the verandah after a while. He was wearing a neatly pleated *dhoti*[1] made of the mercerized cotton from a Manchester mill. His pristine white *Kurta*[2] was buttoned fully. He wore an embroidered blue cap and freshly polished shining sandals.

Before Ruttie could greet him, he was stunned as he saw her.

"Hey! Ruttie! What am I seeing? Wonderful! I cannot believe,"Kanji said excitedly raising his voice.

Ruttie could not understand anything. What was it that made Kanji so excited?

"Really! Am I seeing all this? The same sofa, the same verandah and...andthe electric wires...Oh! This is simply fantastic." Kanji said, his face showing the mixed emotions of surprise, happiness and curiosity.

Ruttie was perplexed. She sat on the sofa and then said, "I did not understand what you are saying. Come, let us talk."

Kanji sat on the sofa facing Ruttie. He was still surprised. He said, "I see you in front of me, yet I cannot believe. Three days ago, I had fallen asleep thinking of you. Then in my dream I saw you in this verandah, laying on the same sofa with the electric wires and the equipments scattered around."

"Really, what are you saying Kanji?" Ruttie said getting curious. "You have seen me in a dream, that is very surprising."

"It is not surprising seeing you in a dream, Ruttie. What is surprising is I saw you in this condition lying on the same sofa. I saw the same electric equipments. In the morning I laughed at the dream. But the next night also I saw exactly the same scene in my dream. I could even hear you speak. You were saying, "Kanji, help me." Today, when I was going home I suddenly felt that we have not met for quite sometime. Then I turned the car this way, though I did not have a prior appointment. As I entered the house, the servant told me that you would not entertain any guest as you were not keeping well. When I was about to turn back, the servant asked for my visitor's card. Then he told me to come here. And then I was surprised to see you lying on the sofa the same way I saw in my dream." Kanji explained in detail.

Ruttie listened with keen interest to Kanji. If what he was saying was true then she must have asked for his help. In fact, she was eager to experience the mystical power that Kanji talked about. And therefore, she wanted to take his help and learn the art.

"This is a very big psychic experience," said Ruttie, "This is an indication of my wish being fulfilled. Now you have to help me. Teach me the magic of experiencing what you had experienced."

At that time Jinnah joined them. On seeing Kanji, he felt surprised and happy. Three of them spent a long time together, drinking the champagne.

Ruttie gradually learnt the mystical art from Kanji. Sometime she would think in a strange manner that she had not ever imagined earlier. Whenever she met Kanji, he would ask her whether she had any such thought. She would be dumbstruck wondering how he could read her inner feelings.

"Ruttie, this is a kind of accomplishment. I have sent those thoughts to you. You will soon learn the para-psychology of exchanging thoughts." Kanji was opening a new mysterical world to her. Ruttie was gruadually comprehending the realms of the conscious and the subconscious mind.

In the midst of all this, Ruttie had developed a keen interest in communicating with the spirits through some mystical power. To achieve this art of communicating with the spirits lots of serious experiments were required. She would feel thrilled whenever she felt like having received some messages through the equipments kept on her table. But the moment the thrill ebbed, she would shiver with fear. For a long time, she would be frightened to stay alone in her room.

Ruttie got entangled in such psychic experiences. She was greatly influenced by Kanji. And whenever she had such thoughts, she would either phone Kanji or write to him sharing her experience. At times, she would not sleep the whole night and due to which would feel drowsy throughout the next day. And due to the drowsiness, she would experience with eyes wide open that as if she had slipped into a curious dream-world. Then in order to regain her physical and mental composure, she would drink two or three pegs. As her supernatural experiments increased, so also the intake of drinks.

One night, she was dead tired of such an experiement for hours together. Jinnah was out of station attending some political conference. Ruttie was alone in her bed room. Her whole body was aching. In spite of taking the pain killers and the sleeping pills, she could neither get any relief from the pain nor fall asleep. Too many drinks had affected her sleep. The ashtray was filled with the stubs and the ash of the imported cigarettes. She wanted to sleep, but the sleep was eluding her.

At midnight, she woke up unable to bear the chain of thoughts. Suddenly, a sense of fear had overtaken her. She phoned Kanji. And when he heard her voice over the phone, he asked her, "Ruttie, what happened to you at this midnight?"

"Kanji," Ruttie said frightened. "I want to sleep. I am scared. I do not get sleep. Please do something."

Kanji holding the receiver thought for a while and then ordered, "Ruttie, go to sleep. Ruttie, go to sleep. Ruttie, you go into a deep slumber. You must sleep…Ruttie…go…go…to sleep."

As the echoes of Kanji's voice boomed in her ear, Ruttie said, "I am feeling sleepy, Kanji. I am very sleepy, but I do not want to sleep. If I sleep you will go away. Then I will be lonely again. I am scared…but…but…I am feeling very sleepy."

"Yes, Ruttie. You must sleep. You are falling asleep. Just go, go to sleep," Kanji ordered again stressing on each and every word.

Ruttie fell asleep after a while.

NOTES

1. A loose, unstitched cloth, traditionally worn by men in India to cover the lower part of the body down the waist.
2. A stitched garment worn with the dhoti covering the upper part of the body.

28

Ruttie-Fatima confrontation about the pet cats, Jinnah-Ruttie quarrel, Kanji-Jinnah discussion about Dina's education, Ruttie's letter to Kanji on her leaving for London

Fatima had developed a sort of contempt for Ruttie for no obvious reason. Fatima possessive of her brother felt that her brother was snatched away from her after Ruttie's arrival. She would scream whenever she saw the pet dogs and cats moving around the bungalow and the garden. She would become furious about Ruttie's psychic experiments. Ruttie would spend hours on the experiments, ignoring every thing else. After the experiments, her facial expression and behaviour would change totally. All this was irritating to Fatima. She was trying to restrain, but she could not restrain any longer.

One day Fatima was sitting on a bench in the garden. Suddently, the electric bulb in the garden burst, resulting in darkness. When she started walking in the darkness, she stepped on a cat lying on the lawn. A scared Fatima jumped and unable to maintain the blance fell on the lawn crushing the cat under the weight of her body. The frightened cat meowed loudly in pain and started clawing in the air. The claws scratched Fatima's legs. An enraged Fatima kicked the cat hard, causing her to whimper in pain and run away. The servants came running, rescuing both Fatima and the cat.

Fatima's suppressed anger now came out in the open. She blamed Ruttie for what had happened. When Ruttie came out and stood near the cat, Fatima became all the more furious on seeing her. She lambasted her. The servants had applied some ointment on the scratches. It was not sufficient to cool her temper. She said in anger, "Ruttie, you have turned this palatial bungalow into a shelter for stray dogs and cats. Poor brother is too busy to spare any time and you have converted his bungalow into a public place. On the one hand we have these dirty animals prowling all around and the ghosts on the other."

Ruttie was enraged. Fatima not only kicked her pet cat and caused her pain, but was also lambasting her. She said in anger stomping her foot on the ground, "This is my house. What I do in my house or what I keep, is none of your business. Do not ever talk like this again."

Fatima could not bear this humiliation. She felt outraged. The servants and the cat turned quiet and it seemed as if they could sense the sparks flying between the two women.

Ruttie turned her back and went away. But Fatima's wounded pride made her restless. Their unexpressed feelings now took an ugly turn.

Ruttie gave the cat the first-aid in her room. And then suddenly she became emotional. She was deeply hurt by Fatima's behaviour. Fatima was treating her like a maid and not as the mistress of the house. Her father's bungalow located at a little distance was more beautiful than this house. But she was no longer welcome there where she had spent her much pampered childhood and youth. Now she had considered this South Court bungalow as her home. But Fatima said that she had converted it into a shelter for stray dogs and cats. And her psychic experiences with the spirits, Fatima derided as encounters with horde of ghosts. Ruttie could not bear all this. She buried her head in a pillow and lay on the bed crying for a long time.

When Jinnah returned home in the night, Fatima was sitting on the easy-chair near the front door. She had bandaged her injured legs. Jinnah noticed the bandage as he entered. Then he enquired, "Fati, what happened to your legs?" He bent down and touched the bandage gently. He saw the tears rolling down Fatima's cheeks. Jinnah was astonished. He had never seen Fatima crying like this. He handed over his coat to the servant and then, loosening his tie, sat on a chair next to Fatima.

"Fati, are you crying? What happened? Are the legs hurting?"

Fatima's feelings were deeply hurt. She expressed her feelings to Jinnah in a shrewd and calculated manner, "*Bhaijaan*, you have been my world until now. But what I had to hear today was deeply hurting. *Bhaijaan*, you tell me what I should do."

"Fati, you do not have to do anything. First calm down. I will talk to Ruttie. I know her. She is not an egoistic woman," Jinnah assured Fatima.

When Jinnah reached the bedroom, Ruttie was still lying on the bed. Her cats were jumping on the bed. A Pomeranian dog was sleeping under the bed, with legs stretched. Jinnah was not fond of the pets either. He was prejudiced particularly towards dogs. He felt dogs were dirty and disease spreading animals. He was scared from the childhood that dog bites could lead to dangerous diseases like rabbi. However, just to keep Ruttie happy, he had never objected to her pet dogs and sometime even patted them to please her. Now after listenting to Fatima, he too became somewhat irritated about these unwanted pets wandering in the bedroom.

Ruttie stood up suddenly on seeing Jinnah. She said, "Though the legal documents of the South Court are in your name, I have the right to half of its property and if the people staying in this house are not aware of it, please tell them."

Jinnah was stunned by this aggressive attitude of Ruttie. He got angry. It was not in his nature to suppress his anger. Yet, contrary to his nature, he remained calm and said, "Ruttie, I know. But in such matters, it is wise to be tolerant and behave with more understanding."

"That means I am not wise and behaving foolishly," Ruttie said in anger.

"I do not mean that. But if you feel that way then you are free to do," Jinnah said unable to suppress his anger.

"No, that means it has to be decided what I should say and what I should not," Ruttie flared up.

"Do not be foolish, Ruttie. Act like a grown up woman and try to understand. Such childish behaviour is unworthy of you."

"Really! I am behaving in a childish manner!" said Ruttie, "What about you and your sister's behaviour?"

The situation was blown out of proportion. Ruttie turned her face and slept off. Her behaviour had made Jinnah angry too. He made no effort to make her understand or pacify her.

*

It had become necessary to make some arrangement for daughter Dina's education. There was a dearth of good educational institutions in and around Bombay. She had been tutored at home by a tutor so far. It was necessary to secure admission in a regular school for all-round development. Jinnah and his friend Kanji were associated with Annie Besant due to the Home Rule League. Kanji had a keen interest in the Theosophical Society founded by her. She had established a big Centre at Adiyar near Madras. It was running a special school for children with emphasis on mental and spiritual development. It had good boarding facilities. Jinnah himself was never associated with the Theosophical Society. He never visited Adiyar. Kanji visited the centre quite often and was impressed by Annie Besant's educational experiments. Kanji felt that the education imparted at the school would produce altogether a different new generation in future.

When the question of education of Dina came up, Kanji suggested, "Jinnah, if you send Dina to the school run by the Theosophical Society at Adyar, she would not get a better education anywhere else. I have observed the educational system there. It will be a good choice for Dina."

Jinnah was silent for a moment. He was aware of the Theosophical Society. He thought for a while and then said,

"I have no doubt that the school at Adyar will be the best. I accept your suggestion. But…"

"But what?" asked Kanji interrupting.

"At the Adiyar school, nothing about the Islamic religion in the education is imparted. I want Dina to grow up as a Muslim. And then…"Jinnah stopped.

It was unusual for Jinnah to stop while talking. It surprised Kanji. He asked, "And what?"

"You know Kanji," Jinnah said frankly. "Dina is everything to me. I do not want to lose my daughter by keeping her away from me."

"What do you mean?" Kanji asked.

"I must remember what had happened to Dinshaw Petit. Whatever had happened to him in his life, I do not want that to happen to me in my life."

After that Kanji did not press him further. Jinnah also did not raise the issue again.

*

The British government had appointed the Sandhurst Committee to consider the mode of recruitment into the army. Jinnah was appointed as a member of the Committee. He went to London to attend the meeting of the Committee. Ruttie accompanied him. Kanji who was in Poona at that time had sent flowers to Ruttie wishing her a happy journey. She had received the flowers the day before the journey. She suddenly became sad, as she could not comprehend what was happening. She would be leaving the shores of Bombay the next day and would be cut off from the life here for many days. She would not be able to hear the sounds of her pet dogs and cats. She had made special arrangements for taking care of them. She would also miss the special room in which she had carried the psychic experiments. Ruttie suddenly realised that she would be terribly lonely in the days ahead. Some unknown fear had overtaken her.

She regained her composure after a while. She made some decision and wrote a letter to Kanji. "Kanji, I am going to a foreign country for few months. I will be lonely there. Please stay with me for my protection. I request you to create a magnetic protective shield for me and restore the faith that you are with me. I want your protective shield to reside in the stone of my ring."

After sending the letter, Ruttie felt that she was not alone any more. She had no doubt that on receiving the letter Kanji would create the magnetic protective shield for her by his psychic power.

29

Khilafat: Ali brothers' posturing, Gandhi's programme of action against untouchability, Jinnah's efforts to break the Congress and form a new party, Jinnah's communal attitude, Motilal Nehru's introduction of Jinnah to other members of the Central Legislative Assembly

Similarly the Muslims had not succeeded in the Khilafat movement in spite of Gandhi's leadership. Gandhi's non-cooperation movement also had come to an abrupt end without achieving anything. Thousands of the Congress workers had bore the brunt of batons and bullets and went to the prison. The minor skirmishes between the Hindus and the Muslims now turned into full-scale riots. The non-violence which Gandhi emphasised now became a victim. At a place called Chauri Chaura in Bihar, a group of people vented their anger and burnt a police station. Some nineteen policemen on duty were burnt alive. All of them were the Indians. When Gandhi learnt about it, he realised that the people did not understand the non-violent nature of the non-cooperation movement. Having realised that it was a Himalayan blunder on his part, he suspended the non-cooperation movement. On both the issues, Khilafat movement and the non-cooperation movement, Jinnah's stand proved to be right.

The Ali brothers who needed Gandhi's support to the Khilafat movement no longer needed him and the Congress. They had travelled the length and breadth of the country to seek support of the Muslims for protecting the Khalifa. They had appealed, through Aga Khan, to Kemal Ataturk of Turkey to become the Khalifa. They failed in their effort. Kemal Ataturk felt that Islam was the religion of the defeated people and that ever since Turkey became an Islamic country, all its progress came to a standstill. After receiving the rebuff from Turkey, the Ali brothers went to Arabia to plead with its King to become the Khalifa. The king of Arabia had realised that the Khilafat was a hollow concept. He showed the Ali brothers the door. He told them to get independence first, to become free from the slavery and then get involved in the international conflicts.

The Ali brothers had shown their true colours. They declared that even the lowliest of the Muslims was holier than Gandhi and that their Jihad would be incomplete till all the Hindus of India accepted the Islam.

The communal riots spread throughtout the country. The feeling of unity that the Khilafat movement had created among the Hindus and the Muslims now got decimated. The Muslim League and its leaders had reached an understanding with the Congress to press for the political reforms at the behest of Jinnah. Because of this understanding, they had dropped the demand for a separate communal representation and agreed for a common electorate. But under the changed situation, the League felt no need to honour the understanding. Consequently, they revived their old demands. This widened the chasm between the Hindus and the Muslims and created an atmosphere of distrust, animosity and hatred. Gandhi realised that without social awareness among the people, such non-cooperation movement would not succeed in the country. He decided to launch a movement against untouchability. The untouchability was a blot on Hinduism from time immemorial. He wanted to end the practice of untouchability. He announced a programme of action for removal of untouchability. In a population of 250 million Hindus in the country, 50 million were treated as untouchables. He condemned the treatment meted out to them by the Hindus as inhuman and launched a movement to bring about a social reform. The so-called untouchables must enjoy equal rights as the Hindus, he declared.

Jinnah had now developed an intensive hatred and contempt for Gandhi. He did not believe in untouchability. Yet he strongly believed that this was a social problem and it should not be mixed with politics. If Gandhi wanted to bring about a social reform, he must not interfere with the Congress and the politics of the country. The social reform was a different arena, and like religion it should not be mixed with politics. He feared that such social reforms would lead to misunderstanding between the Hindus and the Muslims.

Jinnah's fear proved right. The Islamic organisations were carrying the conversions in full swing until now. If a Hindu converted to Islam through coercion or otherwise wished to reconvert to Hinduism, Hinduism had no provision to re-admit such people. The conversion concept was not existent in Hinduism. It was a widely prevalent belief that a person belonging to another religion could not be converted to Hinduism. Hinduism was a way of life ordained by birth. By practising the conversion, the Islamic and the Christian organisations had increased their strength considerably. This had a harmful effect on politics. In such a situation, some Congress leaders like Lala Lajpatrai and Swami Shradhhanand decided to recovert the people to Hinduism. They started an aggressive *Shuddhi*[1] compaign for reconversion. The Muslims raised a hue and cry against the campaign. The Hindu leaders like Lala Lajpatrai and Swami Shradhhanand declared that if the Muslims put an end to the forceful conversion of the Hindus, they would stop the *Shuddhi* campaign. The Muslim leaders rejecting the offer declared that The Quran permitted the conversion of the *Kafirs* and, therefore, it was the Muslims' right to do so. How could the Muslims give up their rights known as *Tableegh*[2] and *Tanzeem*[3]? They would never give up their rights. But Hinduism had not given its followers the right to convert from another religion. Therefore, if the Hindus were converted to Islam it was a religious practice, but reconverting them to Hinduism through the *Shuddhi* was not a religious practice. Both the communities were getting polarised on this issue.

In such a situation, Gandhi's movement for the removal of untouchability was misconstrued by the Muslims. They declared that Gandhi started the movement to prevent the untouchables from converting to Islam in order to escape the atrocities committed by the upper caste Hindus. The social reform was a ploy. It was a conspiracy to reduce the population of the Muslims.

Jinnah was neither interested in *Tableegh* nor in *Shuddhi*. Gandhi now exercised absolute power in the Congress. The Congress was completely influenced by him. Jinnah had realised that by treading the path of Gandhi he would never become a leader in the Congress. Having worked for so many years in the Congress, he had great faith in Motilal Nehru and Lala Lajpatrai. He would often say that if these two leaders had worked with him it would be easy to secure independence. He even thought of breaking away from the Congress and floating a new national party if Motilal Nehru and Lala Lajpatrai and some other leaders supported him. Jinnah thought that Gandhi deviated from the path shown by Gokhale and Tilak. The new party could start afresh. He mooted the idea with some old guards of the Congress.

Jinnah's idea could not materialise. There were no takers. Under no circumstances would Jinnah accept the path adopted by Gandhi. Nor was he able to break away from the Congress and form a new national party. To him, Gandhi's talk of non-violence, impriosonment, *Khaadi,* celibacy and simplicity was pointless. He was convinced that, in order to establish himself as a supreme leader of the country, Gandhi was collecting a crowd of illiterate and ignorant people around him.

At this stage two important incidents occurred.

The last census of the country showed an imbalance in the population of the Hindus and the Muslims. Until now, no provinces other than the Noth Western Frontier Province and Baluchistan had the Muslim majority. In spite of having more than ninety per cent Muslim population, the Frontiner Province had joined the Congress and the national mainstream due to its leader Khan Abdul Gafar Khan, popularly known as the Frontier Gandhi. Now as per the last census, the Muslims became a majority in the important provinces of Punjab and Bengal. As a result, the representation of the Muslims in the Central and the Provincial Assemblies increased. Though Jinnah was a member of both the Congress and the Muslim League, he was getting elected from the Muslim

Constituency of Bombay. As per the new political reforms, fresh elections were to be held for the Central Assembly. He feared that if he contested as a Congress candidate, he might not get elected due to Gandhi's influence in the Congress. On the other hand, considering the growing population of the Muslims, he might have to accept the leadership of the Muslim League and contest the election. If he had to quit the Congress and his desire to form another national party did not succeed, the Muslim League would be the only sanctuary left out for him. He had decided to keep the sanctuary open to him.At the Lahore session of the Muslim League, considering the atmosphere, Jinnah changed his attitude and gave up his opposition to the separate communal representation. He declared that in the prevailing political situation in the country, the separate communal representation would benefit the Muslims. The other religious communities also should get the representation proportionate to their population. If the majority community was given a free rein and not restrained, the security of the minority communities would be endangered.

Jinnah was known for his secular credentials. The people across the country were shocked by his volte-face. Ruttie was the most disappointed. She was furious at her husband's attitude. She could not understand why Jinnah was adopting such a communal attitude that could divide the country. That the Muslims formed the main minority community in the country, did not mean the Christians, the Sikhs and the Parsees were not the minority communities. Ruttie was stunned that her husband supported the stand that could rupture the entire fabric of the country. When Ruttie confronted Jinnah, he had answered her in brief, "You won't understand all this, Ruttie. You should not get involved in this political game."

Ruttie became more furious. She refuted his answer. Jinnah did not agree with her. Nor did he give any reason for the change in his attitude.

"Instead of telling me that I do not understand anything, why do not you say that you are unable to explain the reason?" Ruttie said in a harsh tone as he questioned her ability to understand.

"You may think so," Jinnah said and ended the talk.

Gandhi felt that the Congress should not have participated in the elections of the Central Assembly. Pandit Motilal Nehru and Chittaranjan Das did not agree with him. The Congress adopted a resolution unanimously endorsing Gandhi's view. However, if Pandit Motilal Nehru and his friends wanted to contest the election without invoking the name of the Congress, they should be allowed to do so. They would not be stopped in the name of party discipline. As a result, Pandit Motilal Nehru established the Swaraj Party. Some forty two members were elected to the Central Assembly under its banner, including the leaders like Motilal Nehru, Chittaranjan Das, Pandit Malaviya, Bipinchandra Pal and Vithalbhai Patel. Jinnah was elected as an independent from Bombay. Besides, twenty two members were elected from other local bodies and the communal organisations. They included a few independents. Jinnah formed a group of independents and other members and became its leader. The leader of the Swaraj Party Pandit Motilal Nehru and the leader of the independents Jinnah decided to jointly confront the British Government in the Central Assembly. The things started to become difficult for the Viceroy.

The elected members of the Swaraj Party were not acquainted with Jinnah and his group. To introduce to each other, Pandit Motilal Nehru convened a meeting. There was no political agenda for the meeting. The meeting was convened to introduce themselves to each other and discuss the things with an open mind. The atmosphere was amicable and friendly. They were happy that their united front created difficulties for the Viceroy. Motilal Nehru, being the senior most, had known almost all of them. He introduced all of them. While introducing Jinnah to a new member, Pandit Motilal Nehru said, "Barrister Jinnah, who in spite of being a Muslim, is a staunch nationalist."

The member stretched out his hand. But Jinnah did not reciprocate. The way Pandit Motilal Nehru had introduced him shook him to the core. Gandhi also had said something similar years ago at a function in Bombay. He had remembered all that. Gandhi had said that Jinnah "in spite of being a Muslim, is interested in serving the country." Thereafter, when he was well acquainted with Gandhi, he found it difficult to understand his personality. But Motilal Nehru was different. Jinnah had considered him as a secular and liberal national leader. He was pained to find out that even Pandit Motilal Nehru harboured a notion that patriotism, nationalism and service to the country were the prerogatives of the Hindus and not of the Muslims. If the prominent national leaders like Gandhi and Motilal Nehru could say such things to a staunch nationalist like him, Jinnah pondered, what worse opinions they must be having about other Muslims.Jinnah was contemplating something in his mind throughout the meeting.

Both the groups functioned cohesively in the Central Assembly. The individual differences were not allowed to surface. A bill to promote industries was presented in the Assembly. The government did not want the Bill to be passed. Both the groups of Pandit Motilal Nehru and Jinnah were united to ensure that the Bill was passed. To discuss the Bill, the Viceroy convened a meeting of the Assembly at Shimla. The government tried to break the Swaraj Party and the group of independents so that some members could vote against the Bill and side the government. The atmosphere was quite tense.

Jinnah was staying at the Hotel Cecil in Shimla. The promiment industrialist of the country, Ratan Tata, was present at Shimla lobbying for the Bill. A member of the Assembly approached Ratan Tata and demanded a bribe of rupees ten thousand to vote in favour of the bill. He warned that if his demand was not met he would side the government. The voting was through a secret ballot. And he was sure that he would not be caught. Ratan Tata told about it to Jinnah.

On hearing this, Jinnah became furious."What? What did you say? Take me to that member who stooped so low for a vote. I will not rest till I drive out that corrupt and rotten member from here."

Ratan Tata somehow pacified Jinnah. The next day, he introduced the concerned member to Jinnah. Without mincing words, Jinnah bluntly asked the member, "Is it true, you have demanded a bribe for voting in favour of the Bill?"

Since Ratan Tata was present there, the member was dumbstruck. His face turned grim. Jinnah gave a final blow seeing his hapless condition.

"You will not get the bribe of even a rupee. The corrupt and greedy people like you should be thrown out of politcs. You go to hell. We will manage without your vote,"Jinnah shouted shaking with anger.

There was silence in the room. The member stood up without any eye-contact with Jinnah.

NOTES

1. The ritual by which converts from Hinduism are reconverted.
2. A practice of converting others to Islam.
3. A method by which Muslims are preventing from getting converted to other religions.

30

Ruttie-Adyar Theosophical Society, Rutti-Jinnah confrontation about Dina's education, Ruttie's addiction to drugs, Jinnah's stand on the Simon Commission, Secretary of State for India Birkenhead's proposals on constitutional reforms

As Ruttie had established the contact with the spirits and gained the supernatural experiences, she developed hightened mental tension. She had no idea what was happening to her. Gradually she was addicted to these experiences. She would get terribly upset if she did not have such experience for a day or two. She would take heavy drinks to control her anxiety.

Ever since Kanji told her that the knowledge of the supernatural was the basic principle of the Theosophical Society. She was eager to attend its annual convention. She got the opportunity this year. Jinnah was to accompany her to its annual convention at Adyar. Annie Besant had sent him a special invitation. Jinnah was never interested in the philosophy of the Theosophical Soceity. He had worked with Annie Besant for many years in the Congress and the Home Rule League. Ruttie was eager to go there. His friend Kanji too had persisted. Therefore, Jinnah was ready to go there. However, suddenly an important political meeting was convened in Delhi at that time. He was required to attend the meeting. Ruttie told him not to attend the meeting. But Jinnah had brushed her aside.

"Ruttie, you must understand the politics is my first priority. I cannot do anything else at its expense."

"That means, you give more importance to the politics than to me" said Ruttie annoyed.

"You assume too much. Nothing of the sort. Being a woman, you do not understand how important is politics to an ambitious man."

"I knew only this much, Jin, that you understand everything else except me," Ruttie said in a quivering voice.

Ruttie went alone with Kanji to attend the convention of the Theosophical Society. She did not take much interest in other activities at the convention. However, her attention was drawn to the school run by the Society. She saw the cute, healthy and agile children like flowers in the garden. She could visualise her daughter Dina among them. After learnig more about the school, she felt the school would be ideal for Dina's all-round development. She had expressed to Annie Besant the desire to admit Dina to the school. Annie Besant encouraged her,

"Mrs. Jinnah, we will be very happy, if your daughter is admitted here."

Ruttie was very happy. She looked at Kanji. His face was grim.

"Kanji, you must complete all the formalities for Dina's admission." Ruttie said entrusting the responsibility to him.

Kanji knew pretty well that he would not be able to discharge this responsibility. He had already made this suggestion to Jinnah. But Jinnah had rejected it. Kanji was very sure that the reason given by Jinnah for rejecting the suggestion would not be acceptable to Ruttie. He was in a dilemma as to what he should say before Annie Besant. However, when Ruttie had entrusted him the responsibility he thought it prudent to tell the truth.

"Ruttie," Kanji said, "I had a talk with Jinnah about Dina's admission to the school here and he did not like the idea."

"Did not like?"Ruttie was surprised. "But why?"

"Jinnah did not want to send his only daughter so far away from him," Kanji said looking at Annie Besant.

Annie Besant laughed and then said, "Oh! That is good news. I am surprised Jinnah has such emotional attachment with his family. I have never heard him talk anything except politics and law."

Ruttie felt that Annie Besant was echoing her feelings.

A little later when Annie Besant went out, Kanji told Ruttie the reason for Jinnah's objection. Ruttie was stunned. She could understand Jinnah's concern that his daughter should not leave him, considering the experience of Dinshaw Petit. But she was shocked to know that Jinnah was thinking in terms of Islam when it came to the education of his daughter. Jinnah was never connected to Islam, except being born a Muslim. He had studied The Quran and the *Hadith* in order to understand the laws of the *Shariat* and fight the cases of his Muslim clients in the Court. The *Quran* had never been a holy book to him. Ruttie had never seen him going to a mosque. He did not offer Namaaz even once a day, leave alone the mandatory five times. He could not do without wine and pork. How could such a Jinnah think of imparting the Islamic education to his daughter? Ruttie could not digest it.

On returning from Adyar, Ruttie handed over the admission form of the school to Jinnah and then said, "I want Dina to study in this school."

The astute Jinnah immediately understood. Ruttie must have come to know the talk he had with Kanji since he was with her at Adyar. He did not know what Kanji had told her. But if Ruttie did not know his views on this, she should know.

"Ruttie," said Jinnah, "There is no trace of Islam in the education imparted in this school. It is good if Dina learns to know about Islam."

"Do you want to bringng up Dina as a Muslim woman?"Ruttie asked him pointedly.

"Yes, what is wrong with that?" countered Jinnah.

"You are forgetting, Dina is not only a Muslim!"

Jinnah could not tolerate Ruttie saying that. He said ascertainingly, "You should know that Dina is a Muslim and the daughter of a Muslim family alone. You should know that. I am the father of Dina and…"

"I am her mother," Ruttie said interrupting Jinnah. "I am not a daughter of the Muslim family."

"Yes, but Ratanbai Dinshaw Petit had become Mariambai on the very day of the marriage. You too are a Muslim. And you must always remember this simple fact."

Ruttie was furious. She had expressed displeasure earlier when Jinnah had abandoned the national sentiment of the common electorate and accepted the separate electorate of the Muslim League. He had scoffed at her saying, "…you do not understand anything." And before going to Adyar this time, he had said that politics was more important to him. This meant Jinnah was now deviating from the national mainstream and joining hands with the Mullahs and the Maulvis. Ruttie was shaken up by this change in him.

She turned her back and went to her room without arguing any further. She lay on the bed and went on gazing at the sea waves through the window, quite for sometime—the same way she used to do in her father's bungalow. It was the same sky, the same sea, but the sound of the waves was different. She bit her lower lip and stood up. She took out a bottle from the cupboard and put some white powder on her palm. She removed a cigarette from a packet lying on the table. She pushed some powder inside the cigarette, skillfully rolled it and then lit the cigarette and started to smoke. She was intoxicated and forgot all the pain. She felt sleepy. She was fast asleep before the cigarette on the table could burn out fully.

The white powder had got the desired effect. It was cocaine.

*

Jinnah became indifferent to the activities of the Congress. His ambition to form a new national party by breaking away from the Congress remained unfulfilled. He was getting involved with the politics of the Muslim League without any reservation. Amidst all this distressing situation, his marital relation with Ruttie was also causing him a lot of unhappiness. His alliance with the Swaraj Party in the Central Assembly was not working well. Now Jinnah was spending most of his time in Delhi. A suite in the Cecil Hotel had become his second home. He made an office there to carry out his day-to-day activities. He carried out his routine work from there even when the Assembly was not in session and there were no court cases to attend.

The British government appointed a Commission to examine the progress of the political reforms introduced in 1919 and to make recommendations for more reforms in India. The Commission comprising of six members was headed by Sir John Simon. All of them were Britishers and there was no Indian member in the Commission. None of them was conversent with the history and the politics of India. There were massive protests against the Commission throughout the country. The Viceroy Lord Irwin announced that an Indian would be appointed to the Commission. Jinnah read this announcement in the newspapers. If he could somehow get appointed as the Indian representative in the Commission, Gandhi and the Congress had to recognise his importance. It was a good opportunity to contain Gandhi. In the last few sittings in the Central Assembly he had split from Motilal Nehru and supported the government on a number of issues. Therefore, he had a good equation with the Viceroy.

Jinnah convinced himself that if the Viceroy recommended his name to the Secretary of State for India he would be appointed as the Indian representative in the Commission.

But Jinnah was proved wrong. The composition of the Commission was already decided. Lord Birkenhead, the Secretary of State, was firm about not including any Indian in the Commission.

Jinnah could barely suppress his anger. He had now decided to protest against the Simon Commission. He supported the Congress call for boycotting the Simon Commission. He convened a meeting of the Muslim League in Calcutta to pass a resolution supporting the boycott. If no Indian was appointed in the Commission, the recommendations of the Commission would not be acceptable to the Indian people. He told the Muslim League to join the boycott. In the meantime, Mohammad Shafi was appointed as the member of the Viceroy's Executive Council. He opposed Jinnah's call for the boycott. That was natural. It would be suicidal on the part of Mohammad Shafi to support the boycott after being appointed as the member of the Viceroy's Executive Council. If the majority of the members of the League supported Jinnah, it would be embarrassing to him. He would be compelled either to support the resolution for the boycott or leave the League. Both these options were difficult for him. Jinnah was particular about getting the resolution passed. On the other hand, Mohammad Shafi was calling upon the members to oppose the resolution.

But the majority was with Jinnah. Realising this, Mohammad Shafi split the Muslim League and convened a parallel meeting of the League in Lahore. All the important members of the League were with Jinnah. If religion was invoked the break away group of Mohammad Shafi could create confusion among the rank and file. Keeping this in mind, Mohammad Shafi appealed to Aga Khan to become the President of his League. Aga Khan did not forget Jinnah's rejecting his invitation to join the Muslim League way back in 1906 and his changing the religious sect. Jinnah had also refused to accept Aga Khan as the religious head. Aga Khan accepted the Presidentship of Mohammad Shafi's League. At the meeting of the League in Lahore a resolution was passed to support the Simon Commission, while the League in Calcutta had passed a resolution to boycott the Simon Commission.

The Secretary of State, Lord Birkenhead, came to know that Jinnah had supported the Congress call for boycotting the Simon Commission. This was at the cost of splitting the Muslim League. He sent a message to the Viceroy to ignore Jinnah and not to give him any importance. And he instructed him to ensure that the Simon Commission meets only the Muslim representatives endorsed by Mohammad Shafi. Besides, the other representatives of the dalits and the backward communities opposed to the Congress could meet the Simon Commission. He advised him to give wide coverage to such meetings in the newspapers to instill a sense of fear among the Hindus.

It was not possible to garner the Muslims support by ignoring Jinnah, as dsesired by Birkenhead. The Hindus were not afraid of such attempts. Wherever the Simon Commission went, it was greeted with protests. The Commission was a total failure. Those who met the Commission as the people's representatives, at the behest of the government, had no influence whatsoever on the public life. It was for the first time since the Khilafat movement that both the Congress and the Muslim League followed a unified direction.

As a result, the Simon Commission could not achieve anything. It created a political turmoil. The poltical reforms could not materialise. The Simon Commission was not in a position to make any recommendation. The Secretary of State for India, Birkenhead, commented sarcastically on the Indian leaders who boycotted the Simon Commission saying that they themselves were not competent to draft a constitution for India. And when the British government was making efforts to draft the constitution for India, they were not cooperating. There were many different political parties and differences of opinion in India. Therefore, they were not able to reach a consensus on the constitutional reforms. Those who had boycotted the Commission should take the responsibility of drafting the constitutional reforms.

This was a challenge for the Indian people. The Indian National Congress, the single largest political party, alone could not do much to drafting the constitutional reforms. Considering the rigid stand of the Muslim League, even the other religious communities of Sikhs, Christians and Parsees and the Hindu Mahasabha, became politically conscious of their rights. The Congress wanted to carry all of them along. An all party conference of some twenty nine big and small parties was held in Bombay. The conference was held under the leadership of Pandit Motilal Nehru. The progress of the political reforms introduced in 1919 was reviewed. The Secretary of State for India had challenged the Indian leadership. The Congress wanted to present a new constitution as a befitting reply to him.

Jinnah stood firm like the rock of Gibraltar amidst all this commotion. He felt mortified. He was deviating from the path he had chosen. He was petrified by the thought. But he had no doubt that he would succeed in public life only through the path that he had now chosen.

His stay in Delhi had been unusually lengthy. In between, he could have gone to Bombay if he had desired. But he was annoyed with Ruttie on the question of education for Dina. As a matter of fact Ruttie, of late, was drifting away from him. And he was feeling quite lonely. On the pretext of a busy political schedule, he went on extending his stay in Delhi. His health deteriorated over the past few days. He was troubled by fever, cold and cough. The smoking and the consumption of alcohol had increased.

When a tired and sick Jinnah returned to Bombay, Fatima told him that Ruttie had left the South Court. She had booked a suite in the Taj Mahal Hotel and started living there separately.

31

Ruttie in Taj Mahal Hotel, Jamshed meeting with Ruttie, Payment of Hotel bills by Jinnah

Jinnah was speechless when Fatima gave him the news. He stood up from the armchair in his drawing room in which he was habituated of sitting and relaxing daily. He gazed at the sky through the window with his eyes wide open. He turned back and started walking as if he had made some decision.

"*Bhaijaan*...,"Fatima called out her brother slowly as he moved towards the front door.

"Fati! You don't worry. I will be back soon," Jinnah answered without turning back and looking at Fatima. And he climbed down the stairs before Fatima could say anything.

The servant unloaded Jinnah's luggage from the car only a few minutes ago. And before the driver could park the car in the garage, Jinnah sat in it and said, "Driver, take the car to the Taj Mahal hotel."

The driver turned around. Jinnah did not look at him. The driver did not dare asking anything going by the facial expression of Jinnah. He steered the car out of the bungalow.

There was an unusual silence on the way. It was a total silence except for the noise of the passing vehicles. It was a pleasant cool day of January. The cool breeze blowing inside the car from the sea on the Queen's necklace was pleasant and soothing, but Jinnah was not in a pleasant state of mind to enjoy it. When the car stopped at the majestic Taj Mahal hotel, built up of huge stones, the driver had to remind Jinnah.

At the hotel reception, Jinnah enquired about Ruttie's suite and reached there. He knocked the door two or three times, as a part of etiquette. Then he pushed the door and entered the room. He stood at the door for a while as he saw the scene inside the room. Ruttie was fast asleep in the sofa. He saw an half empty glass of drink on the tea-poy and some white powder drug scattered and the drug filled cigarette butts in the ashtray. The tools lying around were indicating that Ruttie had communicated with some spirit. Even in this new abode, the pet cats of Ruttie were moving around in such a way as if they understood the grim situation.

Jinnah stood there quietly for some time. It did not take him much time to understand the situation. He felt deeply hurt. And at the same time he closed his lips tightly to appear as if nothing had happened. He turned back without uttering a word and left the room.

Kanji was the only contact that Ruttie had with the outside world. He came to meet her practically every day. Sometime, he would see Ruttie in the same condition in which Jinnah had found her. But, unlike Jinnah, he would not leave the room, but waited until she woke up.

As the days passed, the condition of Ruttie deteriorated and she was lapsing into a state of total loneliness and oblivion. She became totally careless about herself. Returning to her father's house was out of question. Hence, she stopped thinking about it. She did not inform her parents about her condition. She did not even know that Jinnah had visited her. She felt deeply grieved that Jinnah did not bother to enquire about her, in spite of the fact that she was living separately in the hotel.

One day Jamshed came to meet her along with Kanji. Ruttie knew him even before her marriage. Jamshed was quite close to Jinnah. He also had business relation with Dinshaw Petit. Jamshed was a soft spoken but shrewd person. Though Ruttie was surprised to see him with Kanji, she welcomed him nonetheless.

After the formal greetings, Kanji said, "Ruttie, Jamshed has not come just to enquire about your condition, but he wants to tell you something important."

"I know, Kanji. It is not difficult for me to understand that he came here for a special purpose," said Ruttie.

"I have full faith in you," said Jamshed cautiously and continued, "I came here because of that faith."

"Jamshed, say what you have in your mind without any hesitation."

"Thank you, Ruttie. This is what I expected from you," Jamshed said and stopped for a moment. He took a deep puff from the cigarette held in his hand and then said, "Ruttie, I want you to forget all the differences with Jinnah and return to the South Court."

Ruttie had expected this. She said, "Mr. Jamshed, this is your wish. It is nice of you to think so. I am thankful to you. That's all."

"This is not only my wish. This is the wish of all those wellwishers of you and Jinnah. We don't know what differences both of you have and what happened between you. We do not want to know," said Jamshed.

"Jamshed, you won't understand, even if you want to," Ruttie said dejected. "Nothing has happened between us. Jin is a gentleman. I have no complaint against him."

"But then why?"

"Enough, I know this much that we cannot live together any longer," Ruttie said to stop the conversation. Jamshed and Kanji looked at each other. Seeing them looking at each other, Ruttie took the half-empty glass of drink from the tea-poy and gulped it. Then she pulled the cat sitting on her right into her lap.

When Jamshed and Jinnah had met two days ago, the latter had said something similar. Jamshed told Jinnah that he should sort out the differences with Ruttie and bring her back to the South Court. He felt that Ruttie was addicted to drugs due to mental depression. He had seen her grow up, her marriage and her life after marriage. Ruttie was ignorant about the outside world, but she was tender and sensitive. She had liking for art and literature. She loved dance and music. Jamshed felt that she was more innocent and tender than an average person. If she was mentally depressed she ought to receive proper treatment. Jamshed tried to talk to Jinnah frankly on this. Jinnah said something similar to what Ruttie had said,

"Jamshed, I still love her as much as I loved her before the marriage. I do not blame her for leaving the South Court. It is unfortunate that she is surviving on the drugs. This is a misfortune not only for her but also for me, but..."

"But what, Mr. Jinnah?" Jamshed interrupted him, "If you understand this, where is the problem?" He looked at Jinnah with a glint of hope.

"Jamshed, there is only one solution. Our paths are different. We cannot live together any longer. Enough! This is a hard reality and we must accept it," Jinnah said raising his index finger.

Then Jamshed felt that Jinnah's stubborn nature would not permit him to arrive at a compromise even if he wanted. Jinnah did not make any complaint against Ruttie. Nor had he blamed her for anything. Instead he expressed his love for her. In such a situation, if his stubbornness was kept under control, things could improve. Jamshed felt, Ruttie could take the first step. He was confident that Ruttie would be able to handle Jinnah's stubbornness.

However, after talking to Ruttie, his faith in her was shattered. She also did not express any contempt or anger towards Jinnah. Yet, she too had expressed the hard reality—"We cannot live together any longer."

Thereafter Jamshed dropped the issue.

As per the norms of the Taj Mahal hotel, Ruttie had paid some advance amount towards the lodging and boarding expenses. She would receive the bill at the end of every week for the expenses incurred by her. Initially she received the bill. But thereafter she stopped receiving such bills. She forgot about the bills as she became totally isolated and lonely. Most of the time she spent on experiments with the psychic powers. Sometime, she would call for the English poetry from the Taj bookstall and read. And sometime, she would enter into a monologue for hours together with her pet cats. Kanji was the only link she had with the outside world. Whenever Kanji met her, he would deliberately avoid talking about Jinnah. Then Ruttie would ask him, "Kanji. Is it true, Jin is turning communal? Jin should remain a nationalist. I cannot imagine Jin becoming a protagonist of communalism."

"No, Ruttie, Mr. Jinnah is a nationalist. It is the propaganda of the Congress backed newspapers that he is tilting towards communalism," Kanji would say reassuring her.

"That's what I expect from Jin," Ruttie would say satisfied and then tell Kanji,

"Kanji, you take care of Jin and keep me informed about him."

Thereafter, the conversation on Jinnah would come to an end. Even if Kanji wanted to extend the conversation, Ruttie would stop him. Once again the bottle of drink, the imported cigarettes and the drugs would become her companions.

Ruttie suddenly remembered that the hotel had not sent her the bills for so long. She wondered how she forgot the bills for so many days. She might have forgotten the bills, but how could the hotel forget to give the bills? She felt embarrassed. She was not new to the Taj Mahal hotel. She came here more often with her father, her friends and later with her husband to attend the political meetings. Perhaps the manager must be knowing her, but that did not mean he should not send her the bills for her expenses. Feeling embarrassed, Ruttie called the hotel accountant over the phone and said apologetically,

"Gentleman, I regret I could not pay the bills on time. I am surprised, even you have not sent the bills to me. Please now send the bills so that I can make the payment."

"Thank you, madam," the voice over the phone said politely, "All your bills are paid."

"The bills are paid!" Ruttie expressed surprise, "Perhaps, there is some mistake. I have not paid any bills so far."

"Madam, it is true, you have not paid the bills. But Mr. Jinnah has deposited enough money in your account and instructed us to send the bills to him,"the voice over the phone clarified.

Ruttie was taken aback. She did not expect this. All along she was feeling that Jinnah did not bother to enquire about her whereabouts. Jinnah was not only aware of her stay in the hotel, but made the provision for making the payment of her bills. The news was so unexpected that she abruptly disconnected the telephone receiver without thanking the accountant.

Kanji did not turn up for two days. Ruttie grew restless. She tried to talk to him over the phone, but he was not available. When Kanji came to meet her on the third day, tears rolled down from her eyes.

"What happened, Ruttie? Has anything happened?" Kanji asked.

"Yes, something has happened," Ruttie said wiping her tears.

"You have not come to see me for two days. Nor have you contacted me."

"Oh! Ruttie, I am sorry. I was held up somewhere else. I did not get any time at all. To be honest, I was under so much pressure of work that I could not even sleep."

"Oh! Really!" Ruttie said and then slowly continued, "Even I have not slept for the last two nights."

"Come on! Let me put you to sleep. Ruttie go to sleep," Kanji ordered changing his voice suddenly.

"Oh! No! Kanji," Ruttie said stretching her hands.

"Not now, if I fall asleep, you will go away. I want you to stay for some time more. Please do not put me to sleep."

"Okay! As you like. Don't worry and get alright," Kanji accepted Ruttie's wish like an obedient pupil.

"Kanji, can I say something?" Ruttie asked suddenly.

"Yes. What is that you need my permission to say?"

"Kanji, dear, I think you should not have been born in this world to wear a *dhoti* .

You should have been born as someone who could wear a saree or a skirt,"Ruttie said and closed her eyes.

Kanji was stunned and glanced at Ruttie. He could not understand what Ruttie was trying to say.

32

Jinnah's meeting with prominent Muslim leaders in Delhi, Fatima-Jinnah discussion on communalism, Gandhi-Jinnah views on the Shariat, All party meeting in Bombay on the Nehru Report, Jinnah's opposition to the Nehru Report, meeting of the Muslim League, All party meeting in Delhi on the Nehru Report, Jamshed at Delhi station, Hooting of Jinnah in the train

A committee, headed by Pandit Motilal Nehru, was formed in the all party conference of 29 political parties and groups held in Bombay to work out a new constitution for the country. Before the Committee could take a concrete shape, some important events occurred.

The illusory unity between the Hindus and the Muslims that had emerged over the issue of the Khilafat evaporated like the dewdrops in the sun. Now it was evident that the understanding reached between the Hindus and the Muslims in 1916, at the behest of Jinnah, was limited to the issue of the Khilafat. The polarisation between the two communities grew day-by-day resulting in communal riots in different parts of the country. The Muslim League claimed to be the sole representative of all the Muslims in the country. Jinnah had emerged as the supreme leader of the Muslim League. However, he was aware that, except for a few Mullahs, Maulvis, Ulemas, Nawabs and landlords, the seventy million common Muslims in the country had nothing to do with the Muslim League. In such a situation, fresh efforts for brining the Hindu-Mulsim unity might succeed. The communal issue of Khilafat was no longer a relevant issue. Now the bone of contention between the Muslim League and the Congress was over the issue of a separate communal electorate and a common electorate. However adamant the Muslim League might have been on the issue of the separate communal electorate, Jinnah knew pretty well that the common electorate was in the best interest of the country. Jinnah's astute mind knew that the communal electorate was dangerous to the country. His inability to make his voice heard in the Congress and secure its leadership and that he could become the leader of only the Muslim League, had made him abandon the issue of common electorate, as a policy of expediency. Now due to the changed situation, he made another effort to revive his original idea.

Jinnah thought that his fresh effort would succeed if he received the support of the entire Muslim community instead of the support of only the Muslim League. He convened a common meeting of prominent Muslim leaders, groups and institutions in Delhi to achieve that purpose. At the meeting, he had presented skilfully his proposal. A resolution was adopted to the effect that without breaking the national unity, the interest of the Muslims should be protected. It was also agreed upon to give up the separate communal electorate that the Muslim League had secured and accept the common electorate. Jinnah made the Muslims to be a part of the national mainstream. The Muslim League was a party to the resolution. This was a great political triumph for Jinnah.

However, while accepting the common electorate, it was demanded that the Muslims should be given adequate representation in the government. Further it was demanded that the seats in the Provincial Assemblies of Punjab and Bengal, where the Muslims were a majority, should be allotted in proportion to the population, and the Muslims should be allotted one-third of the seats in the Central Assembly. The Congress Working Committee had accepted the demands. Thus, once more the country's two major political parties, namely the Congress and the Muslim League had reached an understanding on the issue of the common electorate. This was personally another achievement of Jinnah.

But Fatima was not happy about it. She was annoyed about her brother making the Muslim League accept the demand for the common electorate. The Muslim League was established to maintain a separate identity from the Hindus. If the Muslim community became one with the other religious communities, the purpose of the Muslims ruling the country for hundreds of years would be defeated. She expressed her unhappiness to Jinnah, "*Bhaijaan*, though you understand politics better, do remember that the talk of unity with the Hindus is dangerous to the Muslims."

Fatima's anti-Hindu sentiment was not unusual. But Jinnah never took it seriously until now. He thought, like the Mullahs and the Maulvis, she had some religious prejudices.

"Fati, the community will survive only when the country is secure. Nobody can harm the seventy million Muslims,"said Jinnah.

"Bhaijaan, you do not understand these Hindus," said Fatima, "They do not even drink water from a Muslim's house. To them, the Muslims are an impure lot. They take bath even if they touch a Muslim. We cannot have any understanding with such Hindus," Fatima said in a firm tone.

"Fati, just as the Hindu saints and priests have created misunderstanding about the Muslims, the same way the Mullahs and the Maulvis have created misunderstanding about the Hindus in the name of Islam. This is the result of that. It is important for both these communities to keep away the religious fundamentalists and come together," said Jinnah.

Fatima did not argue further. She knew that Jinnah, being a successful lawyer, was good at arguments.

Around this time, a raging controversy arose about the conflicting social customs and traditions followed by different religious communities. The government was thinking of bringing about a common civil code that would determine the laws relating to marriage, divorce and inheritance so as to secure justice to all communities. The Muslims were more sensitive about these issues than other religious groups. In the seventh century, Prophet Mohammed had prescribed the social norms and rules codified in the *Shariat,* which the Muslims considered sacred. The educated and progressive Muslims organised a national seminar to discuss the *Shariat.* The eminent social reformists and progressive Muslims and the fundamentalist Ulemas, Mullahs and Maulvis were invited to take part in the seminar. Both Jinnah and Gandhi were invited as the main speakers.

The fundamentalists vehemently opposed to any changes in the *Shariat.* They argued that the Muslims would die to defend the *Shariat.* They were greeted with huge applause.

Jinnah spoke with logic and firmness, "What is there in *Shariat* that cannot be changed? Many changes were made in the *Shariat* already. Then why did not anybody question its sanctity? The government had changed the Islamic law relating to crimes and punishment of criminals. The Islamic law relating to witness and evidence is not considered valid. And the commandment of the Quran to deny the right to inheritance to those who convert to other faiths or punish them with death penalty is no longer practised. Considering all this, it is important to change the *Shariat* law in order to keep pace with the time and secure social justice."

Thereafter Gandhi said in his speech, "The *Shariat* is not only a law, but a sentimental religious order for the Muslims. This order was bestowed by the Quran. It is therefore natural that, as per the tradition, the Muslims consider it as a direct command of God. Taking this into consideration, the government should not contemplate any changes in the *Shariat.*"

The Muslim audience applauded Gandhi and concurred with his views. Jinnah looked at Gandhi with bitterness and contempt.

Jinnah wondered whether it was Gandhi's ploy to keep the Muslims orthodox and backward or a clever move to attract them to his side. How could Gandhi achieve independence for the country with such a medieval mindset? When the people world over were discarding the outdated Shariat law, how could the Indian Muslims keep pace with the modern world by adhering to it? How a shrewd person like Gandhi could overlook this plain truth? Jinnah was perplexed by these thoughts.

*

Jinnah was abroad when the Nehru Committee was formed at the all party conference convened in Bombay by the Congress. In his absence, two members of the Muslim League were selected as members of the Committee. In the very first meeting of the Committee, comprising of representatives from various political parties and interest groups, the Hindu Mahasabha and other religious organisations of the Sikhs, the Christians and the Parsees had raised an important issue. The Muslims demanded allotment of seats in the provincial Assemblies of Punjab and Bengal more than proportionate to their population. This was vehemently opposed by all other groups. As per the last census, the Muslims were a majority in Punjab and Bengal. The Congress had asked the local people to boycott the census, as the census forms sought the information relating to family, religion and caste. The Congress suspected that the government intention behind collecting such information was to segregate the tribals and dalits from the Hindus. Consequently, many Hindus had boycotted the census. Nevertheless the government went ahead with the census, and when the census figures were announced, the Muslims turned out to be a majority in Punjab and Bengal. The Hindu Mahasabha and the other groups contended that the census figures did not reflect the true picture as the Hindus had boycotted the census. They also contended that the Muslims could not be allotted one-third seats in the Central Assembly, more than proportionate to their population. Now the other religious groups also demanded that they too should have reservation of seats like the Muslims. It was a difficult situation for the Congress. The Congress was in a dilemma. The Congress had earlier accepted Jinnah's proposal to reserve seats for the Muslims. However, if this reservation was incorporated in the constitution, the demand of other religious groups should also be accepted or else it would be an injustice to them. The Congress had no option except satisfying all the groups. Hence the Congress did not think it wise to implement the Jinnah proposal. As a result, the Muslim League broke away from the Nehru Committee.

The Nehru Committee had completed its task and sent the draft consitituion to all the members of all party conference for acceptance. Jinnah was still abroad. Mohammed Ali Chagla, a prominent leader of the Muslim League, had accepted the draft on behalf of the League. Pandit Motilal Nehru sent a copy of the draft to Jinnah at his foreign address and asked him to send his views on it. He also told Jinnah to discuss the draft with him before making any public statement about it. Jinnah was enraged when he learnt that the Congress had not acted on his proposal. The Nehru Committee provided for the system of common electorate in the draft constitution, but gave no assurance about representation to the Muslims. Jinnah thought that the Muslim League would never accept the draft. He felt the Congress had betrayed him once again. He had no doubt that the Congress had done this under the influence of Gandhi. He realised that it would not be possible for him to work in the national politics by following the path of Gandhi. To Jinnah, Gandhi's ideas and behaviour were illogical and obscure.

On returning to Bombay, Jinnah contacted Chagla and said,

"Who had authorized you to accept the Nehru report on behalf of the Muslim League?"

Chagla said in a polite and firm tone, "I acted as per my conscience and what I did was in the interest of the community and the country."

"You are wrong on this," said Jinnah in a harsh tone.

"Then let us take it up in the meeting of the Muslim League," Chagla said putting an end to the conversation, "But, please do not make any public statement in haste rejecting the Nehru report."

When the Nehru report was taken up in the meeting of the Muslim League, Chagla and Jinnah argued for and against the report. Jinnah presided over the meeting. Chagla had forcefully argued in favour of the Nehru report. There was a great deal of excitement and commotion among the members. Chagla's argument had an impact on the members. An astute Jinnah immediately understood it. He realised that if the voting was done a large number of members might vote in favour of Chagla. And if that happened he would not be able to claim that he was the undisputed leader of the Muslim League. Taking advantage of the commotion and fearing challenge to his leadership he adjourned the meeting.

When the meeting was reconvened Jinnah succeeded in luring back the members who had broken away under the leadership of Mohammad Shafi on the issue of boycotting the Simon Commission. Jinnah told the members that the Nehru report had not considered his proposal unanimously adopted by the all party Muslim convention in Delhi. Therefore, the Nehru report should be rejected. Jinnah convinced the members and got the resolution adopted that the Nehru report could not be accepted until and unless the Delhi proposal was incorporated. However, there was a rift between the members on this issue. The regional outfits of the Muslim League in Punjab and Bengal adopted a resolution accepting the Nehru report, overruling the central leadership of the League. The political situation was very fluid and uncertain.

Jinnah personally met Motilal Nehru and other Congress leaders. He soon realised that young leaders of the Congress were not happy with the Nehru report, as it had accepted the Dominion status for the country instead of complete independence. The prominent among them those who were not happy with the report were Subhas Chandra Bose and Jawaharlal Nehru. Taking this into consideration, Jinnah thought that he should present his view point once again before the all party conference. He had no objection in accepting the system of the common electorate proposed in the Nehru report. Personally, he was in favour of the common electorate, and even the Muslim League had favoured the common electorate. If the all party conference accepted the proposal for one-third representation to the Muslims, the Muslim League would have no objection in endorsing the system of the common electorate. Presently, the Muslims had twenty seven per cent representation in the Central Assembly. This was also not proportionate to their population. Now, if the Congress accepted a mere increase of six per cent, the common electorate would become a reality. Then the scourge of a separate electorate would be banished and the problem of communal disharmony would be solved once and for all.

An all party conference was convened in Delhi to discuss and take a decision on the Nehru report. Besides the Congress and the Musim League, the Hindu Mahasabha, the Home Rule League and the organisations of the Sikhs and the Christians and the interest groups like the Chambers of Commerce participated in the conference. Jinnah made an emotional appeal to all of them saying,

"Please do not misunderstand me. Nobody should have the slightest doubt that the Hindus and the Muslims should march together for the country's progress. There is no point in the Muslim League accepting this report as the millions of the Muslims in the country have a fear. The truth is that such a fear must be allayed from the minds of the people of every community. We are the children of this land and we all must live together. We cannot live without the mutual feeling of give-and-take. Only those who have something can give. The majority community have something to give. They must give the minority community generously, a bit more, and remove its apprehensions. I appeal to you to understand the Muslims' sentiment and to be generous to them so as to put an end to the Hindu-Muslim problem permanently. The Hindu-Muslim unity is my dream and I would be the most happy person in the country if that is achieved."

Jinnah was not destined to receive success at the conference. The Congress was annoyed with Jinnah making a reference to the Muslim League when he was a member of the former. If the Muslims were given representation more than proportionate to their population, the other miniority groups should also get similar representations. Jinnah's plea on behalf of the Muslims was rejected. The members expressed their disagreement and displeasure and raised slogans intermittently during his speech. Some of them even refused to listen to him. The audience jeered at him with cries of "Jinnah, sit down...Jinnah is communal...Jinnah is the agent of the British government." And when Jayakar spoke against Jinnah he received a loud applause from the audience. Jinnah could not bear all this. Nobody accepted his proposal. When it came to voting, the members of the Muslim League and another Muslim group called the Khilafat Committee staged a walk out. The *Ahmediya* Muslims voted with the majority.

Jinnah realised that now he had no other option. Until now, the Muslim League too doubted him. Jinnah worked with the Congress leaders. He was opposed to the Muslim League right from its inception. Everyone knew that Jinnah was against the separate electorate and favoured the common electorate.

His detractors in the Muslim League kept this issue alive to prevent him from emerging as the undisputed leader of the Muslims. Because of his stand, Jinnah was even nicknamed as *Kafir*. Jinnah had no hope in the Congress. During the past five years, Gandhi concentrated less on politics and more on the programmes of social reforms like *Swadeshi, Khaadi* and the removal of untouchability. He was not present at the all party conference which constituted a committee under the leadership of Motilal Nehru. Jinnah felt that due to Gandhi's inactivity in politics, he would be able to lead the Congress on his terms. He hoped that with the help of the veteran leaders like Motilal Nehru and Lala Lajpatrai and the hot-blooded, young leader Subash Chandra Bose he would be able to reshape and give a new direction to the Congress, without the influence of Gandhi. So he did not leave the Congress, in spite of being associated with the Muslim League.

However, unfortunately, Pandit Motilal Nehru had appealed to Gandhi to be present at the all party conference as the Congress representative and provide leadership to the country. Accordingly, Gandhi attended the conference and made significant contribution to its deliberations.

Jinnah was totally dejected. He realised that he was unwanted in the all party conference. He was convinced that the Muslim League was the only option for him to remain active in national politics. Yet he was indecisive whether to leave the Congress or oppose it from within. It was beneath his stature to work shoulder-to-shoulder with Mohammed Shafi, Aga Khan and Raja Mehmoodabad. The Muslims mocked him as the "agent of the Hindus" and called him *Kafir*. To the Hindus, he was a Muslim communal leader.

Jinnah was heartbroken when he left Delhi Railway station. His friend Jamshed came to see him off. Putting his hand on his shoulder Jinnah said, "Jamshed, it is difficult to imagine what will happen to the country in future. But it is certain that my path is different from today."

The worried Jamshed asked Jinnah politely, "Mr. Jinnah, will you be able to carry your colleagues along on that path."

Jinnah understood that Jamshed was hinting at his colleagues in the Muslim League. These leaders had no political acumen. They were no match to Jinnah's intellect. Jinnah knew it. All these colleagues were influenced by the Ulemas and the Mullahs. But he had no other option. He said to Jamshed, "I have no option except to utilize my resources very skilfully," Jinnah's voice was tinged with pain as he uttered those words.

A few leaders who opposed to Jinnah on the Khilafat movement were travelling in the third class compartments of the same train. As usual, Jinnah was travelling in a first class compartment. Some Muslim supporters of the Khilafat movement saw him in the first class compartment and then started taunting him, "Jinnah Sahib, by travelling in the comfort of a first class compartment, you cannot serve the country or the community. You know that the representatives of the community are travelling in the third class compartments."

Jinna humiliated at the conference got provoked by this taunt. It was impossible for him to ignore it. He raised his index finger and screamed, "I bought the ticket with my own money. You do not have to tell me in which class I should travel. Those who cannot afford even the third class fare, can go by foot, if they wish. I can afford to buy the first class ticket."

When Jinnah reached the South Court the next day, what Fatima had said earlier was lingering in his mind. The Muslims accepted the demand of the Hindus. But the Hindus like Motitlal Nehru were not willing to cooperate with the Muslims. According to Jinnah, Gandhi had no foresight at all. The Hindus had succeeded in assimilating all other communities into their fold. They now want the Muslims to assimilate into the Indian society. He would never allow that to happen. It was Gandhi's conspiracy. Why did Gandhi return to politics from the social services and create such a melee? Jinnah admired Fatima's foresight for the first time. As soon as he saw Fatima he said, "Fati, you are right. But it is not a pleasant thing." And then he added, "Truth may be pleasant or bitter, but it has to be accepted now."

33

Ruttie in Paris for treatment, Chamanlal's poetry, Ruttie at Kanji's house, Ruttie's birthday—death

Ruttie's health was deteriorating day-by-day adding to her loneliness. Her father Dinshaw Petit did not bother to enquire about her condition. It was impossible for him to reconcile with his daughter. However, Ruttie's mother Dinabai could not cut herself off totally from her. After all, she was the only child. Dinabai was worried about her daughter's condition. She met Ruttie out of compassion and arranged for the best possible treatment. She visited Ruttie regularly at the Taj Mahal hotel. She knew that it would not be possible to get Ruttie discharged from the hotel and take her home. Her husband did not obstruct her in any way. Dinshaw Petit did not object to her spending on the treatment of Ruttie. He never enquired about his daughter's health.

Dinabai soon realised that Ruttie was in a very critical condition. Ruttie's addiction to drugs was very alarming. All efforts to rehabilitate her from the drug addiction had proved futile. The doctors treating Ruttie told Dinabai Petit that they did everything possible. Any further advanced modern treatment of such patients was possible only in Paris. The treatment there perhaps could rehabilitate Ruttie from the drug addiction and improve her health. As per the doctors' advice, Dinabai Petit took Ruttie to Paris for treatment.

Dinshaw Petit wanted his wife to return home. He did not like the idea of her staying in Paris for an indefinite period. The treatment of Ruttie was getting prolonged. Consequently, Dinabai arranged for Ruttie's treatment by eminent doctors in a reputed hospital in Paris. Dinabai returned to India. Now Ruttie was left alone in the comfort of a well furnished hospital in Paris instead of the Taj Mahal hotel.

Jinnah's close colleague Diwan Chimanlal, who actively participated in the national politics, was passing through Paris on his way to Canada. He halted for a few hours in Paris and accidently met Dinabai Petit. He happened to stay in the same hotel where Dinabai was staying. She was checking out of the hotel when Chamanlal checked in. It was a surprise encounter to both of them. Chamanlal learnt about the condition of Ruttie from her. He was grieved to know that Dinabai could not stay with Ruttie when she was in such a critical condition. Chamanlal knew Ruttie quite well as a beautiful and affectionate girl who was pampered a lot. Jinnah could not understand her. As soon as Dinabai left the hotel, Chamanlal hired a taxi to visit Ruttie at the hospital.Ruttie was lying semi-conscious when Chamanlal entered her room. The nurse was applying cologne water and ice on her head. Ruttie was holding a book in her right hand. The nurse told Chamanlal that Ruttie had a temperature of 106 degrees. Even in that condition, Ruttie insisted on reading the book and the nurse had to stop her.

After a while, Ruttie opened her eyes and saw Chamanlal. Her eyes sparkled with joy. Her lips fluttered. Chamanlal saw that she was too weak. He went close to her and said, "Ruttie, how is your health? Don't worry, you will be alright. Cooperate with the doctors for the treatment."

Ruttie smiled at Chamanlal. She stretched out the book held in her hand and then said, "Chaman, could you do me a favour? Could you read this poem to me from the book? The nurse is not allowing me to read the book."

Chamanlal was amazed. He stared at Ruttie with helplessness and empathy. He noticed the page in the book which Ruttie was holding with her fingers. It was the poem of her favourite poet Oscar Wilde entitled *The Harlot's House*. Chamanlal could not read the poem immediately. Ruttie got impatient, as if she was in a great hurry, and then said, "Chaman, please read this poem for me immediately. Something is happening to me...please."

Chamanlal started reading the poem. There was an eerie silence in the room. The nurse forgot what she was doing. Chamanlal's voice choked as he read the last stanza of the poem,

> "And down the long and silent street
> The dawn with silver sandalled feet
> Crept like a frightened girl..."

Chamanlal finished the last lines quivering, but was not sure whether Ruttie heard them. She was sleeping in a strange manner with her eyes closed that Chamanlal got scared. For a moment he stared at her and touched her face with his palm.

"Ruttie...Ruttie... are you listening?"

But she was not in a condition to answer. She was unconscious. A frightened Chamanlal called out for the nurse. The nurse ran out and called the doctor. The doctor immediately attended to Ruttie and then assured Chamanlal, "Nothing to worry. She became unconscious due to an overdose of drugs and high fever. Once the temperature comes down she would be alright."

Chamanlal could not stay there for more time. His travel itinerary was already fixed. He contacted Jinnah on reaching London as the latter was in London at that time. He gave the full details of Ruttie's condition. On hearing all that Jinnah said, "I will leave all my work and go to Paris. I will do whatever possible to save Ruttie." Jinnah cancelled all his work and reached Paris. He made all the necessary arrangement to ensure that Ruttie was given the most advanced treatment. When Ruttie regained consciousness, she saw Jinnah. The husband and the wife looked at each other for a long time without uttering a word. Then Ruttie closed her eyes.

After two months Diwan Chamanlal returned from Canada. He contacted Jinnah soon on his arrival. Jinnah was alone in the vast bungalow. When Chamanlal enquired about Rutties's condition, he said nonchalantly, "I understand she is alright. I left Paris only after she had recovered fully."

"Then, why did you leave her in Paris? Why did not you stay back for some more time?"Chamanlal asked eagerly,

"There was no point staying in Paris. Ruttie had become normal and returned to Bombay," Jinnah said impassively.

"But why? What happened? Mr. Jinnah, you both were together…!"

"Yes, That's why it happened. We fought again and then separated. That's all," Jinnah said signalling the end of the conversation.

Chamanlal had nothing else to ask.

After returning from Paris, Jinnah made a change in his daily routine. Whenever he was in Bombay he would visit Ruttie every day in the evening at the Taj Mahal hotel along with Kanji. Ruttie was not happy about Jinnah's visiting her daily along with Kanji. Most of the time, she would lay subconscious on the bed fondling her pet cats. She hardly uttered a word. Jinnah too never said anything to her. He would discuss politics with Kanji. And sometime when both of them enter into a heated argument, Ruttie would fall asleep. She would take the medicine before their arrival so that she could blissfully lapse into subconsciousness for a couple of hours until they left the room. Sometime Kanji would try to make them talk, but it was of no avail. Both of them preferred to not to communicate with each other.

One morning in February, Ruttie felt extremely lonely and depressed. No one had visited her for the past two days. Jinnah went to Delhi to attend the meeting of the Central Assembly. And Kanji was preoccupied due to the arrival of Annie Besant in Bombay. The effect of the medicine taken in the previous evening had gone. Her whole body was aching. She got up from the bed and ordered tea. After taking tea, she tried to play with her pet cats. Then suddenly she changed her clothes and walked out. She stood outside the entrance of the Taj Mahal Hotel and watched the tidal waves of the sea. Though it was not a winter day, the sea breeze was cold. Ruttie sat in a Victoria and went to Kanji's house.

Kanji was surprised to see Ruttie in his house so early in the morning. He had not yet completed his morning routine. He found her agitated.

"Ruttie, what made you to come here so suddenly? Are you alright?" Kanji asked her.

She was staring at him as if she had not heard him. Kanji got worried.

"Ruttie, why do not you say something? What is happening?"

And then suddenly Ruttie dropped on the sofa and started murmuring looking at the ceiling, "Kanji, I cannot bear the loneliness within the four walls. The walls and the ceiling come down and crush me. I find it difficult to breathe. Kanji, please do something. I feel suffocated. Please let the fresh air come in so that I can breathe or else I will die. If fresh air does not come in through the cracks I would stop breathing." She said this much and closed her eyes.

There was an eerie silence in the room. Kanji walked upto Ruttie and put his palm on her forehead. She did not respond. She lay down with her eyes closed. Kanji stood near her for quite some time. When he realised that she was fast asleep he went out. Ruttie woke after four hours. Kanji was reading something. She felt better. She suddenly got up and said to Kanji,"Oh! Kanji, I spoilt your programme today. I am sorry. Now I am alright. Please drop me at the hotel on your way to office."

Kanji said smiling, "Ruttie. You do not have to be apologetic. I am glad that you are alright. Now go and wash your face and have some tea. If you are hungry eat something. Then we will leave."

Ruttie remembered. She did not eat anything last night. She wondered whether she forgot to eat the food altogether. If Kanji had not remembered …

Ruttie felt better after taking the snacks and the tea. Kanji dropped her at the Taj Mahal hotel. While bidding good-bye to him she said, "Kanji, do take care of me."

Kanji came to the Taj Mahal hotel again at around ten in the night. Ruttie was lying unconscious on her bed. A stunned Kanji kept on staring at her. For a moment he thought of waking her up. Then he changed his mind. Ruttie was unconscious because of the drugs. She would be free from any grief as long as she was under the influence of the drugs. Waking her up would mean pushing her back into the world of loneliness and dejection. He stood there for a while and then left the room.

The next day was Ruttie's 29th birthday. Kanji remembered it. He completed his daily routine a bit early and then reached the Taj Mahal hotel. He carried a bouquet of fresh roses to greet her. When he entered the room she was awake. Her face looked pale. On seeing Kanji she tried to get up from her bed, but she was too weak to get up. Kanji presented her the bouquet and said holding her hand, "Ruttie, do not get up."

Ruttie asked him with surprise, "Kanji, why have you brought this bouquet today?"

Kanji was speechless for a moment. Had Ruttie forgotten even her birthday?

"Ruttie, today is a very special day! Forgot ! Today is your 29th birthday. Congratulation. You get well soon—that's what I pray."

"Oh! really! I forgot today was my birthday. Kanji, you have reminded me. You are so good. How do I express my gratitude to you?"

"Don't worry about all that."

"Ok," Ruttie said like an obedient child, "But I have something else to worry. Please do me a favour. When I am no more, please take care of my pet cats...do not sell them."

"Do not say such ominous things," Kanji said to calm her, "It is my wish on your birthday that you live for hundred years."

"And one more thing," Ruttie continued as if Kanji had not said anything, "After my death, please perform my last rites by cremating me." As she said those last words she sealed her lips. Kanji placed his palm on her lips. Ruttie closed her eyes, some moisture emanating from them. Kanji looked helpless.

When Kanji came to the hotel in the evening to meet Ruttie, she was not only unconscious, but was in no position to give any response to him. Her pet cats sat next to her body whimpering in a strange manner. A shaken Kanji put his hand on her forehead. Her body was too cold. Some white powder was seen on her lips. A bottle of morphine was lying open near her pillow. Kanji panicked. He started shaking Ruttie's shoulders.

But Ruttie had moved away too far to respond to anything. Ruttie's life journey of twenty nine years had reached its destination. The bouquet that Kanji had presented her, lay on her bed.

34

Ruttie's last rites, removing Ruttie's belongings

The Central Assembly in Delhi was having its session. Jinnah had an important role to play in that session. He was in the forefront in opposing the budget proposals of the government. Vithalbhai Patel was the speaker of the Assembly. Jinnah had a good equation with him. They worked in unison successfully. The speaker's job was made easy due to the cooperation of Jinnah.

At the end of the session that day, Jinnah went to Diwan Chamanlal's house with him instead of going to his hotel. Chamanlal was also a member of the Assembly. He had a flat in the Western Court. Both of them were discussing the strategy for the next day. Then suddenly the telephone rang. Chamanlal attended to the call. He heard a shaky but familiar voice from the other end.

"Chamanlal, Is Mr. Jinnah there? Please call him on the line, I am Kanji from Bombay."

Chamanlal turned to Jinnah and said, "Mr. Jinnah, Kanji from Bombay wants to talk to you."

Jinnah was very surprised. How could Kanji know that he was in Chimanlal's house! Generally at that time he would be in the Court or in the library of the Assembly or in his room in the hotel. Why did Kanji phone to Chamanlal's residence?

"Mr. Jinnah,"Kanji paused for a moment, "I was trying to trace you. After making calls to three or four places, I came to know that you are with Chamanlal. Please come to Bombay immediately."

"What happened, Kanji?" Jinnah asked nervously. "Tell me, what happened?"

"Something untoward happened. Ruttie…" Kanji suddenly broke down.

"What happened to Ruttie? Please tell me."

"Ruttie is not in our midst any more. She is dead," Kanji said quickly.

Jinnah stood speechless for a moment. And then he said, "Kanji, I am reaching Bombay." Then he put down the telephone receiver.

The next day when Jinnah got down at the Grant Road Railway station, Kanji received him. Kanji on his way narrated to Jinnah the background leading to the death of Ruttie. Jinnah listened to all that quietly.

"And Mr. Jinnah," Kanji said softly. "When I had last met Ruttie, she had the premonition of her death."

"How can you say that?" Jinnah asked.

"Ruttie asked me to take care of her pet cats and also expressed a wish."

Jinnah was surprised. What type of wish could it be?

"Ruttie's last wish was that..." Kanji paused for a moment and then said, "...her body be cremated."

Jinnah's face betrayed no emotion. Whatever might be the nature of the last rites, they would make no difference to the reality. Jinnah remembered the time spent with Ruttie. That indescribable meeting amidst the mountains of Darjeeling...a sixteen year old girl defying her father till she turned an adult...then giving birth to Dina...all these flashed in his mind with the speed of a lightning. Ruttie had never demanded anything nor had expressed any wish. Then why should he object to her last wish to cremate her body? For a moment he thought that it was his duty to fulfill her wish.

But if Ruttie was cremated and not buried in a cemetery as per the Islamic tradition, the Muslim League might oppose it. Jinnah was a representative of the Muslims in the Central Assembly. He now chose a path different from that of the Congress. The Congress was transformed completely under the influence of Gandhi. Now his political future was linked with the Muslim League. He had many detractors in the League because of his opposition to the Muslim communalism. If Ruttie was not buried as per the Islamic tradition, his detractors would have a political score over him. He had already lost his position in the Congress. Therefore, it was not a wise thing to give his opponents in the Muslim League a political advantage on the question of the last rites. Whether the dead body was cremated or buried in a cemetery, what difference would it make to Ruttie?

As the car stopped, Jinnah and Kanji got down. Jinnah said to Kanji in a firm tone, "Kanji, forget that now. Ruttie must be buried in a cemetery as per the Islamic tradition. She was Mariam and not Ratanbai."

Kanji did not say anything. What he could do except conveying Jinnah the last wish of Ruttie? The Mullahs and the Maulvis had gathered to dispose the dead body as per the Islamic tradition. Some verses from the Quran were chanted. Jinnah stared blankly at the motionless dead body of Ruttie. He was surrounded by friends. Mohammed Ali Chagla, who had left the Muslim League due to his differences with Jinnah over the Nehru report, was also present at the cemetery. A grave was being dug for the burial. Jinnah was lost in talking to people. He narrated to Kanji and Chagla how his group in tandem with the Swaraj Party had blocked the budget proposals of the government. He kept on saying how complicated the political situation became after the all party conference had accepted the Nehru report. He did not mince any words in expressing his anger at how the country was heading towards a political disaster under Gandhi. The preparations for the burial took three hours. Jinnah went on discussing the politics so stridently as if he came to attend the funeral of some stranger.

However, his mask of detachment was uncovered. The mask of bravery that he wore on his face peeled off. When the body of Ruttie was lowered in the grave and covered with the soil, Jinnah suddenly broke down. When he put a handful of soil as per the tradition, being the nearest relative, he was heartbroken. It was as if a stone had melted. He cried incessantly. He could not stand by the grave. Kanji and Changla tried to console him.

No family member except the estranged husband came to bid a last farewell to Ruttie. Not a single person from her father Dinshaw Petit's family came to pay the last respects to their daughter Ratan.

When Jinnah returned home after the burial, Fatima was waiting for him. While climbing the stairs of the South Court, Jinnah remembered the days when Ruttie used to wait for him along with Fatima. Now Ruttie would not wait for anyone any more. He felt as if Ruttie was still sitting in the easy chair in the drawing room. Her pet dogs and cats were no longer seen, yet he heard a cat's meow.

Jinnah went straight to his room. He had not read the newspapers since the morning. All the newspapers were kept intact in the room. He flipped through the newspapers and looked at the headlines. For the first time, no piece of news interested him. Even the news of the Congress or Gandhi did not interest him. He picked up the champagne bottle. He felt better after gulping a few sips of the drink. He kept on pacing in the room for a long time. It was their bed room. He sat down on Ruttie's bed, which he had never done before.

He went to another room that contained the wardrobe of Ruttie. After Ruttie had left the house, he had never opened that room. He looked around. A variety of cosmetics were lying on the dressing table. He saw very expensive, fashionable and modern clothes hung in the wardrobe, a testimony to Ruttie's elegant and sensible taste. The wardrobe contained the party clothes that Ruttie wore quite often. The party wears included the Parsee attires, the garments suitable for the Muslim and the English women and the party wears of the Hindu queens and princesses. Jinnah gazed at them. Then he opened Ruttie's cupboard. It contained a rich collection of jewels that Ruttie used to wear. The jewels contained the sparkling diamonds of red, yellow, pink, purple and other shades. Jinnah tried to recall when Ruttie wore those ornaments.

By leaving the wardrobe and the cubboard, Jinnah looked at the wall. He saw two attractive frames with beautiful photographs of Ruttie hanging. Jinnah remembered a frame with their joint photographs hanging in the bedroom. He saw an album of many such photographs. He picked up the album and started looking at the photographs. Ruttie's photographs in different poses and styles right from the Darjeeling days stared at Jinnah. He closed the album.

Jinnah turned back and walked into his bedroom. He took the half empty bottle of champagne that he had left on Ruttie's bed. He gulped down the throat a couple of glasses of wine and then made a decision.

Jinnah had a Hindu servant called Bhagwan Dhonde. He stayed in the servants' quarters in the courtyard. Since the time Ruttie had left the house Jinnah was sleeping alone in the bedroom. He instructed the servant to sleep in the passage outside his bedroom. Jinnah trusted him a lot. The servant knew Jinnah's nature and his temperament quite well. And Jinnah liked him.

Jinnah suddenly stood up from Ruttie's bed and called out softly, "Bhagwan..."

He was half awake. He immediately got up and presented himself before Jinnah.

"Yes, Sahib."

"Go and get two or three empty trunks from the godown," Jinnah ordered.

The servant could not comprehend the order. Why he asked for the trunks, it was beyond his comprehension. Yet it was impossible to ask Jinnah anything. He said softly, "Yes, Sahib." The servant obeyed the order of the master immediately.

Jinnah ordered the baffled servant, "Remove all the photographs of the Memsahib and put them in the trunk."

"Yes, Sahib," the servant stared at him surprised. He had seen many families where the portraits of the dead were garlanded as a mark of tribute. Here he was aghast to get the order to remove the photographs from the walls. He could never imagine this.

"And listen carefully,"Jinnah said clarifying futher. Pointing out to the other room he ordered, "Put in the trunks Memsahib's clothes, jewels and cosmetics on the dressing table and all that you remove from that room. Take care nothing is left out."

As the servant lifted the huge trunks, Jinnah ordered again as if he remembered something suddenly, "And look! Take away all the books of Memsahib from her study room and put them in the trunks. And deposit all these trunks in the attic in the room near the verandah." Having ordered thus he lay on his bed.

The servant was shocked and became numb for a while at the behaviour of his master. He knew that the Memsahib had left the house. But he had experienced many a time her generous and affectionate nature. Now such a nice Memsahib was no more. He was unable to reconcile to the fact that a husband like Jinnah was getting rid of all her possessions. He turned his back helplessly.

"And Bhagwan," Jinnah suddenly gave the last instruction, "You finish all this work right now and then report to me. Take care nothing is left out. Go ! Make it fast! I am very sleepy." He closed his eyes.

When Jinnah opened his eyes in the morning, nothing connected to Ruttie could be seen anywhere in the South Court.

35

Congress refusal to participate in the First Round Table Conference, Breaking of the Salt Law by Gandhi, partition in the Round Table Conference by other parties, Jinnah in London, Willingdon as the Viceroy of India

The national political scene was getting murky.

Most of the countrymen, except the Muslim League, had accepted the Nehru Report as the basis of the future constitution. The draft constitution, known as the Nehru Report, was prepared as a response to the challenge thrown up by Lord Birkenhead, the Secretary of State for India. Yet the British officials in London had not paid any attention to it. Instead they were initiating some political reforms on the basis of the recommendations of the Simon Commission which was totally boycotted. The Indian National Congress, which was under the total influence of Gandhi, had decided to oppose any such move. The Nehru Report had demanded Dominion status for India. The Congress had declared that if the British government did not accept the demand for the Dominion status within the stipulated period, it would demand complete independence. The British government was given one year time limit to accept the demand. The time limit had expired and the government had not made any announcement accepting the demand. Therefore, the Congress under the Presidentship of Jawaharlal Nehru adopted a resolution for *purna swaraj*[1] in its session held in Lahore on the banks of the river Ravi. The Congress authorized Gandhi to take all necessary steps to attain the goal.

In the meantime, the British government, in order to find a solution to the political impasse in India, had announced that it would hold a Round Table Conference in London. However, it made no mention of the Nehru Report. Nor did the government spell out its intention to grant Dominion status to India. The Congress put a condition that if the government agreed to consider its demand for dominion status it would participate in the Round Table Conference. The government rejected the condition. Consequently, the Congress refused to take part in the Round Table Conference.

Thereafter, Gandhi announced to launch a new movement called the Civil Disobedience to attain the goal of *purna swaraj*. To make it a mass movement and win the support of the common people, he announced the *Salt Satyagraha*[2]. The salt was a basic necessity of the people. It could have been made freely available. The government had imposed a tax on the salt. The common people could not afford it. Gandhi announced 22nd March as the day for breaking the salt law. He called upon his countrymen to break the salt law on the appointed day and be ready to receive the punishment for breaking the law.

Jinnah was startled by the announcement of Gandhi. He did not forget the non-cooperation movement launched a few years ago and its consequences. Jinnnah could not understand mobilizing the illiterate masses in the name of public awareness. He believed that the politics was not meant for the illiterate masses. It would be easy to become popular by inciting the masses, but it would be difficult to control the mob fury. Then the main objective would be lost and the mob would be rendered leaderless. He condemned Gandhi's programme as an act of madness and invitation to mob frenzy.

Jinnah was the master of law. He was good at arguing endlessly by quoting innumerable examples. With his logical acumen, he was capable of proving an innocent person guilty of a murder and vice versa. Once he made up his mind he would take up a case without bothering whether the client was right or wrong. He would charge heavy fees. He did not think that it was unethical. He believed that a lawyer's job was to fight the case for his client and not to judge whether the client was right or wrong. In contrast, Gandhi as a laywer, was totally different. According to him if Gandhi is believed and the lawyers fight only for truth, the skills of the lawyers, the law books and the courts—all would become irrelevant. As a defender of law, Jinnah was interested only in legal battles. The masses should not be allowed to break the law.

Jinnah knew his limitation. Unlike Gandhi he was a very successful lawyer. However, Gandhi had reached the peak of popularity very rapidly. And unlike Gandhi, Jinnah could not easily mingle with the masses. Jinnah could never understand how anyone could mingle with the untidy and illiterate masses. He ridiculed Gandhi's way of mixing with the masses and talking to them on petty matters.

Taking all this into consideration, Jinnah made a written appeal to the British Prime Minister Ramsay MacDonald to act firmly and decisively against the Civil Disobedience Movement launched by the so-called nationalists.

Meanwhile, the British government was going ahead with the Round Table Conference. The government invited some thirteen representatives from different political parties and sixteen representatives from the princely states. These included the Kings of Bikaner, Bhopal and Kashmir as well as Ranjit Singh of Jamnagar, who was a reputed international cricket player. Besides, some important landlords, industrialists, religious groups and prominent individuals were also invited. These included the Ali brothers, who shot into national prominence due to Gandhi's support on the Khilafat movement, Sir Mohammed Shafi, the leader of the break away group of the Muslim League, Aga Khan, the religious head of the Ismaili Khojas, Dr. Munje of the Hindu Mahasabha who had left the Congress in support of radical Hinduism and Dr. Babasaheb Ambedkar, the leader of the untouchables who considered the untouchables different from the Hindus and the moderate leaders Sapru and Jayakar. Barrister Jinnah was invited as a special representative of the British India. It was certain that the Congress was not taking part in the conference. Jinnah doubted whether the conference would achieve anything.

It had been almost twenty five years since Jinnah entered politics. Initially, as a dedicated Congressman he had worked as a private secretary to Dadabhai Navroji, the grand old man of the Indian politics. Moreover, he had worked shoulder to shoulder with the leaders like Gokhale, Tilak, Pherozeshah Mehta, Motilal Nehru and Chittaranjan Das in the freedom movement. He had differences of opinion with them, but he felt that he had a place among these senior leaders. When Tilak had been charged with sedition by the British government, it was Jinnah who fought his case. Gokhale called him the ambassador of the Hindu-Muslim unity. He had worked with Pherozeshah Mehta. He had rejected the invitation of Aga Khan to join the Muslim League. And when he joined the League years later he did not leave the Congress. After joining the League, he had dissuaded it from adopting a confrontationist approach and persuaded it to become a part of the national political mainstream. He always insisted that the Muslims should keep away from religious bigotry and extremism and become a part of the political mainstream by keeping faith on the Hindus. Because of this he was called a *Kafir* by the Muslims. He believed that, in the interest of the country, the Hindus should be generous to conceded a little more than their share to the Muslims. The majority community would achieve nothing by sidelining the Muslims and the former must win the confidence of the latter. Jinnah had been trying to bridge the gap between the Congress and the Muslim League. But now he realised that he had failed to bridge the gap.

His ire was against Gandhi. When Gandhi returned to India in 1915, Jinnah had spent about a decade in the Congress politics. Yet as soon as Gandhi entered politics he became a supreme leader in the Congress. Gokhale, Tilak and Pherozeshah Mehta were no more. Motilal Nehru and Chittaranjan Das became the disciples of Gandhi. Jawaharlal Nehru and Subhas Chandra Bose were young radical leaders. Sardar Patel entered politics a few years ago and owed his meteoric rise to Gandhi. How could Jinnah accept Gandhi's leadership like them? Moroever, he firmly believed that the path chosen by Gandhi was disastrous.

On the other hand, he had observed that the leaders in the Muslim League did not have the foresight. They always adopted a communal line of thinking. If he wanted he could become a supreme leader in the Muslim League and enjoy the position similar to that of Gandhi in the Congress. But he was conscious of the fact that his supporters in the Muslims League did not have the calibre and the stature of the leaders in the Congress who supported Gandhi. A few persons like Liaqat Ali Khan were an exception.

Jinnah felt a vacuum in his personal life too. After Ruttie's death, he did not have a family. As a matter of fact, he was never a family man. Although Fatima stayed with him right from her childhood, she was never a part of his family. To him she was a necessity. He needed her as a house keeper. And by the time he realised the importance of a family, it was too late. Ruttie had made the South Court a home for a brief period. Now it became only a house once again.

Jinnah was greatly disillusioned. Gandhi's path of *Satyagraha* was taking the Indian politics to total destruction. It was not possible for him to follow the Gandhian path. He was not prepared to break the law and go to jail and sacrifice and suffer. He had two options before him—either to live as an insignificant person in India or invite further acrimony by remaining in the midst of petty minded people. He felt he had gained enough experience both in the Supreme Court and in the Central Assembly. If he left India and settled in London, he could make his future more bright. He could take up the cases in the London Privy Council. He could register as a barrister in the Privy Council. The Indian cases that came up before the Privy Council were very important. And if he could take up those cases he could earn huge money, besides name and fame. If he settled in London, he could also enter the British politics. He weighed the pros and cons of all this and then decided that settling down in London would be more rewarding than staying back in India. Jinnah accepted the invitation for the Round Table Conference and set off for London. He boarded the ship *Viceroy of India* in Bombay on 4th October, 1930.

As expected, the Round Table Conference failed. Everyone knew that without the participation of the Congress the Round Table Conference was bound to fail. But nobody wanted to admit this openly. Admitting this would have meant accepting that without the consent of the Congress, nay Gandhi, nothing could be achieved. In order not to concede this reality, everyone right from King George VI to Aga Khan had continued to make lengthy speeches. The Indian representatives started forming themselves into small interest groups to seek petty concessions. Jinnah kept himself away from all that. Everyone knew that Jinnah's support was crucial. But nobody was sure where he would agree or disagree. All they knew was that it was more easy for Jinnah to disagree rather than agree. And that was what actually had happened.

As announced earlier, every speaker in the Conference was required to deposit a copy of his speech in advance with the organisers of the Conference. The purpose behind was to avoid unnecessary repetitions and mutual accusations. Accordingly, all the speakers had deposited their copies with the organisers. Jinnah did not bother to observe this norm. He did not deposit a copy of his speech. Then he said in his speech at the Conference,

"I would like to tell His Excellency the Prime Minister, that we have had enough discussions on the question of political reforms in India. Now the time has come to act upon them. I understand Britian has a special interest in India. It is natural because Britain derives commercial and economic benefits from India. But you must understand that we have a greater stake in India than you. For us it is not a matter of commercial and economic benefits. India means everything to us. It is our misfortune that we the Indians have not been able to reach any understanding on the Hindu-Muslim issue. The main issue is not that of a common electorate or a separate communal electorate. The real issue is that the Hindu majority is not courageous enough to address the apprehensions of the Muslims. It is important to note that the Muslims do not trust the Hindus. However, I must say in no unambiguous terms that I am an Indian first, and that I am a Muslim is a different matter altogether. My Hindu friends should remember that they can not serve the country by sidelining the Muslims."

At the end of such verbal exchanges of three months, everyone realised the futility of all the efforts. No progress was made in the direction of independence for the country. When the conference failed, the Muslim League leader Mohammad Shafi said that the views expressed by Jinnah were his personal views as he had no support from the Muslims of the country. Jinnah would never agree with anyone.

When everyone was returning to India, Jinnah was in a dilemma. During the course of the Round Table Conference, he had renewed his contacts with the British Labour Prime Minister MacDonald. Aga Khan had a cordial relation with the British opposition the Tory Party. Taking advantage of this, Jinnah tried to befriend the opposition party. Aga Khan was a political rival of Jinnah in India. But when Jinnah sought his goodwill and cooperation he extended it hoping to extract a pound of flesh from him later. If Aga Khan could help Jinnah by exploiting his influence, his permanent political adversary would be obliged to him. And, in return, he would be able to use him later in the Indian politics.

In the midst of this game of political intrigue, Jinnah was unable to decide whether he should stay back in London or return to India. However, an announcement of the British government helped him to make a decision. He had no doubt that in the next few years the political situation in India would worsen and that he would have to contend with more failure than success.

Jinnah did not forget the bitter encounter that he had with Lord Willingdon when he was the Governor of Bombay. And he was quite sure that Lord Willingdon would not have forgotten it either. The same Lord Willingdon was going to India as the new Viceroy.

NOTES

1. Complete independence.
2. A movement to break the salt law.

36

Iqbal's meeting with Jinnah in London, Second Round Table Conference, Gandhi-Jinnah meeting in London

When the participants in the first Round Table Conference were returning to India, a Muslim League representative Sir Muhammad Iqbal met Jinnah. They met several times formally during the course of the conference. The three month long conference could not reach any understanding on the Hindu-Muslim issue. This made Iqbal think that if Jinnah became the sole leader of the Muslims, his own views on the issue could be crystallized. Iqbal was a poet. He was a staunch supporter of the Hindu-Muslim unity when he had joined politics some two decades ago. It was during those days that he had written the most popular patriotic and heart rendering song *Sare Jahan Se Acchha, Hindustan Hamara*[1]. The sentiments expressed in the line *Hindi Hain Hum Vatan Hain Hindustan Hamara*[2] of the song had a mass appeal. But Iqbal had changed now. He had changed the lyrics in the song from *Hindustan Hamara* to *Muslim Hain Hum, Vatan Hain Sara Jahan Hamara*[3]. Now he was not an Indian, but a Muslim. India was no longer his motherland. Instead the whole world was a pan-Islamic motherland. Iqbal had studied the Indian communal problem and came to the conclusion that a separate nation for the Muslims was the only solution. He had proposed that a separate nation comprising of Punjab, Sindh, Baluchistan and the North West Frontier Province should be created for the Muslims. But he knew that he did not have the capability to propose this either to the Congress or to the Hindu groups and confront them. There was no supreme leader in the Muslim League who could understand his vision. Only Jinnah was capable of doing this. Therefore, immediately on the conclusion of the Conference, Iqbal had an exclusive meeting with Jinnah when he brought out the idea of a separate nation for the Muslims.

Iqbal cautiously expressed his idea, "The British type of democracy is dangerous to India. In such a democracy, the Muslims will always remain a minority and the community which was ruled once will now become a majority community and take revenge on the Muslims."

Jinnah dismissed Iqbal's idea in a lighter vein, "Mr. Iqbal, you better write good poetry. Politics is not a subject for poetry. Whatever may be the population of the Hindus, the seventy million Muslims is not a small population." "I think the Indian communal problem cannot be solved without the creation of a separate nation for the Muslims. I want you to consider this idea," Iqbal persisted.

"Look, the nations are not created on the basis of maps alone. It requires a very careful planning. It is difficult to sustain a nation created in this fashion. The Hindus and the Muslims have no option except to unite and gain independence." Jinnah said rejecting Iqbal's idea resolutely.

Iqbal was a responsible and prominent leader of the Muslim League. After listening to Iqbal, Jinnah realized it would be prudent to settle in London and begin his second innings in politics. Iqbal's daydreaming was devoid of reality. He thought the other members of the Muslim League might be similarly daydreaming. He was convinced that he would not be able to achieve anything in the company of such people.

Hence he was making the move in a new direction. He bought a three-storied building known as the West Heath House on London's Hampsted Heath Road and made it his new residence. Fatima and Dina joined him immediately. He soon earned a name among the legal luminaries of London. He realized that his talent would be fully utilized there. He enrolled as an advocate in the Privy Council. He felt there would not be any difficulty in getting the clients because of his past success as an advocate. He completed all formalities of becoming a permanent resident of England so as to ensure smooth entry into the British politics. Fatima managed the house as efficiently as she had at the South Court in Bombay. Jinnah's daughter was admitted to a nearby boarding school.

With the failure of the first Round Table conference, the British government realized that the political crisis in India could not be resolved without the involvement of Gandhi and the Congress. The government while using all its might to crush the *Salt Satyagraha* had got thousands of people arrested throughout the country and sent them to jail. All the prominent Congress leaders were in jail and unless they were released no fresh talks could be initiated. Hence, the Viceroy reached an understanding with Gandhi. And as per the understanding, all the political prisoners were released and the charges against them were dropped. As a goodwill gesture, the Congress suspended the Civil Disobedience movement. The government announced the convening of the Second Round Table Conference and expressed the willingness to discuss all the issues, except the issues of defence, foreign affairs, finance and minorities. Gandhi accepted the announcement on behalf of the Congress.

Some senior Congress leaders expressed unhappiness over Gandhi's decision. There was no mention of self-rule in the announcement. Besides, the important subjects like the defence were left out. The Viceroy, however, conceded that the Congress would have a larger delegation at the Second Round Table Conference than the other groups. Thus, the Congress was accepted as the largest party in the country. After the initial strong reaction, the Congress accepted Gandhi's view and decided to participate in the Conference. However, instead of sending a large delegation, the Congress decided to send Gandhi as its sole representative.

The Second Round Table Conference lasted for nearly four months. Jinnah too received an invitation to participate in the Conference in his personal capacity. Though he attended the Conference, he remained inactive throughout. The British newspapers gave wide publicity to Gandhi's presence in the conference. Gandhi did not attend the first Round Table conference. Yet the British newspapers gave wide coverage of his absence. Aga Khan or Jinnah or any other Indian representative was given so much importance by the British press. Jinnah grew jealous of Gandhi's popularity. Gandhi in his spare time met the leaders of various political parties and social organisations. He interacted with the people dealing with education and other fields. Jinnah felt that Gandhi was cleverly expanding his area of influence.

The Conference threw up the new issue of untouchables in addition to the Hindu-Muslim issue. They were sought to be treated as a separate entity. Gandhi maintained that the untouchables were part of the Hindu society. The Muslim League insisted that Gandhi and the Congress had represented only the Hindus. But Gandhi remained firm on his stand that he was representing the entire country, including the Muslims and the untouchables. This Conference too met the same fate as the first conference. It did not achieve anything.

Gandhi felt it necessary to have a personal meeting with Jinnah to sort out the Hindu-Muslim issue. Jinnah was not a representative of the Muslim League. However, if Jinnah was convinced about the importance of the Hindu-Muslim unity, it would not be difficult to pursuade the League to accept it. Gandhi invited Jinnah for an informal meeting before returning to India. Meeraben, Mahadev Desai, Pyare Lal and Sarojni Naidu had accompanied Gandhi to assist him in the conference. Gandhi sent the invitation to Jinnah through Mahadev Desai. Jinnah was in a quandary. Jinnah was already annoyed with the importance given to Gandhi during the conference. He thought the invitation was like rubbing salt on the wound. He rejected the invitation.

But Gandhi would not give up so easily. Sarojini Naidu and Jinnah had an excellent rapport. Everyone in the Indian politics knew about it. How could an astute person like Gandhi forget the warm and friendly sentiments that Sarojini Naidu had expressed about Jinnah on some other occasion? Therefore, Gandhi sent another invitation to Jinnah through Sarojini Naidu. He was sure that Jinnah would not be able to reject the invitation this time.

Gandhi was proved right. Jinnah could not reject the invitation for the second time. He conveyed the acceptance of the invitation through Sarojini Naidu with a condition. Gandhi was staying at a prominent labour locality at the East End in London. He and his aides were staying in an inn called the Kingsley Hall. Many social activists working for the welfare of the labour class had stayed at the same place. Miss Muriel Lester, the leader of the labourers, was Gandhi's hostess at the Kingsley Hall. Jinnah could not tolerate the idea of squatting on the floor on a mattress and talking to Gandhi. He had seen Gandhi quite often working on the spinning wheel during the course of important speeches at the conference. Jinnah considered it a bad conduct. He felt Gandhi was a hypocrite and dubious character. Yet he could not reject the invitation sent through Sarojini Naidu. But he did not accept the idea of meeting at the Kingsley Hall. He did not like Gandhi's habit of making the visitors take some drinks in the name of health. Keeping this in mind, he said to Sarojini Naidu, "Tell Gandhi that the meeting should not be held in a labour locality like the East End, but in a posh area like the West End. Moreover, I should not be offered any drink other than the scotch and soda."

When Sarojini Naidu conveyed this, Gandhi without getting flustered smiled at her. He instructed Muriel Lester to arrange a suitable place for the meeting at the West End.

"Madam, I stayed in London for three years and after that I visited this place now and then. Yet I don't know how to welcome Jinnah Sahib and provide him the hospitality. Please help me. I am a stranger to the West End and the scotch. Of course, I take soda occasionally," Gandhi said and laughed heartily. Sarojini Naidu could help comparing and contrasting the two persons—the arrogance of Jinnah and the simplicity of Gandhi.

The meeting was held at a place in the West End. Jinnah dressed in a modern suit and wore a monocle. He carried a stick in his hand like a British tourist. Gandhi, as per his daily routine, was squatting on the carpet floor and spinning the wheel. On seeing Jinnah, he put aside the spinning wheel and smilingly gestured him to sit with him. It was difficult for Jinnah to sit on the floor like Gandhi. So he sat on the sofa opposite Gandhi.

"Oh! I forgot Jinnah *Sahib*. It would be difficult for you to sit on the floor with me in that outfit. Look at my *dhoti*. I can sit anywhere comfortably," Gandhi stood up smiling and stretched out his hand to shake. Jinnah shook the hand, but could not smile. Gandhi put his hand on his shoulder and sat on the sofa.

The scotch and the soda were arranged on a teapoy. Gandhi opened the scotch bottle. Then he opened the soda bottle. But he forgot to put the empty glass to the soda bottle when he opened it. As a result the soda water bubbled out and spilt on the teapoy. Jinnah was annoyed. Without feeling embarrassed Gandhi said, "You can see, Jinnah Sahib! How inept I am in these matters! Tell me, which should I pour first in the glass—the scotch or the soda? I will do whatever you say."

Jinnah felt that his last sentence was not a simple statement, but a plot working in his mind. He became alert. He took the glass from Gandhi's hand and prepared a drink himself.

They discussed about an hour the issues that cropped up during the Round

Table Conference. Gandhi was trying to pursuade Jinnah how the Nehru Report could form the basis for gaining independence for the country. And Jinnah was equally insistent on how the proposals made at the Delhi Muslims' conference could form a part of the Nehru Report. At the end of the meeting Jinnah said, "Mr. Gandhi, I think we are avoiding the issue. If this continues, we will remain where we are infinitely. We will not be able to take a single step forward."

"Jinnah Sahib, I am an optimist," Gandhi said without any bitterness, "If we are sincere, we can definitely find a way out."

Jinnah returned home late in the night that day. Fatima was waiting for him anxiously. She was resentful of the fact that her brother had accepted the invitation sent through Sarojini Naidu. She had heard Gandhi could mesmerize even his adversaries by his talk. Fatima knew that her brother was altogether a different type of adversary of Gandhi. Yet she was worried because her brother had not yet got over the illusion of the Hindu-Muslim unity.

When Fatima asked about the meeting with Gandhi, Jinnah said irritably,

"I cannot change this Hindu mentality. And the Muslims do not understand the ground reality. What I consider service to the country, I cannot do it in my own way. If I cannot do anything to the country I love, there is no sense in returning to it. Fati, it is prudent to make London our permanent residence."

NOTES

1. Our India is the most blessed land in the World.
2. We are Indians, India is our motherland.
3. We are Muslims, the world is our motherland.

37

Third Round Table Conference, Jinnah in London—Privy Council, Jinnah's unsuccessful attempt to enter the British Parliament, Jinnah-Rehmat Ali Choudhari meeting, Muslim League in India without Jinnah, Jinnah-Dina on 'Grey Wolf,' biography of Kemal Ataturk

After the failure of the two Round Table Conferences, the British government convened a third Conference to resolve the constitutional crisis in India. Gandhi and the Congress did not participate in the Third Round Table Conference on the ground that unless the government clarified its stand on the demand for independence the conference would serve no purpose. In the meantime, Pandit Madan Mohan Malavya organised another all party conference at Allahabad to find a permanent solution to the Muslim communal problem. The representatives of various religious organisations were invited. The Muslims who demanded 33 per cent reservation of seats in the Central Assembly now climbed down to 30 per cent. The Hindus who were not willing to concede more than 23 per cent seats to the Muslims, in proportionate to their population, now agreed to concede 28 per cent seats. The newspapers reported the progress of the conference daily which had unnerved the government. The difference on the seat sharing between the Hindus and the Muslims had almost watered down. The British officials feared that such an understanding was not in the interest of the government. Therefore, before the all party conference could arrive at an understanding on the issue, the Secretary of State for India, Samuel Hoer announced the convening of the Third Round Table Conference. He had also announced the British government's acceptance of the proposal for reserving one-third seats in the Central Assembly for the Muslims. The government allotted more seats to the Muslims than what they were finally willing to accept. In view of this, there was no point in reaching an understanding with the Hindus. This was a dangerous political game of the British government. The all party conference would have agreed to concede 30 per cent seats to the Muslims. Consequently, the Conference became redundant. And the communal problem flared up once again.

Jinnah could not become a leader of any group or delegation in the First and the Second Round Table Conferences. His approach was different from that of the other Muslim representatives. If Jinnah was of no use earlier, inviting him to the Third Round Table Conference would be very embarrassing to the British government. The Viceroy Lord Willingdon who was preparing a list of invitees for the conference had received a letter from the Secretary of State, Samuel Hoer. The letter read—"Going by the conduct of Jinnah in the last two conferences, it seems he is like a viper. We cannot trust him. Among all the Indians that I have met till date, I can say Jinnah was the most despicable." It was necessary for the Viceroy to consider this. The Congress boycotted the Third Round Table Conference. The government did not invite Jinnah to the Conference as he had no mass support. Jinnah was in London. He was regularly in touch with the British politicians. He was annoyed for being ignored. His isolation was total. None of the Indian delegates participating in the Conference had thought it necessary either to consult him or meet him. It hurt his ego. He felt that now he had no standing in India.

Jinnah was keeping himself informed of the developments in the Conference. A Bill on the constitutional reforms in India was presented in the British parliament. The scheming mind of Jinnah visualized that if he got elected to the British parliament as a candidate of the ruling Labour Party he would be able to make a significant contribution to the constitutional reforms. He had cherished a dream of becoming a member of the British Parliament. Some four decades ago, as a student, he had seen Dadabhai Navroji in the British Parliament. He took interest in the politics due to his influence. And if he could occupy the place that Dadabhai had he too could become the grand old man of Indian politics like him.

Prime Minister MacDonald was greatly disappointed by the individualistic approach adopted by Jinnah in the previous two conferences. Though Jinnah was an old friend, he declined to offer him a seat as a Labour Party candidate in the Parliament. Jinnah had two or three meetings with MacDonald, and when he realized that the Labour Party was not interested in his candidature, he made overtures to the opposition Conservative Party. Aga Khan had a cordial relation with the opposition leaders. Though Jinnah did not have good rapport with Aga Khan, he developed the contacts with the prominent opposition leaders through the latter. He tried to contest the bye-election on the ticket of the Conservative Party.

However, the fortune did not favour Jinnah. The Conservative Party also had rejected the candidature of Jinnah. He was greatly disappointed. He was frustrated and angry at his repeated failures, at his inability to achieve anything.

Having failed to become a member of the British Parliament, Jinnah started thinking on a different line. He could not make his mark in the Privy Council as an advocate. In the Indian Courts, an advocate's oratory skill rather than his logical argument mattered the most. This did not work in the Privy Council. Jinnah now realized that mere oratory skill without the power of logic would not help him to succeed. Most of the cases in the Privy Council were related to India. He tried to get himself appointed as a judge on the panel of the Privy Council. However, getting into the panel of the Privy Council needed some political backing. He had all the requisite qualifications required of a judge. But the fortune did not embrace him. This dream also remained unfulfilled. The British politicians on whom he banked had only used him as a pawn to serve their own political interest in India. It looked as if all the politicians cutting across the party lines had an unspoken understanding on how to use him as a pawn in their political game. They were unanimous in their opinion that Jinnah did not deserve to have any special respectable position in the British political or social life. The reason behind could be a matter of speculation.

Around this time, the Indian Muslim students studying in the Cambridge University were hotly debating the political situation in India. They formed a small group and debated fiercely on how the Muslims, though in the minority, could rule India. The Muslims ruled India before the advent of the English people. They feared the consequences of the Muslim minority community being left at the mercy of the Hindu majority. Rehmat Ali Chaudhari, a student from the Punjab, was a leader of this group.

General Dyer, infamous for the Jallianwallah Bagh massacre in 1919, was spending a retired life in London in those days. When he was put to trial for the inhuman act, the English people in London came to his defence. They had collected a sum of fifty thousand pounds to defend his case. The Secretary of State for India, Montagu said that General Dyer had acted in good faith and what he had done was justified under those circumstances. Thus, both the British people and the government had tried to justify the massacre.

This had boosted the morale of General Dyer. He was favouring the Indian Muslims on the communal issue. Most of the people in the Congress who demanded independence were the Hindus. And most of the people who died in the Jallianwallah Bagh massacre were the Hindus and the Sikhs. He thought that the Congress which condemned the massacre had favoured the Hindus. The Muslim League did not condemn the massacre. He was of the opinion that the Hindu majority would crush the Muslim minority. General Dyer, seeing the struggle for independence intensifying, realized that the British government would have to leave India some day. He believed that it was in the interest of the British people to separate the areas where uneducated fanatic Muslims living below the poverty line were dominated. He was waiting for an opportunity. Rehamat Ali Choudhari provided him the opportunity. The Muslim radical group of the Cambridge invited General Dyer to address them. Dyer giving vent to his vengeful thoughts said, "The British people had conquered India and took away the authority from the Muslims. If they had to leave India, they should hand over the authority to the Muslims who were the original rulers of India. If that does not happen the Hindu majority would crush the Muslim minority. The only justifiable solution to this was to carve out an independent and separate nation for the Muslims. Therefore, the regions where the Muslims are a majority should be brought together to create an independent nation."

General Dyer was carrying out the work of dividing India started years ago by Principal Bacon and Principal Archibald of the Aligarh Muslim University. The regions with the Muslim majority he was talking about consisted of the people who were illiterate and impoverished. He felt the British industries could exploit those regions. Rehmat Ali Choudhari was pleased by the suggestion of Dyer.

The Round Table Conference was in progress. The Muslim League in its annual session at Allahabad was considering the possibility of having a separate administrative system in the Muslim dominated regions within the British rule. Rehmat Ali Choudhari felt encouraged by this development. He had a plan of merging the regions having the Muslim majority. He proposed merging of the Northern and the Western provinces where the Muslims were in a majority. He worked out a blue print of the regions that could form a Muslim nation. As per the blue print, the Punjab, the North West Frontier Province, Kashmir, Sindh and Baluchistan could constitute into an independent Muslim nation called *Pakistan*. Jinnah was in London those days. Rehmat Ali Khan thought that if Jinnah accepted his blue print, the Muslim League could start a movement in India. He vehemently argued that the concept of India as one nation was misconstrued. The Muslims should not be fooled into accepting that.

Rehmat Ali Choudhari had sent his blue print to Jinnah. Jinnah scoffed at his proposal. He had dismissed the proposal of an Islamic nation of the poet Iqbal as "a daydream." He now dismissed the proposal of an independent *Pakistan* of Rehmat Ali Choudhari as "a student's fantasy." Rehmat Ali Choudhari made several efforts to meet Jinnah to discuss the proposal but the latter refused to meet the former on the ground that such meetings had no meaning.

*

In India, the Muslim League without Jinnah was split into two factions—one headed by Hafiz Hidayat Hussein and the other by Miyal Abdul Aziz. The League was getting into political oblivion. Owing to the factionalism, the number of delegates attending its annual conference declined drastically. Once it even posed a problem of quorum forcing the League to amend the rule reducing the size of the quorum. It was now decided that fifty delegates would be enough to carry out the business at the annual conference. The leaders of the Muslim League were having a tough time. The Constitutional reforms were announced. If the Muslim League remained in such a disarray, it would not be able to protect the interest of the Muslims. Even if the British government bestowed favour on the Muslims, there was no leader to take advantage of it to benefit the community. Both the factions of the Muslim League were engaged in a cut throat competition.

Some prominent Muslim leaders felt that if Jinnah returned to India it would benefit the Muslims. They wrote a letter urging him to return. Miyan Abdul Aziz went to London to plead with Jinnah to return to India. Jinnah gave a stern reply, "Going by the present situation in the country, it is not possible for me to work in the manner I wish to. If my return does not serve any purpose, it's better I do not return to India."

In fact, Jinnah was waiting for the right time to return. The success that he had expected in London, he did not achieve. The people from India were urging him to return. He could gauge the despair and fear among the Muslims in India. Moreover, the Muslims were excited by the idea of Pakistan mooted by Rehmat Ali Choudhari. Jinnah had made a serious note of the demand for a separate administrative system put fourth by the Muslim League at Allahabad.

*

Jinnah generally did not read any books other than the books on law and politics. One day he read a review of the book *Grey Wolf* in the supplement of *The Times*. The book was the biography of Mustafa Kemal Ataturk who abolished the Khilafat and established a progressive regime in Turkey. He had become its dictator. Jinnah got so excited about the book that he immediately went out to a bookshop and bought a couple of copies of the book. He was engrossed with the book and finished reading in two days. He was so impressed by the book that he called out his thirteen year old daughter loudly. Dina who stayed in the school hostel had come to meet her father.

Dina was surprised to hear her father shouting. She found his voice somewhat strange. It sounded unnatural that he should call out so loudly. Before she could reach his room, he called her out very loudly again.

"Oh! What is it, Daddy? I see you shouting like this for the first time,"the darling daughter said putting her arms around his shoulders.

"You are right, dear. This book is so wonderful that I wanted to share with someone."

"Wonderful! What is that you read, Daddy? You have read so many books, but you never reacted like this."

"The book is like that. You must read this," Jinnah held out the book.

"Grey Wolf!" Dina laughed loudly on reading the title of the book.

"Daddy, you too are like a wolf. Instead of reading the book, I will call you by the pet name 'Grey Wolf.' " Then she affectionately held her father's hand and said,

"Daddy, I have come here to spend my vacation, not for reading books. Take me to a drama or to a theatre."

But Jinnah was not in a mood to go to a drama or theatre. He thought his own personality was reflected in Kemal Ataturk. Ataturk's mother was an illiterate woman. Kemal Ataturk was a very reserved child without any friends. Whenever he was prodded by his classmates to join them to play the games, Ataturk would tell them, "I am not like you. I am different from all of you." Jinnah felt how true was this of him.

When the youth in Turkey had launched a struggle for reforms, Ataturk became their respected leader and the ruler. Jinnah was inspired by the life of Ataturk. He was so deeply touched by the message that Ataturk gave to his countrymen after establishing a new stable government in Turkey that he pondered over it for a long time.

The future of a country or a people could not be shaped by mere sentiments and fantasies. It was important to stop daydreaming and accept the reality. A country would have to pay a heavy price for sentiments, day dreams and fantasies.

Jinnah felt that this gave him hope for a new beginning.

38

Liaquat-Jinnah meeting in London, Jinnah's return to India, Jinnah-Shahidgunj mosque in Lahore

Though Jinnah made London his permanent address, he was not mentally prepared to accept it as his final decision. He became a British citizen. His idea was to settle in London and work for India through the British Parliament. But he did not succeed in this. He realized that there was no possibility of this happening in the near future. He did not consider himself like other leaders. He believed that he was a different leader altogether. Till now he had never met with anything but success. During the past four decades he had succeeded at whatever his hands laid on. Ever since he drew the attention of Dadabhai Navroji in the corridors of the British Parliament, he felt he had some special qualities in him which others did not have. He had achieved remarkable success in the legal profession in Bombay. At the age of thirty five, he was elected uncontested to the Imperial Legislative Council. He was accepted by the Muslims of the country as their sole leader. He could not lead them because of their medieval mindset. He occupied a prominent position among the Hindu leaders before the advent of Gandhi. Gandhi alone was singularly responsible for his losing that position.

Presently, he was nothing more than an advocate in London. He regularly met the British politicians and discussed politics with them. He was quite often invited to deliver lectures. In spite of all this, he could not achieve anything remarkable. After all, India did provide him some opportunity. Although Gandhi and the Congress did not give him much importance, the millions of Muslims in the country and the Muslim League had accepted him as a leader and followed him. The only thing that he would have to compromise was his nationalist agenda. If only he could give it up and instead embrace the communal agenda that he had rejected till now, he could achieve success. Jinnah gave more importance to the sentiments of the Muslims than to the reasoning. He could sway their sentiments by his oratory skill.

He was waiting for an opportune time to return to India. The factionalism in the Muslim League had reached a feverish pitch. The future of the League was at stake.

The situation in 1933-34 was similar to the one that prevailed in 1910 when he was elected as a representative of the Muslims to the Imperial Legislative Council. In 1910 the Muslims got the seat for the first time. The two Muslim factions in Bombay had fought bitterly for that seat then. And when they were unable to reach an understanding as to who should contest the seat, Jinnah's name suddenly cropped up as a compromise. That was how he had entered politics due to the infighting between the two factions.

Now the two warring groups of the Muslims were seeking a third person to lead them. Barrister Muhammad Ali Jinnah became acceptable to both the groups. Everyone in the Muslim League had accepted his indispensibility in the Indian politics. The opposition to him in the League was due to his unwillingness to accept the communal agenda. He was a nationalist. He had declared many a time that he was an Indian first and then a Muslim. Now after his exile, if he could give up the nationalist agenda and lead the Muslim League, he would receive a hearty welcome.

Among the members of the Muslim League, Liaqat Ali Khan was the closest to Jinnah. When both of them met for the first time in 1928, the latter was about thirty years old. Liaqat's sensibility and style of functioning had attracted Jinnah. He had graduated from the Aligarh Muslim University and then studied the law in London. After becoming a barrister he married Begum Rana at the age of thirty five. And her charisma had contributed to his rise in stature. Considering the situation of the Muslim League, Liaqat Ali Khan too wished that Jinnah returned to India. He was not a senior leader in the League. Hence, he was not in a position to exert much influence in the League. He went to London for his honeymoon.

Liaquat contacted Jinnah in London. In his very first meeting, he spoke unabashedly to Jinnah, "The Muslim League is in a disarray. No one else except you could rescue the League. Today, the League needs a leader who can think of the welfare of the community and nothing else. And only you are such a leader."

Jinnah was flattered. Liaquat's words soothed his bruised ego. During the past four years of his stay in London, he had never heard anything that could boost his ego. His hurt ego was rekindled.

It was Friday evening at the West Heath House. Fatima was welcoming the guests from India very enthusiastically. She was well versed with the politics of the Muslims. She agreed with Liaqat Ali Khan. She thought if Jinnah accepted his request, the illusion of the Hindu-Muslim unity would disappear forever.

"And I assure you, Jinnah Sahib!" said Begum Rana in a very sweet voice, "I will mobilize the support of all the Muslim women behind you."

Jinnah looked at her. She sat with her elbows placed on the table and her face cradled in her palms. In the shade of twilight, she looked as lovely as the Greek statues adoring the room. The pictures of Monalisa and Cleopatra hung on the wall and a statue of Venus was displayed on the showcase just behind Begum Rana. Jinnah kept staring at her speechless.

She smiled at him and said, "I have not taken any active part in politics. And if you return, I would be happy to work with you."

"Both of you are young and inexperienced. You have no knowledge of the real world," Jinnah said and then turned to Begum Rana, "Madam, it is not as easy to mobilize the Indian Muslim women as you think."

"You are more experienced, Jinnah Sahib. But I am confident, I would succeed," she said confidently.

Jinnah was impressed by her self-confidence. He felt that when he was of her age, he too used to talk so confidently. What he said to her betrayed his lack of self-confidence. He was shocked. He wondered whether his lack of self-confidence would taint his image among the Indian Muslims.

"If you and Liaqat are with me, nothing will be impossible,"Jinnah said as if to arrest the damage.

Fatima was serving the food on the dining table. Her eyes focused on Begaum Rana. The words of her brother were ringing in her ears. Rana suddenly looked at Fatima. There was a strange look in her eyes. Fatima served the food as if nothing was amiss.

The Round Table Conference ended without any success. Now the round table that Jinnah saw was his own dining table. And four of them ate the food to their content.

*

On his return to India, Jinnah tried to take stock of the organisational strength of the Muslim League. The warring groups had compromised and agreed to accept him as the leader. The constitutional reforms were overdue. After the Round Table conference and the Civil Disobedience Movement, Gandhi and the Congress leaders were mainly occupied with the social reforms like the campaign against untouchability. Gandhi had made an important decision. He had resigned from the primary membership of the Congress in order to distance himself from the party politics. The organisational discipline of the Congress had obstructed his work. In order to give more time to the social reforms and make himself free from the rules of party discipline, Gandhi parted company with the Congress.

It was a quirk of fate. At a time when Gandhi voluntarily relinquished his supreme position in the Congress, his arch adversary Jinnah became the supreme leader in the Muslim League.

Jinnah's greatest drawback was his inability to communicate with the masses. He was aware of his weakness. The Congress could reach out to the nook and corner of the country, because of the mass contacts that Gandhi had developed. The Muslim leadership had no such charisma. Whenever Gandhi made any announcement, be at the Sabarmati Ashram or at Wardha, millions of people across the country would come out on the streets in his support. Jinnah was aware of this. Jinnah now realized that if he had to secure the support of the Muslims he would have to reach out to the masses like Gandhi. Jinnah who hated the crowds was now longing for an opportunity to mingle with them.

Fortunately, he soon found such an opportunity.

The Muslims and the Sikhs were on loggerheads on the question of control over the Shahidgunj mosque in Lahore. The Sikhs claimed that the mosque complex belonged to them and that it was originally a *Gurudwara.* However, after a military victory, the Muslims had captured it and transformed it into a mosque. The mosque was situated in the Sikhs locality. Several communal riots had taken place on this issue creating a tense atmosphere for the past so many years. In spite of several rounds of talks, no solution could be found. One day the Sikhs captured the mosque and hoisted a flag over the mosque with the words *Sat Shri Akal.* The Muslims could not tolerate this. In protest the Muslims went on a rampage in Lahore. A militant Muslim organisation called Ittihad-e-Millat, under the leadership of Maulana Zafar Ali Khan, had launched an agitation to recapture the mosque. The angry mobs of the Sikh community resorted to arson and killings. The Muslims retaliated. They looted and terrorized the people. They offered a stiff resistance to recapture the mosque. The law and order deteriorated in Lahore day-by-day.

A clever Jinnah saw an opportunity in this. He thought if he could discuss the issue with the concerned people and find an amicable solution, he would become a popular leader not only among the Muslims, but also among the Sikhs. Until then the Sikhs were opposed to the Muslims in all the movements. They supported the Congress. Jinnah thought that if he could find a solution to the problem of the Sahidgunj mosque, he would make a dent in the support for the Congress.

Jinnah reached Lahore immediately.

He addressed the agitated Muslims. Had it been some other time, he would have met the Muslim representatives in an air-conditioned hotel room or in a luxurious conference room. But now he had to change that to succeed in his chosen path. Jinnah had decided to call a public meeting to understand the problem.

But he faced a hurdle at the very first meeting. The people who attended the meeting knew only two languages—Punjabi and Urdu. And Jinnah could not speak either of the two languages, except uttering a few sentences at random. His fluency in English might have been alright in conference rooms, but here in the audience no one could understand a word of English. Without a good interpreter at his very first public meeting, he would not be able to communicate with the people. Nor would they understand him. In a jam-packed meeting held at a public ground, Jinnah in his trade mark suit and monocle looked like a foreigner.

39

Jinnah in mosque with shoes, settlement between the two communities in Lahore, political reforms, New Viceroy Linlithgow, Central Assembly in Delhi-Jinnah's views

After establishing the contact with the Muslims, Jinnah also tried to reach out to the Sikhs and the Hindus. The Sikhs were so agitated that they were not willing to listen to any advice of giving up their control over the Sahidgunj. Jinnah noticed that the Hindus supported the Sikhs. Yet all the parties wanted to find some solution and restore the normalcy. The British government in Punjab was in a difficult position. Neither any party was interested in taking the matter to the court and settle the issue nor anybody was prepared for any third party mediation. Both the parties had made it a communal issue. The situation in the entire province was getting worse. There was a fear of the situation going out of control and resulting in violent communal riots. Hence, the governor welcomed Jinnah's peace efforts and assured him full cooperation. The atmosphere created was such that it seemed as if the governor himself had invited Jinnah to initiate the peace efforts.

On the other hand, the Muslims in the city had resorted to acts of violence. The Sikhs retaliated. The government insisted that both the communities must abjure the violence. Both the parties had come out with pre-conditions. The Muslims insisted that unless the Sikhs surrender the Sahidgunj mosque, they would not agree to any negotiation. The Sikhs remained equally adamant in their stand that the question of surrendering the mosque did not arise. The situation worsened. As the violence remained unabated, hundreds of people belonging to both the communities were arrested and sent to jail. Lots of discussions were held, but the solution was evasive. Jinnah was eager somehow to find some solution to the problem so that he could become a leader of both the Muslims and the Sikhs. He expressed his wish to visit the mosque where the Muslims used to offer their prayers. The Sikhs agreed to this.

The next day Jinnah visited the Sahidgunj mosque complex along with a group of Sikhs, Hindus and Muslims. The part of the complex used by the Muslims for prayers was closed. The other part of the complex was a *gurudwara*.

The Sikhs who were waiting to receive Jinnah raised the slogan *Sat Shri Akal.* The Muslims not to be left behind raised the slogan *Allah-o-Akbar*. Jinnah entered the mosque with a group of Muslims. The verses from the Quran written on the walls were white washed. The Hindus did not enter the mosque with Jinnah. The group of people accompanying him suddenly stopped and stared at each other. There was some commotion. Jinnah entered the mosque without removing his shoes outside, as per the well established Islamic tradition. He defiled the mosque. It was difficult for anyone to call him back and ask him to remove the shoes. Everyone knew how arrogant Jinnah was. He would not hesitate insulting the people, if he was asked to remove his shoes. It might disturb the situation.

"Why nobody is stopping him? He is defiling the mosque by enter the mosque without removing his shoes," a young man, barely out of his teens, shouted from behind. Nobody had expected this. All of them suddenly turned back and looked at him.

He shouted, "It looks, Barrister Jinnah had never visited a mosque, because he is a Khoja. The Khojas have nothing to do with the mosques. Their place of worships is the community hall." The young man ran towards Jinnah and said, "Mr. Jinnah, please go out and remove your shoes."

The crowd was stunned. The young man was right. But his aggression was frightening. The situation could turn grim, if he attacked Jinnah. Some people in the group held him and took him away. Jinnah turned back and saw the young man being dragged out of the complex. He understood the enormity of the situation. He immediately came out pretending as if nothing had happened.

The Sikhs were neither prepared to surrender the mosque nor willing to accept any third party mediation. They claimed that it belonged to them. In such a situation, finding a solution to the problem became very difficult. Jinnah doubted his ability to find any solution. He could not afford to spend more time on this. He had other important work to attend. As a last effort, he held parleys with the Hindus in search of an amicable solution. They were also affected by the situation. Their trade and industry were badly hit by the communal riots. If the violence continued unabated, it might result in a communal flare up throughout the country and ruin the economy. Considering all this, the Hindu leaders made a suggestion to Jinnah that he should impress upon the Muslims to withdraw the agitation first. If the Muslims abjured the violence, they would prevail upon the Sikhs to accept the mediation of a third party. Jinnah should bring pressure on the governor to release the people arrested in this connection. He realized that no solution would be possible through violence or force. And if he left the place without finding a solution, it would harm his image as a leader among the Muslims of the Punjab and in the Muslim League.

Jinnah met the Muslim leaders and urged them to withdraw the agitation. The Muslims realized by now that it was not easy to use force against the Sikhs. They were prepared to withdraw the agitation provided the Sikhs agreed to a third party mediation. If the Sikhs agreed to the mediation, it would mean they were accepting that the mosque was a disputed structure. It would mean victory to the Muslims in a way.

Once the agitation was withdrawn, the parleys would take long time to yield any result and the people would calm down. The Sikhs suggested that instead of a third party mediation a joint committee comprising of the Sikhs, the Muslims and the Hindus of Lahore be formed to find an amicable solution.

The parties reached an understanding. Jinnah met the governor. It was to release all the prisoners immediately on withdrawing the agitation. And the charges against them would be dropped. Even for the governor the agitation posed a big problem. He was responsible to the Viceroy for maintaining the law and order. He had no objection in releasing the prisoners once normalcy was restored in the city.

As a matter of fact, the Hindus had no stake in the issue. It was a dispute between the Sikhs and the Muslims. However, the Hindus as a neutral party could facilitate the dialogue between the two parties. The Hindus agreed to get involved in the public interest to restore peace and tranquility. The Muslims withdrew the agitation. The government released the prisoners. A joint committee comprising nine members—four Muslims, three Sikhs and two Hindus—was formed.

While leaving Lahore, Jinnah addressed the Muslims assembled for the Friday prayers at the Royal mosque, where he said, "There is no question of the Muslims giving up their right over the Sahidgunj mosque. Like the Muslims, the Sikhs are also a valiant community. I am sure that the joint committee will come out with a solution and ensure communal harmony between the two communities. In the meantime, maintain peace in the city. And call me whenever I am required." (In 1938, the Court decided that the Sahidgunj was a gurudwara, and not a mosque).

It was obvious that Jinnah could not succeed in finding a lasting solution to the problem. At least, it established the fact that on an issue like this he could become a leader acceptable to all communities. Where the government had failed, he could succeed in containing the communal passion, though temporarily.

*

A bill on the constitutional reforms in India was presented in the British Parliament. The British Conservative Party leader Winston Churchill tried to stall the reforms. As per the proposed reforms, the British provinces in India would have autonomous governments. Churchill believed that the Indians were not competent to rule. However, the British Parliament passed the bill with a thumping majority due to the efforts of the Labour Party Prime Minister Ramsay MacDonald. Certain sections in the Act still had the potential to disturb the communal harmony. It prescribed certain qualifications like education and economic status as the basis for eligibility to vote. The seats in the Provincial Assemblies were reserved for some seventeen communities. The criteria for eligibility to vote was different for the Muslims and the non-Muslims. A fresh Muslim graduate with less income could be eligible to vote, but that was not so with regard to the other non-Muslim communities. Out of the three hundred million population in the country, the Muslims constituted seventy million. But the percentage of the Muslim electorate rose to thirty three per cent. And only twelve per cent of the people were enrolled as the voters.

The population of the country was segregated on the basis of religious affinity. Besides, the people were also segregated on the basis of castes and sub-castes. The government defended that this was done to protect the interest of the minorities. Criticizing this policy of the government, Jinnah said, "The segregation of the voters on the basis of religion is not a good thing. Protecting the interest of the minorities is alright. But the religion alone cannot be the basis of determining the minorities. It is possible a particular religious community is a minority in a particular region, but the language, caste and culture also make a people minority. It is important to protect their interest also. Considering all this, the government should not make protecting the interest of the minorities a religious issue, but a political issue."

At a time when the elections were being held under the new Act, the Muslim League was in a disarray. Its organisation was weak. Its financial position was not sound. It depended mainly on the donations by the philanthropists. To improve its financial position, Jinnah had co-opted many rich Muslim industrialists into the Working Committee of the League. They included, Ismail Chundarigar, a noted and wealthy advocate from Bombay, Liaqat Ali Khan from the United Province and Suhrawardy from Bengal—all the three having a notch above the rest. Jinnah tried to free the League from the clutches of the Nawabs and the Maulvis by bringing the people with modern educational background.

Yet Jinnah was in a dilemma. Though he was the supreme in the League, he was not sure about its success. He was still prepared to reach some understanding with the Congress. He wanted the Congress and the League to contest the elections jointly under the new Act. The Muslim League was in such a bad shape that he doubted whether it could form the governments on its own even in those provinces where the Muslims were a majority.

However, he was disappointed by the speech made by the new Viceroy Lord Linlithgow. In his first speech he said that he was absolutely neutral and unbiased on the communal issues. He said just as the Hindus, the Muslims, the Christians, the Sikhs and the untouchables were the children of mother India, they were like his children too. God had given him the opportunity to look after them and he would make full use of that. All were equal to him. And that he would not discriminate between them.

When Jinnah heard the speech, he became furious, "This means, the Muslims will not be rewarded for their loyalty to the British government. If all are equal, what is the meaning of loyalty? If the special privileges conferred upon the Muslims are withdrawn, in the name of neutrality and justice, we will resist."

Jinnah got an opportunity to confront. He was elected to the Central Assembly. He was re-nominated as a Muslim representative from Bombay, before he took up the reins of the Muslim League. The Congress members had raised an issue in the Assembly. The Congress leader Subhash Chandra Bose was arrested. The Congress contended that he was arrested without any reason only to disturb the peaceful atmosphere. It moved a motion censuring the government in the Central Assembly. The government needed the support of Jinnah and his group to defeat the motion. Jinnah wanted to demonstrate that the Muslims could not be equated with the other communities and that without the support of the Muslims the British government could not run the country.

But this did not mean that his group would vote in favour of the motion. Jinnah was willing to support the motion provided he extracted a pound of flesh from the Congress. If the Congress was not willing to pay the price, the government would have to pay. But the Viceroy had already declared his neutrality. Jinnah chose a middle path. He and his group abstained from voting on the censure motion. Jinnah chose to adopt the same neutrality the Viceroy had advocated and posed a challenge to him—"You will not be able to run the government without the cooperation and the support of the Muslims. Your neutrality will simply lead to the Congress riding roughshod over you."

The Congress censure motion was passed by a majority in the Central Assembly. It was an embarrassing situation for the Viceroy.

40

Jinnah-Khurshid meeting, face lift to the 'South Court', Jinnah's conversation with a friend's son throughout the night, Jinnah-Khaliquzzaman-Rafiq Ahmed Kidwai

Jinnah was unhappy about the poor calibre of his colleagues in the Muslim League. He wanted to induct the educated, intelligent and fearless young people into the League. He was looking for the talented young people. He suddenly spotted to two such young men.

Jinnah and Pandit Jawaharlal Nehru were scheduled to address a public meeting. Both of them expressed their views on the prevailing political situation in the country. At the end of the meeting, Jinnah descended from the dais and was heading towards the gate. A Muslim youth Ibrahim Habibullah was walking alongside Jinnah. Noticing something striking in the young man, he asked him,

"Don't you think, what Jawaharlal said was utter nonsense?"

"Not at all," the young man answered in a firm tone. "On the contrary, I totally agree with all that he said."

"If we accept what Jawaharlal had said, we will have a law of the jungle in the country. That you have not realized it is a sheer madness."

"Jinnah Sahib," said the young man with more firmness. "The progress of the mankind had started from the jungle. If you do not understand that, forgive me, it's your madness."

The stunned Jinnah stared at the young man who was hardly twenty five years old. No one could talk to him so boldly. He suddenly stopped, put his hand around the young man's shoulder and asked,

"Young man, what is your name?"

"Ibrahim Habibullah."

"Oh! That's a very good name," a pleased Jinnah said thoughtfully.

"What is good about it? It is after all a name!" said the young man.

"The name Ibrahim is very important to me. I want to draft the bold and the intelligent young men like you into the Muslim League. I think you are the young man I am looking for."

Habibullah was enthralled. Jinnah was not only a prominent leader of the

Muslims but also an influential politician in the country. Jinnah's offer was an opportunity to Habibullah. He immediately accepted Jinnah's offer. The young man who found Jawaharlal more sensible and logical in his address at the public meeting than Jinnah had no qualms in joining hands with the latter. He soon became an important colleague of Jinnah.

In the same way, Jinnah found another bright young man called K.H. Khurshid. He was from Kashmir. He worked as a reporter in a local newspaper. He was the leader of the students' movement in Kashimir. Jinnah was present at a function of the Muslim students. Khurshid had acted as Jinnah's host. When both of them were introduced, Jinnah said," Young man, you are connected to the Press. You must keep me informed every day about the activities of Gandhi."

This was a golden opportunity to Khurshid to reach out to Jinnah. He started briefing Jinnah regularly on the activities of Gandhi. Jinnah was pleased about his sincerity. He was collecting all the news about Gandhi a day before the newspapers published it.

Khurshid was greatly impressed by the speech that Jinnah had delivered at a students' function. Jinnah had said that the Muslims had only one God, one holy book The Quran, one pilgrimage and only one Prophet Muhammad. Now they must have one organisation, one platform, one flag and one leader like Prophet Muhammad. And if the Muslims were united, no one could stop their progress. After the function, Jinnah attended another function of the Kashmiri youth. Khurshid accompanied him. This function was not meant for any particular community or class. The Hindus were present in a large number. The chairman of the youth organisation Shivnarayan Fotedar, introducing Jinnah to the gathering said,

"I am the leader of the minority community in Kashmir. But I am not a Jinnah of Kashmir."

Jinnah understood the hint, and then retorted very quietly,

"I wish, you become one. My good wishes are with you."

Khurshid was impressed by Jinnah's wit.

Jinnah stayed in Kashmir for three days. While returning he asked Khurshid, "Would you like to work as my private secretary?"

Kurshid did not react immediately. The offer was unexpected.

"I will pay a salary of hundred rupees a month."

Hundred rupees was a big money those days. It was an honour to work as a private secretary to an eminent leader like Jinnah. He immediately accepted Jinnah's offer.

"Sir, I am honoured that you have reposed faith in my talent. But I do not have any place to stay in Bombay."

"Oh! That is no problem. You can stay in my bungalow whenever you are in Bombay. But..." Jinnah said cautiously, "whenever you travel with me outside Bombay, you will have to make your own arrangements."

Khurshid accepted the condition. But he could understand its implication only when he started staying with Jinnah in Bombay. Jinnah would stay hardly a few days in Bombay. Most of the time, he spent in travelling across the country. No special arrangement was made for Khurshid's stay in Bombay. When Khurshid discussed the problem with Jinnah the latter suggested that the former could convert the passage between the kitchen and the bathroom into a room and stay there. Khurshid remained a close associate of Jinnah till his last breath.

Jinnah was now about sixty. He was involved in several activities, had amassed great wealth and earned name and fame. A lot of people visited him everyday at his bungalow on the Mount Pleasant Road. He found his residence inadequate and uncomfortable. He planned to erect a new grand building in its place. Beside politics, Jinnah took keen interest in the Bombay Stock Market and the Mahalaxmi race course. Sometime he adjusted his work schedule to go to the race course in Bombay and Poona. He had investments in the real estate in the cities of Bombay, Lahore, Delhi and Karachi. He engaged a renowned architect Claude Batley to design and construct a new house. He instructed that the material to be used for the house should be of a very high quality and purchased only after his approval. He decided to shift his residence to his other bungalow at Mayfair Gardens till the new house was ready.

In the midst of all these activities, Jinnah would often feel lonely. He would spend his private moments in the courtyard of his bungalow and in his room. A small incident which occurred at the South Court could give a glimpse of what loneliness had meant to him.

A childhood friend of Jinnah, who had studied with him in the school at Karachi, had sent his son and his friend to Jinnah's house. The two young men came to Bombay in connection with some examination. They were strangers to Bombay. Hence, Jinnah had arranged for their stay in his bungalow. He would enquire every day about their examination and the experience in Bombay. They would meet at the breakfast table and in the garden in the evenings. This was a routine for about ten days.

The night before they were to leave, Jinnah had engaged them in a conversation for a long time. Then both of them retired to their room and soon were fast asleep. Jinnah could not sleep. He was suddenly overwhelmed by a feeling of loneliness that he had never experienced before. Had it been any other time he would have sought refuge in a bottle of scotch or whiskey. He got up from the bed and walked quietly into the room where the two young men were sleeping. A dim night bulb lit the room. Yet, Jinnah switched on the bright light. The young men woke up due to the sudden flash of light. They were astonished to see Jinnah in *pyjama* and dressing gown standing in front of them. Jinnah sat on one side of the bed and said gently to them,

"I am sorry to disturb your sleep, my children," he said with an uncharacteristic mellowness. "Since you are leaving tomorrow, I thought I could talk to you for a little more time."

Both of them were very surprised. They could not understand what a busy and important person like him would talk to the youngsters in that midnight? They looked at him curiously.

"I remembered my student days in Karachi..." He narrated his student days. He also narrated his experiences as a student in London. He talked freely for hours. Then he got up suddenly from the bed and said patting them,"Enough, it is too much. You sleep for sometime," and then he said while switching off the light, "If I had a son like you..."

*

It was time to implement the new Act passed by the British Parliament. The stage was set for the election to the Provincial Assemblies. About thirty million electorate would elect more than 1500 members, out of which, 485 seats were reserved for the Muslims.

Jinnah realized that the Muslim League would not be able to form the governments on its own even in those Provinces where the Muslims were a majority. Jinnah knew that the League was far behind the Congress in terms of organisation, resources and manpower. Sikandar Hayat Khan of Punjab had formed a separate party and attracted the Muslims, the Hindus and the Sikhs into its fold. In Bengal, Suharawardy and Fazalul Haq had refused to toe the line with Jinnah. Allah Baksh in Sindh had also challenged his leadership. Nobody doubted that the Congress in the North West Frontier Province, under the leadership of Badshah Khan, would sweep the poll. In the United Province, the Mullahs and the Maulvis and the Nawabs had rallied behind Liaqat Ali Khan. He was Jinnah's right hand. He claimed to be the sole leader of the Muslims in the United Province and insisted that he would choose the candidates of the Muslim League. He wanted to keep his detractors under check.

But Jinnah did not agree with this stand of Liaqat Ali Khan. The United Province had a large Muslim electorate. If the Muslim League won the election there, it would have an impact all over the country. Jinnah formed an Election Committee for the United Province to select the candidates, much against the wishes of Liaqat Ali Khan who was not even made a member of the Committee. Khaliquzzaman was appointed the Chairman of the Committee.

Khaliquzzaman had been closely connected to the Congress politics for two decades. He was a close friend of the Congress leader Rafi Ahmed Kidwai. He had held various positions in the Congress. Though he was with the Muslim League, his political allegiance was with the Congress. He had played a major role in the Khilafat movement and in the Home Rule League. Now under the influence of Jinnah, he left the Congress and was totally devoted to the cause of the Muslims.

Thus, Khaliquzzaman became the incharge of the election campaign of the Muslim League in the United Province, while his close friend Rafi Ahmed Kidwai was his counterpart in the Congress. The Muslim League was not in a position to make substantial gains in the Province. Jinnah was trying to reach an understanding with the Congress to fight the elections jointly. Khaliquzzaman tried to reach an understanding with Rafi Ahmed Kidwai. He suggested to Kidwai, "Rafi, we can reach an understanding. Let the Congress and the League form a coalition government in the United Province. Though we may contest the elections separately, let us keep that in mind."

Rafi Ahmed did not find anything objectionable in the suggestion. He felt it would be much easier to oppose the British government if the Congress and the Muslim League acted in unison. He said to Jaman, "Your suggestion is good. We can make some arrangement after the elections."

None of them knew that their decision would take a decisive turn in future.

41

Jinnnah-Jawaharlal Nehru correspondence, Jinnah as the permanent President of the League, Muslim League session in Lucknow, change in Jinnah's dressing style, refusal to accept a toy free of charge

Liaquat Ali Khan was a very influential person in the United Province. Jinnah had sidelined him. This made Liaquat Ali Khan quite unhappy. Jinnah thought that since he was a colleague, he could pacify him somehow. The people who opposed to the politics of the Muslim League in the United Province had formed a separate party called the Unionist Party. In the Punjab too, the people opposing the Muslim League had formed a similar Unionist party under the leadership of Sikandar Hayat Khan. Jinnah tried to appease the Unionist Party of the United Province to win over it to his side. Everybody knew that Liaquat Ali Khan owed his rise in politics to Jinnah. However, no one had doubted his power and strength.

A clever Jinnah realized that if a close colleague like Liaquat Ali Khan could become unhappy, it would be difficult for him to stamp out the dissent. The only solution was to have all the power vested with him. Keeping this in mind, he got elected himself as the President for life of the Muslim League at its annual session, before the commencement of the elections. Nobody had the guts to challenge him. A totally relaxed Jinnah, then got a resolution passed vesting all powers with him. Now he became an undisputed leader and exercised absolute power. No one could challenge his actions legally within the League. Jawaharlal Nehru, the Congress President, wanted to reach an understanding with Jinnah since he was the whole and sole of the Muslim League. When it was proposed in the party to have talks with Jinnah, Nehru reacted saying, "I have no objection in talking to Jinnah, but he has a closed mind. He knows only law and politics. I doubt whether he knows anything about human civilisation and culture. He has a strong negative frame of mind. Negativity cannot find solution to any problem. However, I will take the first step to have a talk with him with an open mind and good intention."

Nehru took the first step. In his letter to Jinnah, he said, "I do not think that we have any differences which cannot be resolved. If you can tell me the issues where we differ, I shall try to resolve them."

Jinnah, in his reply, said, "you should be aware of our differences. There is no need to enlist them, because you knew where we differ. However, if you want to meet me, you can do so on my return to Bombay."

Thereafter, Jinnah commenting on the correspondence exchanged between them said, "Jawaharlal is an extremely learned son of my colleague Motilal. He should have been a Professor of English in a college instead of entering the politics. He is the *Peter Pan* of the literary world."

When the election campaign reached its feverish pitch, the Muslim League made an issue of the word *Ramraj* used by Gandhi while referring to the *Swaraj*. The League leaders twisted the word to mislead the illiterate Muslim masses that Ram was a Hindu God and Gandhi was trying to make Him a God of all communities. A fear psychosis was created among the Muslims that if the *Ramraj* became a reality, Islam would be endangered. And if the majority Hindus rule the country, they would force the Muslims to give up wearing *pyjama* and make them wear *dhoti* and destroy the Islamic culture. The Congress leader Maulana Azad convened a meeting of the Mulllahs, Maulvis and Ulemas to dispel the misgivings of the Muslim League.

Jinnah became furious about the Ulemas assisting the Congress in clearing the misgivings of the Muslim League leaders. He coined a new slogan "Islam is in danger" for fighting the election. This became the main election plank for the Muslim League.

Jinnah travelled across the length and breadth of the country for the election campaign. He reached Lucknow a day before his scheduled public meeting. He was a guest of a local prominent Muslim League leader Raja Mahemoodabad. Jinnah was still travelling in his modern western suits. If he had to address three to four meetings a day, he would change his suit after every meeting. He would not wear any suit for more than four to five hours. His audience mainly comprised of the illiterate and the semi-literate Muslim masses who dressed in the traditional Islamic outfits. He looked completely out of place in his well tailored suits and English hat. As a result, though huge crowds turned up at his meetings, there remained a huge distance between them. Jinnah who had hated the crowds now came to them, but could not become one among them.

Before the scheduled meeting at Lucknow, Raja Mehmoodabad had suggested to Jinnah, "If you do not mind, I would like to make a suggestion. Your western dress looks strange to the Muslim masses. They come in a large number to see you or listen to you. But they are unable to connect to you. They hesitate in connecting to you."

Jinnah was lost in thought. He pondered over the suggestion. For a moment, he thought of wearing a small loin cloth like Gandhi. But he was horrified at the thought. Perhaps what endeared Gandhi to the Hindu masses. Jinnah looked at Fatima, standing next to him.

"*Bhaijaan*! Raja Sahib is right," concurred Fatima. "Just as Gandhi connects to the masses, you too can connect to the Muslim masses if you wear the Islamic dress *Sherwani*. The Hindu leaders pretend to appease the masses. You should do the same to appease the Muslim masses."

Jinnah felt that Fatima's suggestion was quite sensible. He ordered for *Sherwani* and *salwar*. This was totally a new experience to him. Since his days as a student in England he had never worn anything except the western attire. For the first time he was going to address a public meeting in this new dress.

Fatima's words were ringing in his ears till he reached the venue. It was impossible for him to wear a *dhoti* like Gandhi. Jinnah suddenly remembered that Gandhi initially used to wear a *khaadi* white cap. That cap called the 'Gandhi cap' became extremely popular among the people. Though he did not wear it any more, the millions of his followers popularised it across the country to spread his message. Jinnah thought the Muslims had no such common cap. He thought that if he could wear a cap that goes with his *Sherwani*, it could become popular among the Muslim masses. He saw a prominent Muslim leader Nawab Mohammed Islam Khan standing near the venue. He was wearing a black Iranian cap. A thought suddenly flashed in his mind. Why not present it as a model cap for the Muslims to counter the Gandhi cap? He whispered something in his ear.

"Nawab *Sahib*, as suggested by Raja *Sahib*, I wore this dress to identify with the Muslim masses. But I think this dress is incomplete without your cap. Can I try your cap today?"

The Nawab was stunned. He was astonished to see Jinnah in *Sherwani*. And if he wears the black cap, the crowd would not be able to recognize him. But they would be excited once they recognized him. Without hesitating for a moment, the Nawab took off his cap and put it on Jinnah head. The people around cheered him "*Janab Jinnah Zindabad*."

The Nawab's guess proved right. When Jinnah climbed the dais, for a moment the crowd did not recognize him. But when he started greeting the people on the dais in the Islamic tradition, the joy of the crowd knew no bounds. They were used to seeing him all these years in modern expensive suits. Now in this traditional dress, he sounded like one among them. They cheered him.

The meeting was a great success. His supporters in the Muslim League thronged the market in search of his cap. The cap that was available for a rupee the previous day was not available even for five or ten rupees the next day. Those who managed to get the cap were excited. They cried out, "Look! This is 'Jinnah's cap.' It is much better than the Gandhi cap!"

*

The Muslims were a majority in Baluchistan and the North West Frontier Province. But they were different from their co-religionists in India. Racially and culturally, they were closer to the tribals of Afghanistan. They were against the British rule. They admired the Congress for its fight against the British rule and condemned the Muslim League's opposition to the Congress. They were known as the Pathans. The British government had introduced administrative and educational reforms in the British provinces, but these tribal regions were left untouched. The Pathans were a fierce, brave and valiant people. They would not hesitate to take up arms to fight. The British government had tried to fuel infighting among them and took undue advantage of the situation. It tried to settle the disputes among the warring tribal chieftains. Once the chieftains were managed, the Pathans would simply obey their orders. The Congress was most popular in the North West Frontier Province due to the influence of Badshah Khan and his band of *Khudai Khidmatgaars*. The Pathans of Baluchistan had no experience of elections until now. Jinnah made a lot of efforts to strengthen the Muslim League in these two regions.

To this end, a meeting was arranged at Quetta, the capital of Baluchistan. With the help of the British government, the chieftains of various tribal groups were contacted. The efforts were made to collect as large a gathering as possible. Jinnah's host in Quetta was a modern and educated family. It was absolutely necessary for the women to wear the *burqah*. The lady of the house, though well educated, could not go out without wearing the *burqah*. As usual, Fatima accompanied Jinnah. She had never worn the *burqah* in her life. However, if she attended the meeting without the veil, it might cause a furore. And the fury of the Pathans could prove fatal to the Muslim League. Hence, the host suggested to Fatima, "Madam, it will be better if you do not attend the meeting."

Fatima could not understand this. The lady of the house, being an educated woman, was against this system of *burqah*. She thought if Fatima could move out without the *burqah*, she would be able to defy this practice. Opposing her husband's stand, she told him, "Why are you saying that? That Jinnah Sahib is here, it is an opportunity to get rid of this medieval practice. What is wrong if the Muslim women go out without the veil?"

Jinnah, who heard the conversation, said sternly to the hostess, "What are you saying? I have been trying to bring the Muslims together for the past three years. You want me to fail in my efforts. I cannot afford to pay such a heavy price for changing this practice. I do not want my efforts to fail. Fatima and you can stay at home."

There was a time when Jinnah took exception to the slightest insinuation of Lady Willingdon about his late wife Ruttie's revealing outfit. The same man was now ordering his sister to wear the *burqah*. He had no other option. In order to put an end to the conversation, Jinnah took the four year old child of the host in his arms and then asked, "Do you like chocolate?"

The child ran his hand over Jinnah's cap and said, "Jinnah dada, please get me a rocking horse. I like it."

After the meeting, Jinnah stopped at a toyshop. As he got down from the car, the people recognized him. A crowd had gathered around the shop. They were excited that Jinnah was buying a toy from the shop. They went on cheering him. The shop keeper packed the toy neatly and feeling overwhelmed by the fact that a great man like Jinnah came to purchase the toy from his shop. He said,

"*Janab*, you have done me a great honour. Please accept this as a token of love and respect from me. You do not have to pay anything for it."

Jinnah was annoyed. Instead of taking the toy, he turned back. The shop keeper was stunned. He took up the parcel in his hand and tried to hand it over to Jinnah.

"Why do you want to gift it to me? Have you got this toy free? Or do you want to gift it to me and expect some big favour from me, in return?" Jinnah shouted at him.

The crowd cheered him. The shop keeper had nothing to say. He quietly accepted the payment for the toy.

42

Elections of Provincial Assemblies (1937), Jinnah-Begum Rana meeting in Lucknow, Gandhi-Jinnah meeting postponed

The results of the Provincial Assemblies showed mixed fortunes both for the Congress and the Muslim League. The Congress secured a clear majority in the Provinces where the Hindus were a majority. The Muslim League did not get the success as anticipated in the four Provinces where the Muslims were a majority, namely Sindh, North West Frontier Province, Punjab and Bengal. Although these four Provinces overwhelmingly elected the Muslim candidates against the reserved seats, most of them were opposed to the Muslim League. In Punjab and Bengal, the local parties opposed to Jinnah's Muslim League secured the most of the seats. In Punjab, the Muslim League emerged as the single largest party, but did not secure enough seats to form a government on its own. In the North West Frontier Province, Badshah Khan's *Khudai Khidmatgaars* secured victory for the Congress. Although a very few Hindus were elected in this Province, the Muslims were elected against the seats reserved for Muslims under the Congress tickets. Though the Muslim League was defeated badly in the elections, Jinnah had a reason to feel satisfied. Out of 485 seats reserved for the Muslims in the country, the Congress managed to win only 26 seats, 19 of which came from the North West Frontier Province alone. Thus, the Congress could win only 7 seats against the reserved seats in the rest of the country. The Muslims throughout the country rejected the Congress. It was not difficult for Jinnah to demonstrate that the Congress did not represent the Muslims and that it represented the Hindus alone. In spite of the debacle of the Muslim League at the hustings, Jinnah had rejoiced for the fact that the Muslims had rejected the Congress. It was important to capitalize on this anti-Congress sentiment among the Muslims and somehow cajole them to come under one banner. Jinnah, the shrewd political player, understood this pretty well.

After some initial hiccups, the decks were cleared for the formation of the Congress governments in the Provinces having the Hindu majority. Jinnah had another plan. He thought that the Congress and the Muslim League could form the coalition governments to ensure the Hindu-Muslim unity. Based on the verbal internal discussion between Khaliquzzaman and Rafi Ahmed Kidwai, he proposed a coalition government of the Congress and the Muslim League in the United Province. Similarly, he had a broad oral understanding with B.G. Kher, the Chief Minister of the Bombay Province to induct two Muslim League members into his ministry. However, this was subject to approval by the Congress, particularly Vallabhbhai Patel.

Jinnah's efforts to share power did not succeed. Jawaharlal Nehru, the Congress President, did not approve of the informal understanding in the United Province. The so-called discussion in the United Province was between two friends and not between two parties. However, as a goodwill gesture, he agreed to include two Muslim League members in the provincial government provided they agreed to certain conditions. Jawaharlal Nehru insisted that the Muslim League members to be inducted into the ministry should resign from the Muslim League. The Muslim League did not accept this as it would mean the League members were joining the government as independent members. The Congress leadership also opposed the Muslim League joining the government in the Bombay Province. Thus the opportunity of bringing in communal harmony between the Hindus and the Muslims through coalition governments was lost once again.

The Muslim League had a special reason to form a coalition government in the United Province. The landlords and the Nawabs were responsible for disunity among the Muslims. These feudal lords dominated politics in the United Province. During the election campaign, the Congress, particularly Jawaharlal Nehru, had promised to protect the interests of the country's farmers, landless labourers and peasants and workers. Naturally, this did not augur well with the landlords. Once the Muslim League realized that it could not form a government in the United Province, it was looking for a backdoor entry into the government. If no single party won majority, two or three parties could come together to form a coalition government. But in the United Province, the Muslim League suffered heavily in the election. It won only 27 of 64 seats reserved for the Muslims. And the Congress had a clear majority in the Assembly. Nehru did not want the feudal elements to enter the government and obstruct its functioning. Jinnah knew this quite well. Yet, he carried a nationwide campaign that the Congress wished to sideline the Muslims. He worked out a two-pronged strategy.

He tried to bring the anti-Muslim League elements together in Sindh and Bengal Provinces. He tried to reach out to Fazalul Haq of the Krishak People's Party in Bengal, Sikandar Hayat Khan of the Unionist Party in Punjab and Allah Baksh, who had revolted against the Muslim League and formed a government with the support of the Congress in Sindh. Liaquat Ali Khan who rebelled against the Muslim League and contested the election as a candidate of the Unionist Party was defeated. There was a pressure on Jinnah to expel him from the League for breaking the party discipline. Jinnah understood the importance of Liaquat

Ali Khan. He tried to placate the detractors of Liaquat Ali Khan. Liaquat Ali Khan created a situation of rebellion in the League. Jinnah did not want to expel him from the League and invite more troubles.

Jinnah had not forgotten Liaquat Ali's wife Begum Rana. He still remembered the pleasant encounter with her in London. She had then assured him that she would mobilise the country's Muslim women behind him. Jinnah thought she could help him in winning over Liaquat. He had met her quite often. Now there should not be any difficulty in meeting her. It was not so easy to forget Begum Rana's attractive persona, her amiable manners and her logical and pleasant talk. He got an opportunity to meet her.

Jinnah had to halt for a few hours at the government guest house in Lucknow. Coincidentally, Liaquat Ali Khan and Begum Rana were also present there. Begum Rana was sitting in the lobby and reading something. Liaquat was in his room with his colleagues. Begum Rana noticed Jinnah as he entered the guest house. To both of them, this was unexpected. She stood up and greeted Jinnah courteously and said,

"Jinnah *Sahib*, this morning is so lucky for me. I could not imagine I could meet you so unexpectedly."

Jinnah was surprised to see her alone. He thought this was the godsend opportunity to use Begum Rana to placate Liaquat.

"I am more lucky, because ever since I have learnt that you are also annoyed with me like Liaquat I wanted to meet both of you,"Jinnah said cautiously and then continued, "Begum, politics is a strange thing. It is a game of dice that can alienate even friends like you."

"Jinnah Sahib, this is your misunderstanding. I do not understand politics. But how could you think that I am annoyed with you?" Begum Rana said feeling offended.

"The truth is, ever since I met you, you have a special place in my heart."

To Jinnah, this response was not only unexpected, but very positive. Then he proceeded as per his plan, "If that is so, Begum, do I take it like you Liaquat is also a good old friend of mine? Can not you do something to create the same feeling that you have about me in Liaqat?" Jinnah spoke out his mind very cautiously.

"You have just said, politics is a strange thing. I said I don't know anything about it. But I know that Liaqat and I have the same feeling towards you. If you think Liaqat is annoyed with you, I shall be happy to clear the misunderstanding."

"Oh! Begum. You have unburdened me. I shall be grateful to you."

"But, I have a condition."

"Condition! What condition!" Jinnah wondered whether she would bind him with something.

"The condition is very simple. You please listen carefully."

"Yes, I have always heard you carefully."

"Then listen. Jinnah Sahib, you have lived a lonely life. I would like you to get married again," Begum Rana said with a mesmerizing look.

"I have no objection in fulfilling your wish. But I too have a condition," Jinnah said gazing into her eyes.

"I will accept your every condition, if you fulfill my wish," said Begum Rana generously.

"Then listen, Begum," Jinnah said with emphasis on each and every word, "I am willing to marry, if you find another Begum," Jinnah said raising his hand as a gesture and walked towards his room.

Jinnah did not wait to see the impact of his words on her. Begum Rana astonished turned back her face and she saw Fatima standing outside Jinnah's room. Fatima already reached the room with the luggage from the rear entrance. She saw Begum Rana talking to Jinnah. Her elegant charm, her body language and her proximity to Jinnah infuriated Fatima. Begum Rana noticed the rage on Fatima's face.

"Bitch," she muttered to herself and then said to Fatima loudly raising her hand and bowing her head, "*Aadab Arz* Fatimaji!"

Fatima returned the greeting with an induced smile, but her eyes betrayed her feelings.

*

The 1937 elections saw a major shift in India towards the provincial autonomy. New governments were formed in the British Provinces. But the Muslim League could not form a government on its own in any province. In Sindh, Alla Baksh broke away from the Muslim League and formed a government with the support of the Congress. In Punjab, Sikandar Hayat Khan of the Unionist Party formed a coalition government of the Hindus, the Muslims and the Sikhs. And in Bengal Fazalul Haq of Krishak People's Party formed a similar government. To Jinnah, this new political map of India was shocking. In the United Province and the Bombay Province, the Congress refused to share power with the Muslim League, in spite of what Jinnah called an understanding. If the situation remained like this, any talk of unity would be futile. Khaliquzzaman, who had an understanding with the Congress for sharing power in the United Province, said to Jinnah despondently, "If we cannot share power with the Hindus, how can we stay with them in the country?" His words hit Jinnah like a dagger. The Hindus would always remain an overwhelming majority in the country. Therefore, whenever democratic elections were held, the Muslims would never be able to capture power in the country. Jinnah thought seriously about it. Jinnah, who had considered democracy as the best form of government until now had a second thought.

Diwan Chimanlal, a member of the Central Assembly and a friend of Jinnah, tried to bridge the chasm created by the election. He tried to bring Gandhi and Jinnah together once again. Chimanlal mooted the idea with Jinnah. If these two reach an understanding, it would ease the communal tension in the country.

Jinnah heard Chimanlal patiently and then said stiffening his position, "Why should I meet Gandhi? If Gandhi wishes, he can meet me," Jinnah said raising his index finger, "Gandhi should take the initiative."

Chimanlal was aware of Jinnah's nature. However, he felt happy that Jinnah was not averse in meeting Gandhi if the latter took the initiative. Gandhi would not feel belittled. It was not in his nature. Chimanlal approached Jawaharlal Nehru to arrange a meeting between Gandhi and Jinnah. "I appreciate your good intention," Nehru said, "If Jinnah meets Gandhi in the present situation, it might raise his stature among the Muslims, but it would not serve any purpose. I knew Jinnah quite well. He always talks negatively."

"Nevertheless, please convey my proposal to Gandhi. He might accept my proposal," Chimanlal insisted.

Jawaharlal Nehru briefed Gandhi about Chimanlal's proposal. He also shared his personal views about the meeting. Though Gandhi did not completely agree with Nehru, he too felt that a meeting with Jinnah at that stage would not serve any purpose. He thought it necessary to wait for some more time. He had no objection in meeting Jinnah once the atmosphere became peaceful.

Jinnah's ego was hurt when he came to know Gandhi was not interested in meeting him immediately. He thought Gandhi must pay the price for his imprudence of ignoring him.

Jinnah got an opportunity within a short time to settle the score.

43

Hue and cry about alleged injustice to Muslims, Gandhi's letter to Jinnah, Gandhi-Jinnah meeting in the South Court, Jinnah's refusal to accept inquiry into alleged atrocities against Muslims, Pirpur report, Jinnah's press conference

The steps taken by the Congress Provincial Governments to improve the governance were a testimony to their organisational skills. The new educational system proposed by the eminent Islamic scholar Zakir Hussein was introduced, with the blessings of Gandhi, in the Congress ruled provinces. It was known as the Wardha plan. The song *Vande Mataram* which practically became the national anthem was accepted by the educational institutions. These changes were unacceptable to the Muslim League. Jinnah denounced the new educational system as the Hindu system. When his attention was drawn to the fact that the new system was proposed by an Islamic Scholar, Jinnah reacted angrily, "The Congress has kept a few disloyal Muslims as puppets. They are not the real Muslims." Somebody asked him, "Can you tell us who is a real Muslim?" That person knew that Jinnah did not have much faith in Islam, the Hadis or the Quran. "There is no point in talking about something that everybody knows and which needs no proof," Jinnah answered bluntly without any hesitation.

The Muslim League raised a hue and cry about the reforms introduced in the Congress ruled provinces, dubbing them as anti-Muslim. It was alleged that the Hindus beat drums outside the mosques during the prayers and that the Congress governments did nothing to stop it. The Hindus took away the cows whose sacrifice was an important religious ritual for the Muslims. It was further alleged that the Congress governments were giving training in arms to the Hindu youth in camps to force the Muslims to flee. And citing the cases of the Muslims arrested for the serious criminal offences like rape or murder, the Muslim leaders tried to project all that as a plot to destroy the Muslims.

At this stage, Gandhi thought that it was important for the Congress President to meet Jinnah and clear the misunderstandings. Jinnah was in Calcutta. Gandhi wrote a letter to him asking for a convenient time for the meeting. Jinnah did not forget Gandhi rejecting Chimanlal's proposal for a meeting a few months ago. He thought it was an opportunity to give a befitting reply to Gandhi. He wrote to Gandhi, "My meeting the Congress President will not serve any purpose. You are not even an ordinary member of the Congress. Yet the Congress cannot do anything without your approval. You know you cannot act as a bridge and remove these misunderstandings. However, if you wish to meet me you may do so."

When Gandhi received the letter, he called a woman from his Ashram to send a reply. The woman called Amtussalam was associated with the Ashram work for a long time. When Gandhi started dictating the letter, she drew his attention to a Urdu newspaper that carried a news item on Jinnah. The newspapers introduced Jinnah as the *Quaid-e-Azam*. On reading the news item Gandhi said, "Brother Jinnah is really well versed with the law. It is befitting to call him the *Quaid-e-Azam*."

Then he said, "Let us make a good beginning by addressing him as *Quaid-e-Azam*. Write, Brother *Quaid-e-Azam* Jinnah... You know Amtus," Gandhi said, "This title was used in the Muslim League meeting at Lucknow in 1916. It was used for Kemal Ataturk of Turkey. Now he is no more. But we can surely use the title Quaid-e-Azam for Jinnah."

Gandhi said in his letter to Jinnah, "I have no objection in meeting you. We can meet and sort out the differences or misunderstandings. I would request you to stop at Wardha on your way to Bombay." The letter was written in Gujarati. Jinnah rejecting Gandhi's request wrote, "It will be difficult for me to break my journey at Wardha. My itinerary has been fixed already. If you wish to meet me, you can come to Bombay after fixing a date sometime in April. I would like to remind you that I can't read or understand or speak in any language other than English. I would request you to come alone. Please do not bring Maulana Azad with you."

Though Jinnah outrightly rejected Gandhi's request, he was very happy to accept the title *Quaid-e-Azam* bestowed on him by Gandhi. When their correspondence was published in the newspapers, the title given to Jinnah by Gandhi became popular throughout the country. Barrister Jinnah now came to be known as the *Quaid-e-Azam*.

The meeting took place in Jinnah's bungalow in Bombay. In spite of Jinnah's rude behaviour, the meeting lasted for more than three and a half hours. The South Court bungalow was reconstructed. Its conference hall was modern and furnished with exquisite furniture and art pieces. Gandhi sat down on the carpet in the middle of a room, without any discomfort as if he was in his own house. Jinnah was surprised to see Gandhi sitting on the carpet instead of the plush sofa. But he controlled his temper and sat down on the sofa. Gandhi asked for a cushion for support as he was not keeping well. Jinnah provided him a large round cushion and Gandhi relaxed his head and back against it. Then he took out a package of black mud from his bag and placed it on his open stomach. Jinnah became contemptuous at these antics of Gandhi. A few drops of mud fell on the carpet. For a moment, Jinnah felt that no talk could be possible with Gandhi. "Jinnah *Sahib*," Gandhi addressed, "My health has improved after I have started using this mud pack instead of the modern medicines. If you follow this, your health will improve."

"I have no health problem," Jinnah said.

The meeting achieved nothing. At the outset, Jinnah made it clear that he was the President of the Muslim League and that the League was the sole organisation representing the entire Muslim population of the country and their interests. He insisted that the Congress represented only the Hindus. Gandhi refused to accept that the Muslim League alone represented the Muslims of the country and that the Congress represented only the Hindus. Gandhi claimed that the Congress was a national organisation that protected the interests of all religious communities and classes of people in the country. Both Jinnah and Gandhi remained firm on their stand.

Emerging from the meeting after three and a half hours, Gandhi said to the waiting journalists, "I had come here with confidence that I would be able to convince Jinnah Sahib about my views. But I haven't succeeded. I have failed to convince him about my views."

After the failure of the talks, Jinnah became more vocal in accusing the Congress Provincial governments of committing atrocities on the Muslims. The Congress President, Rajendra Prasad, refuted the allegations. He demanded that if any atrocities were committed against the Muslims they should be listed and made public. He also offered to have an inquiry conducted by Justice Maurice Gwyer, the Chief Justice of India. If the inquiry established the charges, the Congress governments would accept any punishment.

But Jinnah had made up his mind. It was not possible to have a cordial relation with the Congress, leave alone returning to the Congress. If he could not acquire a stature above that of Gandhi, he should at least hold a position equal to him. He was unable to forget the fact that he was a more senior leader than Gandhi in the Congress. Jinnah could not come out of the notion that Gandhi was responsible for his failure in the Congress and the national politics. He was not willing to accept the other Congress leaders like Jawaharlal Nehru, Sardar Patel, Rajendra Prasad or Subhas Chandra Bose as his equals. He considered the Muslim leaders in the Congress like Maulana Azad as mere puppets. He felt this was his last struggle to prove his worth. The goal was more important than the principles or the means. And the goal would not be realised without the Muslim League. It was important to mobilize the millions of the Muslims across the country to realize the goal.

Jinnah rejected Rajendra Prasad's offer for an inquiry. Instead he demanded that the Viceroy or the Secretary of State for India should appoint an Inquiry

Committee. The Viceroy had already expressed the view that there was no need for an inquiry. But, when Jinnah insisted on the appointment of an Inquiry Committee, the Viceroy Linlithgow wrote to him,

"Please do not insist on any inquiry. Because if any such inquiry is conducted, you and the Muslim League would be embarrassed. The Governors of the Provinces have not made any such complaint against the Congress government."

This enraged Jinnah. He decided to fight more aggressively. He accused the Viceroy of being partial. He declared that the Congress had always acted against the interests of the Muslims. It was a life and death issue for the Muslims to check the atrocities of the Congress. In order to prove his charge of atrocities, Jinnah asked a Muslim League member, Nawab of Pirpur, to prepare a report on the alleged atrocities. He instructed him how to write and what to write in the report. The Nawab prepared the report and submitted it to him. Jinnah scrutinized the report, made the corrections and the necessary modifications and released it to the newspapers. Jawaharlal Nehru reacting to the coverage of the report in the newspapers, issued a public statement challenging Jinnah, Fazalul Haq, Liaqat Ali Khan or any one else to accompany him to any part of the country to establish the truth about the charge of atrocities on the Muslims. Jinnah rejecting the challenge said, "You cannot make a goat a camel. The goat or camel needs no proof. What has happened is clear to everybody, it does not need any more evidence. If you do not want to see all that, that is your choice."

Sir Francis Wylie was the Governor of the Central Province. He reacted to Jinnah's accusation, "Jinnah's accusation that the Congress Ministers are prejudiced against the Muslims and the evidence presented by him is as absurd as saying that rabbits have horns."

Jinnah had to face barbed questions from the reporters on the report published in the newspapers. Jinnah said that the song *Vande Mataram* had hurt the religious sentiments of the Muslims as India was portrayed as a Goddess in the song. The reporters asked him, "Quaid-e-Azam, you were an important leader of the Congress for twenty years. This song has always been sung in the meetings of the Congress. Surely, you must have sung the song."

"No, I have never sung the song because it was against Islam."

"You must be aware that this song was sung in the meetings that Gandhi had with the Mullahs and Maulvis during the Khilafat movement," another reporter drew his attention to the fact.

"The leaders of the Khilafat movement only can answer this. I was not present in their meetings."

"The new educational system that you are opposing is jointly prepared by Dr. Zakir Hussein and Khwaja Saiyuddin, the former Director of Aligarh Muslim University. What do you have to say on this?"

"Zakir Hussein! Who is Zakir Hussein?" Jinnah asked feigning surprise, "I don't know him. And the name of Khwaja Saiyuddin I am hearing for the first time."

"You must be knowing at least that both of them are Muslims," said an impertinent reporter.

"The Congress always keeps a few such Muslims who are of no significance.

The very title of the education system shows the malafide intention of the Congress. It is called the *Vidya Mandir* educational system. The words *Vidya* and *Mandir* show the malafide intention of the Hindus. Gandhi himself formulated the new system," Jinnah said without mincing words.

"What is wrong if the Congress tries to reach out to the Muslims? If it does not reach out to them, it will be accused of neglecting the Muslims," asked yet another reporter, as if there is no end to the questions.

"The Congress is misleading the Muslims. Its intentions are malafide," Jinnah said confidently.

44

Beginning of World War II, Viceroy's appeal to Gandhi-Jinnah for cooperation in war efforts, Resignation of Provincial governments, observing the 'Day of Deliverance and thanks giving', Linlithgow-Jinnah parleys, Muslim League session in Patna, Viceroy's rejection of Jinnah's suggestion to form Provincial governments

The Second World War began in September 1939. Soon the entire European continent became a war zone. One by one, the countries like Germany, France, Holland, Britain and Italy got entangled in the war. Britain and France had vast colonies all over the world. It was very difficult to protect them. India was one of such big colonies of Britain. It was surrounded by the sea on three sides. Owing to the technological advancement, the war was not confined only to the land. Even the aerial and the naval routes were not safe. The British government was worried about the security of India. The Indian army was deployed on various war fronts. The Viceroy Linlithgow had sought the cooperation of the Congress, the largest party in the country, in fighting the war. Most of the British provinces were ruled by the Congress. The Viceroy sought the support of the Congress in the war efforts of the British authorities.

The experiment with the provincial autonomy was not a complete success. The Congress was not happy with the residuary powers vested in the Governors under the new Act. The divide between the Hindus and the Muslims had deepened. The Congress found the political reforms inadequate and demanded complete independence.

The Congress leaders raised a legitimate question. When the whole country was enslaved, how could the Congress support the government in its war efforts? The Congress refuted the claim of the British government that it was fighting the war to uphold democracy and freedom. Using the Indian army for the war was to insult India. The Congress declared that as long as India was enslaved, it would be ridiculous to fight the war for somebody's independence.

The Viceroy invited both Gandhi and Jinnah for a discussion on the issue.

It was for the first time that he invited both of them for a meeting. All the talks the Viceroy had till then were either with individuals or with various representative groups. Sometime common meetings with various religious groups were held. But it was for the first time that Gandhi and Jinnah were invited as the supreme leaders of the two main political parties in the country.

The Viceroy's invitation was so unexpected that an otherwise dispassionate Jinnah became excited for a moment. The Viceroy accorded him the status equal to that of Gandhi. He had never dreamt of this. The war in Europe became a blessing in disguise. He felt confident that he would be able to make Gandhi taste defeat hereinafter.

Gandhi clarified the Congress stand on the war in his very first meeting with the Viceroy. He made it clear that as long as the British government did not declare its intention to give independence to India, the enslaved India could not call the war meant for upholding democracy and freedom. Jinnah saw a ray of hope for his success in Gandhi's unequivocal stand. He thought leaving some ambiguity in his stand would be more beneficial. If the Congress refused to cooperate with the Viceroy in his war efforts, he would have no option but to seek the cooperation of the Muslim League—the Muslim League meant Jinnah himself. Calculating this, Jinnah said to the Viceroy, "I have to consult the other leaders of the Muslim League. Then only can I make my stand clear."

Both Jinnah and Linlithgow knew that the Muslim League meant Jinnah and vice versa. Yet Jinnah wanted to keep the Viceroy in guessing without commiting himself. The Viceroy also knew that this was a clever ploy of Jinnah. It was very obvious that if Jinnah did not support the British government in its war efforts, it would mean he was endorsing the Congress stand. Therefore, the Viceroy thought that even if the Congress did not support him in the war efforts, Jinnah would support him. If he could not garner support from the whole country, he would at least get a partial support. A friendly game of cat and mouse was started.

The British government refused to link the issue of independence of India with the aims of the war. Gandhi and the Congress leaders retaliated. Britain declared that India, as a British colony, would fight the war. India had no enmity with Germany, Italy or any other country who were the enemies of Britain. In such a situation, if India was fighting war on behalf of Britain it would mean the provincial governments supported the Viceroy in his war efforts. The provincial governments represented majority of the people in the country and, therefore, even an indirect support to the British government would prove disastrous. It was inevitable that the Congress provincial governments would resign to dissociate from the war. The Congress leaders were divided on the issue. Some senior leaders feared that this would give a free rein to the Muslim League and the British government. This could be very dangerous. Gandhi felt it was a moral issue. He was opposed to any immoral action for the sake of temporary gain. As usual, his view prevailed. The Congress provincial governments resigned en masse.

Jinnah saw yet another golden opportunity in this. The Muslim League extended the support to the Viceroy. The British government accepted all the conditions of Jinnah. Jinnah was very happy about the resignation of the Congress governments. He declared that the country would observe a 'Day of Deliverance and Thanksgiving'. He said it was a relief from the atrocities of the Congress governments. Even the Hindu Mahasabha, an extremist Hindu organisation, extended support to him in this celebration. The Hindu Mahasabha felt that the Congress provincial governments were unnecessarily favouring the Muslims and they were upset that the provincial governments did not implement the ban on cow slaughter. The Muslims were anti-Hindu and if the Congress governments adopted a lenient policy towards them, the Hindus would not be able to voice their grievances. The Hindu Mahasabha considered the Congress an obstacle in fulfilling its goals. Hence it joined the Muslim League in celebrating the 'Day of Deliverance.' It was the first and the last time that these two organisations had acted in unison.

The Viceroy called Jinnah for a meeting to discuss the modalities of the Muslim League cooperation in the war efforts. The Viceroy knew that except Jinnah, the Muslim League had no other leader who could match with the stalwarts in the Congress. He thought it would be better if Jinnah involved other Muslim leaders in this. The Viceroy said, "Mr. Jinnah, I want all the prominent and intellectual Muslims to be associated with the war efforts."

"You will find such Muslims in the Muslim League only," Jinnah told the Viceroy.

"I want the Muslims to support our war efforts."

"Your wish will be fulfilled. The Muslims will take care of the British interest in the Central Assembly, and your governors should take care of the Muslims' interest in the provinces."

The Viceroy understood the conditional support of Jinnah. Such an understanding could not be put in black and white, but it remained as an implicit understanding. The Congress boycotted the war efforts. In such a situation, the Viceroy had no option, but to depend upon Jinnah. The Viceroy gave him a diplomatic smile. It suited Jinnah.

After this, Jinnah made an aggressive lengthy speech at the annual session of the Muslim League in Patna. He still had a problem of communicating with the masses. But his rhetoric and histrionics had the desired effect on the crowd. The Muslims who until now kept an equidistance from the Congress and the Muslim League, realized that with the backing of the Viceroy, Jinnah would reach a new political height. His detractors in the Muslim League in Punjab and Bengal began realizing that their future was more safe in his hands. The Muslim League had started a campaign and listened to Jinnah in Patna. Addressing the gathering, while chalking out a political strategy, he said,"If the eighty million Muslims do not unite and speak in one voice, the Hindu Raj will crush them. We must be determined to fight for our security. The Muslims will not tolerate the vote bank politics in the name of democracy. The western type of democracy will not suit India. In Britain and France, people are homogenous, but in India the Hindus and the Muslims are two different communities. The interests of both these communities are poles apart. The beef is a delicious food to us, but the Hindus worship the cow. Until now, the Muslims, as a minority community, were given some concessions as charity. The Hindus and the British government should realize that the Muslims are not a minority community. They are the equal citizens like the Hindus. The Muslims are a nation, not a minority. They cannot be secure unless they are equal partners in the governance of the country. If we accept the western type of democracy, we will never be able to capture power by remaining with the Hindus. Who is responsible for our miserable condition?"

Nobody in the crowd could answer the question. The speech was translated simultaneously into Urdu by an interpreter. The crowd was more dazzled by Jinnah's histrionics and the rhetoric. He was cheered now and then. Jinnah himself answered the question, "If there is anyone responsible for this condition, it is Gandhi. He had destroyed the principles of the Congress. He has reduced the Congress which had been established to protect the interests of the whole country into an organisation of the Hindu revivalists. The Congress is now a party of the Hindus aiming to establish the rule of the Hindus. We will not allow this to happen. The Muslims are a separate nation and they will fight for it as their right."

After the Congress provincial governments had resigned, Jinnah thought the Muslim League as the second largest party would be able to form the governments in those provinces. In Sindh, Allah Baksh, who had formed the government with the support of the Congress, was murdered. Subsequently, the Muslim League formed the government there. In the North West Frontier Province, the Congress had formed the government with the help of Badshah Khan's *Khudai Khidmatgaars*. But some members of the Assembly were arrested and imprisoned by the British government. Consequently, the Congress was reduced to a minority. Taking advantage of the situation, the Muslim League succeeded in forming its government in the Province with the tacit support of the governor. Jinnah was hoping that similar governments by the Muslim League could be formed in all the provinces. And thus, the Muslim League could extend its rule to the whole country. If the Viceroy accepted this, his dream of establishing the Muslim League Rule in the whole country could be realized.

However, the Viceroy Linlithgow was not prepared to oblige Jinnah. The Congress governments had resigned, but the Congress members had not resigned from their membership of the Provincial Assemblies. That meant the Congress had still a majority in the Assemblies, and the Muslim League was a minority. Even if the League formed the governments in the provinces, it would not succeed in winning the vote of confidence in the Assemblies. In a democracy, no government would survive without the support of the majority members in the Assembly.

Jinnah could not refute the reasons given by the Viceroy. There was no constitutional provision to form such governments as desired by Jinnah. If this truth was accepted the Muslims would never be able to capture the power in the country. He suddenly remembered what Muhammad Iqbal and Rehmat Ali Chaudhari had told him a few years ago. Both of them had told something similar to him. The Muslims would never be able to capture power on their own through a democratic process. There was only one way to make India a *Dar-ul-Islam.*

Jinnah had dismissed the suggestion of Iqbal as a daydream, and he had made fun of Rahmat Ali as a student dreamer. He was unable to digest the bitter truth that in the provinces where there were no governments, the Muslims were unable to form the governments constitutionally.

He felt that perhaps Iqbal and Rahmat Ali were right. Now following their footsteps was the only way to protect the interest of the Muslims and safeguard his own position.

45

Dina-Jinnah conversation about marriage

The Jinnah House until recently known as the South Court became the most prestigious in Bombay. But the whole edifice was rocked by an emotional upheaval. Jinnah's daughter Dina, who called her father 'Grey Wolf' during his years in self-exile in London, now became a pretty young woman of sharp intellect and sensibility. Whenever she came to spend her vacation, Jinnah would make it a point to take out some time to spend with his darling daughter. After Ruttie's death, he never spoke about her to any friend or relative. He did not keep any of her photographs. All her belongings were dumped in the trunks. The trunks were never opened, Ruttie came alive in Dina. She resembled her mother. The pretty, delicate and always smiling Dina would make the otherwise stern Jinnah cheerful. He started noticing the beautiful flowers in his garden. That the flowers could be so colourful and beautiful he realized only after Dina visited him.

One evening when he was sipping coffee with Dina, he suddenly remembered something and became serious. Dina noticed the change on her father's face. She asked him with some anxiety, "Daddy, what happened? What are you thinking about?"

Jinnah was surprised, but felt happy about his daughter's keen observation. He used to think that nobody could read his mind. Even his colleagues found it difficult to understand his political moves. That his daughter could read his mind was a matter of immense satisfaction.

"You are right, my dear. I was thinking about you only," said Jinnah.

"But why are you so serious?"

"After all, I am a father," Jinnah said quietly. "You just look the same way your mother looked when I married her."

"Tell the truth, Daddy. Are you pleased or not?" she asked him a pointed question.

"Well!" Jinnah answered placidly, "I am happy you look like your mother, but I am worried because you are my daughter."

"Worried! Why are you worried, Daddy? What have I done to make you worry?"

"You have not done anything, my dear. As a father, I am worried about your marriage. Where and when can I find a suitable match for you?"

Dina stared at her father's anxious face for a moment. She got up and walked up to him. She closed her lips tightly for a second, as if she was deciding something, and then said softly, "Daddy, I am your daughter. You need not worry. Think, I have relieved you from this worry."

"Means!" asked Jinnah anxiously.

Dina putting her arms around her father and head on his shoulder said, "Daddy, I have chosen a boy whom I want to marry. I was about to tell you about it. Since you have brought up the issue I am telling you now."

"Oh! really," Jinnah said casually. In a way, he was happy that his daughter was thinking about her marriage. "I am sure you must have chosen the right person, my dear. Tell me, who is that person?" he asked.

"Daddy, I am glad you trust my judgment," a relieved Dina dropped her head on his shoulder.

Jinnah put his hand on her head, "You are the only one I trust, my dear." In his life of six and a half decades he was rarely emotional. This was one such moment.

It looked as if the father and the daughter were floating on a cloud of happiness for a moment.

"Tell me, who is that person ?" Jinnah asked his daughter affectionately.

"His name is Neville. He belongs to a Parsee family in Bombay. We both have decided to marry," Dina said.

"Parsee!" Jinnah screamed and stiffened his back. Dina was startled noticing the sudden change in him.

"Yes, Daddy. He is Parsee and the son of Nasarwanji Wadia, a leading industrialist of Bombay and a member of the Governor's Council," Dina said giving the full details. Jinnah knew about the Wadia family. However, he was worried that if his daughter married a Parsee, at a time when the political situation was fluid, the position that he commanded among the millions of the Muslims in the country would be jeopardized. The Viceroy accorded him the status of a supreme leader of the Muslims. He was treated on par with Gandhi, who until recently was considered an undisputed leader in the country. Because of their refusal to cooperate in the war efforts, the Congress and Gandhi fell from the grace of the British government. Now the government depended completely on Jinnah to secure the support of the Muslims in its war efforts. The Muslims, who had been under the clutches of the Mullahs and the Maulvis, now accepted him as their sole supreme leader. These Mullahs and Maulvis, who had never recognized any religion other than the Islam, would never tolerate this marriage. If that happened, he would lose everything. He now understood the Muslim mentality quite well.

"Impossible!" Jinnah pushed his daughter and stood up and said in a stern voice, "This can never happen. You cannot marry a person from another religion."

"Another religion!" Dina asked curiously. "You are saying this, Daddy! What has religion to do with marriage?"

"Yes, it has to do a lot." Jinnah said raising his index finger, "The Parsees are not Muslims. And I want you to marry only a Muslim ."

This was completely unexpected and unimaginable for Dina. She stood up, took a couple of steps back and said looking straight into her father's eyes,

"But... but why, Daddy? Tell me, is anything lacking in the person I chose or in his family?"

"He is not a Muslim. Is it difficult for you to find a young man like Neville from among the eighty million Muslims in the country?"

Dina stood still. She angrily pounded her right fist into her left palm and then said, "Daddy, forgive me, when you married my mother then also there were millions of Muslims in the country. Why did you choose a Parsee girl instead of a Muslim? Was not there any girl like Ratanbai Petit among the Muslims? Or was not there a family like that of Dinshaw Petit?" These words hit Jinnah like bullets.

It was a storm in Jinnah's life. It was the most agonizing moment of his life. It was like a severe earthquake and a storm in the ocean. Be it the Viceroy's Council, the Privy Council in London, the rival leaders in the Congress or his adversaries in the Muslim League, he could confront them all effectively. But now he had no answer. He could not face the bitter truth. How could he explain to his daughter that when he had married Ruttie he was a staunch nationalist but now he turned into a communalist for political expediency?

Jinnah became red faced. Whatever he had to say he had already said and he did not want to argue with her.

"Enough! This is my final decision. You will not marry into a family belonging to another religion," he pronounced his judgment without arguing further.

"If my mother could marry a person from another religion, why cannot I marry?" Dina said. "Daddy, I won't accept your decision."

Jinnah was speechless once again. He suddenly realized that this could have been the agony suffered by Dinshaw Petit because of his daughter Ratanbai two decades ago. This was the same daughter Dina whom he did not want to lose when Ruttie insisted on admitting her to the Annie Besant's school at Adyar.

And the very Jinnah who had never suffered a defeat or conceded a defeat was now bleeding and struggling to come to terms with the reality. Dinshaw Petit's daughter had defied him. The result was that no one in his family had attended her funeral. Now his daughter Dina too...

History was repeating itself.

"If anything like that happens, I will disown you as my daughter," Jinnah gave the ultimatum. His own words sounded strange to him. Perhaps Dinshaw Petit had uttered the same words to his daughter. Could the words produce an echo after so many years?

"If that happens, I will accept it as my misfortune," Dina said with ease.

The shock that his daughter gave him in later years of his life was not only unexpected, but also lethal. He was completely shaken and torn apart, though his nature would not allow him all that. The man who had never conceded any defeat was unable to accept the fact that his daughter had defeated him. This mental strain affected his health. At times he suffered mild fever and occasionally had the attacks of cough and cold. He lost his appetite. He found solace in drinking and smoking. Considering his deteriorating health, the doctors advised him complete rest for some days. He was annoyed with the advice. To accept the doctors' advice was to concede defeat to his daughter. Therefore, he paid no heed to their advice. On the other hand, the political turmoil in the country left no time even to breathe.

Yet, Barrister Jinnah was prepared to meet any eventuality. He made a decision.

46

Dina's marriage, Jinnah's will, Jinnah-Linlithgow meeting, Muslim League-Jinnah strategy for Pakistan-option

Dina married the young Parsee gentleman Neville Wadia she had chosen. The groom and the bride had renounced their religion and embraced Christianity. Their marriage was registered as per the Christian norms. Jinnah could not bear his daughter defying him. He acted upon what he had told her. He disowned her. He refused to recognize the fact that he had a daughter. He became so bitter that whenever he wrote letters to his daughter later, he addressed her as "Dear Mrs. Wadia." The daughter remained "Mrs. Wadia" to him for the rest of his life. And to prove that she was after all her father's daughter, Mrs. Wadia never met him after she had left his house. The only exception was when she came to Karachi to pay her last homage to Jinnah after his death.

Jinnah had a huge fortune. Considering his advanced age and fragile health, he made a will. He had no one in the family except sister Fatima. He had two or three surviving sisters, but he had no contact with them. Jinnah appointed Fatima and Liaqat Ali Khan as the executors of his will. He wrote in the will –

"Whatever I have given to Fatima till now should be treated as a gift from me and she will be the owner of all that. From my remaining property, she should be given a house, a car and two thousand rupees per month for the rest of her life. Besides, all my surviving brothers and sisters should be given hundred rupees each per month during their lifetime."

The will made no mention of Dina. It was an indication of the mental trauma Jinnah had gone through. It was a tussle between a father and an ambitious politician. This was evident from the later part of the will. He did not forget Dina, but he did not take her name in the will. He wrote in the will—"I keep aside two hundred thousand rupees for a special purpose. The interest on this amount will come to twelve thousand rupees per annum. Out of this, one thousand rupees per month be given to my daughter. And after her death, the amount be distributed equally among her children. If she dies childless, the amount be distributed equally between the Aligarh Muslim University, the Islamic College, Peshawar and the Sindh Madrassa, Karachi. Besides, a donation of twenty five thousand rupees each be made to the Anjuman-e-Islam school, Bombay and the Arabic College, Delhi. A donation of fifty thousand rupees be given to Bombay University."

After completing the legal formalities of the will, Jinnah raced towards the final mission of his life at a dangerous pace.

*

The Second World War was spreading rapidly. The Nazi Hitler and the Fascist Mussolini opened new fronts and became strong. Britain was fighting for its survival at a crucial juncture in history. The Congress not only refused to cooperate with the British government in its war efforts, but also directed its provincial governments to resign. In such a situation, Viceroy Linlithgow played his cards quite deftly. In fact, the resignation of the Congress provincial governments could be attributed to his success. The hostile provincial governments would not have been conducive to his war efforts.

At the beginning of the war, the Viceroy had called Gandhi and Jinnah for a meeting and accorded them equal status. This was done with a malafide intention. He asked the governors of the provinces to take charge of the administration, after the resignation of the provincial governments. He constituted a Security Council to coordinate the war efforts. The Congress had already declared the complete independence as its goal. Jinnah pledged the support of the Muslims in the war efforts. But he was silent on the goal of the Muslim League. The Muslims extending their support to the government without making their goal clear could prove to be dangerous for British interest. To find out what was in his mind, the Viceroy called Jinnah for a meeting. In his first meeting with the Viceroy, Jinnah had insisted on safeguarding the interests of the Muslims in return for the support to the government. The Viceroy understood the clever move of Jinnah. His ambition was that he should be considered equal to Gandhi. But unlike Gandhi, he lacked the clarity of putting his thoughts into action and the backing of the people. The Viceroy suggested to Jinnah, "*Quaid-e-Azam*, the British government is thankful to you and the Muslim League for the support in the war efforts, but the common peoples' support will not last unless they are presented with a long-term goal. The Congress had declared complete independence as its goal. The Muslim League was opposed to the Congress, but it had not come out with any alternative programme. It is in your interest that I should make your goal clear to the Secretary of State and the British Parliament. If you have any alternative programme, be assured you will have my support." Jinnah understood the importance of the hidden message behind the Viceroy's suggestion. He accepted his suggestion. He began thinking of a programme that could unite the Muslims and win their support. In the elections of 1937, the Muslims won the majority of the seats reserved for them. But all of those members who won the election were not candidates of the Muslim League. The Muslim League had a minor share in the seats. And the League could not form a single government on its own even in those provinces where the Muslims were a majority. In fact, 95 per cent Muslims in the North West Frontier Province had voted for the Congress. In Punjab, Sikandar Hayat Khan's Unionist Party had bitterly fought against the Muslim League. In his ministry, besides the Muslims, a large number of Sikhs and Hindus were also included. The provincial autonomy of Punjab was more important to the Unionist Party. Sikandar Hayat Khan did not allow Jinnah or the Muslim League to have a foothold in Punjab. At the time of election, Jinnah had tried to befriend him, but did not succeed. Jinnah was so frustrated that he vowed publicly not to take any interest in the politics of Punjab again. Similarly, Fazalul Haq of Bengal was against the Muslim League. His Krishak People's Party had formed the government with the support of the smaller groups and a radical Hindu leader like Shyama Prasad Mukherjee. Fazalul Haq was not willing to forego his fiefdom for Jinnah.

Yet, both Fazalul Haq and Sikandar Hayat Khan knew that controlling their regional fiefdoms was not every thing. If the Muslims' voice was not powerful in the Central Assembly at Delhi, the British government would bow to the dictates of the Congress dominated by the Hindus. It was important to strengthen the Muslim voice in the Central Assembly to arrest this. Everyone knew that only Jinnah could present such strong a voice of the Muslims. Though they disliked Jinnah personally and opposed him, they knew that they could not run the provincial governments without the support of Jinnah in the Central Assembly.

The Muslim majority provinces like Sindh and Baluchistan were dreaming of becoming independent nations. The Muslims in the predominantly Hindu majority provinces feared that they might be reduced to a minority if the states are carved out on the basis of population. They wanted autonomous Muslim states and a federal government at the Centre where the Hindus and the Muslims would share power equally. The Muslims seemed united in opposing the Congress demand for complete independence, but no one, including Jinnah, could understand what it actually meant.

In such a situation, Jinnah felt that the Viceroy had wanted to know the thinking of the Muslims League under the pretext of alternative programme. The Viceroy knew the narrow sectarian interests of the various Muslim groups. He felt perhaps it was the Viceroy's ploy to remind him of his limitations. Nevertheless, since the Viceroy had assured his support to the alternative programme, he should take advantage of that. Even if the Viceroy wanted to use him he would never allow that to happen. In fact, Jinnah was skillful enough to use others to serve his purpose. He used his skill. He envisaged a plan that could appease one and all—the Provinces like Punjab and Bengal who wished to be autonomous, the majority Muslim provinces like Sindh and Baluchistan who wanted to be independent and the Muslims in the predominatly Hindu provinces who wanted autonomous regions within a federation and even Viceroy Lord Linlithgow.

Barrister Zafarulla Khan of Punjab was an adversary of Sikandar Hayat Khan. He had not succeeded in securing any gains to the Muslim League in Punjab. Jinnah asked him to draft a resolution. He made Zafarulla Khan to draft the resolution in a cleverly worded language that the parties concerned could interpret it in whichever way it suited them. The Sindh and the Baluchistan provinces started dreaming of becoming independent nations. The Muslims in other parts of the country were visualizing the establishment of *Dar-ul-Islam,* and the British government would not be able to reach any understanding with the Congress in future without the support of the Muslims and the Congress dream of securing independence would never be realized. Further, Jinnah would emerge as the sole spokesman of the Muslims in the country to negotiate with the British government on their behalf. It did not matter if some upheavals came in the way. The end was more important than the means to him.

It was necessary to secure the consent of Sikandar Hayat Khan and Fazalul Haq to the resolution drafted by Zafarulla Khan. These two leaders depended upon Jinnah to make their voice heard at the Centre. Taking advantage of this, Jinnah suggested that their parties should merge with the Muslim League. Both of them were seasoned politicians. They knew quite well that they could not afford to say or do any thing against the interest of the Muslims. It was not that they were nationalists or in favour of the Hindu-Muslim unity. They subscribed to the Muslim communalism which they used to realize their personal political ambitions. They agreed to merge their parties with the Muslim League on the condition that the League or Jinnah would not interfere with the working of their governments and that they would enjoy unfettered power in the provinces. In order to realize his ambition, Jinnah who always upheld the constitutional and legal procedures agreed to their outrageous and unconstitutional demands.

After making the final changes in the resolution, Jinnah dispatched Zafarulla Khan to the Viceroy to get his approval. It demanded that the Muslims should be treated as a separate nationality, and not as a religious minority. They should be treated on equal footing and not from the point of a majority or a minority. Besides, the Muslim majority provinces should be separated from India. If required, these provinces could enter into an agreement with the government at the Centre. The resolution was too ambiguous to draw any correct inference. Yet this was what the Viceroy wanted as a long-term agenda.

Having thus done the spade work, it was decided to call a special session of the Muslim League at Lahore to endorse the resolution. It was agreed that Sikandar Hayat Khan would propose the resolution, while Fazalul Haq would second it. They only had to present the draft resolution. It was left to the *Quaid-e-Azam* Muhammad Ali Jinnah to make a keynote address outlining the scheme.

47

Lahore session of Muslim League, demand for Pakistan

In Lahore, the capital of Punjab, the weather was pleasant in the last week of March. But the political atmosphere was heating up. The chilly winter was over. A group of Muslim extremists called *Khaksaars* held the city to ransom. They were opposed to the Muslim League, particularly Jinnah. They were protesting against the League holding its session in Lahore. Their protests turned violent. The city was infamous for communal riots and bloodshed. The government of the Unionist Party of Sir Sikandar Hayat Khan was bitterly opposed to the Muslim League and Jinnah. However, due to the secret understanding he had with Jinnah, his government was obliged to contain the *Khaksaars*. In order to maintain the law and order, the police had resorted to the firing at the protesters. As a result, many protesters were injured and admitted to hospital.

The city of Lahore was engulfed with the protests before the starting of the session. Considering the hostile political situation, Sikandar Hayat Khan requested Jinnah to postpone the session. Some areas in the city were placed under curfew. As per the programme, Jinnah, the President of the Muslim League, had to be taken in a procession on his arrival at the Lahore station by the Frontier Mail. If he was taken in a procession it would create a serious law and order problem in the face of strong protests. The Hindus and the Sikhs were badly hit by the violence in the city. Jinnah turned down the request to postpone the session, but agreed to abandon the procession.

Jinnah was an expert strategist. He knew how to turn the situation to his favour. The *Khaksaars* were responsible for the present situation in Lahore. However, Jinnah saw in this an opportunity to condemn Sikandar Hayat Khan's government for the police excesses committed on the protesters and attract the *Khaksaars* towards him.

When Jinnah got down at the Lahore station, he went straight to the government Mayo hospital to meet the injured *Khaksaars*. He collected beforehand the information regarding the injured persons. He spent more than two hours in the hospital meeting personally every injured person. He enquired with the doctors about their treatment. He criticised the excesses committed by the government on the protesters. He struck an instant rapport with the *Khaksaars*. The *Khaksaars* who supported Sikandar Hayat Khan's government because of his opposition to Jinnah, now turned against the government. This was what Jinnah wanted. The cunning Jinnah thus managed to kill two birds with one stone even before the Muslim League session began.

At Minto Park in Lahore, the favourite city of the Mughal emperors, the Muslims gathered in large numbers. Most of them still sported the red Turkish cap, as a symbol of reverence to the Caliph though the institution of *Khilafat* was abolished. Amidst a sea of Turkish caps, a large number of Muslims were seen wearing the popular Jinnah cap. On one side of Minto Park was the majestic royal mosque in white marble and the main gate of Shah Jahan's fort was on the other. By noon, a hundred thousand Muslims gathered. As 2 p.m., Jinnah dressed in a typical Islamic outfit arrived at the venue. A special seat was arranged for him on the dais. Fatima sat to his right. The sword wielding volunteers of the Muslim League who came from Bombay after attending the Friday *namaaz* took their place in the audience. As Jinnah entered the venue, the air was rent with the cries of *Quaid-e-Azam Zindabad.*

Jinnah spoke incessantly for two hours. When he started his speech, he spoke a few sentences in broken Urdu. But finding it uncomfortable he switched over to English. Instead of saying that he was unable to speak in Urdu, he said that the whole world was watching them and was eager to listen to him. Therefore, they should not object to his speaking in English so that the world could understand what he was saying. But most of the people in the crowd were not willing to accept this excuse. Only a few in the crowd could understand what he was saying. Consequently, a large section of the crowd expressed its dismay and displeasure, resulting in commotion. Nobody could hear what Jinnah was saying. He stopped speaking for a moment. He stiffened and stared sternly at the crowd. And then took out a cigarette and lit it, held it between his two fingers and took a deep puff. This arrogant behaviour of Jinnah had its effect on the crowd. The crowed jeered at him. The commotion stopped. Jinnah continued his speech in English triumphantly,

"We have enough experience of how the provincial governments function as per the reforms introduced by the British government in 1935. We do not accept the constitution which treats the Muslims as a minority community. Mr. Gandhi says that the Hindus and the Muslims are the same to him and that he cannot accept them being treated differently. He calls me his younger brother and tells me that I should not talk anything vain. Today I want to tell Gandhi that what he considers vain is very important to us. I want to remind him that the elder brother has three-fourth of India with him, whereas the younger brother has only the one-fourth. In such a situation, the Muslims will be always dominated by the Hindus. The truth is that the Muslims are not a minority in this country.

They are a separate nationality living in this country for the past thousand years. They should be equal partners in independent India. If Gandhi is willing to negotiate on this, I welcome him as the leader representing all the Hindus in the country. If the British government wants a lasting solution to this problem, it should partition India in such a way that the Muslims get independent states which they can consider their motherland."

Jinnah was cheered. The crowd was cheering and clapping in between the speech without understanding what he was saying. To play on the mob psychology, he was cleverly referred to the words like Islam, Quran, Namaaz frequently during his speech that lasted for two hours. It sounded as if he got a chance to act on the stage as he had done during his student days in London. The art of expressing anger, pain, emotions and aggression that he had mastered as an actor came to his rescue. The crowd mesmerizing by his acting cheered him now and then.

In order to cast his spell on the crowd, Jinnah made a passionate plea at the end of his speech, "The Hindus and the Muslims have nothing in common except the bondage to the British. The Hindus look in one direction to remember their ancestors, places of pilgrimage and culture centres, while the Muslims look in another direction. India is the only motherland for the Hindus, whereas all the places where the Muslims live are our motherlands. The sooner the Hindus accept this gospel truth, the better for all of us."

At the end of the speech, Sikandar Hayat Khan presented the resolution demanding partition of India to create independent and autonomous states for the Muslims. Fazalul Haq seconded the resolution. The resolution drafted by Zafarullah Khan was approved by the Viceroy Lord Linlithgow. Yet the Viceroy was not willing to identify with the resolution openly. The Viceroy and Jinnah had an understanding that no one should come to know that the resolution was drafted by Zafarullah Khan with the approval of both of them.

Zafarullah Khan was an Ahmediya Muslim. The Ahmediya Muslims were the natives of a village called Kadiyan and, therefore, they were also known as the Kadiyani Muslims. The orthodox Muslims considered the Ahmediya sect un-Islamic. In the 19th century, the founder of this sect had raised some fundamental questions about the Holy Quran and the Prophet Mohammed with the Islami Ulemas. The Ulemas had no answers to the questions. Therefore, instead of encouraging an intellectual debate, the Ulemas declared the Ahmediyas as *Kafir* and boycotted them. Zafarullah Khan belonged to that sect. If he was identified as the author of the resolution, the orthodox Sunni and Shia Muslims would not accept it. Keeping this in view, he was very cleverly kept away from the venue of the session.

The resolution was passed unanimously amidst a thunderous applause.

At the end of the session, the enthusiastic and aggressive crowd knew only one thing that after the Moghul Emperor Aurangzeb, the only man carrying the *jehad* for the welfare of the Muslims was the *Quaid-e-Azam* Muhammad Ali Jinnah. A reporter asked an enthusiastic man in the crowd, "What is your opinion on what the *Quaid-e-Azam* has said? Can the country be partitioned in this manner?"

"You ask only the *Quaid-e-Azam* about all this. We know only this much that if he said something it must be true," the man answered innocently.

Both the resolution and the speech of Jinnah had mentioned about independent and autonomous states for the Muslims. It implied that the Muslims should have not one but more independent states. A reporter asked Jinnah, "In the resolution, you have mentioned more states instead of one for the Muslims. Does it mean you are demanding creation of more states for the Muslims?"

"The resolution is absolutely clear. It does not need any further clarification," Jinnah responded.

"What is your idea of independent Muslim states? Tell us how it will be practical to create such states," countered the reporter.

"Whatever necessary has been said. If any further clarification is needed, it will be given at an appropriate time. It is enough for now," Jinnah said this much and walked away.

*

After the resolution was passed, the Viceroy, Lord Linlithgow, in his confidential weekly report to the Secretary of State for India, Lord Amery, said—"As per my instruction, Zafarullah Khan has prepared the resolution. And now the Muslim League has adopted the resolution in the form of a demand. Considering all this, we can now trust Jinnah as our own man. I suggest that we must accept him as the sole spokesman for all the Muslims. I am glad to say that hereinafter the fight of the Congress will not be confined to us alone. It will have to confront Jinnah and the Muslim League as well. This will make our work easy."

48

Generous donations to Jinnah in Ahemedabad, Jinnah-Tej Bahadur Sapru on Quran in a court in Hyderabad, study of Quran by Jinnah, Ban on Jinnah's entry into Gondal

The next day, the newspapers across the country, had reported that the Muslim League and Jinnah demanded the partition of India to create Pakistan. In fact, the Lahore Resolution of the League or the speech of Jinnah did not mention the word Pakistan. Jinnah was not sure whether the creation of Pakistan was feasible. Until now, the Congress was making all sorts of concessions to the Muslims, in the name of minority. Jinnah realized that the Congress had unwittingly contributed to the idea that the Muslims were the only minority in the country. There were many religious communities like the Christians, the Sikhs, the Parsees and other smaller communities. The Congress still gave undue importance to the Muslims, due to their numerical strength. Jinnah was determined to take full advantage of this mentality. He had very cleverly refrained from demanding a single state of Pakistan for the Muslims in the Lahore Resolution. The purpose behind the demand for more Muslim states was to create a fear psychosis among the Hindus. The Muslims were a majority in many districts and provinces. Besides, the Muslims were a majority in many towns within districts and in many areas in cities. Jinnah's intention was to create terrible fear of the Muslims states being created in the areas where the Muslims were a majority. He knew pretty well that Pakistan could not be achieved in this manner. However, this would excite and unite the Muslims across the country in the name of Islam. And Jinnah would become the undisputed leader of the Muslims. This would make the Congress, particularly Gandhi, accept his importance. Jinnah wanted to extract maximum benefit from the British government by holding the threat of breaking India into many pieces. He was well aware of the fact that if India was divided in the name of religion, the Muslims living in different parts of the country could invite the wrath of the Hindus.

The millions of Muslims in the country did not understand what was obvious to Jinnah. The slogans like the "Islam is in danger," and "Pakistan will become Dar-ul-Islam" rented the air. Even those Muslim regions which could never become part of Pakistan were excited and lent their support for creation of Pakistan. One could understand the Muslims in Sindh, Punjab and Bengal supporting the demand for the creation of Pakistan. But even the Muslims living in the United Province, the Central Province and in the cities like Bombay and Ahmedabad actively supported the demand.

Jinnah was touring the country with a hurricane speed to garner support for his demand for the partition of India. He received a tremendous response in Ahmedabad which became a trend setter. He was invited to inaugurate the Bombay Provincial Muslim Education Council in Ahmedabad. Khaji Issah presided over the function. Jinnah was received at the Ahmedabad station by a huge contingents of the Muslims and was taken in a procession. He was put up in a locality of rich Muslims, away from the city. His speech at the inaugural function of the Education Council aroused the religious sentiments of the Muslims. His histrionics and oratory skills proved useful.

Gandhi used to collect donations for public causes like Khadi and social upliftment at public meetings. Gauging the enthusiasm and the passion of the people who had assembled, Jinnah asked for donations to the Muslims League. The response was unimaginable. Notes and coins poured out in a torrent. The volunteers wearing the Jinnah cap went around and collected bags filled with currency notes and coins. This was the first opportunity for collecting the donations from the public. A colleague of Jinnah asked him, "Quaid-e-Azam, the enthusiasm of the community is fantastic. You can capitalize on this. If you can announce some amount as your personal donation, it will not only motivate the Muslims present here to donate but also the Muslims all over the country will be motivated to donate." Jinnah retorted, "You remember one thing. My contribution should not be judged in terms of money. My contribution in terms of time and energy is manifold than the money collected here."

Jinnah carried the sacks filled with money to the place of his stay. He asked his personal staff to count the money. Fatima kept a watch. The counting continued throughout the night till the wee hours of the morning. Only after ascertaining the total amount collected Jinnah went to sleep.

Jinnah was considered an expert in the Islamic law and the rules of the *Waqf* Board. But his knowledge of the *Shariat* was based on his study of law books in English. He had never read even the English version of the Quran, leave alone reading in Arabic, Persian or Urdu. He could utter only the words "*Achha Hain*" in chaste Urdu. Sometimes he would say a few sentences in broken Urdu to impress his audience. One incident made Jinnah to read the Quran.

Jinnah was representing a client in a court at Hyderabad. Sir Tej Bahadur Sapru was fighting the case against Jinnah. Like Jinnah, he was also a reputed advocate and was active in politics. When a witness, from Jinnah's side, was questioned in the court, he quoted a couple of verses from the Quran in support of his case. The Judge did not have any knowledge of the Quran. The Judge asked Jinnah to translate the verses in English for his benefit. It was a very embarrassing situation for Jinnah. He could himself neither understand the verses nor translate them into English. He was in a quandary. The Court asked the witness to repeat the verses to enable the clerk to write it down on a paper. The clerk held out the paper to Jinnah. But Jinnah did not take the paper.

Jinnah said, "Your honour, the court must make its own arrangement to get it translated. The advocate is not expected to do that."

Sir Tej Bahadur had been Jinnah's colleague in politics for a long time. He was aware that Jinnah knew nothing about the Quran or its verses. He knew the reason behind what Jinnah had said to the judge. In order to ensure that the court proceedings are not hampered over the issue, he said, "Your honour, I beg your pardon for interrupting. If the Court wants the English translation of the verses, I can do that. The court can interpret its meaning."

The judge gave Sapru the permission to translate the verses into English. Sapru translated the verses with ease. The court proceedings continued. The next day the local newspapers in Hyderabad flashed out the news in bold letters on the front pages, *Maulana Tej Bahadur explains the verses of the Quran, not Pandit Muhammad Ali Jinnah.* Jinnah realised that it was imperative to study the religious texts like the Mullahs and the Maulvis whom he abhorred. He bought a copy of the Quran in English and read it thoroughly.

*

The region of the Gujarat popularly known as via Viramgam in the Bombay Province was known as the Kathiawad. It had more than two hundred princely states. The region was not under the British rule. Even then the British government controlled it through its agents. Gondal was one of the important princely states. The kings of Gondal had the foresight of taking advantage of modern education and science and technology for the benefit of the people.

The people in the princely states were not directly influenced by the freedom struggle. However, they were affected by the communal flare up in the country. The voice of the Quaid-e-Azam echoed in the Kathiawad region. The towns of Upleta and Dhoraji of Gondal state had a sizeable Muslim population.

Bhagvat Sinhji, the King of Gondal, had banned the cow slaughter. The Muslims of Dhoraji defiled the King on the ground that the ban went against their religious practice. The British Agency's headquarters was then situated at Rajkot. The British Resident Officer kept a vigilance over the princely states and entertained the peoples' complaints. The Muslims of Dhoraji had lodged a complaint with the Resident Officer against their King. The complaint was forwarded to the Governor of Bombay for appropriate action. The British government was against the ban on cow slaughter, but it did not want to oppose it openly fearing that the Hindus might think that the government was favouring the Muslims. Moreover, this matter pertained to a princely state and the princely states were independent to handle their own matters. If the British government interfered and lifted the ban imposed by the King of Gondal, its relation with the princely states would suffer. Considering this, the Governor of Bombay dismissed the complaint against the King of Gondal on the ground that it was an internal matter.

The Muslims of Dhoraji did not accept this stand of the Governor. They represented themselves to the Viceroy's Council. And finally they took up their case with the Privy Council in London. The Privy Council had set aside the Order of the King of Gondal on the ground that it went against the religious practice of the Muslims. After winning the case against their King, the Muslims invited Jinnah to Upleta and Dhoraji. Jinnah accepted the invitation. He had not forgotten that Paneli near Upleta was the native place of his ancestors. He remembered his wedding procession in Paneli at the age of seventeen before he had left for London. He immediately decided to tour Upleta and Dhoraji.

It was natural for the King of Gondal to be annoyed with his people. He thought that if a communal leader like Jinnah addressed the people it would disturb the communal harmony in his state, besides antagonizing the Hindus. He wanted to prevent that. He also wanted to avenge the people going against him. He banned the entry of Jinnah on the ground that it would disturb the communal harmony in the state.

The Kathiawad Mail was the only train connecting Kathiawad with the British Provinces. Jinnah arrived in a special coach attached to the train at Jetalsar, the first station on the border of the state of Gondal. The Muslims from Upleta, Dhoraji and Junagadh were present in a large number on the platform to welcome him. As Jinnah got down from the train, people rushed towards him with garlands. A police officer from Gondal along with his associates were standing at a distance. Before Jinnah could step into the soil of the state of Gondal, the police officer served him the Order of the King banning his entry into the state. Jinnah read the Order bearing the royal seal. He became angry and tight lipped. He crushed the Order with his two hands and threw it away with contempt.

49

Jinnah in Junagadh and Gondal, Jinnah in Karachi, meeting with the students of law

The intervention of the police officer was unexpected by the Muslims who stood on the platform with the garlands in their hands. They thought the King might have sent the police officer to welcome Jinnah on his behalf. When Jinnah threw the paper angrily, they realised the issue was something else. They inched closer to listen to the conversation between Jinnah and the police officer. These Muslims came from well-to-do families. They were aware of the royal traditions. They heard Jinnah speaking loudly in an angry voice, "Officer, tell your King that the Quaid-e-Azam Muhammad Ali Jinnah does not care about the order. I do not accept the Order."

"Whether to accept the Order or not, that is up to you, but I have to obey the order of the King," the officer said firmly.

"What do you mean?" Jinnah stiffened and asked him pointedly.

"Sir, I want to tell you that if you defy the King's order and enter the border of the state of Gondal, I will be forced to take you in custody," the officer said in a stern voice.

Jinnah never imagined that an ordinary police officer of a princely state could talk to him in this manner. He retorted sternly, "Do you understand the consequences?"

"Sir, I do not have to bother about the consequences. It is for you and the King to worry about the consequences. I am the officer on duty and I will act as per the order," the officer said with determination.

"You are forgetting one thing, officer," Jinnah said suddenly changing his tactic.

"I am a native of Paneli. Hence I am a citizen of the state of Gondal. As a citizen, I have the right to enter Gondal."

"No, Sir!" said the police officer interrupting Jinnah, "You are not a citizen of the state of Gondal. Your ancestors were the subjects of Gondal and now they are the subjects of the British empire. Hence, you are a subject of the British government and not of our state."

Jinnah's hosts, who listened to the conversation with concern, had a difficult situation. It was true Jinnah was their guest, but the guest would depart within a day after accepting their garlands and making one or two speeches. Thereafter they have to live as the subjects of the King in Gondal. If Jinnah defied the order of the King and the police officer took him into custody, they would face a very precarious situation. A few prominent persons in the crowd had made a quick decision and then said to Jinnah, "*Quaid-e-Azam*, such a skirmish with the state will ruin our programme. You can attend the programme arranged for you in Junagadh and you can reach Junagadh from another route without entering the state of Gondal. In the meantime, we will meet the King and make suitable arrangements for your arrival in the state."

Jinnah did not like the suggestion. However, he realised that if he forcefully entered the state of Gondal, these people could be in serious trouble. And if he got embroiled with the petty problems of the local Muslims, his attention would be diverted from the national issues. Considering all this, Jinnah accepted the suggestion to reach Junagadh through another route.

After Jinnah departed, a delegation of Dhoraji's Muslims met the King as his subjects. They pleaded with him that banning the entry of Jinnah, a national leader, into the state was not a wise thing. Moreover, Jinnah's ancestors were the subjects of the state of Gondal and, therefore, it would be prudent to allow him to enter the state. The King heard them patiently. But he knew the mindset of his subjects, who had challenged his order banning the cow slaughter in the Privy Council. The King did not like the idea of Jinnah making an inflammatory communal speech in his state. The King suggested to them via media, "I appreciate your concern for the state. I have no objection in welcoming Jinnah as a State guest. But I cannot tolerate any communal clash between the Hindus and the Muslims or any breach of law and order."

"We assure you nothing of the sort will happen. You trust us, we will live together amicably."

"I fully trust you," said the King diplomatically, "I do not want to hurt your sentiments. You get an assurance from Jinnah that he will not carry out any political activity and make any speech in the State of Gondal. If he accepts this condition, I will lift the ban on his entry."

The Muslims leaders accepted the King's condition. They had no other option. They immediately went to Junagadh and obtained the assurance from Jinnah. He accepted the condition. When Jinnah's acceptance was convened to the King, the ban on his entry was lifted.

*

As the days passed by, Jinnah succeeded in turning the tide of the Muslims sentiments in his favour. He had no qualms about using any means as long as they served his purpose. He followed the maxim that the end justifies the means. In spite of his advancing age and failing health, he travelled extensively to meet the people from Kashmir to Kanyakumari and from Calcutta to Kathiawad.

Jinnah, who considered mingling with the crowd beneath his dignity until recently, would now grab every opportunity to mingle with the crowd, though he could not become one among them. He knew that these surging crowds would be his greatest weapon in his fight ahead. Now he very cleverly adopted the Islamic dress code and the Islamic mannerism. The Muslim students of law and the advocates arranged a public speech by Jinnah in Karachi.

He said in his speech, "The people of the country knew that I had left the Congress politics and settled in London. I did not take part in the Third Round Table Conference. However, when the Government of India Act of 1935 had provided for the Provincial Assemblies, I realized that the Provincial governments formed on the basis of minority and majority could create a grave situation for the Muslims. I wound up my residence in London and travelled seven thousand miles to return to India. I rejoined politics for the sake of the Muslims of the country. The Hindus and the Muslims can never co-exist since there is nothing common between them except the bondage to the British. I cannot understand how any self respecting Muslim could tolerate governments in the Muslim majority provinces run on the whims of Gandhi sitting in Sevagram. It is a sheer nonsense."

After the speech, a bright student asked him, "Why did you prefer to become a barrister?"

"Oh!" Jinnah in a dramatic gesture raised his two hands and looked around. "To tell you the truth, it was the wish of Allah. After so many years you have reminded me. I had no intention to study the law in the 'Lincoln's Inn.' It so happened that when I was passing through the campus of the "Lincoln's Inn," I saw the names of the great legal luminaries written at the main entrance. I saw the name of the Prophet Mohammed among them. Then I felt that I should study the principles propounded by the Prophet. That was how I became a student of law."

He was greeted with loud cheers.

Another sharp student asked him, "The Hindus and the Muslims have been living together in every village and street in this country for a thousand years. What do you say on this?"

"Country? Which country? There is no country here. We have the Hindus and the Muslims and both of them are completely independent nations. You do not need any proof of this," Jinnah said in an aggressive tone.

"The British government had always been anti-Muslim. The Hindus form three-fourth of the population in the country. In such an adverse situation, do you think it is possible for the Muslims to secure Pakistan?" yet another question was put to him.

"That is the only correct solution. There is no other way except the partition," said Jinnah very confidently. "You all are advocates and as advocates it is your duty to fight the case of your clients to the best of your ability. Before taking up the case decide whether it is right or wrong. But once you take up the case, you must believe that you are right and fight with determination and win the case. If you do not win the case, you do not become a successful advocate." And then he added cunningly, "And you all are aware, how I am fighting as an advocate to secure an independent Pakistan for the Muslims. You are also aware that professionally I have been a successful advocate. I am not a failed advocate like Mr. Gandhi."

A crackle of laughter filled the auditorium.

"Do not you think that after the partition of the country, the two nation theory will haunt us? Even after the formation of the two new nations—India and Pakistan—the Hindus and the Muslims will be at loggerheads with each other in every province, every town, every village and every street. Are you talking about creation of such nations?" someone from the audience asked a pointed question presenting a grim picture of the future.

"Yes, it is an issue of two nations being at loggerheads with each other in every province, every town, every village and every street. But the partition is the only solution," answered Jinnah without the slightest hesitation.

"*Quaid-e-Azam*, don't you think that it will create a very dangerous situation?" asked a concerned member of the audience.

"Perhaps it will be a very terrible situation. But that is the only solution to the communal problem," Jinnah said as if it was his final decision.

At the end of the meeting when Jinnah was getting down from the dais, Liaquat Ali Khan whispered softly in his ear, "Quaid-e-Azam, you said that you had seen the name of the Prophet Mohammed at the entrance of the Lincoln's Inn. I too had studied there, but I had never seen any such name."

"How could you see the name?" Jinnah said shrewdly, "when there was no such name," Jinnah marched quickly.

Liaquat Ali Khan was speechless. It was Liaquat Ali Khan who had persuaded Jinnah in 1934 to return to India. And yet he was talking as if he had made a great sacrifice for the sake of the Muslims. Besides, he was taking the name of the Prophet Mohammed to impress upon the audience. Liaquat Ali Khan tightened his lips and clenched his fists. He was lost in a serious thought.

When Jinnah left for the annual session of the Muslim League at Madras, he was troubled by constant bouts of cough. His blood pressure was abnormal. The doctors had advised him rest for some days. But it was not possible for Jinnah to accept the doctors' advice. He invited Ramaswami Naickar, the leader of the Dravid Kazhagam, who was demanding a separate Dravidistan. Jinnah was to support the demand for Dravidistan so that Ramaswami Naickar could reciprocate by endorsing his demand for Pakistan. This bargain could create a rift between the Hindus and weaken the position of the Congress. In South India, the anti-Brahmin Movement gained momentum. Ramaswami Naickar made a cruel joke on the *Ramayana*—a holy book of the Hindus. Jinnah wanted to take full advantage of the situation.

50

Madras session of Muslim League, the question of a separate Dravidistan, Jinnah in Ooty, appointment of Muslims as members of the War Council by Linlithgow, Jinnah in Kashmir, Tej Singh: question answer, Gandhi's advice to Hitler

Jinnah reached Madras, a day before the scheduled programme. He went against the doctor's advice and travelled to Madras in a special coach attached to the train. Fatima and his personal staff were with him. He became bed ridden for hours before reaching Madras. He could not sleep a wink during the entire journey. He coughed incessantly. The strong medicines could not provide any relief. He became unconscious due to the bouts of cough. Fatima got worried. She gently shook him, "Bhaijaan, Bhaijaan, what happened to you?" Jinnah did not answer. The medicines prescribed were administered, but there was no improvement in his health.

The train was about to reach Madras station. There were no other stops in between. When the train reached the station, hundreds of Jinnah's supporters were waiting on the platform. As the train entered the platform, Fatima was gesturing to the crowd to keep quiet with a finger on her lips. The crowd started chanting *Quaid-e-Azam Zindabad* and *Allah-Ho-Akbar*. Fatima said in a shaky voice urging them to keep quiet,

"Quaid-e-Azam's condition is very serious. He is bed ridden, not able to come out. Please arrange an ambulance and call a doctor."

The crowd was stunned. The doctor was summoned. Jinnah was taken in an unconscious condition to the hospital for emergency treatment. After the treatment, he regained consciousness, but was still weak. As the news of his illness spread, a huge crowd gathered at the hospital. Jinnah was worried that if he did not attend the League's session, Ramaswami Naickar would not turn up at the session. If Ramaswami Naickar did not turn up, his dream of creating a rift between the Hindus and getting support from a section of the Tamil Hindus would remain unfulfilled. Hence, he told the doctor that it was absolutely necessary for him to be present at the session. Let the doctor take every precaution, but his presence at the session was a must.

"You will be permitted to be present at the session on only one condition," said the doctor, "You will not make any speech. It will strain you and you might lapse into unconsciousness again."

"Look doctor," Jinnah said raising his index finger, "My address at the session is more important than my presence. Thousands of Muslims will turn up to listen to me."

"Bhaijaan, you must assure that you will speak as little as possible," suggested Fatima.

"You are right," Jinnah responded knowing that it was left to him to decide how long to speak, "I assure you I will speak as little as possible."

But the right to determine this 'little' was solely with Jinnah only and he exercised this right when he stood up to address the crowd. He thrust one hand in the pocket of his white *sherwani* and held the mike in the other hand so that it could prevent him from collapsing. He spoke continuously for two hours. During these two hours, he neither coughed nor felt any uneasiness. He did not sip water even once from the glass placed near the microphone. He took repeatedly the name of Ramaswami Naickar who sat to his right and declared his support for the movement for a separate Dravidistan. About one hundred thousand Muslims and the supporters of Naickar were present to listen to Jinnah, while the green flags of the Muslim League and the blue flags of the Dravida Kazhagam Party fluttered all over the pavilion. Jinnah said, "I am glad that, after the downfall of the Mogul Emperor Aurangzeb, the Muslims of India are united for the first time as a force. We are not a minority. We are an independent nation. As a nation, we have our own flag, religion and culture. Nobody can stop us now. Do you think the movement of the supreme Congress leader Gandhi is a movement for independence? No!" he said answering his own question sarcastically, "Gandhi's satyagraha is meant to create trouble for the British government. Britain is fighting the war with Germany and Italy for its survival. At such a time, Gandhi wants to establish a Hindu raj in the name of freedom. The British government must understand this and instead of trusting Gandhi, it must trust the Muslims who were loyal to it and accept their legitimate demands. Then the Indian Muslims can support the government in its war efforts."

Jinnah drawing sustenance from his pent up anger and passion managed to complete his speech without any hindrance. But he collapsed as he finished the speech. The doctors advised him to go to the nearby hill station Ootacamand and take complete rest. Now he had no excuse. He left for the hill station. But he was not to rest in peace there. The Congress had refused to cooperate in the war efforts. The Viceroy constituted a War Council comprising the representatives of the Muslim League, the princely states and some prominent citizens who were not associated with the Congress. He appointed the prominent Muslims from the provincial governments of Sindh, Punjab, Bengal and Assam as members of the War Council. In addition, he nominated three or four prominent Muslims into the Council. Some of the members appointed were connected with the Muslim League. The Viceroy sent the list of the members appointed by him to Jinnah for information before making it public. Jinnah became furious. He was under the impression that the Viceroy would not appoint any Muslim to the Council without his consent. He thought that nobody except him had the right to speak or act on behalf of the Muslims of India. He ought to remove any doubt if at all the Viceroy or anybody else harboured on this. The Muslim representatives who accepted the appointment without seeking his permission had committed a breach of discipline. He sought their explanation from Ootacamand. As a result, some of them resigned from the Viceroy's War Council. And for those who did not resign, Jinnah invoked his power as the President of the Muslim League and expelled them from the League.

This was a decisive moment for the Viceroy. The Congress which enjoyed the massive support of the people had refused to cooperate right from the beginning. If Jinnah remained adamant, he would lose the support of the Muslims as well. He could not dismantle the War Council in the midst of the War. The War Council was in the interest of the British government. The Viceroy accepted Jinnah's position. It proved beyond doubt that he was the supreme leader of the Muslims in India. Even the leaders like Sikandar Hayat Khan and Fazlul Haq, opposed to him, were forced to fall in line in order to get the Muslims support to remain in politics. Jinnah's communal sentiments suppressed until now suddenly gushed out like the water from a soda bottle.

A youth organisation of Kashmir invited Jinnah to discuss the political situation in the country. It was an opportunity for Jinnah to intensify his campaign for Pakistan. Most of the members of the organisation comprised of the Hindus and the Sikhs. He accepted the invitation and said that a delegation of the organisers could meet him at the place where he was staying. He was staying in a modern and well-furnished houseboat called Elizabeth. The delegation of seven young men was led by Taja Singh. Jinnah welcomed the delegation. He shook hand with every one of them. After exchanging the formal greetings in the pleasant atmosphere of Kashmir, Taja Singh said, "Quaid-e-Azam, we have been looking for an opportunity to meet you to understand your idea of Pakistan."

The temperate and placid Jinnah suddenly became alert and turned serious.

"The idea of Pakistan is not clear to us, you may call it our misunderstanding. We want you to clarify."

"Ah!" Jinnah shook his head.

"Do you really believe that in this age of democracy, an elected government can commit atrocities on the eighty million Muslims? We think the Muslims fear this and that is why they are demanding Pakistan."

"There is no doubt that in a democracy, an elected government having the support of the majority can commit atrocities on the minority. But the Muslims are not demanding Pakistan out of any such fear. They are demanding Pakistan because the Muslims are a separate nation in terms of culture, lifestyle and ideology."

"But Sir, you often spoke of such fear in your speeches," Teja Singh pointed out.

"No! No! There is no such thing. The majority can impose its will upon the minority."

"Could you please give an example so that we can understand?"

"For that, you must read my speeches."

"Sir, I have read them. That is why I am asking this."

"Then, you must get answer to your question."

"I have not got the answer. Hence this question."

"That means you have not read my speeches," Jinnah persisted in evading the answer.

"I reiterate that I have read your speeches very carefully," Teja Singh insisted.

"Then, you must read them again," Jinnah said.

"But Sir, you are the only leader who could clear the misconception about Pakistan."

"I have not come here to waste my time with such futile arguments. Please allow some one else to speak," Jinnah commanded to silence Teja Singh.

Teja Singh had nothing more to say.

"Quaid-e-Azam! What is your opinion about the formation of a democratic government in Kashmir?" asked another young man.

"It is a matter between you and your King," said Jinnah.

"Can not we solve the Indian problems in the manner the Soviet Union did?" Teja Singh asked another question.

"Which India are you talking about? You do not have to worry about the British India. Gandhi and I can take care of that. You worry about Kashmir only as you are a Kashmiri."

"No, Sir!" Teja Singh said politely but firmly, "I am a Punjabi settled in Kashmir. But I am an Indian first."

"Indian!" Jinnah feigned surprise, "There is no Indian here. The people here are the Hindus, the Muslims, the Sikhs, the Punjabis, the Bengalis and the Kashmiris. There is no country called India."

"Do you think we can achieve independence by following Gandhi's satyagraha and non-violence?" asked another young man diverting the conversation.

"Satyagraha! What is satyagraha?" Jinnah asked aggressively, "Working on the spinning wheel for five hours a day, offering the prayers in the morning and the evening, breaking the law and going to jail and then fasting to ruin the health and then getting released from the jail in the name of poor health—do you call all this satyagraha? I do not believe in all this." Then he said with great contempt, "The Hindus of the Congress must come out of this magic spell of Gandhi."

"Why do not you tell the Hindus?... You have good friends among the Hindus. Some of them are good and understanding."

"Forget it,"Jinnah said interrupting the young man, "No Hindu can be good and understanding. And if you are talking of Gandhi, see today's newspaper." He picked up a newspaper from the table and showed the news item marked with blue ink. It related to the meeting between Viceroy Lord Linlithgow and Gandhi.

The War that started in Europe now became a World War. The most powerful countries in the world jumped into the fray. The Viceroy in his meeting with Gandhi requested him not to create more political problems during the course of the War. In response, Gandhi said, "I do not believe that anything could be achieved through the violence. The British government should give up its armed resistance to Hitler. Instead, it should resist him with non-violence. The force of non-violence is the most powerful."

The Viceroy was stunned by Gandhi's advice. The meeting ended abruptly. The Viceroy's ADC had escorted Gandhi to his car. The Viceroy was so shocked by Gandhi's idea of offering non-violent resistance to Hitler that he forgot to say goodbye to Gandhi.

Jinnah pointing out at the news item said with a triumphant smile, "This is your Gandhi. And these are his ideas."

The meeting ended there.

51

1942 'Quit India Resolution', arrest of Gandhi, Jinnah's reaction, Gandhi's letter to Jinnah, Jinnah's refusal to sign appeal demanding Gandhi's release, attack on Jinnah

The World War had now spread to Asia and America, besides Europe. The world was divided into two groups—the Axis and the Allied powers—bent on destroying each other. Britain, which claimed to be fighting the war to defend freedom, had refused to free India. Gandhi and the Congress did not wish to remain inactive in the struggle for freedom any more. Having decided not to cooperate with the British government in its war efforts, they could not afford to be inactive or else it might lead to political inertia. Gandhi insisted that though the granting of independence might not be possible during the war period, the British government should at least declare a fixed time period for granting independence to India after the war. In the meantime, the government should give more powers to the Indians in order to secure their support for its war efforts.

The British government, being unhappy with the stand of the Congress, leaned more towards the Muslims for their support. Gandhi announced the launching of the final struggle for independence to end this stalemate. The Congress session held in August 1942 at the Gowalia Tank, Bombay gave a clarion call to the freedom struggle across the country. Initially, an influential group of leaders within the Congress felt that it was not an opportune time to launch such a struggle. The group included the senior leaders like Jawaharlal Nehru, Acharya Kripalani, Maulana Abdul Kalam Azad and C. Rajagopalachari. Gandhi was firm in his decision. The movements launched in 1921 and 1931 had not achieved the desired results. The Non-Cooperation Movement in 1921 had to be withdrawn as it turned out to be violent compelling Gandhi to concede that it was a "Himalayan blunder." The Civil Disobedience Movement in 1931 had resulted in millions of people receiving the police lathicharge or going to the jail and in the loss of lives. Yet, the success of the political reforms thereafter was attributed to the Round Table Conference. Because of the movement, Gandhi could not take part in the First Round Table Conference. Though he subsequently participated in the Second Round Table Conference, it did not achieve anything substantial. Rajagopalachari and other leaders were not sure whether this final struggle would yield the desired result. They felt that it might lead to greater public awareness, but at a time when Britain was fighting a life and death war, the government might go all out to quell any dissent. A large section of the Muslims in the country now turned against the Congress and the Hindus. If Gandhi's struggle was launched, these Muslims might not only remain aloof from the struggle, but might even oppose it and instigate communal riots.

But Gandhi did not heed to all that. As usual, all the Congress leaders fell in line and requested him to lead the struggle. C. Rajagopalachari was the only exception. He refused to support any such struggle and declared that if the Congress launched any such movement he would quit the Congress.

8th August, 1942

The Congress adopted the "Quit India" Resolution in its session held at the Gowalia Tank, Bombay. Gandhi gave the clarion call of *Karenge ya Marenge,* that is, 'Do or Die' to all the Indians. It was a *mantra*[1] to every Indian that he would either free India or die in the attempt. It was his duty to reject any forms of slavery to the British. If required he should sacrifice his life, but fight till he liberated India from the bondage of the British. Gandhi said in support of the Resolution, "It is good if the British government can free India and leave the country. And if they have any doubt as to whom to hand over the power, I would say let them leave India in the hands of God. It might lead to anarchy and civil war. But the real India will emerge as a result of this trial by fire. I would like to remind the people who are indulging in the vilification campaign. The more I try to reach out, the greater is the vilification. If we, the Hindus and the Muslims, sincerely wish to achieve unity, we must first fight unitedly to liberate India from the shackles of the British empire. Mr. Jinnah says that the British had taken India from the Muslims and, therefore, India should be entrusted back to the Muslims, that is the Muslim League. India had never been a country of one single community. Though the Hindus may be majority in this country, it belongs to all the people living in the country."

The Congress Working Committee had unanimously adopted the "Quit India" Resolution with a clarion call. The British government had arrested all the leaders of the Working Committee past midnight.

Jinnah was looking at the "Quit India" movement from a different angle. If the movement became successful and the British government handed over the reins of powers to the Indians before the end of the War, the stock of the Congress and Gandhi would rise. In such an eventuality, the Congress would get major share in power and the attitude of the British government towards the Muslims, on whom it counted for support till now, would change. If the Congress joined in the war efforts, Jinnah and the Muslim League would be sidelined. This was what had happened at the Round Table Conference. Jinnah did not forget that.

In the absence of Gandhi, the First Round Table Conference could not achieve anything. Gandhi participated in the Second Round Table Conference and he became the focal point of the media and the government publicity. Gandhi did not take part in the Third Conference and the British government thought it wise to ignore Jinnah. Jinnah became apprehensive that now after a decade a similar situation was emerging. If due to the "Quit India" movement the British government joined hands with the Congress, the "veto" power that he was exercising would be destroyed. He was desperate to avoid that happening.

He immediately reacted to the movement as the President of the Muslim League, "The Quit India movement is an attempt to force the British government to accept the Congress Rule. This entire movement is the result of an enraged and desperate mind. By starting this movement, Gandhi has challenged the very existence of the millions of Muslims in India. The Muslims must accept this challenge. Gandhi has created a terrible and dangerous situation."

When Gandhi came to know about Jinnah's reaction to the "Quit India" movement, he met a Muslim friend called Meklai, who was also a friend of Jinnah. Making use of his goodwill, Gandhi once again took the initiative of reaching an understanding with the Muslim League. He wanted Meklai to convince Jinnah that he was determined to maintain the Hindu-Muslim unity at any cost and that Jinnah should have an open mind to discuss the issue. When Jinnah heard this from Meklai, he replied to Gandhi in the general meeting of the Muslim League, "If Gandhi really wants to discuss the issue with me, it's worth welcoming him. But such a discussion can be fruitful only if Gandhi has a change of heart. He must write to me without taking the help of any intermediary. Whether Gandhi is in jail or the government is all powerful, no one would dare to block a letter written to me."

Gandhi was not deterred by this contemptuous speech. Without making it a prestige issue, he wrote to Jinnah from the jail, "I don't know about a change of heart. God alone knows the inner feelings of a man. I want you to accept me as I am. Let both of us try to solve the communal problem to our mutual satisfaction. Why not we work with all those who are interested in this?"

However, the government had censured the letter. Only a gist of the letter was sent to Jinnah. Forgetting the public challenge he had thrown at the government, Jinnah said, while reading out the gist of Gandhi's letter,

"Gandhi makes no mention of the demand for Pakistan in his letter. It was a ploy of Gandhi to pit the Muslim League against the British government and secure his release."

Thus, the issue ended before it could be discussed.

As anticipated, the Quit India movement brought the law and order situation in the country on the brink of collapse. Thousands of people courted arrest rendering the jails inadequate to accommodate them. The incidents of violence and the communal riots occurred in several parts of the country. The Viceroy declared in unambiguous terms that what had happened was due to Gandhi and that he was responsible for it. Gandhi wrote to the Viceroy that if he could assure that he was responsible for all that had happened he would compensate for it. What followed was a lengthy correspondence between Gandhi and Jinnah, but it failed to infuse mutual trust and goodwill. Gandhi had announced that he would go on a fast from the jail.

The entire country was anxious and worried about the announcement by a frail seventy five year old Gandhi. An all party meeting was convened in Delhi to discuss the situation arising out of his fast. Jinnah was invited to the meeting as a President of the Muslim League. But he refused to accept the invitation on the pretext that it was a ploy of the Congress to get Gandhi released from the jail. The all party meeting released a public statement urging Gandhi to give up his fast and appealing to the government to release him from the jail due to his deteriorating condition. The appeal was signed by the leaders of various parties and communities. They urged Jinnah to sign the appeal, but he refused to associate with such an appeal.

The war situation was worsening day-by-day. The German army had conquered half of Europe and invaded Russia. Japan, which joined the Axis powers, had conquered Rangoon and was about to capture Burma. The British troops were not able to resist the Japanese. The Japanese troops had entered the eastern border of India. There was a wide spread panic that the Japanese war planes could attack any Indian city any time. Jinnah feared that if the British government failed to protect India and left the country abruptly by handing over the power to the Congress, the position of the Muslims would be very precarious. Before this could happen, some protective measures were necessary. Keeping this in mind, he made a very alarming demand at the annual session of the Muslim League,

"The Muslims have a condition that before the British government leaves India, it must hand over to us an independent and sovereign Pakistan. I want to tell the British government that before thinking of independence, think of partition of India. Our response to Gandhi's Quit India movement is first divide India before you leave. First divide and then leave. I would go to the extent of saying that if you do not want to leave the country after dividing India, you may not leave, but you cannot leave without dividing India."

At this time, an incident occurred that stunned the entire country.

It was the month of July and it was raining heavily in Bombay. Jinnah arrived at the Victoria Terminus Station after a very hectic tour of Karachi and Baluchistan. He reached his bungalow at the Mount Pleasant Road. He spent the whole day going through the important files and correspondence. His health was deteriorating. He had been constantly suffering from cough, cold and fever. He lost his appetite. He found a refuge in smoking and drinking. And in spite of all this, he travelled extensively. His work increased manifold.

Around 2 p.m. Jinnah emerged from the room which he used as his office. He was holding some papers and files. While browsing through a file, he felt the need for some more information and documents which his private secretary was in possession of. Instead of calling the private secretary to his room, Jinnah went to his room. A tall and lean young man of thirty years was standing there. With his long beard and cap, he looked like a Muslim. On seeing Jinnah, the private secretary stood up. After getting the details that he wanted as Jinnah turned back, the young man came forward and punched him in the face. Jinnah was stunned. He stumbled. As he regained balance, the young man pulled out a dragger from his waistband and pointed at Jinnah's throat.

NOTE

1. Spell.

52

Rafiq' arrest, Rafiq-Jinnah dialogue in court, Rajagopalachari's formula

Jinnah understood the gravity of the situation. The dragger could slit Jinnah's throat. He grabbed the assailant's waist with one hand and clutched the wrist holding the dragger with the other hand. In the meantime, the blade had cut his jaw slightly. The stunned private secretary rushed to Jinnah's rescue and held the assailant with his two hands. He struggled hard to break free. In the scuffle, the dragger fell down from his hand, grazing Jinnah's shoulder and tearing his coat.

On hearing the shouts of his private secretary, the servants and the guards in the bungalow came running. The assailant managed to break free and jumped out of the window into the garden. The gardener and the chauffeur were taken aback. They managed to catch hold of him. The other servants came running and overpowered the assailant.

Within a few minutes, a convoy of policemen from the Gamdevi police station arrived. Jinnah sat down calmly, his coat, shirt and colour showing the clots of blood. He was not yet given any first-aid. The doctor who accompanied the police treated him. The police arrested the assailant and took the statements from all those present. The frenzied assailant chanted some verses from the Quran and screamed at the servants,

"Brave! You are the loyal servants. Unfortunately, I could not succeed in accomplishing my mission. But remember I am not a mercenary killer. I came here to kill *Quaid-e-Azam* with the blessings of *Allah*. He is a stooge of the British Imperialists. He is an obstacle in the path of India's independence."

The police stopped him from speaking further and took him away.

After a few days, the trial of the assailant on the charge of attempted murder begun. The prosecution presented the charge sheet along with the statements of Jinnah and his staff. The accused himself defended his case.

The accused Rafiq Sabir Gaznavi hailed from Lahore. When Jinnah had visited Lahore a few years ago, he entered the mosque without removing his shoes. Rafiq Sabir was present there. He was enraged to see Jinnah defiling the mosque. Had the people not stopped him, he would have attacked Jinnah in a fit of anger. He had no intention to kill him at that time. He just wanted to push him out of the mosque.

Though Jinnah claimed to be a leader of the Muslims, he knew nothing about Islam or the Quran. He led a life in total contrast to the Islamic principles. Rafiq Sabir in his statement to the police said that he had written several letters to Jinnah drawing his attention to his contrasting lifestyle. Jinnah had never bothered to reply to any of his letters. Jinnah's family belonged to the Ismaili Khojas and hence they had nothing to do with a mosque. Therefore, by entering the mosque at Lahore, Jinnah had deeply hurt the sentiments of the orthodox Muslims. Rafiq Sabir also said in his statement that Jinnah was a pawn in the hands of the British and had become an obstacle on the road to the country's freedom.

Rafiq had come to Bombay a week ago with an intention to kill Jinnah. Since Jinnah was out of station, he waited for him to return. He stayed in an Inn run by the Haji Islam Haji HabibTrust in Pakmodia Street. He wrote his name as Mohammed Sadiq and gave the reason that he came to Bombay in search of a missing relative.

He wanted to kill Jinnah at the railway station, but he did not get the chance as Jinnah was surrounded by his supporters. Hence he decided to go to his bungalow and kill him on the pretext of meeting him. When he reached the bungalow, the guard stopped him. He told the guard that he had come to take an appointment for meeting Jinnah from his private secretary. Then he entered the bungalow and went to the private secretary and requested for an audience with Jinnah. The private secretary asked him his name and address and identity. Rafiq gave him an evasive reply and told him that he was a very ordinary Muslim and that his identity should not matter.

The private secretary asked him, "Look! Quaid-e-Azam is very busy and he cannot meet anyone without a prior appointment. You may write on a piece of paper what you want to say. I will pass it on to Jinnah Sahib. He will then decide."

Rafiq thought for a moment and then took a piece of paper from the table and wrote,

"Respected Jinnah *Sahib,*

Amen! I have crossed many hurdles and reached Bombay to meet you. I have some important work. I shall be grateful if you could spare a few minutes.

Rafiq Sabir Gaznavi."

As Rafiq finished the writing, Jinnah suddenly entered the room. To him it was a Godsend opportunity. He thanked Allah and suddenly attacked Jinnah as he turned back.

During the course of the trial, Rafiq decided to cross examine the witnesses himself. When the victim *Quaid-e-Azam* Barrister Muhammad Ali Jinnah stood in the witness box, Rafiq started the cross examination.

Rafiq : I had sent you several letters and telegrams, which you had never answered. Do you agree?

Jinnah: I don't know. I receive hundreds of letters every day and I travel a lot. Hence, I am unable to read all the letters.

Rafiq : Is it true that you have asked Maulana Hazrat Mohini to leave the meeting of the Muslim League at Allahabad?

Jinnah: No! This is not true.

Magistrate: What has this question to do with the case?

Rafiq: Your honour, this question is important because Jinnah Sahib considers himself the leader of the Muslims.

Magistrate: Alright, you can proceed.

Rafiq: You have not clarified the meaning of Pakistan? Please clarify the word Pakistan?

Jinnah: The meaning of Pakistan is clear to those who want to understand it. No one can explain it to those who do not want to understand it.

Rafiq : Is it true that you and Liaquat Ali Khan started the Delhi based newspaper *The Dawn*?

Jinnah : Yes. I am the founder of *The Dawn* and Liaquat looks after it.

Rafiq: Is it true that you pay three thousand rupees per month to Liaquat Ali Khan for looking after it?

Magistrate: This question is not relevant to the case.

Rafiq: Jinnah Sahib, is there any personal enmity between us?

Jinnah: No. I do not think so.

Rafiq: Then can you tell me why I attacked you?

Magistrate: This question is unnecessary.

Rafiq: Your honour! Can I ask Jinnah Sahib what happened at the time of his daughter's marriage?

Magistrate: No. Not at all.

Rafiq: Jinnah Sahib, is it true that you have received hundreds of copies of the Quran as gifts?"

Jinnah: Yes.

Rafiq: Do you know why they are gifted to you?

Jinnah: As per the Islamic tradition, the gifting of the Quran is bestowing an honour.

Rafiq: No. These copies are gifted to you so that you could quit the politics of manipulation and study the Quran and lead a better life in the old age.

Magistrate: This is not relevant to the case.

Rafiq: Do you remember that you had entered the Sahidgunj mosque in Lahore with the shoes?

Magistrate: We are not here to condemn the behaviour of Quaid-e-Azam. We are here to investigate the attempted murder on him.

Rafiq: Your honour, Quaid-e-Azam has just said there is no enmity between us. We have no dispute over any property or woman. Then why should I attack him?

Magistrate: Alright, you can proceed.

Rafiq: Jinnah Sahib, your lifestyle is not according to the principles of Islam. Then how can you be a leader of the Muslims?

Jinnah: You must put this question to the Muslims of the country.

Rafiq: You are not conversed with the real conditions of the Muslims. Have you ever thought about their poverty and illiteracy and why they turn to begging, theft and gambling? I wanted to meet you only to ask this question. Then he turned to the magistrate and asked an important question,

Rafiq: Does the blood on the dragger match with the blood of Jinnah Sahib? Why no chemical test is carried to match the blood samples?

Magistrate: You are right. This should have been done.

Rafiq: Then, cannot we say that Jinnah Sahib has fabricated the incident to gain the sympathy of the Muslims and the publicity in the press to boost his image?

Magistrate: The court will consider this.

Rafiq: Your honour! Jinnah Sahib says that the dagger in my hand fell down in the room. But his chauffeur says in his statement that he wrested the dragger from me when I jumped into the garden and handed it over to Jinnah Sahib. I draw your attention to this contradiction. The Court pronounced its verdict. Rafiq Sabir Gaznavi was found guilty of the charge and sentenced to five years rigorous imprisonment.

*

C. Rajagopalachari who had distanced himself from the "Quit India" movement tried to find a solution to the Indian problem. When all the leaders of the Congress were in jail, he worked out a formula that could be acceptable to both the Congress and the Muslim League. As per the formula, the Muslim League should support the Congress in its freedom struggle and become part of a national government. The formula proposed plebiscite in the provinces where the Muslims were a majority. If the majority wanted an independent state, it should be conceded. This raised the hope for the creation of Pakistan in future.

He met Gandhi in Yervada jail in Poona and obtained his approval for the formula. Gandhi had already made it clear that if any region did not want to be a part of the Union of India, it should not be forced to stay within the Union. If the Muslim League cooperated with the Congress, it would not be difficult to achieve independence. In the meantime, an interim national government could be formed. Taking all this into consideration, Gandhi approved the formula of Rajagopalachari.

However, Jinnah rejected the formula when Rajagopalachari presented it to him. He said that the formula did not provide for Pakistan. Nevertheless, he agreed to place the formula before the Working Committee of the Muslim League for consideration. But Rajagopalachari knew that when Jinnah had already rejected the formula, taking it to the Muslim League would serve no purpose. Then he released the formula to the press together with the reaction of Gandhi and Jinnah. He said in a letter to Jinnah, "The private parleys end here. And now it is necessary to take the people into confidence."

53

Gandhi's release from jail, Gandhi's letter to Jinnah, Jinnah's health, Jinnah's instruction to Dr. Jaal Patel to keep his disease a secret

On a scorching summer morning of 1944, Gandhi was released from the Aga Khan palace before the expiry of his prison term. During the two years of prison, he lost his most trusted Secretary Mahadev Desai and devoted wife Kasturba. His health deteriorated due to the fast and the illness. There was a widespread apprehension that he might not survive the prison term. The British officials in London, Delhi and Bombay even conferred on how to perform his last rites and pay him tribute.

But fortunately for the country, such an eventuality did not arise. After the release from the jail, Gandhi spent a few days convalescing first at Panchgani and then at Juhu beach in Bombay. He wrote a letter to the Viceroy to find some solution to the political problem. The Viceroy asked for Gandhi's suggestion to end the political impasse. Gandhi wrote, "How can I give my suggestion without discussing with the senior leaders of the Congress Working Committee? However, if you are serious about the formation of a national government, we can meet."

In reply the Viceroy said, "As long as the Hindus and the Muslims do not have an understanding, our meeting will not serve any purpose."

The letter that Gandhi had written to Jinnah from the jail had never reached him. The government had passed only a gist of the letter to him. Jinnah had reacted very rudely and even accused Gandhi that the purpose of writing such a letter was to get him released from the jail. Jinnah's statement in this context had received a wide coverage in the newspapers across the country. Yet in the interest of the country and without making it a prestige issue, Gandhi wrote another letter to Jinnah suggesting that they should have a meeting with an open mind to resolve amicably the problems between the Hindus and the Muslims. Jinnah wrote to Gandhi from Srinagar, "I have a busy schedule till the middle of August. Hence, I cannot spare any time for such a meeting. However, I will be glad to meet you after my return to Bombay." He suggested that Gandhi could determine the time of meeting at the Jinnah house.

When Gandhi received the letter from Jinnah, Sir Tej Bahadur Sapru, a prominent moderate leader of the Congress, was present. Sapru was a close friend of Jinnah. Both of them quite often fought against each other in the Court. When he came to know the contents of Jinnah's letter he reacted, "Bapu, you alone can pay the price of meeting him this way."

In the meantime, Jinnah was worried about the news reports in the foreign newspapers, particularly the American newspapers. A strong belief was gaining ground in the political circles in America that the rigid stand of the Muslim League became a stumbling block to the independence of India. The American President Roosevelt suggested to the British Prime Minister Churchill to resolve the issue of India's independence in a democratic manner. Churchill did not like the American interference. Jinnah and the Muslim League were excuses for him to delay the independence of India. Jinnah thought that if he could have parleys with Gandhi without giving up his rigid stand, he would not be accused of being a puppet in the hands of the British government. It was obvious that the British government would not be happy if the Congress and the Muslim League reached any understanding. But Jinnah wanted to use this opportunity to counter the impression carried in the foreign newspapers.

In the middle of August Jinnah returned to Bombay. The meeting with Gandhi was fixed for 19th August at Jinnah House. Gandhi was staying in the Birla House, at a distance of two kilometers. People were excited about the ensuing meeting between the two.

However, the meeting could not take place as per the schedule. Jinnah felt very weak after a very hectic tour. He had a high fever. He could hardly eat anything. He started coughing and vomiting blood. The medical examination and the treatment had not yielded any positive result. Jinnah was confined to bed as he became sick.

Dr. Jaal Patel was an eminent doctor in Bombay. Jinnah was acquainted with him. Many prominent persons had been his patients. Jinnah decided to have a thorough medical check up by Dr. Patel. The doctor got all the necessary tests done, like the x-rays and the spit and the blood samples. The doctor asked certain questions relating to his past history of health.

"Doctor, I used to have diarrhea now and then. But I understand that it was due to my irregular eating habits," told Jinnah.

"Did you have any other problem?"

"Yes, I used to get chest pain sometimes. But it was due to muscular pain and I used to get relief with some medication," Jinnah once again spoke about his ailment and the treatment.

"Oh!" the doctor paused for a moment and asked, "Any thing else?"

"Sometimes I get serious bouts of cough. That could be due to my hectic travels in different climatic conditions."

The doctor paused again for a while.

"Oh! Yes. I was getting fever now and then for the past few years. That could be due to my advancing age and increase in the workload," Jinnah said confidently.

The result of the tests stunned the doctor. Jinnah was in the last stage of tuberculosis. His lungs were damaged completely due to heavy smoking and drinking. He also had blood cancer.

Dr. Patel was in a predicament. Considering the advanced stage of the disease and the treatment available, nothing could be done to lengthen the life span of the patient. At the most, the patient could live for another two or three years. No scientific breakthrough could help the patient who is about seventy years. The question now was how to convey the bad news to him.

Jinnah was almost bed ridden. He was not in a condition to hold the scheduled meeting with Gandhi. Dr. Patel started the treatment and told him that he needed complete bed rest at least for three weeks. Accordingly, the meeting with Gandhi was adjourned to 9th September.

The entire country was waiting with a bated breath for the parleys between Gandhi and Jinnah to begin. The Hindu Mahasabha was strongly opposed to any such talks between them. Even some senior Congress leaders were unhappy about the manner in which Gandhi requested for a meeting with Jinnah and the latter's discourteous response. Gandhi setting aside his personal prestige wanted to make a last effort. A few days before the scheduled meeting, Jinnah released a press statement saying that he would meet *Mahatma* Gandhi and make sincere efforts to reach an agreement on the question of the independence of India. The word *Mahatma* used in the statement unnerved the British officials. During the past fifteen years, Jinnah had always addressed him as Mr. Gandhi, although sometimes he addressed him as *Gandhiji* out of respect. But he did not consider him *Mahatma.* That was an open secret. Even the British officials sometimes addressed Gandhi as *Mahatma*. But for Jinnah, he was a Mr. Gandhi of the Hindu Congress. Hence, the British officials were taken aback that Jinnah addressed Gandhi as *Mahatma.* This raised a new hope among the Indian people, while it made the British officials in India and London restive. The war became very destructive. There seemed to be no end to the war and victory or defeat remained uncertain. In such circumstances, if the parleys between Gandhi and Jinnah succeeded and the Hindus and the Muslims reached an agreement, it would bring more trouble for the British government.

Dr. Patel was committed to his profession, but he was also politically conscious. He knew that the country was passing through a critical stage and the role of Jinnah in it. Yet, his main concern was to diagnose the disease and give the best medical treatment possible to cure the patient. The scheduled parleys between Gandhi and Jinnah could cause more mental stress to the patient. Considering this, the doctor thought it wise to tell the truth to Jinnah. When Jinnah's health improved somewhat, the doctor called him to his consulting room on the pretext of having some more tests.

"Quaid-e-Azam," the doctor started cautiously, "I think you have abused your body and totally neglected your health."

"May be," said Jinnah, "Though I am lean, I remained healthy. Now the advancing age must have affected the health."

"Excuse me, Quaid-e-Azam. It is very serious."

"Means!" Jinnah asked anxiously, "Tell me clearly."

"Jinnah Sahib, I am sorry to say that you are in an advanced stage of a fatal disease," said the doctor.

Jinnah became speechless for a while. His face betrayed some inscrutable emotion. Then he said, "Doctor, tell me clearly what you want to say without any hesitation."

"Quaid-e-Azam, I know you quite well," the doctor said at last, "That is why I want to tell you the truth. You are in the last stage of tuberculosis. Not only that, you also have blood cancer."

Jinnah was stunned.

"And we must accept the bitter truth that the way the disease has spread, even the modern medical science cannot cure it," said the doctor.

There was an eerie silence in the room. Jinnah sat silently for a long time as if his mental faculties were paralysed for a while. Realising his condition, the doctor said, "But God is great! We can only give you the treatment. You are understanding enough. God willing, we may find some cure. Let us not lose the hope."

"Doctor," said Jinnah firmly as if he made some decision, "Though I have always remained an optimist, I am not averse to pessimism. I want to ask you a question. If the disease of the patient has reached such an advanced stage, how much can you lengthen his life span?"

"Quaid-e-Azam. No power on the earth can lengthen the span of life. Life is determined by destiny on birth. We doctors try to keep the patient healthy as long as he lives. Whatever the modern science may say, you can live hundred years if God had willed it," the doctor said cleverly.

Jinnah was not satisfied with the doctor's reply. He asked with greater clarity,

"Doctor, please tell me without bringing God into this, how long can I survive?"

"Quaid-e-Azam you try to complete your unfinished task in two or three years. I think you cannot live more than three years," the doctor said frankly.

Jinnah was lost in a deep thought. He felt pain in his chest. His heart beat increased. His blood flew faster through the veins. In a state of mental turmoil he said,

"Never mind, doctor. You can continue the treatment, but..." Jinnah looked around and said cautiously, "You must promise me one thing. And you will not break the promise till I die," Jinnah said and held out his right hand to the doctor for the first time in his life.

The doctor grieved by the emptiness on his face put his right hand into his hand.

"You don't worry. Quaid-e-Azam. We doctors have certain professional ethics. You can say what you want to without any hesitation."

"This knowledge of my life span should remain between you and me. No third person should come to know about my disease," Jinnah said, his voice quivering.

"This is part of my professional ethics. I promise you, no one will come to know anything about your health."

"Then, in order to fulfill the promise, you must ensure..." Jinnah said with great imagination, "that my x-rays, the reports and the medical prescriptions do not bear the name of any patient . Even, by chance, if any one comes across this file he should not be able to know the name of the patient."

The doctor was astonished by the precaution of Jinnah. The doctor was aware of the precarious political situation in the country. He understood the implications of the promise. He was an Indian. Yet he considered his professional duty more important than his duty towards the country. He assured Jinnah,

"You don't worry, Quaid-e-Azam. I will ensure that."

54

Fatima's knowledge of Jinnah's disease

The adjournment of the 19th August meeting to 9th September between Gandhi and Jinnah gave rise to all sorts of speculations. Everybody knew that Jinnah was not keeping good health. Even Gandhi was not in a robust health to shoulder the burden of work. After the death of his wife Kasturba, a companion for sixty years, and Mahadev Desai, who was like his son, it was not the same Gandhi. The people suspected that there might have been some political reason behind the adjournment of the meeting.

Dr. Jaal Patel advised bed rest at least for three weeks. However, Jinnah for obvious reasons decided not to meet anyone during this period. He did not want to give the people any chance to make political calculations based on his health. He decided not to entertain even his close colleagues like Liaquat Ali Khan, Abdul Rab Nishtar and Khaliquzzaman. When it came to the pressing matters, he preferred correspondence.

Initially, Fatima thought that his sickness was due to the heavy workload. She had studied the medicine at the Christian school in Bandra. She was a qualified dentist. Hence, she could not be kept in the dark about the treatment given to Jinnah. She made enquiries about the medical reports and the prescriptions of the medicines. While Dr. Patel managed to evade her questions, Jinnah told her the half-truth. He thought it better Fatima had some inkling about his health, in case he slipped into a coma.

Liaquat Ali Khan had rebelled against Jinnah at the time of elections to the Provincial Assemblies in 1937. And he had contested the election against the Muslim League in the United Province which he had lost. In spite of the pressure to expel Liaquat Ali from the League, Jinnah did not take any disciplinary action against him. He had not forgotten his meeting at that time with Begum Rana in the government guest house at Lucknow. Jinnah had subsequently pacified the detractors and allowed Liaquat Ali Khan to enjoy the position of number two in the Muslim League.

Liaquat Ali felt that if Jinnah was not keeping good health and unable to handle the pressure of work, he could share the burden as his heir, though temporarily. He thought that in case Jinnah was seriously ill, a change of guard was inevitable. Jinnah was nearing seventy, where as he was fifty. Whether Pakistan would become a reality or not, he had a long political career ahead. God forbid, if something happened to Jinnah, there would be a huge vacuum among the Muslims of the country. The Congress had many leaders of Gandhi's calibre. It had the leaders like Jawaharlal Nehru, Sardar Patel, Rajendra Prasad, and Rajagopalachari. Hence, Gandhi's absence would not create any vacum. However, the situation was different with the Muslim League. To discuss this, Liaquat Ali Khan sought an appointment with Jinnah.

But he could not get the appointment. He received a letter signed by Fatima that in the present condition Jinnah would not like to meet any one. Liaquat Ali was annoyed. In spite of his being the second in command in the Muslim League, he was not permitted to meet Jinnah. Dr. Patel was issuing the medical bulletins on Jinnah's health from time to time. But the bulletins were couched in such medical terms that no one could understand them. Jinnah's presence in Indian politics was a foregone conclusion, but his absence from the political scene could create a new and unpredictable situation. Liaquat Ali Khan felt that something should be done to deal with such an eventuality.

*

Jinnah's health improved. The doctor's treatment, the complete bed rest and the constant care by Fatima had contributed to the improvement of his health. However, the doctor, Jinnah and Fatima—three of them—knew pretty well that what was apparent was not real. The tests did not show any positive change.

The scheduled meeting between Gandhi and Jinnah on 9th September raised the political temperature again. Gandhi was staying at the Birla House in the Malabar Hills for this purpose. He had undergone an operation after his release from the jail. Because of the operation he became weak. In the meantime, he was corresponding with the Viceroy and the British Prime Minister. His colleagues in the Congress were still in jail. He suggested that if they were released the Congress Working Committee could meet and decide the future course of action. The government rejected his suggestion.

Meanwhile, the British Prime Minister Churchill called Gandhi a *naked fakir*. The newspapers gave a wide publicity to it. The newspapers in Britain took pride in reporting that this *naked fakir* of India should be crushed. Gandhi was in Panchgani at that time. He wrote a sarcastic letter to Churchill,

"Dear Prime Minister,

It is reported that you have called me a *naked fakir* and that you wanted to crush me. It is extremely difficult to become a *fakir* and that too a *naked fakir.* I have been trying to become one for a long time. I accept your saying as a compliment, although it was never expected. I would request you to trust this naked fakir and avail of his service for your sake, for the sake of his people and through them for the sake of mankind.

Your true friend,
M.K. Gandhi."

As soon as the countdown for the Gandhi-Jinnah parleys began, the British government released to the press all its correspondence with Gandhi. If the talks between the two succeeded, it could put a spoke in its plans. The enmity between the Hindus and the Muslims would benefit the government. While releasing the correspondence to the press, the government had also declared that the communal problem in India was not confined to the Hindus and the Muslims alone, but it also encompassed a large section of the society—the Dalits. Its intention was clear. The government wanted the parleys between Gandhi and Jinnah to fail. Jinnah was not aware of the correspondence exchanged between Gandhi and the British government. Hence, the government wanted Jinnah to know about the correspondence before the meeting began.

The provincial government of Bombay made elaborate security arrangements for the meeting. The Congress leaders like Jawaharlal Nehru, Sardar Patel and Maulana Azad were not happy about Gandhi's decision to meet Jinnah. A section of the people also felt that it was humiliating for Gandhi to meet Jinnah on the latter's terms. But Gandhi was firm. The situation was quite tense. The government restricted the entry of the vehicles and the people in the Malabar Hills area for the duration of the talk. The residents of the area were issued special permits. The government declared that if any person wanted to enter the area he should obtain a special permission. Both the Birla House and the Jinnah House were provided adequate security.

Gandhi arrived at the Jinnah House at 9 a.m. on 9th September. A group of people, breaking the security cordon, tried to prevent him from leaving the Birla House. The police took them into custody. This created the widespread impression that Gandhi was extending the hand of friendship to Jinnah much against the will of the Congress and the will of a large section of the people in the country. Jinnah instructed his staff not to allow anyone to enter the house during the talks. No reporter or photographer should be allowed beyond the garden.

The reporters and the photographers jostled as Gandhi entered the House. The security personnel could control them. Jinnah stood on the steps of his house to receive Gandhi. Both of them shook hands warmly. Gandhi put his right hand on Jinnah's shoulder to draw him closer. Gandhi wore a white *dhoti* and covered the body with a white cloth. In contrast, Jinnah wore a very expensive imported suit with a matching tie and shoes. Gandhi's simple sandals were an indication of his simplicity, while Jinnah's shoes and socks were a testimony to his expensive tastes. Both of them stood smiling on the steps of the House for a while, when the photographs clicked the photos of their historical meeting. They looked relaxed and eager to achieve something concrete. The pressmen hoped that they would be the first ones to share something with the rest of the world.

Jinnah's favourite wine and cigarettes were kept handy in the conference room. Gandhi, due to the illness, was drinking boiled water. He generally carried the boiled water with him. However, this time he decided not to carry the water. He feared that if the water was brought along, Jinnah could make an issue of it. Jinnah said many a time publicly that the Hindus wash their hands after shaking hands with the Muslims and that they neither eat food nor drink water in a Muslim's house. Jinnah should not assume that even Gandhi did not drink water from a Muslim's house. Gandhi quietly took a glass of water from the table and drank it calmly.

When the door of the room was closed, four hundred million people across the country from Kashmir to Kanyakumari, Calcutta to Kathiawad waited anxiously with bated breath.

55

Gandhi-Jinnah parleys, Wavell's reaction to the parleys

"I have not come here only hoping to find a solution, but I am determined to find a solution. Hope you are with me on this," said Gandhi beginning the talks.

"I assure you, I am with you. We have no option, but to find a solution," Jinnah reciprocated.

Gandhi : I must accept that you have great influence over the Muslims of the country.

Jinnah : Just as you have the influence over the Hindus.

Gandhi : Since you have by and large agreed with the formula of Rajagopalachari, can we take that as the basis of our talks?

Jinnah : I do not have any objection. But I wish to make one thing clear at the beginning.

I am talking to you as the President of the Muslim League on behalf of the Muslims of the country. I would like to know in which capacity you are talking to me?

Gandhi : You can consider me as the representative of the entire country.

Jinnah : How can that be possible?

Gandhi : Why not? Every Indian must strive to become a representative of the entire country. Whether he succeeds or not is a different thing. If you wish, you can talk to me as an individual.

Jinnah : You cannot find a solution this way. The problem is not between two individuals, but between two nations living in one country.

Gandhi : That means you consider the Muslims of the country a different nation.

Jinnah : That is a well known fact. The Muslims are not a minority in India. They are totally different from the Hindus in terms of religion, race, tradition, culture and lifestyle."

Gandhi : In that case, how can we separate the Muslims living in every Indian province, district, city and street? The millions of Muslims bear the names of the Hindus.

They have retained the Hindu surnames like Pandit, Rai, Choudhary, Majumdar and Patel even after converting to Islam. You must have visited the villages in Bihar. There, the Hindu and the Muslim women wear the same type of clothes.

Jinnah : That is not true. The Muslims are a separate nation. You must first accept the Lahore Resolution of the Muslim League for partition of the country.

Gandhi: That Resolution does not speak of Pakistan. Please clarify your demand for Pakistan?

Jinnah : The demand is very clear. If you read the League's Resolution once again, you will understand it.

Gandhi : My son got converted to Islam. Do you think now he belongs to a different nation?

Jinnah : That is your personal matter. It has nothing to do with my belief.

When both of them emerged from the meeting that lasted for three hours, the eagerly waiting press reporters asked Gandhi, "*Bapu*, what have you brought for us?"

He held out the flowers in his hand to them and said, "Now I have brought only these flowers."

Thereafter the talks continued on a day-to-day basis, with a break in between for one reason or the other. They met fourteen times in eighteen days. Both of them also corresponded to clarify certain matters. During the course of the talks, Rajgopalachari asked Gandhi, "Can you tell us, what is the progress of the talks?"

"These talks are really testing my patience. I am astonished about my patience. As you know, I am optimistic even under the most depressing circumstances."

When Jinnah did not succeed in making Gandhi accept his two-nation theory, he said to him, "I thought you had changed. But now I think you are still the same person that you were in 1939."

Gandhi : Yes. I have not changed. I am the same person. But if you can change my ideas, I will support you wholeheartedly."

Jinnah : I have been able to change the ideas of not only the Muslims of the country, but also of many Hindus and foreigners. I am confident that if I change your ideas you will become my *Ali.* You for once accept Pakistan and leave non-violence. You leave to us, how to deal with the British government. Please do not beat around the bush.

Gandhi, whose knowledge of Islam and the Quran was far superior to that of Jinnah, was vexed by Jinnah mentioning *Ali.* He was surprised that Jinnah wanted to become the Prophet. He continued, "Then are you trying to cross examine me?"

Jinnah : No. I have been a lawyer all my life. The manner of my talking might have given you that impression.

Gandhi : Please give me in writing if you have any objections to the formula of Rajagopalachari?

Jinnah : There is no need for that. My objections are well known.

The talks could not continue due to the *Eid* festival. On the occasion of the *Eid*, Gandhi sent some special dish to Jinnah as a gesture of goodwill. Jinnah accepted it, but did not eat.

During the course of the talks, Gandhi's private secretary Pyarelal and two or three aids would come every day and sit in a separate room. They used to chat with the staff of the Jinnah House. One day Pyarelal invited them for tea as a gesture of goodwill. K.H. Khurshid was Jinnah's private secretary. He said he would respond to the invitation the next day. Pyarelal received the reply the next day, "We thank you for the invitation. We think it is not appropriate to accept the invitation at this stage. We regret, we cannot accept the invitation."

The reports about the progress of the talks published in the newspapers across the country generated lot of excitement and anxiety. At one stage, the question of the formation of Pakistan also came up during the talks.

Gandhi : The Pakistan that you are demanding, do you think it can be formed voluntarily like the two brothers agreeing to separate with mutual understanding.

Jinnah : Once you accept the two-nation theory, we can discuss the details.

Gandhi : But have you thought of its political system?

Jinnah : Pakistan will be a democratic nation. All the people—Muslims, Hindus, Sikhs, Christians—will be equal citizens.

Gandhi : Your answer raises two doubts in my mind. Until now, you have been opposing democracy in India. You said democracy means the rule of the majority over the minority. If we apply the same logic to Pakistan, will it not mean the rule of the Muslim majority over the Hindus, the Sikhs and the Christians minorities?

Jinnah : Not at all. That will not happen. If the minorities in Pakistan wish, they can have separate electorate. The democracy that I oppose is the one imposed from outside. Democracy in Pakistan will be of its own.

Gandhi : But if these minorities put forth the two-nation theory and demand for separate independent nations, what will be the response of Pakistan? Then what have you thought of the thirty five million Muslims who will be living in India even after the partition?

Jinnah : Those Muslims can be exchanged for the Hindus living in Pakistan.

Gandhi : But it will be gigantic and almost impossible task!

Jinnah : Then I can trust you for the safety of these thirty five million Muslims.

Gandhi : As per the formula of Rajagopalachari, we must achieve independence first because when two brothers part they should not be enslaved to any one.

Jinnah : How is that possible? You have launched the "Quit India" movement against the British without taking the Muslims into confidence. You want the British to leave the country and hand over the reins of power to the Hindus. You must first withdraw the movement.

Gandhi : The movement is not against the Muslims, it is against foreign rule. The formula of Rajagopalachari makes it clear that once India achieves independence, the provinces will have the right to separate if they so desire. I wish we stay together, but I will not force any province to remain in the Union of India against its will.

Jinnah : The Muslims in the provinces which will form Pakistan have already given their verdict. The British government will have to grant independence not only to India, but also to Pakistan. It is not that Pakistan is separating and India is getting independence. Both the nations will become independent at the same time. Considering this, I can say that your movement is actually against the Muslims.

Gandhi : You are the Quaid-e-Azam. I have heard that you understand the minute aspects of law. If you think the Quit India movement is against the Muslims, I suggest you take the opinion of any legal luminary of your choice about it and then let us accept whatever he says.

Jinnah : When I myself know the law, why should I take somebody else's opinion?

Gandhi : There should be plebiscite in those provinces which want to separate. That is the essence of a true democracy. This cannot be considered an imposition from outside. Let the people in the provinces of Punjab, Bengal, Sindh, Baluchistan and other provinces decide through plebiscite whether they want to join Pakistan.

Jinnah : There is no need for the entire population of these provinces to take part in such plebiscite. It concerns the Muslims only. In case of plebiscite, only the Muslims will vote and not others.

Gandhi : It is a strange democracy that gives the right to self determination only to a section of the people and not to everyone. In that case, the provinces like Punjab and Bengal will have to be partitioned.

Jinnah : These provinces cannot be partitioned. Punjab and Bengal are the Muslim majority provinces, hence they should be merged with Pakistan just as the Hindu majority provinces will remain with India.

One day during the course of these talks, Jinnah escorted Gandhi to the front door. Gandhi noticed him limping. Gandhi stopped on the steps and asked Jinnah,

"Quaid-e-Azam, it looks you have pain in your leg?"

"Yes," Jinnah said. "It seems I have sprained my ankle last night."

"I have a medicine that can cure it. It is as effective as the *Rambaan*. I will send it to you tonight. You apply it over the sprained portion and the pain will disappear by the morning."

Jinnah did not react. But he registered the word *Rambaan.* This proved what a Hindu protagonist Gandhi was. Jinnah accepted the medicine sent by Gandhi, but did not apply it. Because the medicine was connected to the Hindu God Ram.

Even after several rounds of talks, nothing concrete was achieved. The country wide excitement was receding rapidly into despondency. In spite of the failure of the talks, both the leaders made yet another attempt.

Gandhi : There is nothing unusual about two brothers parting ways. But their father remains the same. Even if India is partitioned and Pakistan is created, as per your wish, cannot we agree to have a common defence and foreign relations?

Jinnah : No, that is not possible. An independent Pakistan should have the right to fight a war against India, if required, to protect its interest. I wish that does not happen. Pakistan will serve as a protective wall for India on it north-western frontier and India as a protective wall to East Pakistan.

Gandhi : I am shocked by your idea. How can we talk of independence and the war at the same time?

Jinnah : You have not brought any new proposal for reaching an agreement. I have agreed for the talks with an intention to reach an understanding. You do not have the right to take any firm decision to reach an understanding. Under the circumstances, there is no point in continuing our talks.

Gandhi : I have failed to understand you. However, I would request you to give me an opportunity to present my views to the Working Committee of the Muslim League or in its open session. Whether my views would be accepted or not, you will at least not be held responsible for the failure of the talks.

Jinnah : Your suggestion is very extraordinary and unprecedented. Only the members or the representatives of the Muslim League have the right to participate in its meetings.

Gandhi : In the past, the Congress leaders had addressed the meetings of the League and the leaders of the League also had attended the meetings of the Congress.

Even the British Parliament invites eminent persons who are not its members to address. It cannot be that a person of your stature is not aware of this.

Jinnah : An organisation may make such an exception through a special invitation. The Muslim League has not made any such exception and I do not think it is necessary now.

There was no common meeting ground to continue the talks. On the last day of the meeting, Gandhi expressing despair said that there was no common meeting ground between the two except ill-will.

At the evening prayers on 27th September, a dejected Gandhi acknowledged the failure of the talks. However, he expressed the hope that something positive would emerge. He said, "I have knocked the door of the Quaid-e-Azam, but I failed. I believe in truth and non-violence. I do not get disheartened by failure. What is good for all of us, only God knows."

Jinnah was in a completely different frame of mind. Once he realized the seriousness of his illness, his focus changed drastically. It was clear to him that he would not survive for more than two or three years. He wanted to take recourse to such an action that would give him maximum benefit. If he could extract Pakistan by taking a rigid and unequivocal stand, it would be a great personal achievement. Jinnah felt that the Quit India movement had no impact on the British government. It was possible that both Gandhi and the Congress had run out of steam. He wanted to exploit the situation to his full advantage. Even if he did not succeed in securing Pakistan immediately, at least he would be able to block the Congress demand for the independence of India. In that event, the position that he now enjoyed would not alter. And in case he died, he will have an exalted status. Jinnah wanted a unique place in history after his death.

The day after the talks were declared a failure, the newspapers across the country published two reactions. Gandhi's reaction—

"Our talks have not failed, but adjourned sine die. These talks have helped us to understand each other better. I have no doubt that Mr. Jinnah is a gentleman. I hope we will meet again."

And Jinnah's reaction—

"I have agreed to meet the 'seeker of truth' so that he could see the true light and join the company of the righteous people. I regret I have not succeeded in my efforts. Yet I must admit that Mr. Gandhi was truthful and candid in his views."

Lord Wavell, the Viceroy of India, wrote in his personal diary, "I hoped that something substantial would emerge from the talks. But the talks have failed to achieve anything. The talks made Jinnah's task easy. He had to simply reject every proposal of Gandhi. He had nothing new to offer. Jinnah had succeeded in his efforts. Gandhi must accept the blame for the failure of the talks. Gandhi's leadership has proved inadequate, while Jinnah has gained in stature. There is no doubt that Jinnah has gained in stature at the cost of righteousness."

56

Jinnah in magistrate's court in Agra to fight the case of Shyamlal—recommended by Vasant Kripalani

After his return from England, Jinnah had devoted more time to the communal politics with a remarkable success. At the same time he was also practicing the law. But the provincial assembly elections in 1937 and their aftermath did not leave him much time to spare for the legal profession. Moreover, his health also deteriorated. Consequently, his legal profession almost came to an end. However, in the midst of hectic political activity, due to an incident, he had to appear before a magistrate as a defence lawyer.

A trader named Seth Shyamlal from Agra was supplying tents and other goods to the British government during the Second World War. He was manufacturing the goods, as per the government norms, and supplying them to the British resident officer Major Martin and the district Collector Shivdasani.

The Collector wanted to please the provincial governor Maurice Hallett in order to get a promotion. He and Major Martin had come out with a plan to weigh the governor in gold and the proceeds from the sale of the gold to be donated to the government towards its war efforts. The Collector was abusing his position. He told the contractors supplying the military goods to collect the gold collectively in one lot and donate it to him. Seth Shyamlal was one of the contractors. He was a supporter of the Quit India movement and the Congress. He was reluctant to support the war efforts in this manner. He expressed his inability to donate the gold. As a result, Major Martin rejected his supply of goods on the pretext that they did not conform to the prescribed standard and declined to pay for the goods. The value of the goods estimated to be around three lakhs rupees.

Shyamlal's son Kesarichand met Major Martin in this connection. He argued that until then their company had supplied the same goods and no objection was raised. But Major Martin refused to listen to him. Instead he demanded a bribe of three thousand rupees for accepting the goods. Kesarichand was tempted. After all by shelling out just three thousand he would get the business worth three hundred thousand rupees. Both of them had reached an understanding. It was agreed that Kesarichand would carry the amount the next night and leave it on Martin's study table and entering his bungalow through a backdoor on his signalling by lighting a cigarette.

This was a conspiracy hatched by Shivdasani's fertile brain. He wanted to teach a lesson to Shyamlal by getting his son arrested on the charge of attempting to bribe. When Kesarichand reached Major Matin's bungalow the next day to hand over the amount, Shivdasani came out from the adjacent room and got him arrested.

As per the ordinance issued by the Governor during the war, all such cases had to be tried in a magistrate's court instead of a regular court for speedy trial. A person convicted and punished under the ordinance had no right to appeal in any other court. Accordingly, Kesarichand's case was presented before a special magistrate in Agra.

Seth Shyamlal was very depressed. A young Sindhi called Vasant Kripalani handled his company's business in Bombay. He was a clever and practical man with a lot of common sense. Shyamlal called him to Agra to seek his advice. Kripalani understood the situation. He searched out a distant relation with the collector Shivdasani from his sources. He met him to seek his help in the shelter of this relation in Kesarichand's case. But Shivdasani refused to help him.

Shyamlal was looking for a reputed advocate who could impress the magistrate, Major Martin and Shivdasani. Kripalani suggested the names of Sir Tej Bahadur Sapru, Kanaiyalal Munshi and Sir Chimanlal Setalvad. But Shyamlal had somebody else in mind. He said, "Kripalani, if we can engage Barrister Jinnah for this case, his very presence will ensure our victory. Go to Bombay and talk to him."

Kripalani was stunned for a while by the suggestion. Jinnah was not only a reputed national and international advocate, but an important leader in national politics. It would not be possible to pursuade him to take up this ordinary case in a magistrate's court. Shyamlal insisted on Jinnah and asked Kripalani to go to Bombay to pursue the matter.

Kripalani's father was a trader in Karachi years ago. He used to supply the goods to M/s. Punja Valji Takkar—the firm of Jinnah's father. They had good business relation. During the festivals they used to visit each other. Kripalani came to know from his father that Zinabhai's son Maamad had become a great barrister and a political leader. Kripalani made use of this connection to meet Jinnah.

Jinnah's private secretary Khurshid asked Kripalani why he wanted to meet Jinnah. Kripalani knew that if he told the truth he would not succeed in meeting Jinnah, since he had stopped accepting the cases. He said, "Please tell the Quaid-e-Azam that a son of his father's business associate in Karachi wants to greet him."

Khurshid took his address and telephone number.

When Kripalani received a phone call at 9.00 in the morning the next day from Jinnah himself, he started sweating. Jinnah asked him, "Who are you, my friend, reminding me of my father's company in Karachi. Do come. I will be happy to meet you." Kriplani was ecstatic. He was so stunned that he could not utter anything beyond saying, "Yes, sir." "And listen," Jinnah continued, "Come at nine sharp. We will have tea together."

Jinnah had created two types of images about himself. To the millions of the Muslim masses in the country, he was a messiah. But to most of the Hindus, Sikhs, Christians and the Europeans he was an insincere, arrogant and ambitious and unscrupulous person. What Kripalarni experienced now was totally a different dimension of Jinnah's personality. As a matter of fact, Jinnah was too busy to meet Kripalani. He had forgotten his teenage days spent in Karachi long ago. As a national political leader he had visited Karachi twice or thrice. But he never had the chance to visit his home at Vazir Mansion again. Kripalani rekindled in him the memories of the Vazir Mansion in Karachi, his father Jinabhai's business and the horses in the stable that the teenage Maamad loved to ride. Jinnah became nostalgic about all that, which was uncharacteristic of him. His insistence on talking to Kripalani himself over the phone had surprised even his secretary.

Kripalani reached Jinnah's house at the appointed time. Khurshid led him with courtesy to the visitors' room. In a short while, a tall, lean and stiff Jinnah wearing an immaculate suit entered the room, wearing a monocle on his right eye and holding a lighted cigarette in his left hand. On seeing him, Kripalani stood up. Jinnah held out his right hand and then said, "Hello! Mr. Kripalani. You are welcome. You have rekindled the forgotten memories of my days in Karachi."

Kripalani was awestruck. Jinnah enquired about him for a while. He could not recall Kripalani's father. He was reminiscing his past. He took Kripalani to Fatima's room and introduced him to her. Then he personally offered him a cup of tea. This was an extraordinary experience to Kripalani. Jinnah asked him about his profession,

"I am working for a firm, but I intend to dabble in the share market."

"Oh, no! No wise man should ever think of that. I have experienced it. Many brilliant young men were ruined by the lure of the share market."

"But, Sir, some people have made a fortune," said Kripalani.

"Those who seem to have made a fortunate are only struggling to save themselves from sinking. Of all the professions I knew the share market is the most unstable profession," said Jinnah. "The position of the race course is the same. I have the experience in both these. And I can say that those who want to lead a happy and healthy life should stay away from both of them."

Kripalani felt at ease after the conversation. Now he told him the purpose of his visit. He explained at length how Shivdasani had trapped Kesarichand. Jinnah listened to him patiently and then said putting his hand around his shoulder,

"Friend! You know that I have now given up the legal profession. Why do not you talk to Setalvad or Munshi?"

"Sir, Seth Shyamlal wants you to rescue his son. No one else can rescue him."

Jinnah thought for a while and then asked, "Is Acharya Kripalani related to you?"

"Yes Sir," replied Vasant Kripalani, "He is my distant uncle."

"Then are you politically affiliated to him?"

"No Sir. My politics is centred around my livelihood. I hardly meet him."

"Why? He is a fine gentleman. I know him quite well." Then he checked his diary and the programme.

"Vasant, I am very busy. Yet, I cannot say no to you. Get the case adjourned by the magistrate. And meet me after fifteen days when I come to Delhi."

To Kripalani, this consent was as good as acquittal of Kesarichand. When Seth Shyamlal came to know about this his joy knew no bounds.

After fifteen days both Kripalani and Shyamlal met Jinnah in Delhi. Shyamlal took off his turban and placed it on Jinnah's feet and sitting on the floor he said in a choked voice, "*Sahib*, the life of my only son is in your hands."

Jinnah did not expect this from him. Placing his hand on his shoulder, he said, "Don't worry, Seth. Saving your son is not my only concern. Shivdasani is a stooge of the British. Major Martin is a corrupt official. I want to expose both of them."

Jinnah had gone through the papers relating to the case on his way to Agra from Delhi. On hearing about his presence in the country, a huge crowd had gathered outside the court room. Some four military legal advisors came from Delhi to assist the public prosecutor Mishra. They sat next to the magistrate.

"Who are these gentlemen? Why are they sitting next to the magistrate?" Jinnah asked in a stern voice.

The public prosecutor and the magistrate did not expect this pointed question. The public prosecutor replied politely,

"They are the military legal advisors. They have come to assist me in the case."

"Very good !" said Jinnah. "I welcome them. They too will learn a lesson today."

Then Jinnah proceeded to cross examine Major Martin,

"Major Martin, how much salary do you draw in a month?"

"Three thousand rupees."

"That means you wanted a bribe equivalent to one month salary!"

"That is not true. I never asked for a bribe. Kesarichand wanted to bribe me and get his shady work done."

"How can you call it a shady work? You had wrongly stopped his payment of three lakhs rupees. What is wrong if a shrewd businessman wishes to spend three thousand rupees to get his work done?"

"Bribing is a crime," Major Martin said, "His goods were not as per the government norms, and he wanted to get his work done by bribing."

"It means Kesarichand did not succeed in getting his work done, but you have managed to trap him."

"Sir, arresting the corrupt person is not a trap."

"That is what I want to say. Nothing is wrong in arresting the corrupt person. Can you give us a list of the assets acquired by you with a monthly salary of three thousand rupees?"

Jinnah's question hit Major Martin like a bullet from an automatic rifle. He fainted for a moment. He could not say anything. Taking advantage of his condition, Jinnah asked, "If you cannot remember, I can hand over the list of your assets to the court. We can work out how and when you acquired the assets in India and England and how much you paid. I can help you in this."

"It is my personal matter. It has nothing to do with the case," said Martin.

"Yes, it has. How can a man earning three thousand rupees a month acquire the assets worth millions of rupees without taking bribe? You are a corrupt official and you have acquired the assets illegally by misusing your position. You had demanded a bribe from my client and then got him trapped."

"I do not accept this."

"If you do not accept this you are not telling the truth."

Major Martin was stumped. He felt fighting in a combat was much easier than continuing the war of words with Jinnah.

Jinnah drawing the attention of the magistrate to the Ordinance published in the gazette said, "Your honour! This ordinance was published after the charge sheet was filed against Kesarichand. Any law can be applied only prospectively and not retrospectively. This ordinance cannot be applied to Kesarichand. If at all he had committed any offence, he could be tried in a regular court. This court has no jurisdiction to try his case."

There was a commotion in the court. The crowd outside the court room cheered Jinnah loudly. The magistrate had no option but to concur with Jinnah. This was Jinnah's last legal battle. When he returned to Delhi triumphant that evening, his servant Bhagwan served a special dish of pork for his dinner.

57

Jinnah-Khizar-Hayat Khan of Punjab Unionist Party, Roosevelt's pressure on Churchill, Liaquat-Bhulabhai understanding, Gandhi's stand on the understanding

Jinnah was well aware that he stood on a shaky ground against Gandhi and the Congress, the British government and the Hindus. His ammunition against them was completely ineffective. He was counting the last days of his life. The Muslim majority provinces, whom he claimed to represent, were opposed to him vehemently. And the leaders of Bengal and Punjab provinces had refused to accept his authority. Jinnah got a temporary respite when the leader of the Punjab Unionist Party Sikandar Hayat Khan died. But Khizar, the new leader of Punjab, became more troublesome to him. The Unionist Party which ruled Punjab had Hindu and Sikh ministers. Khizar's colleagues who had enlisted themselves as the members of the Muslim League refused to quit the Unionist Party. They refused to accept the central authority. After a great deal of persuasion, Jinnah wrote to Khizar, "You must dismantle the Unionist Party and join the All India Muslim League. You being a member of the two political parties at the same time, is like having a mistress when there is a wife at home."

But Khizar was not a person to accept such a taunt. He gave him a befitting reply, "The Islamic law does not forbid a man having more than wife. In fact, the Prophet permitted a man to have four wives at a time. Hope you must be aware of this fact."

This was too much for Jinnah to tolerate.

The leaders of the Muslim League in Punjab urged Jinnah to declare Pakistan as an Islamic state. Jinnah had never wanted to have a theocratic state. His aim was to ensure that the Congress and the British government accepted him as the sole spokesman of the Muslims in India. Once this was accepted, he was willing to compromise on anything. Gandhi refused to accept his claim, resulting in the failure of the Gandhi-Jinnah parleys. The provincial leaders wanted Jinnah to invoke the religious sentiments among the illiterate Muslim masses in the countryside. He reluctantly issued a statement in the form of the Lahore Resolution leaving a lot of ambiguity so that everyone could interpret it in the manner that suited him. Jinnah said, "The people of Pakistan will draft a constitution of their choice." There was no mention of the Quran or the Shariat. At the same time he offered the carrot to those who could not think beyond the Quran or the Shariat.

The war had engulfed the world. The countries ranging from Japan in the East and America in the West had entered the war. America was on the side of Britain. This had boosted the morale of Britain. But Japan proved to be a formidable enemy of Britain. Japan posed a serious threat to the British empire in India. The Japanese troops had entered Burma. If Japan conquered India, it would be a severe blow to Britian. It would lose the military might of the Indians. In that eventuality, Britian would find it difficult to defend London from the invasion of Germany. At this stage, the American President Roosevelt tried to exert pressure on the British Prime Minister Churchill, "You will not be able to stop the invasion of India by Japan without the support of the Indian people. You say you are fighting the war to defend democracy, but when the democratically elected provincial governments have resigned, the Indian people will not support the war. The world will not accept your claim that the war is fought to defend democracy. To resolve this deadlock, you must try to remove the obstacle in the path to India's independence."

To Churchill this was a bitter pill to swallow. At this time, the British ambassador in Russia Sir Stafford Cripps, through his diplomatic skills, succeeded in making the iron man of Russia Joseph Stalin a British ally in the war. Churchill wanted to avail the services of Stafford Cripps in resolving the Indian political issue. He dispatched the Cripps Mission to India to find out a solution acceptable to both the Congress and the Muslim League. The Cripps Mission failed to achieve a break through. Gandhi described the proposals of the Cripps Mission as "a post dated cheque of a failing bank." The Congress insisted on forming a national government during the war with control over the defence and the foreign affairs. The Muslim League rejected the Cripps proposals on the ground that they made no mention of Pakistan. Thus, the Cripps Mission failed.

*

The political deadlock remained unresolved. There seemed no way out. Almost all the Congress leaders, except Gandhi, were in jail. The Viceroy had rejected Gandhi's proposal of a discussion with the members of the Congress Working Committee. The Congress leaders like C. Rajagopalachari and Bhulabhai Desai were opposed to the Quit India movement and the individual Civil Disobedience. Bhulabhai Desai was the leader of the Congress in the Central Assembly, while Liaquat Ali Khan was the leader of the Muslim League. It was a coincidence. They were good friends. They often visited each other's house. Bhulabhai talked to Liaquat in order to break the political impasse.

Liaquat saw an opportunity in this. He was also eager to find some viable option. He did not forget how seriously ill Jinnah was before the Gandhi-Jinnah parleys and his refusal to meet him. Though now Jinnah appeared to be in good health, Liaquat suspected about his health as he had declined to entertain any visitor for a month. The information that he had clandestinely collected about

Jinnah's health made him believe that Jinnah was indeed suffering from a serious disease.

The news that Liaquat had received made him to think about it again. Jinnah had to leave Delhi for Bombay due to the sudden sickness. All his programmes were suspended. Even his meeting with Viceroy Wavell had to be cancelled. His doctor in Bombay Jaal Patel issued a press statement that Jinnah was suffering from asthma and fever for the past ten days. The news alarmed Liaquat. He tried to contact Jinnah to find out the actual position. But he could only talk to his private secretary Khurshid. Then he read in a newspaper that Jinnah was suffering from pleurisy. This sort of conflicting reports only added to his suspicion. He also heard that Jinnah's health had deteriorated drastically and that he had no chance of survival. As if to give credence to the rumour, Jinnah had decided to take bed rest for one full month. And a press release stated that he would not entertain any visitor or accept any public programme during this period.

If all this was true, it was important that Liaquat made some decision. He firmly believed that Jinnah's personal ambition and prejudice had prevented him from reaching an agreement with the Congress.

Liaquat wanted to secure his position by reaching an agreement with the Congress, in case Jinnah died suddenly. An independent Pakistan was a distant dream. He was eager to get what was feasible. He knew Jinnah would not be willing to reach any such agreement. Hence, he did not want to take Jinnah into confidence. In view of Jinnah's fragile health, he was looking for an opportunity to reach an agreement with the Congress. Fortunately, Bhulabhai provided him the opportunity. He told Bhulabhai his willingness to reach an agreement, if possible.

Most of the members of the Congress Working Committee were unhappy with Bhulabhai for having distanced himself from the Quit India movement. Initially, some other members were also opposed to it, but ultimately they fell in line with Gandhi. But Rajagopalachari and Bhulabhai remained firm and opposed the Quit India movement.

Encouraged by Liaquat's response, Bhulabhai raised the matter with Gandhi. They discussed the idea of forming a national government with the Congress and the Muslims sharing the power equally. It meant that the twenty five per cent Muslims would have the same representation in the government as the seventy five per cent Hindus. This was implicit in Jinnah's insistence that the Muslims were not a minority but a separate nation. Gandhi cautioned Bhulabhai, "Be very careful in whatever you do. Only the Congress Working Committee can give the final consent. Whatever you discuss with Liaquat, ensure that he has the prior approval of Jinnah."

Thereafter Bhulabhai Desai and Liaquat had a series of private talks and prepared a draft agreement. Liaquat assured Bhulabhai that in principle he had the prior approval of Jinnah, but he would obtain his consent once they reached an agreement. An astute Bhulabhai fumbled to grasp the meaning of his friend's jugglery of words.

As per the agreement reached between them, it was decided that the Congress and the Muslim League would form a national government and share the power equally. Further it was agreed that once the government was formed all the members of the Congress Working Committee would be released from jail and that the Congress and the League would form coalition governments in the provinces.

All this was an indication that the Congress was now tired and worn out and was anxious to secure peace by hook or crook. As per the agreement, a concession was made that even in the provinces where the Congress had a majority and formed the governments on its own the League would be a coalition partner in the government. Most importantly the acceptance of the demand for equal representation of the Muslims in the government went against the democratic principle of the rule by the majority. Moreover, the members of the Congress Working Committee were to be released only after the formation of a national government.

Bhulabhai signed the agreement and handed over a copy to Liaquat. Liaquat did not sign the agreement and told Bhulabhai that he would show it to Jinnah and after getting his signature he would return it to him. Thus Bhulabhai had no evidence that suggested Liaquat was a party to the agreement, whereas his signed copy of the agreement as a leader of the Congress Party in the Central Assembly remained with Liaquat. Bhulabhai, who was considered a brilliant lawyer, was deceived in the name of friendship.

This agreement between Bhulabhai and Liaquat was reached in the house of a Muslim League leader called Mohammed Yamin Khan. The news of this agreement was somehow leaked out to the media and the journalists started making their own conclusions. When Jinnah came to know about it, he was enraged. His health had improved somewhat. It seemed as if he came alive from the jaws of death. This was a very difficult situation for Liaquat. Jinnah's influence over the Muslim League and the Muslims of the country was unrivalled. Liaquat feared that his political career might end.

When an enraged Jinnah asked Liaquat to clarify the reports appearing in the newspapers, Liaquat flatly denied having entered into any such agreement. He had no other option. He stated in unequivocal terms that neither he had entered into any agreement with Bhulabhai nor had he talked to him on this issue. Liaquat managed to save his political career, but for Bhulabhai Desai it was the end of his public life. He could have refuted Liaquat. But he was not in a position to do so as Liaquat did not sign the agreement. He could not afford to enter into any controversy. If the signed copy of the agreement reached the Congress Working Committee, Bhulabhai's position would become untenable. He had no option but to keep quiet. Bhulabhai had done this with the knowledge of Gandhi. However, Gandhi did not come to the rescue of Bhulabhai in the Congress Working Committee. Bhulabhai bowed out of the public life for ever.

58

Simla Conference, Wavell-Jinnah—June 1945, Prime Minister Attlee's address, elections of 1945, Jinnah-Iskandar Mirza-North West Frontier Province, Nawab of Bhopal

By May 1945 the Allied powers had won a decisive victory over Hitler and Mussolini. Japan was the only Axis power which still offered resistance on the eastern front. It was certain that Japan would be defeated soon. The fear that Japan might attack India from its eastern border had almost disappeared. In June, the Viceroy had invited the leaders of various political parties and the representatives from the princely states for a conference in Simla to discuss the communal issue. Jinnah demanded that the Muslims as a separate nation should be given fifty per cent representation in the government. It meant the remaining fifty per cent would be represented by the seventy five per cent Hindus and the other religious minorities. When the Viceroy asked how this could be possible, Jinnah answered, "I accept that there are other religious minorities in the country, besides the Muslims. But in practice all of them, except the Muslims, live with the Hindus. The interest of the Muslims can be safeguarded only by representation on the fifty-fifty basis."

If Jinnah's demand was accepted, it could raise a lot of contentious issues. Yet the Congress accepted the demand in principle to find a solution somehow to the vexed issue.

The Viceroy then asked the Congress and the Muslim League to suggest the names of their representatives to be appointed to his Executive Council. The issue once again reached a dead end. Jinnah insisted that the Congress should not suggest any Muslim as its representative. If the Congress included a Muslim as its representative it would mean it was a party representing all communities in the country. That would give the Congress the right to speak on behalf of all the communities. It would also disprove the claim that Jinnah and the Muslim League alone represented the entire Muslim community in the country. Jinnah insisted that the Congress should represent the Hindus alone. And it was for the Viceroy to nominate the representatives of other religious minorities like the Sikhs and the Christians.

Khan Abdul Gafar Khan of the North Western Frontier Province was present at the conference. He questioned Jinnah, "You say that the Congress is a party of only the Hindus. I am a Muslim, but I am with the Congress. What do you have to say on this?" To this Jinnah answered, "No true Muslim can ever be with the Congress. Those who defiled the Islam alone can join the Congress. They are not Muslims."

The political stalemate continued. In the meantime, the staunch opponents of the Congress and India, Churchill and his Conservative Party were defeated in the post war general elections held in Britian. The peoples' verdict was an indication that Churchill who had won the war for Britain would be of no use in the time of peace. The Labour Party under the leadership of Clement Attlee formed the new government. Attlee was eager to end the political stalemate in India. Britain had suffered a huge loss in the war in terms of military power and other resources. It was no longer in a position to sustain its rule in India. The public opinion in Britian also favoured the end of the British rule in India and the reconstruction of Britian after the war. Taking all this into consideration, Prime Minister Attlee said in his address to the people, "The people of India have the right to draft a constitution as per their will. We cannot stop the people's progress. No minority can exercise a veto power to stop the peoples' progress. Nor can a majority afford to overlook the interest of the minorities."

It was a clear message to both the Congress and the Muslim League. The Congress should be more generous in addressing the concerns of the Muslims. And the Muslim League must give up its negative attitude to reach a political settlement. This enraged Jinnah. It meant that if the Muslim League did not adopt a positive attitude, the British government would go ahead and take appropriate steps to resolve the political stalemate. Jinnah became cautious.

*

Viceroy Lord Wavell was a protégé of Wiston Churchill—a staunch protagonist of imperialism. During the war, Churchill had appointed Wavell as the Viceroy keeping in mind his imperialist policy. When Wavell left for India, Churchill gave him a piece of advice, "If you cannot take care of what you have, destroy it instead of handing it over to the enemy."

Wavell exploited the communal disharmony between the Hindus and the Muslims. But now the rulers in London had changed. The British public opinion too had changed. The new government of Attlee had a different agenda. Since the war had ended, it became necessary to hold fresh elections to the Central Assembly. These elections would give the two major political parties a chance to demonstrate their strength and the peoples' support. The elections began in December 1945. For nearly two months, the elections were held in various parts of the country in a very tense atmosphere. Only ten per cent of the population was eligible to vote. After the last elections, the Congress could form its governments in eight provinces, whereas the Muslim League could not form a government even in a single province. The Muslim League could not win a single seat in the North West Frontier Province though 95 per cent of its people were Muslims. It had the Congress government. Jinnah was not worried much about Punjab, Bengal and Sindh as the Muslims in these provinces were not with the Congress. They either supported the local Muslim parties or the Muslim League. Jinnah was plotting to change the equation in the North West Frontier Province. This Province linked Afghanistan and Russia to India. Viceroy Wavell considered it strategically important. Jinnah knew this. He worked out a plan.

Iskandar Mirza was the Commissioner of Peshawar—the capital of the province. He was a Pathan and being a native was quite popular. Jinnah appointed Khan Aurangzeb as the President of the Muslim League in the province. But he was a pigheaded corrupt person. He invoked fear among the people by intimidating them. But he could not sway the voters. When Jinnah realised that Aurangzeb would not fit into his scheme of things, he tried to reach out to Mirza.

The Nawab of Bhopal, a princely state in Central India, was a friend of Jinnah and a supporter of the League. As per the plan, the Nawab had invited Iskandar Mirza to Bhopal on the pretext of a tiger hunt. In the meantime, Jinnah had an understanding with Viceroy Wavell and the Governor of the province Cunningham on utilizing the services of Mirza. A meeting of Jinnah with Mirza was arranged at the royal palace. After the exchange of formal greetings, Jinnah cleverly expressed sympathy and enquired about the health of Mirza's mother. Mirza was touched by this. Jinnah then said confidently, "The Muslims in India are at the crossroad at this juncture. Don't you think that for the first time in twelve hundred years since Mohammed Bin Kasim invaded India in the eighth century, the Muslims are facing a crisis of survival?"

"Yes," said Mirza, "There is no doubt about it. Now that you are our leader, we shall overcome it."

"Then, can I take it that you consider me the undisputed leader of the Muslims of India after the Prophet?"

"Undoubtedly," Mirza was trapped like a fly in a spider's web, "No one can deny that."

"Then, as the sole leader of the Muslims in India, I would like you to make every possible effort to form a Muslim League government in the North West Frontier Province. For this, you will get whatever help you need."

"Quaid-e-Azam, this is not possible as long as you have the corrupt leaders like Khan Aurangzeb."

"I know Aurangzeb is corrupt. But he has muscle power which can be of use. We cannot get rid of him," Jinnah was slowly unfolding his plot.

"In that case, I am willing to help in whatever you may decide for the Muslim community. But as a gazetted officer of the government, it will be difficult for me to do anything unless the governor consents to it."

"I will take care of that. The governor Cunningham will back your efforts.

You do not bother about the expenses. The Nawab sahib will meet all the expenses."

Mirza was a practical worldly man. He was not a fool not to extract the price when a rich Nawab was willing to foot the bill.

"The task is quite expensive. The Pathans accept the diktats of their tribal chiefs only. The Mullahs, the Maulvis and the Ulemas also exercise a great deal of influence over them."

"I am aware of it," Jinnah said, "You have a free hand in this. You give whatever money the Maulvis and the Ulemas demand or fix some monthly allowance for them. But through them, you have to ensure that the message that the Islam is in danger reaches to the illiterate Pathans and they get stirred up to die in defending the Islam."

The meeting proved successful. And it was agreed that the Nawab would deliver ten million rupees to Mirza at Peshawar for the noble cause. And the Nawab handed over twenty thousand rupees to Mirza for meeting petty expenses.

When Mirza reached Peshawar, he received a message from the governor asking him to meet him immediately.

Though Mirza was a government officer, he had no difficulty in working for the Muslim League on behalf of Jinnah. As per the understanding, the governor had turned a blind eye on his activities. The Viceroy wanted the Muslim League to extend its area of influence to the North West Frontier Province at any cost. The *Khudai Khidmatgaars* of Badshah Khan were bitterly opposed to the British government. They were the descendants of the Afghans. And ever since the British rule was established in India, they had skirmishes regularly with the British government. The Britishers wanted to contain the influence of Russia in Afghanistan. They were allergic to the communist rule in Russia. The Pathans were more close to the Afghans on the other side of the border than to the Muslims of Punjab on the eastern border of their province. They were more anti-British than pro- Muslim League. The Muslim League since its inception had never opposed the British rule. In fact, its leaders turned pro-British to safeguard their vested interests. They spared no stone unturned to extract every possible benefit by repeatedly proclaiming their loyalty to the British empire. The Congress was opposed to the British rule, hence the Pathans had developed an affinity with it. Both Jinnah and Wavell had understood this. Hence, this plot was hatched to mislead the illiterate Pathans in the name of Islam. The Pathans were largely an illiterate community. They were divided into numerous groups and clans known as *Jirgas*. And each group had its own chief and his order was obeyed by all. These chiefs had a great faith in Islam and the Quran and this turned out to be their weakness. Jinnah was banking on this weakness. Mirza was engaged to exploit their weakness.

Mirza succeeded in his task. The tribal chiefs were carried away by the propaganda unleashed by the hired Maulvis and the Ulemas that Islam was in danger and that if the Hindus came to power the mosques would be destroyed and that there would be restrictions for offering *Namaaz* . Mirza by luring the Mullahs and the Maulvis with the largesse offered by the Nawab of Bhopal had succeeded in fooling the tribal chiefs. And the propaganda had its desired effect.

Jinnah was impressed by Mirza's success. He met him again. He had another plan for him. He wanted him to instigate riots among the Hindus and the *Khudai Khidmatgaars*. "Mr. Mirza, you have really served the community so well. I congratulate you. I expect you to serve the community more."

Mirza received the reward for his service. He had diverted the funds received from Bhopal to his personal accounts. Jinnah knew it. Now he was a totally changed man. He was no longer the same person, who twenty years ago lashed out at a member of the Central Assembly for demanding a bribe of ten thousand rupees. Now the end was more important to him than the means. To achieve the end he would go to any extent. Cunningham too was pleased with Mirza's successful accomplishment of the task. Mirza was promoted as the Secretary to the Defence Minister. He thought that if he could serve Jinnah more faithfully his future could become even brighter.

"Mirza," Jinnah said, "Now you do not have to work. You leave the job and devote all your time to the North West Frontier Province. You must incite the Pathans to carry out *jihad.* You know Pakistan will be created soon. And I need people like you in the new nation of Muslims."

Mirza started dreaming of becoming a minister in Pakistan. He had accepted Jinnah's advice and resigned from the service. He devoted all his time to incite *jihad* in the North West Frontier Province.

59

Election results, the naval mutiny in Bombay, Cabinet Mission, Jinnah-Pethic Lawrence meeting, discussion with Stafford Cripps

The elections came to an end in the midst of an atmosphere of hatred, animosity, anger and violence. The country had to face the consequences of the ill feelings. The country was badly affected by the communal riots spread out from Karachi to Calcutta and Multan to Madras. Jinnah travelled across the country raising the demand for Pakistan. He had not clarified till then what Pakistan actually meant. But the elections made him spell out the composition of Pakistan. He presented a political map of Pakistan that would include the entire provinces of Punjab and Bengal, besides Assam, Sindh, Baluchistan and the North West Frontier Province. He knew that this could never be secured. But it was essential to present such a map to appease the Muslims in Punjab and Bengal who were opposing the Muslim League. Jinnah also knew that the elections result could spell doom. If the Muslims in Punjab, Bengal and Sindh lean towards the local Muslim leaders, his claim that he was the sole spokesman of all the Muslims could come under scrutiny. He also wanted to appease the Muslims in the Hindu majority provinces. The Muslim industrialists found it difficult to compete in business with the leading industrialists like the Tatas, the Birlas and the Dalmiyas. The Muslim industrialists of Bombay welcomed the idea of an independent Pakistan so that they could become industrial giants in the new nation. The Muslims of the United Province and the Central Province were eager to migrate to Pakistan lock, stock and barrel. And the slogan 'Islam is in danger' had a mesmerising effect on the poor and impoverished Muslim masses. Jinnah tried every possible trick to woo the voters of all classes. His efforts paid off.

The election results raised his leverage and clout among the Muslims. The results revealed that ninety per cent Muslims had voted against the Congress and favoured Pakistan. The Muslim League won all 300 seats in the Central Assembly. Besides, it won 427 seats out of 507 in the Provincial Assemblies. Yet the League was not in a position to form government on its own in any of the provinces.

This was because the League won most of the seats in the provinces where the Muslims were a minority. The Muslims in these provinces were lured by the idea of Pakistan. This meant the Muslim majority provinces did not vote for the Muslim League, instead they preferred the local Muslim parties. The North West Frontier Province again voted for the Congress, although the League had improved its position. However, the results had sent out a clear message that the Muslims in the country were overwhelmingly in favour of Pakistan and that Jinnah was their sole spokesman.

Viceroy Wavell wanted to form an interim government. He invited Jawaharlal Nehru to form the Viceroy's Executive Council. The Congress and the League could not reach an agreement about the representation in the Council. Nehru wanted an assurance from the Viceroy that he would remain as a symbolic head of the interim government and that he would not tolerate interference in its day-to-day functioning. This was not acceptable to the Viceroy.

*

An important sudden development made the British government realize that it would not be able to hold on to India any longer. The naval ships returned from the war were positioned in the waters of Bombay and Karachi harbours. A minor incident sparked off a naval mutiny in the Bombay harbour. Some three thousand naval men revolted against the British officers. They captured two ships positioned in the sea. They lowered the British flag Union Jack and unfurled the flags of the Congress and the Muslim League. This was repeated at the Karachi harbour. The Air force personnel at the Ambala Air base had also revolted against their British officers. This mutiny was extremely dangerous. By capturing few ships independence could not be gained, as the British forces were far more powerful. General Lockhart warned that if the rebels did not surrender, their ships would be sunk. The patriotic naval men contacted Sardar Patel to seek the Congress support. With the permission of the government, Sardar Patel boarded the ship and addressed the rebels, "Any kind of indiscipline among the armed forces is not good. You cannot withstand the might of the British forces. We are on the threshold of getting independence. And this type of revolt can create more problems for the country. You must surrender. The Congress will try to solve your problems."

A section of the navy had also contacted Jinnah to get the Muslim League support. Jinnah's emissaries returned in the midnight with a message. He concurred with Patel's views. He felt any such revolt did not abode well for a new nation. If the armed forces leave the barracks and enter politics, the country will have a military rule instead of a government by the people. He advised the rebels to give up the resistance.

Though the naval mutiny was crushed, the British government was jolted to the hilt. It realized that any further delay in granting independence to India would be disastrous. Prime Minister Attlee announced the dispatching of a three member

Committee called the Cabinet Mission, headed by Pethick Lawrence, the Secretary of State for India, to India to reach a political settlement. Sir Stafford Cripps, who had earlier tried to reach a settlement, was a member of the Mission. He was reputed for his political acumen. Now he was accompanying Pethick Lawrence for a specific task.

On reaching India, the Cabinet Mission undertook a hectic tour of India. They had travelled the length and breadth of the country for 17 days. They had 182 meetings and met as many as 472 leaders of various political parties. The political parties realizing that the Mission had come with a specific task of finalizing the modalities of independence, started pushing their own agenda. Pethic Lawrence invited Jinnah to present his point of view. Jinnah had already made up his mind. The Cabinet Mission had proposed that the British Provinces in India be formed into three groups. The provinces of Sindh, Punjab, Baluchistan and the North West Frontier were to form into one group; the provinces of Assam and Bengal were to be included in the second group and the remaining provinces in the third group. The princely states were free to join any of these groups keeping in view the geographical contiguity. These groups would enjoy autonomy. However, the subjects like defence, foreign relations and communications would remain with the Central government. These groups could elect their representatives to the Constituent Assembly to draft a constitution for India. Besides, the provinces would be free to secede from the Union of India, if they so desired. Thus, the demand for an independent Pakistan was rejected. But at the same time the Congress demand for a strong unified India was also diluted. However, it gave a chance to the Muslim majority provinces to secede from the Union of India to form Pakistan. This could have met Jinnah's demand to some extent. Similarly, the Congress could have succeeded in establishing a federal India without partitioning the country.

Jinnah wanted to meet the Cabinet Mission as the sole representative of the Muslim League. When Jinnah expressed this to the Working Committee of the League, Liaquat Ali Khan had a reason to doubt. He thought instead of Jinnah meeting Pethick Lawrence alone and then conveying what transpired, it would be better if he accompanied him for the meeting. Unlike the other members, who agreed with Jinnah, Liaquat expressed his desire.

"Quaid-e-Azam, do not you think I could be of some assistance to you at a critical time like this? Considering your health, such assistance is necessary," he said cautiously.

Jinnah glanced at Liaquat. He thought that his protégé was trying to get better of him. He knew why he wanted to accompany him. He said, "If I need any help I will send a message. Now I do not need any help. Liaquat, you don't worry." Liaquat became speechless. He could make out that Jinnah understood his intention.

Jinnah accepted the proposals of the Cabinet Mission, though the proposals had rejected the demand for Pakistan. The difficulty was that the Muslims in the Hindu majority provinces were more enthusiastic about Pakistan. Now if he gave up the demand for Pakistan, these Muslims would desert him. The Muslim League had no influence in the Muslim majority provinces like Bengal, Punjab, Sindh and the North West Frontier. The local Muslim leaders in these provinces were defying the authority of Jinnah. Because of the Muslim majority, these local chieftains had no fear of the Hindus or the Congress. The Congress was ruling the North West Frontier Province due to the influence of Badsha Khan and his brother Khan Sahib. As per the groupings proposed by the Cabinet Mission, many prominent Muslim leaders, including Jinnah and Liaquat would figure in the Hindu majority provinces. If these provinces were asked to chose their representatives for the Central Assembly, the position of these Muslim leaders would be very precarious. Moreover, Jinnah wanted to keep the important portfolios like the defence and the foreign affairs in the Central Executive Council with him. He thought the Congress would not accept the proposals of the Cabinet Mission since the provinces were given the right to secede from the Union of India. He thought by accepting the proposals he would become the Prime Minister of the country.

The Cabinet Mission spent three hours with Jinnah. The talks did not yield any positive result. Jinnah wanted to drag them into his scheme of things. He intended to create such vortexes wherein the members are dragged and then slowly take them out as suits him. He asked Pathick Lawrence how these proposals could be implemented if the Congress rejected them. To which Lawrence said, "Considering the aspirations of the people, these proposals cannot be stalled any longer. Even if both the parties reject the proposals, we will have to find some way out."

It was a very diplomatic answer. Jinnah wanted to confuse the Mission, but he himself was baffled by this answer. He inferred that if the Congress rejected the proposals, the Muslim League alone would be able to form the government. The dream that he had nourished for fifty years could be realized at last. In the groupings of the provinces, leaving aside the group having the Hindu majority, the other two groups had the Muslim majority due to Bengal and Punjab. Since Assam, Sindh and the North West Frontier Province were sparsely populated, Bengal and Punjab would be able to rule over them without considering their opinions. Further, the federal government would be weak and powerless. Taking all this into account, both Jinnah and Viceroy Wavell thought that the Congress would not accept the proposals of the Cabinet Mission. The interests of both seemed to converge.

When Jinnah mentioned the Lahore Resolution during the course of talks, Sir Stafford Cripps said, "I do not understand how the creation of Pakistan could solve the problem of the majority and the minority. A large number of Hindus will remain in Pakistan and the Muslims will be a bigger minority in India than they are now. This will be an unnatural partition of the country."

"Country? Which country?" asked Jinnah, "India had never been a country. The British have assimilated hundreds of independent states into an empire and yet there are many independent princely states today. Right from the Chandragupta Maurya till date, India had never been a single country."

"We may debate the political and geographical point of view, but we must not forget the cultural heritage of India that goes to the dawn of civilisation," Cripps argued.

"The cultural heritage is a myth created by the Congress," Jinnah retorted, "The culture of the Hindus and that of the Muslims are totally different. The Hindus consider Sanskrit as the language of their culture, whereas the Muslims regard Arabic as the basis of their culture. The Hindus consider the Himalayas or the Kanyakumari as the centre of their faith, while the Muslims consider Arabia or Iran as the centres of their faith."

"But as an Indian, do you really believe that the partition of the country would result in communal harmony between the two communities?"

"This question does not arise when there is no such country as India. I do not become an Indian simply because I was borne in this land. I am not an Indian," Jinnah said sternly as if he was giving an ultimatum.

The meeting ended. Sir Stafford Cripps wrote in his diary, "We talked to Jinnah for three hours today. What we wanted to discuss could have been done in an hour. I must admit that we have wasted two hours for nothing."

60

June 1946—Second Simla Conference, Jinnah-Maulana Azad handshake, Pethic Lawrence-Jawaharlal Nehru-Jinnah, Jinnah aborts understanding, Cripps-Jinnah clash, Jinnah's deteriorating health, Cripps-Alexander enquiry about Jinnah's health, Dr. Jaal Patel-Jinnah

Simla, the summer capital of the British in India for nearly a century, was suddenly buzzing with activity. The Viceroy and his Secretariat usually shifted to the cooler place of Simla in the months of April and May to escape the scorching heat of Delhi and Calcutta. The Mall Road, on which the Vice regal Lodge was located, was buzzing with activity in June 1946. It was a locality where no Indian was allowed to enter unless he wore the western clothes. The locality had the expensive hotels catering to the tastes of the British officials and their wives and the Indian bureaucrats. Simla, situated in the lap of the beautiful snow capped Himalayan mountains, was a picture of nature's abundant beauty that captivated the people. When the sun rays fell on the snow covered roads and the mountains, a golden glow spread all over and it looked as if a heavenly body was descending on to the earth.

Viceroy Lord Wavell convened a special conference of the two main parties—the Congress and the Muslim League—to discuss the proposals of the Cabinet Mission. He invited Gandhi to take part in the conference. Gandhi declined the invitation stating that he did not represent any political party. Then the Viceroy wrote to him, "The Conference should benefit from your experience and wisdom. Even if you do not wish to attend the conference, please make yourself available in Simla during the conference so that we can seek your advice and suggestion in any situation of crisis. I will make the arrangements for your stay in a separate bungalow near the Vice regal Lodge."

The Viceroy sent a formal invitation to Jinnah as the President of the Muslim League. But he did not send a similar invitation to Maulana Azad, the Congress President. Perhaps he thought that the invitation to Gandhi was a formal invitation to the Congress. That was a mistake on his part. Gandhi said in his reply to the Viceroy, "I accept your invitation. I would like to make it clear that you must also send the invitation to Maulana Azad, the President of the Congress."

The Congress President received the invitation from the Viceroy. The Congress had nominated Maulana Azad, Jawaharlal Nehru, Sardar Patel and Badshah Khan as its representatives. Jinnah, Liaquat Ali Khan, Nawab Ismail and Abdul Rab Nishtar represented the Muslim League. Among the eight statesmen, who assembled to write a new history of the country, only two Hindus represented the seventy five per cent population, while the other six represented the twenty five per cent Muslims. The Viceroy had invited Sardar Baldev Singh as the representative of the Sikhs.

The Viceroy inaugurated the conference on 25th June in the imposing hall of the Vice regal Lodge. As per the protocol, he formally introduced the persons. They shook hands and greeted each other. But Jinnah, who otherwise was very particular in observing the Western etiquette, refused to shake hands with Maulana Azad. In fact both of them being the Presidents of the two main parties were introduced first. Maulana Azad held out his hand, but Jinnah did not reciprocate. All the gentlemen sitting across the table were stunned. Jinnah sat nonchalantly, his lips sealed and the face downcast. He sat with his two hands folded. A humiliated Maulana withdrew his hand. According to Jinnah, Maulana was a puppet. The fact that the Congress President was a Muslim refuted Jinnnah's claim that the Congress was only a party of the Hindus. Jinnah could not tolerate this. He would not have got a better opportunity than this to belittle Maulana. Thus, the atmosphere was vitiated even before the talks began.

At the outset, Jawaharlal Nehru sought a clarification from Pathick Lawrence, the Secretary of State for India. He wanted to know whether the purpose of the conference was to consider handing over the power to the representatives of the people of the country. Pathick Lawrence responded, "Yes, I would like to say on behalf of the British government that we want to grant complete independence to India and then leave the country. But our problem is that as a responsible government we cannot push the people of this country into anarchy. Whom should we hand over the power?"

"If you really want to hand over the power, you may hand it over to any person you consider worthy of. Even if that person is Muhammad Ali Jinnah we have no objection. Our aim is to achieve independence for India," said Jawaharlal Nehru putting his cards on the table without any hesitation.

Jinnah and Lawrence found Nehru's suggestion explosive enough. Lawrence looked at Jinnah.

"I am ready to discuss this matter further with Jawaharlal," Jinnah said.

At this stage, Lawrence suggested suspension of the talks. He said that both Nehru and Jinnah should discuss among themselves the modalities of the transfer of power and come out with a concrete proposal. Both the leaders discussed the various options. The next day they came out with a mutually agreed formula. The Congress and the Muslim League would form a national government together, and any differences on policy matters would be referred to a three member Committee. Of the three, one each would be chosen by the Congress and the League and the third—a neutral member—would be appointed by the Viceroy. Both the parties would suggest three names each to the Viceroy who could appoint one among them to the Committee.

Two days later, Jinnah retracted his stand and said that he was not in favour of any such Committee. Both the leaders had agreed that the neutral member should not be either a Hindu or a Muslim, but could be a Sikh, a Parsi or a Christian. When Jinnah started looking for suitable persons, he realized his own limitations. He feared that in controversial matters, the third neutral member could take the side of the Congress thereby reducing the Muslim League member to a minority. He flatly denied that he had ever reached such an agreement with Jawaharlal Nehru.

This denial shocked Badshah Khan, the Congress leader in the North West Frontier Province. He dreaded the idea of his province with ninety five per cent Muslim population merging into Pakistan, in the event of the country not remaining united. The Muslim League leader Abdul Rab Nishtar was also a Pathan. Before he joined the League, he was a supporter of Badshah Khan and a staunch opponent of Jinnah. Badhshah Khan appealed to him, "You know that Jinnah had in fact reached such an agreement with Jawaharlal. It is in the interest of all of us that the country remains united. Please persuade Jinnah not to back out from the agreement." Abdul Rab Nishta assured Badshah Khan that he would talk to Jinnah. He knew that Jinnah had agreed to the appointment of a neutral third member. He made efforts to persuade Jinnah, but in vain.

Jinnah met Sir Stafford Cripps a couple of years back with his idea of a political settlement. Cripps did not have pleasant memories of Jinnah. He used to tell his friends that Jinnah was a very unreasonable man and that there was no logic in his arguments. Cripps felt upset by the arrogant behaviour of Jinnah in refusing to shake hands with the Congress President, Maulana Azad. He could not stand the rudeness of Jinnah. He told him, "Mr. Jinnah. It is only when you respect others, you receive respect."

"I know the manners. I do not have to learn the manners from any one," rebuked Jinnah.

"It is not enough to know the manners. It is important to practice them," countered Stafford Cripps.

Jinnah was affronted. He could not tolerate Cripps' insinuation. He got up angrily,

"Quaid-e-Azam," Cripps said quietly, "Political conferences are not the places to take offence. Every one is expected to behave in a matured manner. If you get up like this, neither will India become independent nor will Pakistan be achieved."

An insulted Jinnah turned back and started walking towards the door. Liaquat took the situation in his hand. He went after Jinnah and pacified him. Jawaharlal also got up from his seat and tried to placate Jinnah. Jinnah returned to his chair as if his bruised ego had been nursed.

The two parties could not reach an agreement due to certain fundamental differences. The conference failed. Pethick Lawrence declared that though the conference had failed, the British government could understand the different perceptions of both the sides and that the government would come with a formula to reach a political settlement.

Jinnah's health had deteriorated due to the physical and mental strain of the conference. Had the conference lasted a few days more, it would have been impossible for him to talk or even attend the conference. He cancelled all his engagements and returned to Bombay with his sister Fatima and his personal staff. He travelled in a special first class compartment in the Punjab Mail from Delhi. He had a difficulty in breathing and during his entire journey he coughed incessantly. Because of too frequent bouts of cough he could not lie down and sleep. He sat for hours together with the support of the pillows. He was almost unconscious. He could not eat anything due to high fever. Realising the seriousness of his condition, Fatima sent a telegraphic message to Dr. Jaal Patel in Bombay from a nearby railway station asking him to be ready for an emergency treatment. No one except Dr. Patel knew anything about the disease of Jinnah. A large crowd of his supporters gathered at the railway station in Bombay to welcome him. Because of the uncompromising stand that he took at the Simla conference, the Muslims who had been opposed to the idea of Pakistan earlier, now came under his influence. They realized that he was the only fearless and aggressive spokesman who could protect the interest of the Muslims. What was Pakistan? And what would happen to the Muslims who live in India after the partition? They thought Jinnah must have had answers to all this. Even the Muslims leaders in Punjab and Bengal began accepting the indispensability of his leadership. To secure their future these leaders now turned to the Muslim League.

On receiving the message from Fatima, Dr. Jaal Patel realized how serious the condition of Jinnah was. He felt that if Jinnah got down at the Bombay main railway station his supporters would surround him and that would create more physical and mental discomfort to him. Not only that, the seriousness of his condition would spread like a wildfire throughout the country. Considering all this, the doctor thought it would be advisable that Jinnah got down at some station before reaching the main railway station in Bombay. The doctor boarded the train with all necessary equipments at Igatpuri, the last stop before entering Bombay. He asked his assistants to keep an ambulance ready at Dadar, the first stop in city of Bombay.

Everything went off smoothly as per his plan. The doctor's apprehension turned out to be true. Any treatment could give only a temporary lease of life to the crumbling edifice. Jinnah was almost unconscious. He was shifted to the ambulance at Dadar station and taken to a hospital.

When the third member of the Cabinet Mission Alexandar came to know about Jinnah's serious condition, he talked to him over the phone, "Mr. Jinnah, perhaps the cool climate of Simla has aggravated your breathing problem. Lord Pethick Lawrence and Sir Stafford Cripps are worried about your health."

"Really!" Jinnah responded sarcastically. He did not forget the insult heaped on him by Stafford Cripps. "Then they can come here and meet me," Jinnah quipped.

Dr. Patel was present there. He knew his patient. He felt that it was the effect of his disease.

When the private secretary to the governor of Bombay enquired about his health, Jinnah said to him,

"His Excellency the governor seems to be so busy that you are enquiring on his behalf."

"Sir, he is busy with an important political meeting."

"Then tell him that just as he cannot spare the time to talk to me, I too do not have the time. I just cannot talk to anybody," Jinnah said and then banged the receiver.

After very careful treatment for several days, Jinnah's health showed some improvement. But Dr. Patel knew that it was only superficial. When he felt that Jinnah was in a position to bear the strain of a talk, he told him,

"Quaid-e-Azam. Please do not be under any illusion that your health has improved. The improvement that you see is not real. It is the effect of the medication. It can only conceal the reality, it cannot alter it."

"Doctor, you are unnecessarily worrying," said Jinnah confidently. "I will not die until I achieve my goal. If you want me to live longer, you must push my goal still further."

"Quaid-e-Azam, I don't know anything. I am only a doctor. As a doctor, whatever I see, I advise the patients accordingly," the doctor said dejectedly, "You must change your lifestyle. One cannot live on will power alone. You must understand that smoking and drinking have seriously damaged your health."

"They have been my companions for the past six decades. Leaving them now would be disgraceful," Jinnah said unmoved, "I cannot change my lifestyle now. Besides, I have brought the Muslims of the country to such a stage, from where I have no option but to move ahead."

"You alone can decide about it," said the doctor, "My advise is you must leave all your work and go to some sanatorium in a hill station and take complete rest."

"Doctor, I know that my sanatorium is now in a cemetery," Jinnah said without betraying any emotion. "While treating me, you must ensure that no one, particularly no Congress leader, should know about my disease. If they get any inkling of my disease they would prefer to wait till I die. That would shatter my dream."

A stunned doctor started looking helplessly at the blue skies through the glass windows. His professional duty had taken precedence over his duty towards the country.

61

Pethic-Lawrence-Jinnah-Jawahar-Maulana meeting not materialising, Nizam-Jinnah meeting, Cabinet Mission proposals, Jinnah in a dilemma, Mullahs-Maulvis, Cabinet Mission's approval for interim government, Congress—interim government, Jinnah's call for 'Direct Action'

When Jinnah's health improved a little, meeting the Nizam of Hyderabad was his first priority. Hyderabad was the largest princely state in the country. A vast majority of the people in the state were Hindus, but the ruler Nawab Nizam-ul-Mulq was a Muslim. Even when Pakistan became a reality in future, there was no possibility of the state merging with it as it was surrounded by the Hindu majority provinces from all sides. In such a situation, it would be desirable if the state remained independent. The Nizam was a staunch Muslim and a sympathizer of Pakistan. His Prime Minister Mirza Ismail was known for his liberal attitude. Jinnah knew that once the country became independent, the question of the princely states merging with the rest of the country would come up. In that event, it would be better to have a staunch Muslim as the Prime Minister in a predominately Hindu state rather than a liberal minded person. Jinnah wanted to pressurise the Nizam to replace Mirza Ismail as the Prime Minister. The Nizam was perhaps the richest Nawab in India, but led a life of austerity. His austerity was not due to any principle like that of Aurangzeb, but because of his miserly nature. Jinnah wanted to prove himself superior to the Nizam and impress upon him. A meeting was arranged and accordingly Jinnah walked into the visitors' room of the Nizam, wearing a very expensive modern suit, a monocle on his right eye with an expensive cigarette in his hand. The Nizam had not yet arrived.

In order to impress the Nizam, Jinnah lit the cigarette and sat in an armchair with his feet stretched out on the tea-poy. He did not change his position even when the Nizam entered the room. As if that was not insulting enough, he took a deep puff of the cigarette and released the smoke into the air. The Nizam was shocked by this appalling behaviour. He was furious and yelled at his bodyguard, "Who is that man sitting there? No one can misbehave like this in front of me. Ask him to leave the place at once."

Jinnah was shaken for a moment. He might be a supreme leader of the Muslims of the country, but here he was sitting in the palace of an independent princely state. The Writ of the British Raj or the Muslim League did not run here. He came to his senses. He immediately withdrew his feet from the teapoy and straightened his back. He got up from the chair as if he had not heard the Nizam and offered his hand in a gesture of friendship.

Jinnah was humbled. He could not forget the lesson that he got from this meeting for the rest of his life.

*

Pethick Lawrence wanted to make a final effort to make the two main political parties reach an agreement before announcing his formula for a political settlement. He wanted to share his formula with the respective Presidents of the Congress and the Muslim League. If both of them could reach an agreement his task would become simple. Accordingly, he had invited Maulana Azad and Jinnah for a meeting, but Jinnah expressed his resentment against the presence of the Congress President at the meeting. He could not forget the insult heaped on him by Stafford Cripps in front of Maulana at the Simla Conference. Jinnah had a contempt for Maulana and considered him a puppet of the Congress. He found it beneath his dignity to accept Maulana as his equal at the negotiating table. Therefore, he accepted the invitation with a rejoinder, "I cannot talk to Maulana Azad. He is a traitor for the Muslims. He is a puppet in the hands of the Congress. If the Congress is really serious about the talks, it should replace him as its representative."

Gandhi wanted to resolve this tangle somehow. He knew Jinnah was desperate and lost the sense of balance. He overlooked the insult meted out to the Congress President and instructed Jawaharlal Nehru to represent the Congress.

Jinnah assumed that since he had refused to talk to the Congress President, there would be no meeting. He was sure that a nationalist and esteemed party like the Congress would not tolerate the insult of its President. After the rebuke by Cripps, he did not want to talk to the Congress again. This was an excuse for him to stall the talks. But now he was in a quandary. So he came out with another condition saying, "Before I could talk to Jawaharlal, there must be some common meeting ground. Or else it will be a sheer waste of time and efforts. If the Congress accepts our condition that the Muslims will have fifty per cent representation in the proposed interim government and that the Muslim League will nominate the Muslim representatives, then the talks can continue."

This had the desired effect. The meeting did not materialize.

The Viceroy Lord Wavell wanted to stall the process of independence for two years. This was what his mentor Churchill desired. Churchill somehow wanted to stall the independence of India. If at all the independence became inevitable, he wanted an independent state of Pakistan for the Muslims so that the two new nations were constantly at loggerheads with each other. The new Labour government of Britain was aware of this game plan of the Viceroy. Prime Minister

Attlee realised that Wavell was an impediment in the way of the independence of India. He was in search of a suitable Viceroy.

The Cabinet Mission had declared its proposals. The proposals contained the formation of an interim government, the election of members to the Constituent Assembly and the subjects like the defence and the foreign affairs were also to remain with the central government. Besides, the provinces would form into groups and they would reserve the right to secede from the Union of India, after ten years if they so desired.

Jinnah hoped that the Congress would not accept the proposals. The reason was obvious. The proposals did not clarify that the Viceroy would remain a mere constitutional head of the interim government and that he would not interfere in the functioning of the government. Moreover, his demand that the Muslim League alone would nominate all the Muslim members in the interim government could prove lethal for the Congress. Jinnah was right. The Congress expressed its reservations on the proposals. It demanded an assurance that the Viceroy would not interfere in the functioning of the government and that he would not veto the decisions of the Central Assembly.

This was what Jinnah had wanted. The British government made its stand clear that if any party did not accept the proposals, the government would go ahead with them unilaterally. This made Jinnah to announce the acceptance of the Cabinet Mission proposals on behalf of the Muslim League.

The Congress was in a dilemma. Jinnah believed that since the Muslim League had accepted the proposals, the Viceroy would invite him to form the interim government. But an adverse situation had stalled his dream.

Jinnah was aware of the gravity of his illness. Until now, he held the card of Pakistan close to his chest, as it was his ace to silence all his opponents. He thought he could become the Prime Minister of a unified India, without the Congress. He knew his days were numbered. Therefore, he wanted some solution to the communal problem during his lifetime. He also knew that even if Pakistan was formed, the communal problem of India would never be resolved. He understood that the population of the Muslims who would continue to live in India after the partition would be equivalent to the entire population of Pakistan. He also understood that Pakistan which he was banking upon would not be a modern state of his vision, but a medieval theocratic state dominated by the Mullahs and the Maulvis. The Mullahs had already declared that Pakistan would be governed by the Shariat law. Jinnah began to realize that the creation of Pakistan would not benefit the Muslims, but would be detrimental to their interest. His colleagues in the Muslim League were Islamic fundamentalists. Considering all this, if he became the Prime Minister of India, he could give up the demand for Pakistan.

But his destiny willed it otherwise. Some powerful leaders in the Muslim League and the Ulemas, who had great hold on the Muslim masses, had vehemently opposed Jinnah's acceptance of the Cabinet Mission proposals, as it would mean foregoing the demand for an Islamic state of Pakistan for ever. The resentment was building up. But nobody dared to defy Jinnah openly. Jinnah was confronted with a grave problem.

The situation turned worse when the Viceroy did not invite Jinnah to form the interim government in spite of his acceptance of the Cabinet Mission proposals. The British authorities in London believed that if the Congress which represented seventy five per cent of the Indian population did not join the government, it would not be prudent to ask the Muslim League to form the government. Because of this, the Viceroy could not invite Jinnah to form the government.

Thus, Jinnah was caught between the devil and the deep sea. On the one hand, his colleagues in the Muslim League were annoyed with his acceptance of the Cabinet Mission proposals and on the other hand his plan of forming the government failed. Knowing well that the elected members of provincial assemblies and office bearers of Muslim league were mentally annoyed, Jinnah invited all of them to Delhi for a conference to discuss the political situation in the country. It was just a diplomatic move to placate them.

At the conference, very cleverly he made a fierce speech, "Our goal is to achieve Pakistan. We all are united and committed to achieve this goal. Let us swear by the *Holy Quran* and in the name of *Allah* that we will fight for Pakistan till the last drop of our blood"

Jinnah knew that once he invoked the name of the Quran and Allah, the dissent would die. The man who had never accepted the Quran and Allah now cleverly played with the religious sentiments to curb the dissidence against him. All of them solemnly took the oath one after another.

*

In the meantime, the Secretary of State for India, assured the Congress that the Viceroy would remain only as the constitutional head and would not interfere with the functioning of the interim government. The Congress in turn agreed to join the interim government and help in the formation of the Constituent Assembly.

Once the Congress and the Muslim League accepted the Cabinet Mission proposals, the Viceroy invited the President of the Congress Jawaharlal Nehru to form the interim government. The Viceroy's Executive Council would consist of thirteen members—five each from the Congress and the Muslim League, one from the backward classes nominated by the congress and one each from the Sikhs and the Christians. One additional member was added to the Council raising its strength to fourteen. Jinnah once again took a rigid stand that the Congress should not nominate any Muslim member to the Council. This was not acceptable to the Congress. It nominated Sir Shafat Ahmed Khan as its member to the Council. Consequently, the Muslim League refused to join the interim government. Nehru formed the interim government by leaving two seats to the Muslim League in the Executive Council if they intend to join at a later stage. He formed the government with twelve members, instead of fourteen. Sir Ahmed Khan, a Congress nominee, was appointed as a member of the Executive Council. A tragic event occurred the very next day after he was sworn in. A fanatic Muslim youth murdered Ahmed Khan for daring to join the interim government. A few years ago, Allah Baksh who broke away from the Muslim League and formed the government in the Sindh province with the support of the Congress, was murdered in a similar fashion. His murderer was never apprehended. Similarly, the conspiracy behind the murder of Ahmed Khan was never unearthed.

In the meantime, Jinnah was looking for an excuse to abort the Cabinet Mission proposals. If he could not become the Prime Minister of a unified India, he would play the card of Pakistan once again. Nehru had unwittingly provided him the golden opportunity.

Nehru declared at a press conference in Bombay that the Constituent Assembly would be able to amend the Cabinet Mission proposals by a majority vote in a democratic way. This was interpreted by Jinnah as the intention of the Congress to bring changes as per its will by using its majority in the Assembly and that Nehru wanted to establish the Hindu Raj in India. It gave him an excuse to abort the Cabinet Mission proposals. He declared that since the Congress had intended to establish a Hindu Raj in India, the Muslim League withdrew its acceptance of the proposals.

This was a serious setback for the efforts to reach a political settlement. The Congress Working Committee had debated the political fall out of Nehru's press statement. If it had contradicted his statement, it could have amounted to belittling the President of the Congress. And if it did not clarify its stand, the political stalemate would continue. It passed a resolution stating that the Congress had accepted the Cabinet Mission proposals and it had no intention to back out. But Jinnah needed no such clarification. He killed two birds with one stone. He sent out a loud message to the British rulers that a Congress government would not last if the Muslim League was sidelined. And secondly, he assured the radical elements in the League that the ultimate goal was to achieve Pakistan. He made an aggressive and highly inflammatory speech at the meeting of the League's Working Committee. He said, "From today, we say farewell to the constitutional way of struggle. We are facing two-fold attacks, from the British Government as well as congress empowered with a machine gun of majority aimed at us. As such no political settlement is possible. Both are our enemies. This is a life and death struggle for us. The Muslim League has carried out a lawful and peaceful struggle till now. Now we will have to answer with a bullet for a bullet. The Muslims do not accept non-violence. No victory ever comes without a bloodshed. We will now resort to *Direct Action* and launch an unlawful struggle to achieve an independent state of Pakistan. Our guns are loaded and it is the time to fire. Now we have no option but to shed the blood of others for every drop of blood shed by the Muslims."

The Muslim League had declared 16th August, 1946 as the day of *Direct Action*.

62

Direct Action: Riots in Calcutta, Muslim League in the interim government, Liaquat-Jawaharlal—Budget

Jinnah claimed that until now he had carried out a lawful and peaceful struggle and that now he would resort to *Direct Action* and launch an unlawful struggle. This was a great blunder on the part of Jinnah who had been a defender of law. So far, a barrister from 'Lincon's Inn' of London and obstinate for the legal methods. He displayed the unlawful streak in him which was suppressed for long. He could not comprehend that no government could tolerate the unlawful activities. When the newspapers published the Resolution of the Muslim League, the reporters cornered Jinnah and asked him to clarify what he meant by the "unlawful struggle." He was caught on a wrong foot. He immediately corrected himself, "It means unconstitutional. Our protest is not against any law. It is a protest against the constitution." To this another reporter asked, "When the constitution is not framed, how can you protest against the constitution. The laws are enacted. And anyone who breaks the law would invite the punishment. Can you clarify what you mean by protest against the constitution?"

"No. I cannot give you any more clarification right now. You will understand it in due course," thus, as usual, Jinnah abruptly put an end to the conversation.

The Muslim League had already decided to observe 16th August, 1946 as the day of *Direct Action.* In Bengal, Suharawardy's government had unleashed an orgy of violence and mass murders on that day. Twenty years ago, Suharawardy had represented the Congress in Calcutta. He was elected as a member of the Central Assembly on the ticket of the Swaraj Party under the leadership of Motilal Nehru. The same man now turned against the Congress and the Hindus and became a communalist and a staunch supporter of the Muslim League. He had been opposed to the interference of the League and Jinnah in Bengal politics for many years. Now he was a totally changed man. The political expediency made him to toe the line with Jinnah. Like all other Muslim leaders, he subscribed to the view that Jinnah alone could lead the Muslims and make their voice heard by the British government. As a head of the government in Bengal, he ordered the transfer of the police officers in all the twenty four police stations. He placed twenty two police stations under the charge of the Muslim officers. All the Hindu police officers were transferred. After the Friday prayers, the armed Muslims from the mosques marched into the Hindu residential areas and went on a rampage by carrying out looting, arson, rape and murder. Jinnah earlier declared that the *Direct Action* day would be observed peacefully to express the sentiments of the Muslims. Trusting his words, the Hindus and the Sikhs remained indoors. The Bengal government declared 16th August as a public holiday. All the government offices were closed. Suharawardy himself went to the police control room to monitor the *Direct Action*. A large number of Hindus and Sikhs were massacred. No police help was provided. The dead bodies were thrown on the roads. The Hindu temples were torched. And the properties of the Hindus and the Sikhs were set on fire with no firemen to douse the flames. This mayhem continued unabated for two days. No provincial police or army came to the rescue of the innocent victims.

When Hindus and Sikhs realised that no government protection was forthcoming and that they would be slaughtered mercilessly if they did not retaliate, they launched a massive counter attack on the third day. The Muslims and the government were not prepared for this. The retaliation was swift and brutal. Hundreds of Muslims were butchered and their property destroyed. If the situation was not brought under control immediately, the position of the Muslims in Calcutta would have worsened. The governor asked the Viceroy for the army assistance. On the fifth day, the army took control of Calcutta. But by then thousands of people were massacred and the mutilated corpses littered the streets. The smoke still billowed out from the houses set afire. The killings in Calcutta sparked the violence across the country. The communal violence erupted in Bihar and other parts of the country. Jinnah had no idea that the communal flame would spread out to so many places so rapidly. He had never been a leader of the masses. In fact, he preferred to stay away from them. He could never understand the mass psychology. It was easy to receive the applause from the crowd by making fiery speeches. It was impossible for him to control the violent and he took the stand that this violence was an expression of an uncontrollable passion of the Muslims for Pakistan. He warned that the country would plunge into a civil war if the demand for Pakistan was not conceded.

The Viceroy Wavell tried to make the interim government a scapegoat for the mayhem. In his letter to the Secretary of State for India, he said that Nehru's interim government would not be able to function without the Muslim League joining it. Jinnah also had realised the harm done in not joining the interim government. If Nehru could run the government smoothly for some more time, it would mean the League's support was not required. Jinnah never wanted that situation to arise. If he remained inflexible in his stand, the Muslims would have a difficult situation and would not be achieving much, leave alone achieving Pakistan.

The Viceroy suggested to Nehru that he should invite the Muslim League to join the interim government. Nehru met Jinnah. But they could not forget the earlier bitterness and their meeting did not yield any result. The Viceroy continued to make efforts to ensure that the League somehow joined the government. The reason was that his relation with Jawaharlal Nehru, particularly Sardar Patel, was not cordial. Moreover, it was humiliating for the bureaucrats to take the orders from these leaders whom they had considered traitors until recently. Nehru and Patel expressed to the Secretary of State and the British Prime Minister that they lost faith in Viceroy Wavell and requested them to replace him immediately. The Viceroy felt that if the League's representatives joined the government, they could control Nehru and Patel. He arranged yet another meeting between Gandhi and Jinnah. At this meeting, Jinnah resented the supreme position that Nehru occupied in the government after the Viceroy. It meant that the Congress was more important than the Muslim League. Jinnah was not willing to accept this position. Further, he insisted that the Muslim League was the only organisation representing the entire Muslim community in the country. He demanded that if the League joined the interim government, it should be given the important portfolio of the Home Ministry.

Gandhi adopted a middle path. He suggested that the Congress should concede that the League had represented the majority of the Muslims in the country and that the League in return should accept the right of the Congress to nominate a nationalist Muslim as its representative in the interim government. He somehow wanted to resolve the deadlock. But Sardar Patel did not accept this compromise formula. He was of the opinion that Jinnah's firmness was only a façade and that he was desperate to join the government. He warned that if he had to give up the portfolio of the Home Ministry, as a result of the compromise, he would quit the government.

The Viceroy had another round of discussion with Jinnah. Thereafter, Jinnah declared that the League would join the government in deference to the wishes of the Viceroy. He said that the five members of the League in the interim government would maintain a separate entity under the leadership of Liaquat Ali Khan and that for the working of the Ministries under their charge they would be responsible to the Viceroy and not to Jawaharlal Nehru, the head of the government.

This was a strange situation. The interim government was no more a single entity with a collective responsibility. It was divided into two groups, each pursuing its own agenda. Liaquat Ali Khan had made his intention clear before joining the government. He said in a public speech at Karachi, "The Congress did not want the Muslim League to join the government. The League is joining the government to thwart the Congress efforts. Our aim is to divide the government from within and work towards our goal of achieving Pakistan."

Jinnah maintained that the Ministers representing the League would function as a parallel government. He also said the League had joined the government to stop the massacring of the Muslims by the Hindus. When he realized that the Leauge would not be able to wrest the Home Ministry, he insisted that the portfolio of the Finance Ministry should be given to Liaquat Ali Khan. Chaudhari Muhammed Ali was the Principal Secretary of the Finance Ministry. He was a supporter of the League . He knew how the Finance Ministry could put hurdles for all other Ministries. It was he who convinced Jinnah that the Finance Ministry was more important than the Home Ministry. All other Ministries in the government would get the funds allocated by the Finance Ministry. The Congress leaders were not acquainted with the intricacies of running a government. Chaudhari Mohammed Ali exploited their ignorance and was instrumental in handing over the Finance Ministry to Liaquat Ali Khan.

Liaquat Ali Khan successfully used his Ministry of Finance to break the government from within. Most of the proposals for funds received from the Congress Ministries, particularly the Home Ministry of Sardar Patel, were either totally rejected or cut down to the bare minimum. Sometime the files were returned seeking more clarification. It was an impossible situation.

It became extremely difficult for any Congress Minister to function. Sardar Patel was the most frustrated among all the Ministers. It began to sink in his mind that if this non- cooperative attitude of the League continued in the interim government, it was better to partition the country rather than keeping it unified.

As if this was not enough, Liaquat Ali Khan held a parallel meeting of the Ministers of the League whenever Jawaharlal Nehru convened weekly meetings of the Executive Council. This violated the principle of collective responsibility. Nehru found it difficult to make the members of the Executive Council responsible. He wrote to the Viceroy drawing his attention to the flagrant breach of discipline. The Viceroy did not respond.

Nehru talked to Liaquat to put an end to the non-cooperative attitude of the Muslim League. He told Liaquat that the government would not be able to function with a dual leadership and that in a democracy the government functioned on the principle of collective responsibility of Ministers.

"Excuse me, *Panditji*, what you call a government is not a government in reality. This is the Executive Council formed only to assist the Viceroy. It is not a democratically elected government," Liaquat responded sarcastically.

"Khan *Sahib*, if you want to call it the Viceroy's Executive Council, I have no objection. But its working is not different from that of a Council of Ministers in a democracy. The ideal that we have to follow is that of a collective responsibility of a democratic government," Jawaharlal tried to reason out.

"What can I say to you, *Panditji*? What is merely the Viceroy's Executive Council cannot become a democratic government simply because you want it to be so."

Thereafter Nehru did not argue. The matter ended there.

Liaquat Ali Khan presented the annual budget in the Central Assembly. Since he did not accept Nehru as the head of the government, he did not discuss the budget proposals with him. Nehru was ignorant about the budget proposals. One of the proposals in the budget was that the rate of income tax would be raised by twenty five per cent on the businessmen whose annual income exceeded one lakh rupees. Thus, he targeted the Hindu businessmen as most of them came under this income group. Since the Hindu businessmen supported the Congress it was aimed to punish them. The Congress supporters and the businessmen across the country became livid about this.

The government was paralysed. In the meantime, the Constituent Assembly was convened to draft a constitution for India. The members of the Muslim League were a minority in the Constituent Assembly. Jinnah boycotted the Constituent Assembly on the pretext that it was not a representative body of the Muslims and demanded that the Muslims should have a separate Constituent Assembly. His goal was to achieve Pakistan. He wanted a separate Constituent Assembly for Pakistan. He wrote to Viceroy Wavell that he preferred a small Pakistan to the groupings of the provinces into the Hindu and the Muslim majority as suggested by the Cabinet Mission.

63

Failure of Jawaharlal-Jinnah-Attlee parleys in London, Churchill-Jinnah correspondence: pseudo name, Jinnah-Baldev Singh talks, Jinnah-Muslim Conference in Cairo, Mountbatten-Edwina acquaintance, Wavell's welcome to Mountbatten, Mountbatten-George Catleen: perception of Gandhi-Jinnah

Wavell could not resolve the deadlock on the issue of the Constituent Assembly. He sought the intervention of the Secretary of State and the British Prime Minister. In this context, Nehru and Attlee exchanged the correspondence. The British government was interested in reaching a political settlement in India. Attlee had decided to convene a conference in London. He instructed Wavell to ask the representatives of the two political parties to attend the conference in London. Accordingly, Wavell sent invitations to Jinnah and Acharya Kriplani, the President of the Congress. As the President of the Muslim League, Jinnah immediately accepted the invitation. However, the Congress had some reservations. It did not accept the invitation as it felt the conference would not serve any purpose. Attlee as British Prime Minister wrote to Nehru as the head of the interim Indian government inviting him to attend the conference. The Congress accepted his invitation and authorized Nehru and Patel to attend the conference. But Patel was of the opinion that the conference would serve no purpose at that juncture. He felt Attlee's invitation was just a courtesy. He believed that unless the Muslim League changed its attitude, the trip to London would be futile. Nevertheless, he clarified that Nehru could represent the Congress, but he himself was not interested in attending the conference.

Jinnah was annoyed that Attlee had personally invited Nehru. He felt he deserved a similar treatment from the British government. He realised that he was in haste in accepting the invitation of the Viceroy. The correspondence between Nehru and Attlee gave rise to suspicion in his mind. He now came out with new conditions. He declared that he would not attend the conference unless Attlee sent him a personal invitation. Further, the correspondence exchanged between Nehru and Attlee be released so as to understand the basis for discussion at the conference. Attlee accepted his conditions. He sent personal invitation to Jinnah. Viceroy Wavell left for London along with Jinnah and Liaquat Ali Khan, as the representatives of the Muslim League, Jawaharlal Nehru as the Congress representative and Sardar Baldev Singh as the representative of the Sikhs.

Sardar Patel's prophecy turned out to be true. The London conference failed. The Muslims remained a minority in the Constituent Assembly. Neither Jinnah nor the British government had any magic wand to convert a minority into a majority. Jinnah persisted with his demand that the British government should concede the demand for Pakistan. Then the Muslims would elect their own Constituent Assembly to draft a constitution for the new nation. Nehru responded to this saying that if the Muslim League did not want to join the Constituent Assembly, it had no right to continue in the interim government. The interim government and the Constituent Assembly were the two parts of the same scheme. No party could accept one part and reject the other part. Thus, both the parties once again failed to reach a settlement.

At the end of the Conference, Jinnah realised that, unlike the Conservative government under Churchill, the policy of the Labour government under Attlee was not beneficial to the Muslims. The Labour government was eager to leave India at the earliest. Churchill was not prepared to let go off the jewel in the crown of the British Empire. If it became inevitable for the British government to leave India, he wanted the demand of the Muslims to be accepted even if it meant going against the interest of the Hindus. He had a personal meeting with Jinnah. Though Churchill was the opposition leader in the British Parliament, he exercised considerable influence in the matters of governance. He assured Jinnah that he would oppose any proposal for granting independence to India. According to him, the Indians were not capable of governing themselves. He expressed the apprehension that if the British government left India, without creating Pakistan, it would lead to a civil war in the country.

Churchill's fear revived Jinnah's dream. He felt assured that Churchill would protect the interest of the Muslims in the British Parliament. Both of them agreed to remain in touch with each other.

"An awkward position in India," Churchill said as a precaution. "There is a way out. We can correspond in fictitious names so that nobody will come to know about it."

Jinnah appreciated Churchill. He accepted the suggestion.

"My pseudo name will be Miss Juliet," said Churchill. "You can write letters to me addressing me by this name."

"And my pseudo name will be Miss Mariam. You can address to me by this name while writing," Jinnah responded. Mariam was the name he gave to his wife Ruttie after he converted her to Islam.

Since then both the friends—Miss Juliet and Miss Mariam—continued to exchange the correspondence until India was partitioned and Pakistan was created.

Jinnah had a personal meeting with Sardar Baldev Singh before returning to India. Jinnah knew that if Pakistan was created, the Sikhs of Punjab would prefer to live in India. That would divide Punjab. Master Tara Singh, the President of the Akali Dali, had already demanded that if Pakistan was created for the Muslims, a separate state of Sikhistan should be carved out of Punjab for the Sikhs. If the Sikhs could be won over, the entire province of Punjab could be merged into Pakistan. Under this situation the Sikhs would be reduced to a minority and then they would not create any problem for the new nation. This calculation made Jinnah to coax Sardar Baldev Singh. He said to him,

"*Sardarji*, I may or may not realize my dream of Pakistan. I will accept a moth eaten Pakistan. I sincerely seek the support of the Sikhs. If you join hands with me, we can merge together and create a bigger and stronger state that can even usurp the power in Delhi."

Sardar Baldev Singh was wise enough not to get trapped by Jinnah. Socially and religiously, the Sikhs were closer to the Hindus. The Sikhs had very little in common with the Muslims. In fact, historically both these communities shared a common heritage of hatred and hostility. It was ironical that Jinnah who always insisted on a separate state for the Muslims was now talking of creating a larger state with the help of the Sikhs.

On their way back to India, Jinnah and Liaquat stopped in Cairo, the capital of Egypt. Cairo was hosting a conference of the Islamic nations. Both of them participated in the conference. Jinnah said in his address to the delegates,

"If we fail to achieve Pakistan, India will extend its border up to Egypt. The Muslims live in the western part of India. The majority Hindus will overpower them in no time. There is a threat looming over Afghanistan, Iran and Egypt. The Pan Islamic Organisation can succeed only when Pakistan is created. We seek your support in our struggle."

It was the same Jinnah who had opposed the Muslim League and Gandhi on the Khilafat movement some twenty five years ago. The contradiction comes out when what he said now was juxtaposed to what he had said then. The nationalist Jinnah had opposed Aga Khan and said there could be no Pan-Islamic Organisation of the Muslims and that Islam as a religion had nothing to do with one's nationality. The Khalifa was a ruler of Turkey and it was a universally accepted norm that the victor would depose the vanquished. Jinnah who had said all this so vehemently was now a totally transformed man.

*

The British Prime Minister Attlee had no faith in Viceroy Lord Wavell. The Prime Minister and the Secretary of State for India were convinced that Wavell was still pursuing the imperialist policies of his mentor Churchill. They thought Wavell would not be able to ensure smooth transfer of power in India. He was recalled. And Lord Louis Mountbatten was appointed as the Viceroy of India. Mountbatten was responsible for the British victory in the Second World War as a naval commander. Attlee felt that Lord Mountbatten's charisma, intelligence, negotiating skills and his knowledge of India would be quite useful during the transition period. A young Moutbatten at the age of twenty two had visited India when his cousin Lord Reading was the Viceroy. Then he met Edwina, the niece of Lady Reading. They fell in love and decided to marry, although Lady Reading had reservation about the choice of her niece. She thought "the girl was making a mistake. There is nothing special about Mountbatten."

However, Lady Reading was proved wrong. The Commander of the British Navy and a World War hero was now assigned the toughest job in the history of the British Empire. It was the month of March and the temperature was soaring in Delhi. Mountbatten took over as the last Viceroy of India and the thirty-fourth Governor General. He was conferred special powers which his predecessors did not enjoy. He brought with him the most trusted and competent staff to accomplish the specific task assigned to him.

While bidding goodbye Lord Wavell said to Lord Mountbatten, "You have a very difficult task in hand. I regret I could not succeed in completing the task. You must remember that you are entering into a madhouse and you will have to deal with all sorts of mad people. I wish you success in your new assignment."

Before undertaking his task, Lord Mountbatten wanted to get acquainted with the Indian leaders. He wanted to work without any prejudice. George Catleen, a British official, was well acquainted with the Indian leaders. Mountbatten wanted to know from him how he should deal with the two important leaders of India—Gandhi and Jinnah.

"Look," said George Catleen sharing his experience, "When you meet Gandhi, give him enough time to express his views. He will sound like a philosopher when he talks about the ideals you may feel that all that creates a psychological problem. You might feel that after Buddha, here is a saint who remained untouched by the passage of time. After hearing him patiently, ask him a question to make him realize the ground reality."

And then he advised Mountbatten, "Never trust Jinnah. He can change his stand any time. Lord Wavell never accepted my advice. That is why the British government and India are caught in this impasse. Jinnah can disown in no time what he agrees upon and you will have no evidence to prove what he agreed upon. If you want to avoid such embarrassing situation, always ensure the presence of a third person whenever you talk to Jinnah."

Keeping in mind the advice of George Catleen, Mountbatten invited both Gandhi and Jinnah for a first formal meeting.

64

Mountbatten-Gandhi-Jinnah parleys, Edwina-Fatima meeting, Jinnah-Mountbatten talks regarding division of Punjab and Bengal, Jinnah's declaration on the question of majority-minority in Pakistan, Gandhi's reaction

When Gandhi reached the Viceroy House in Delhi, the temperature soared to 110 degree Fahrenheit. He wore a short dhoti and covered his body with a thin shawl. The bones on his lean body were clearly visible. The Viceroy's ADC led him respectfully to the visitors' room.

Jinnah arrived soon. He noticed Gandhi as he entered the room. Gandhi gave him his characteristic smile and nodded the head. Jinnah acknowledged the greeting by waving his hand. He looked around. He saw a sofa at some distance. He sat on the sofa. There were some sofas and chairs near Gandhi which Jinnah avoided.

Viceroy Lord Mountbatten entered the room. He looked at both the guests. Gandhi sat straight in the chair, while Jinnah sat relaxed in the sofa. The Viceroy greeted both of them and shook hands. He was in a dilemma for a moment. Both Gandhi and Jinnah were sitting at such a distance from each other that if he talked to Gandhi, Jinnah would not be able to hear and vice versa. A teapoy was lying between the two. Mountbatten pulled a chair and sat in the middle near the teapoy maintaining an equidistance from his guests. This was an indication of the task that he had come to perform.

The formal meeting ended on a cordial note. But the Viceroy asked Jinnah to meet him again the next day. This time Fatima accompanied Jinnah. Fatima was introduced to the Viceroy. Lady Edwina Mountbatten was also present.

"Mr. Jinnah," said Mountbatten beginning the conversation, "We are on the threshold of an important turning point in the Indian history. If we do not take proper decision now, the future generations will hold us guilty. I want to have your clear and candid opinion on this issue."

"Before we talk about the issue, I have a condition..."

Mountbatten was taken aback. The smile on his face disappeared and he became serious.

"Mr. Jinnah, I do not want to listen to any condition. It is better if you can say whatever you want without any condition," he said in a firm tone.

Jinnah was stunned. For a while he did not know how to react. But he would not give up easily.

"It is true that the Muslims are a minority in the country. Nevertheless, the Muslims ruled India for eight hundred years, before the arrival of the British," Jinnah said.

Mountbatten was astonished. What was Jinnah saying? Mountbatten knew the Indian history. He wondered what Jinnah's intention could be in invoking the history.

Jinnah noticed the change in the facial expression of Mountbatten. He realized that the Viceroy could not understand the context of his statement. He thought his approach was right. Then he went on talking enthusiastically for quite sometime.

"The root cause of all the problems is the Hindu communalism," said Fatima joining the conversation, "The Hindus are so extreme and violent that no peace loving person can ever live with them. They do not understand how to co-exist."

"Madam Fatima," Lady Edwina responded, "This morning I visited the Lady Irwin College in Delhi. This women's college is functioning in a very efficient and harmonious environment. The class I visited has sixteen girls, fourteen Hindu girls and two Muslim girls. Yet, the girls unanimously elected a Muslim girl as their class representative."

"You do not be deceived by this," Fatima retorted, "This is a policy of the Hindus giving a little consideration to the Muslims so that they always remain under their thumb."

"If that is so," Lady Edwina continued the argument, "the Hindu girls could have tormented the two Muslim girls. Nothing of that sort happened. Instead they elected a Muslim girl as their class representative. We must look for an answer to this."

"The answer is clear," said Fatima, "We have not been able to reach out to colleges to tell the truth. And once we tell the Muslims students about the Hindu mindset this will not happen again."

Lady Edwina was surprised and shocked by this line of thinking of Fatima. The Viceroy was quietly listening to their conversation.

When the guests finally left, Mountbatten turned to his wife and said,

"Oh my God! It is impossible to meet this man twice in a day. It is difficult to understand what he wants to say and what is going on in his mind."

"I have never seen a more fanatic person with such prejudice towards the Hindus than this woman," Edwina expressed her opinion.

The Viceroy and Jinnah met again after a week.

"Mr. Jinnah," said the Viceroy beginning the conversation, "The partition of the country is not a solution. I do not accept the partition."

"There is no other way out," Jinnah said in an aggressive tone, "We cannot trust the Hindus any more. We have had enough experience. If the British government transfers power without partition, we have nowhere to go. We will have to live at the mercy of the Hindus."

"That won't happen. This is your imaginary fear. Jawaharlal Nehru and his colleagues are noble men. They cannot allow that to happen."

"You are saying this, but I have a bitter experience of Nehru. It was Nehru who had blocked our power sharing formula in 1938-39. The only solution to the communal problem is creation of a viable Pakistan. You must give the provinces of Punjab, Sindh, Bengal, Assam and North West Frontier and a corridor connecting the East and the West Pakistan."

"Look! Mr. Jinnah, you are right. What you are saying is that the majority will rule over the minority and that you are against it. Is that right?"

"Yes, you understood rightly."

"Good. You know there are many districts in Punjab and Bengal having the mixed population of the Hindus and the Muslims. If we create Pakistan, as per the principle propounded by you, we have to divide Punjab and Bengal. You cannot include the Hindus of these districts in Pakistan," Mountbatten said with a cool determination.

Jinnah was stunned. He realised that this astute statesman was using his own argument against him. He understood that the Viceroy was using the same principle, which he had used for demanding Pakistan, for dividing Punjab and Bengal.

"I want you to understand one thing clearly," said Jinnah, "There is no such thing as Punjab or Bengal. These two provinces have a separate nationality. Every person living in these provinces is a Punjabi or a Bengalee first before he is a Hindu or a Muslim. These provinces which have a common cultural heritage cannot be divided. If they are divided, it will lead to more trouble and bloodshed."

"You are right, Mr. Jinnah. I agree with you," Mountbatten said cautiously.

Jinnah did not expect this. He was surprised that the Viceroy accepted his argument.

"Thank you," said Jinnah, "I am happy, you agree with me."

"Any understanding person must accept the truth," said Mountbatten. "You have just said that the people in these provinces are the Punjabis or the Bengalis first before they are the Hindus or the Muslims. But first they are the Indians. That being so, India can never be divided."

The Viceroy's argument stumped Jinnah. During his career spanning forty years, he as a public figures played the game of politics with many Viceroys, Prime Ministers, statesmen and politicians. But he had never been defeated as decisively as by Mountbatten today.

"I think you have not understood me, let me clarify ..."

Mountbatten knew what Jinnah was going to say. He would repeat the same thing in a different way. To stop him from doing so, he said,

"Look, Mr. Jinnah. You want to divide the country!"

"Yes, that is the only solution."

"Then, the same principle that is used to divide the country shall be applied to divide Punjab and Bengal."

"That means, you want to give a moth eaten Pakistan," Jinnah asked dejected.

"No. In fact, I do not want to give you any Pakistan. I want you to live with freedom in undivided India."

"No, this is not possible. I will accept Pakistan in any form rather than living with atrocities meted out by the Hindus."

The talks ended. Both of them had their own reason to feel satisfied in a way. Jinnah was satisfied that the Viceroy had accepted in principle the creation of Pakistan, but he was stung by the fact that the Viceroy used the same principle to counter him. Mountbatten felt satisfied that he made Jinnah to realise how weak the premise for his demand for Pakistan had been.

There were heated arguments and debates over the issue of partition of the country. There was a serious concern about the security of the Hindus who might be left behind in Pakistan and the Muslims living in India. There was an apprehension that the majority communities in both these countries would not be able to forget the acrimony and would have to live forever with hatred and hostility. It was doubtful whether these two countries would be able to live without enmity. All these apprehensions were natural. But there seemed to be no other way out going by the hostility and violence unleashed in the country.

As the days passed by, Jinnah was quite agonized over the issue. It was impossible that the Muslims in India would migrate *en masse* to Pakistan. Even after the partition about forty million Muslims would still remain in India. Of the sixty million Muslims who would form Pakistan, about thirty million alone would remain in the divided Bengal. Another fifteen million Muslims would live in the divided Punjab. The other regions of Pakistan would be sparsely populated. If all the forty million Muslims in India decide to migrate, Pakistan would not be able to offer even a single room to each one of them. Pakistan would not be able to bear the economic burden of resettling them. Taking all this into account, Jinnah released a public statement,

"I assure the minorities in Pakistan, particularly the Hindus, that they would be treated even better than the Muslims. The Hindus in Pakistan will be equal citizens and there would be no masters or servants. There won't be any problem of majority or minority."

The day when this statement was published in the newspapers, Gandhi made a reference to it in his prayer meeting at Patiala. Welcoming the statement, he drew a new inference from it,

"If Jinnah *Sahib* assures that Pakistan will treat the Hindus better than the Muslims, why cannot he adopt the same principle in India? If that happens, the entire country will welcome it and then India itself will become Pakistan. Then the question of dividing the country shall not arise."

65

Noakhali, riots in Bihar, Mountbatten's suggestion for joint appeal for peace, Gandhi's consent, Jinnah in a dilemma, Viceroy-Gandhi on transfer of power, Jinnah's reaction, Churchill's advice to Mountbatten on the partition

The Muslims were caught unawares by the retaliation of the Hindus in Calcutta, following the communal riots. The Muslims suffered heavily. They did not expect this. They thought that the Hindus would not be able to retaliate as the Suharawardy government was on their side and that the Muslims would not have any problem of security. The Muslims wanted to avenge this and Noakhali, a predominantly Muslim township, became a soft target. The Hindus were attacked brutally. There were no villages of the Hindus nearby to seek shelter. The news of the attacks on the hapless people shocked the country. It spread like a wild fire and the Hindus in Bihar retaliated against the Muslims, resulting in communal riots on a large scale. Jawaharlal Nehru, the head of the interim government, was deeply grieved by the developments. He rushed to Patna and gave a stern warning that if the riots did not stop the government would not hesitate in firing at the rioters and even bombarding them. The riots were quelled with the might of the security forces. Many innocent Muslims shed their blood and the situation was quite tense. The atmosphere was further vitiated by the tales of woes narrated by the Hindus who fled to Bihar from Calcutta and Noakhali. Besides, the news of atrocities committed against the women in Naokhali and the forceful conversion of the Hindus had spread like the lava of an erupted volcano. Anytime it could spread across the country. The communal upsurge was spreading in other parts of the country.

The Congress and the Muslim League represented ninety nine per cent of the people in the country. The Muslim League had the support of ninety per cent Muslims and Jinnah remained their undisputed leader. Mountbatten realized this. He thought that the situation could be brought under control if the Congress and the Muslim League issued a joint statement appealing to the people to maintain peace. He felt it appropriate to moot the idea first with Jinnah. The next day when Jinnah came to meet him, he asked him, "Mr. Jinnah, will you issue a joint statement with the Congress appealing to the people to maintain peace and not to resort to violence as a means to achieve a political end?"

Jinnah thought for a moment. He doubted whether the Viceroy was acting with an ulterior motive. He wondered whether it was a ploy by Gandhi or Nehru to use the Viceroy as a pawn.

"The violence is always condemnable and the people who instigate violence are the criminals. The innocent people shed their blood. This is what I have always said in my speeches." said Jinnah.

The Viceroy understood. Jinnah was evading the question and buying time. The Viceroy wanted the appeal to be issued so that it could have a deterrent effect. He said, "Mr. Jinnah, we know all that. I just want to know whether you would agree to issue the joint appeal."

"The way the violence is spreading is regrettable," Jinnah stretched the issue. "The attacks on the Muslims in Bihar are condemnable. Any civilized government ought to curb the violence. The Congress government in Bihar did nothing to curb the violence."

Mountbatten stared at him. Jinnah condemned the violence in Bihar, but conveniently forgot that the seeds of the violence were sown in the communal riots of Calcutta and Naokhali. Mountbatten wondered how the Muslims had accepted the leadership of such a man.

"Look, Mr. Jinnah, if you think issuing a joint appeal is not in your interest, then forget it. All that I want to know at this moment is whether you would agree to issue the joint appeal. Please give me a clear answer." Jinnah realised that now he had no other option. He said, "The idea of a joint appeal is good. I agree with your idea." Then, the Viceroy showed him the draft of the appeal. He asked Jinnah that if he had no objection, he could sign it as the President of the Muslim League. He assured him that he would obtain the signature on it of Acharya Kripalani, the President of the Congress.

Jinnah was under the impression that the joint appeal would be signed by him and Gandhi. He wanted to show that he considered only Gandhi as his equal. It would also demonstrate that Jinnah represented the Muslims and Gandhi the Hindus. Jinnah always maintained that the Congress and Gandhi had represented only the Hindus and the joint appeal could prove that. But if Kripalani signed the joint appeal, it would disprove his illusion once and for all that he was equal to Gandhi. He was not prepared to accept that. He told the Viceroy in unequivocal terms,"Though Kripalani might be the Congress President, I do not consider him as a man of any influence. If any person other than Gandhi signs the joint appeal, I refuse to be a party to it."

The Viceroy was bent on getting the appeal issued. The next day Gandhi was leaving for Patna. Once he reached there and moved among the victims of the communal riots, lot of time would be wasted in contacting him. He immediately called Gandhi for a meeting. Gandhi read the draft of the appeal. He was in its favour. He suggested a couple minor changes and then signed the appeal. While handing over the signed appeal to the Viceroy, he said,

"I appreciate your gesture. This appeal is necessary. However, just as Mr. Jinnah signed the appeal as the President of the Muslim League, it is but natural and legitimate that his counterpart Acharya Kripalani, President of the Congress, should also sign the appeal. Since Mr. Jinnah insisted on my signature, I have signed the appeal. But as a matter of legitimacy, you must also obtain the signature of Kripalani on it," Gandhi paused for a moment and then said, "You know, I am not even an ordinary member of the Congress. I have no right to speak on its behalf. You and Quaid-e-Azam must understand the position."

The Viceroy knew that Gandhi was right. But Jinnah was almost fanatical in insisting on Gandhi's signature. It was Jinnah who said during his parleys with Gandhi two years ago that Gandhi had no right to speak on behalf of the Congress as he was not its member. Now the same Jinnah was insisting on Gandhi's signature on behalf of the Congress. Gandhi signed the appeal, but Jinnah was not willing to accept the signature of Kripalani as the Congress President. He was not prepared to concede that Kripalani was his equal. Thus the appeal was delayed.

The Viceroy sent a cable to Gandhi in Patna asking him not to insist on Kripalani's signature. In reply, Gandhi said that whatever the Viceroy and Nehru together could decide would be acceptable to him. When Nehru came to know about it, he became furious. He asked the Viceroy how, as a matter of principle, could such a joint appeal be issued without the signature of the Congress President? The Viceroy had no answer to it. He said, "Jinnah and logic do not go together. He is his own counsellor. He does not listen to anyone. Please do not insist on Kripalani's signature. The innocent people are shedding blood, let us stop it. This is not a political issue, it is a question of humanity."

Nehru did not make an issue of it. The Viceroy obtained Jinnah's signature and the joint appeal was released. The newspaper *The Dawn* in its editorial commented that the fact that the appeal was signed by Gandhi as the representative of the Hindus and Jinnah as the representative of the Muslims meant that both the communities were different nations. The Congress accepted that the Muslims were a separate nationality. Now the only option was to accept the Muslim League's demand for a separate Pakistan.

*

Viceroy Mountbatten worked at a breakneck speed. The British government gave him the deadline of June 1948 for granting independence to India. The Viceroy set March 1948 as his deadline. The Communal violence in the country took a dangerous turn and the leaders were worn out due to long years of struggle. An astute Mountbatten gauged the mood of the leaders. The experience in the interim government made the Congress leaders realize that the Muslim League was bent upon wrecking the government from within. They now realized that it would not be possible to keep India united. Jinnah was convinced that his dream of forming Pakistan would be realised soon. Mountbatten declared that if a solution was not found to the vexed problem through a consensus, he would go ahead with his own solution and that would not be reversed. He too realized that the partition of the country was the only solution.

However, before proceeding with his plan, Mountbatten wanted to meet Gandhi to find out his reaction. If Gandhi did not agree with his plan, the Congress leaders would not endorse his plan of partitioning the country. Even if the Congress agreed to partition, Gandhi alone could mobilize the people of the entire country to oppose the partition. That could create another more serious problem than the one sought to be resolved. Therefore, it was important to convince Gandhi about the partition of the country.

When Gandhi learnt that the Viceroy was planning to divide the country into two independent nations and hand over the power to them, he said, "The main issue is the transfer of power. I understand that now the British government should not have any problem on that."

"You have understood rightly," said Mountbatten, "I will be happy if India remains united. But I am unable to decide whom to hand over the power in united India. The distrust between the Congress and the Muslim League is making my task difficult."

"I will offer you the solution," said Gandhi. "You invite Jinnah to form the government of the united India. Let Jinnah be the Prime Minister. I will persuade the Congress to accept this," Gandhi put forth a startling proposal.

Mountbatten, a seasoned British diplomat, was stunned for a moment. What was Gandhi saying? If the Congress was ready to accept this, why did it carry out the struggle for independence for so many years?

Mountbatten conveyed Gandhi's proposal to Jinnah. He thought it would be better to avoid the partition of India in this way. The partition would create serious problems with regard to the division of the power, the assets and the army. And dividing the army would mean destroying its discipline and strength. Moreover, the security of innocent people would be endangered. Gandhi's amazing proposal offered solution to all these problems.

Jinnah was not surprised a bit by this. Even if he became the Prime Minister of India, it would not make a difference to the fact that the Muslims were a minority. The animosity and distrust would not disappear overnight. Even if the British government handed over the complete power, Jinnah knew that he could live hardly for a few months more. And once the British government left India, Jinnah had no doubt, the Congress would get a vote of confidence passed against him by virtue of its majority in the Central Assembly and wrest the power from him. Jinnah thought that Gandhi must have kept this option in mind when made the proposal. He always thought that Gandhi was a cunning fox. He felt that Gandhi had an ulterior motive to entrap the entire Muslim community. Until now, he was single handedly combating Gandhi, the Congress and the British government on behalf of the Muslims. He knew that this was heading nowhere. Now it was a matter of time that either he would ultimately succeed in his efforts or fail. There was no other Muslim leader of his stature to succeed him. He wrote to the Viceroy rejecting Gandhi's proposal, "The Muslims will not accept anything short of an independent and sovereign Pakistan. The stage of discussion and compromise is over long back. Now the only option is partition."

The Viceroy considered the pros and cons of the partition. He worked out a plan for partition. Before the plan was sent for approval of His Majesty's Government in Britain, it was necessary to get it approved by the Congress and the Muslim League. Mountbatten showed his plan first to Jawaharlal Nehru. He studied the plan. He was shocked.

"I am shaken," he said, "I do not dare to imagine the consequences of such a partition. Agreeing with this plan is to concede that our struggle is futile. Even after the partition, there is no guarantee that the two countries will live in peace and harmony. If this is the only solution, I will ask my colleagues to accept it as the most tragic chapter of our history."

When Jinnah received a copy of the plan, he met Mountbatten and expressed his dissatisfaction.

"Your proposal to divide Punjab and Bengal is very dangerous. You have ignored the history, the economy, the geography, the culture and the language. You have considered only the religion and the race. If this is the criterion for dividing, it should be applied in every province of the country."

A stunned Mountbatten said,

"Mr. Jinnah, do you understand what you are saying. We cannot divide every district, village and street."

"Then, please note that we will never accept Bengal without Calcutta and Punjab without Lahore."

"And what if Calcutta is not given to East Pakistan!"

"Then it should remain as a free port city like Hong Kong. But it should never be handed over to India," Jinnah said firmly, "Besides, you must give us a corridor linking the East Pakistan with the West Pakistan."

"Mr. Jinnah, this demand is very dangerous. If the East Pakistan is linked with the West Pakistan in this way, India will be further divided into two parts. Have you thought of it?"

"That is India's problem. It is for India to solve it," said Jinnah.

After listening to both the sides and making some modifications, Mountbatten prepared a final plan. The British Prime Minister Attlee approved the plan. Churchill, the leader of the opposition, advised Mountbatten—"You must pressurise both the parties. Withdraw all the British officials from the government. Hand over the soldiers without the British commanders. Ask them how they will protect India and Pakistan and how they will govern them. Ask Jinnah how long Pakistan will survive once the British government withdraws its support. Tell him if he is adamant for Pakistan only, he will not get anything more than this."

Considering all this, the Viceroy convened an all party meeting on 2nd June, 1947 to get the consent to his plan for the partition of India. Liaquat Ali Khan and Abdul Nishtar joined Jinnah. Jawaharlal Nehru, Sardar Patel and Acharya Kripalani represented the Congress. And Sardar Baldev Singh represented the Sikhs.

66

Viceroy's house—partition plan, Mountbatten's advice to Jinnah, Jinnah-Viceroy late night talks, Jinnah's nod for the partition, Jinnah-Nehru-Mountbatten broadcast on All India Radio, Punjab, Bengal, North West Frontier Province on partition, date for independence

Though the atmosphere at the Viceroy's House at New Delhi was normal, any keen observer could sense a quiet tense situation. In the North Court of the vast hall, the Viceroy's personal staff were seen making some special arrangements. After the formal greetings with the leaders of the Congress and the Muslim League, the Viceroy presented the final plan for the partition of the country, as if he was opening a Pandora's box. He clarified the intricacies of the plan for two hours and then said,

"Gentlemen, I know the gravity of the decision that we are about to make. Both His Majesty's Government and the opposition have consented to the plan. Now I do not like any delay in its implementation. I want your consent to the plan by midnight today. If that does not happen, the British government will hand over the power to whichever party consents and leave India."

Mountbatten did not want to give any chance to these leaders to discuss the plan in his presence. He feared that such a discussion would sideline the main issue and result in a verbal duel. To avoid that situation, he gave them the time till midnight. He declared that the meeting was over. When all the leaders got up with grave face without uttering a word, Mountbatten turned to Jinnah and requested him to wait for a while. Jinnah looked at his colleagues, Liaquat and Nishtar. The Viceroy understanding Jinnah's dilemma said to them, "Both of you may leave. Mr. Jinnah will join you a little later."

Mountbatten conveyed to Jinnah the message of Churchill. Jinnah had a great support in Churchill. Now it was clear to him that if he did not accept Pakistan offered to him, he would lose even the support of the opposition in the British Parliament. Chruchill was no friend of India, the League or Jinnah. The British Empire and the British interest were of utmost importance to him. In the changed scenario, Jinnah had to decide for himself. When a crestfallen and dejected Jinnah turned back, Mountbatten said quietly to him, as a matter of warning, "Mr. Jinnah, you must remember one thing clearly that though Gandhi is called the *Mahatma* and may look like a saint, he can become a Trotsky when the situation demands. Donot forget that."

Jinnah became immobile. What was the Viceroy saying? What was the motive of his warning? The Viceroy accompanied him to the door. His ADC escorted Jinnah to his car.

Some fifteen years ago, when a student in London Rehmat Ali Chaudhari presented a political map of Pakistan, Jinnah had dismissed it as the dream of a student. When the poet Mohammed Iqbal presented his vision of Pakistan, Jinnah had called it a poet's fantasy. Now the British government was presenting him the same Pakistan. Jinnah himself had described the idea of Pakistan as a political stunt. He never imagined that the stunt could become a reality. When he demanded an independent and sovereign Pakistan at the Lahore session of the Muslim League, seven years ago, he had no idea about its shape. The people who then supported Pakistan had interpreted it in the manner that suited them. Jinnah transcended all that and persisted with his demand for Pakistan with the Congress and the British government in order to derive the maximum political mileage. His main objective was to ensure that Gandhi and the Congress accepted him as the sole leader of the Muslims in the country. Now he got choked up.

The Viceroy fixed the deadline. But Jinnah was vacillating and wanted to buy time. If the Congress rejected the plan, his task would become easy. He had some superficial discussions with his colleagues in Delhi. But they left the final decision to him. It was a bitter pill to swallow that Punjab and Bengal would be divided if they wanted Pakistan. If these provinces were divided, it would lead to violent communal clashes. The Muslims in these provinces might even revolt against the leadership of Jinnah.

The time was running out. Jinnah's colleagues waited for his reaction. They could not decide till ten thirty in the night. Hardly any time was left for the deadline given by the Viceroy. Jinnah felt that time had conspired against him. He reached the Viceroy's House alone at eleven in the night. He could see the lights in the Viceroy's office and his study room.

The Viceroy greeted Jinnah with a grave face. He was expecting him. He had already received the consent of the Congress. To Jinnah who converted successfully the negativity into an instrument of political success until now, this was the most testing time. He did not have the habit of consenting to anything, but this time he was in a position to disagree. He knew that the Viceroy would not accept anything other than 'yes' or 'no.' Yet he wanted to make a last attempt.

"Mr. Jinnah, hope you have brought the letter of consent from the Muslim League," the Viceroy enquired cautiously.

"Your Excellency, you know that the Muslim League is an organisation that believes in the democratic method. It can be decided by a majority vote only after the matter is discussed in its Working Committee."

Mountbatten gave a mischievous smile. He looked at Jinnah and then said, "I know what is a democratic method. You know better than me what a democratic method means to the Muslim League. Please do not try to jeopardise the plan at the last moment."

"Even if I want, I cannot give a written consent immediately, without the consent of the Working Committee of the League. And I need at least ten days to convene the meeting of the Working Committee."

"Ten days!" asked, a surprised Mountbatten. He looked at the clock on the wall and then said sternly, "Look! you do not have even ten minutes. You have got your Pakistan. I know this is not what you wanted. I have received the consent of the Congress. It is conditional that if you do not give your consent by the midnight today it would withdraw the consent. Think of the terrible consequences, if that happens."

"But... but I am not the Muslim League. How can I give a written consent on its behalf?" Jinnah at last attempted to stall.

Mountbatten gave yet another mischievous smile. Suppressing the smile he said,

"Mr. Jinnah, do not tell me. You may fool the whole world but not me. I know what the Muslim League is."

There was an eerie silence in the room for a moment. The Viceroy took a deep breath and said, "Mr. Jinnah I want to tell you something. I understand your problem is that of giving a written consent. I know that you personally accept the plan."

Jinnah's face lit up with a glimpse of hope. He said somewhat enthusiastically,

"Your Excellency has understood me properly. My problem is that of giving a written consent."

"Then I would suggest a solution that would solve our problem."

Jinnah was curious.

"When we meet tomorrow morning, I would say that the Congress had accepted the plan with some reservations and that I would satisfy the Congress. Then I would say that I had a long and candid discussion with Mr. Jinnah last night and that he had personally consented to the plan and that he would obtain the consent of the League shortly."

Jinnah was stunned. What was the Viceroy saying? The Viceroy continued, "Then I will turn to you. You may not say anything. But just nod your head to show that you agree with me. But remember that if you do not give the gesture of agreement everything will collapse. And you will never get anything again. Pakistan will be aborted before its birth. This is not a threat. This is a prophecy. And if the things do not work out this way, go to hell."

The Viceroy spoke in such a harsh tone that Jinnah could not say anything. His face turned pale. No one ever talked to him before in this manner. When the clock struck twelve, Jinnah walked down the steps quietly with his head bowed.

The next day the things passed off as they had been planned. As decided the previous night, Mountbatten announced at the meeting that he had received the consent of the Congress and that Jinnah had consented on behalf of the Muslim League. He looked at Jinnah who nodded his head reluctantly in agreement. And with that all the parties consented to the partition of the country. It was decided that the news of the partition would be broadcast on the All India Radio that evening and that Mountbatten, Nehru and Jinnah would announce the partition of the country on behalf of their sides. Three of them agreed to read out a common written speech to avoid any misgivings about the partition. It was suggested that Mountbatten would make the announcement in English, Nehru in English and Hindi and Jinnah in Urdu. Nehru accepted the suggestion. But Jinnah could not accept the suggestion. Mountbatten knew that most of the Muslims considered Urdu as their mother tongue, but he did not know that Jinnah could not speak Urdu. He thought that just as Nehru would be able to reach most of the people by speaking in Hindi, Jinnah too would be able to reach his Muslim audience by speaking in Urdu. But Jinnah proved him wrong.

"Your Excellency, I will speak in English on the All India Radio. I am not comfortable in speaking Urdu."

A surprised Mountbatten asked, "But the Muslims don't know English, how will they understand your speech?"

"Those who know English will convey to them," Jinnah answered sarcastically.

The three leaders' speeches were broadcast that evening on the All India Radio. But Jinnah added the words *Pakistan Zindabad* at the end of his speech.

Now began the most difficult task of demarcating the boundaries of the two nations and the division of the assets of India. The Viceroy took swift and effective steps to ensure that the task was completed on time. Separate special committees were set up to do the job. Mountbatten wanted to transfer the power as soon as possible. He remembered 15th August 1945 when he had secured the surrender of Japan during World War II on behalf of the Allied powers. To ensure that the four hundred million people of the Indian subcontinent celebrate that day as a day of victory, he chose 15th August 1947 as the day for transfer of power.

*

No one doubted that Sindh and Baluchistan would remain in Pakistan. It was also certain that Punjab and Bengal would be divided. The elected members of the provincial Assemblies of these two provinces were asked to decide the issue. The Provincial Assemblies of Sindh, Punjab and Bengal could decide by a simple majority whether they wanted to join India or Pakistan . In the eventuality of failing to do so, the Muslim and the non-Muslim members of these Assemblies would decide separately about the issue of dividing the provinces. The Sindh Provincial Assembly voted to join Pakistan. But the people of Punjab and Bengal were not in a position to decide the issue. In Bengal, the arch rivals, the Congress and the Muslim League, joined hands and opposed the division of the province and instead demanded an independent Bengal. Suharawardy and Saratchandra Bose supported the idea of an independent Bengal. Soon most of the political parties in Bengal started supporting the idea. The provincial Muslim League in Bengal appointed a sub-committee of six members to discuss the idea with the Hindu leaders and reach an agreement. They tried to seek Gandhi's support for an independent Bengal. Gandhi advised them to remove the mutual distrust. It was obvious that if the demand for an independent Bengal was conceded the other provinces and the princely states would also raise similar demands and then the situation would be difficult to contain.

The real problem was the North West Frontier Province. Though ninety five per cent of the population in the province consisted of the Muslims, the Congress had the majority in the Assembly. If this province was given the right to determine its future, like Punjab, Bengal and Sindh, there was no doubt that the Assembly of the North West Frontier Province would vote overwhelmingly to join India. Jinnah wanted to avoid this situation at any cost. He knew quite well that if the North West Frontier Province with ninety five per cent Muslim population opted to join India, his two-nation theory would fall flat.

67

Violence in the Frontier Province, Khurshid in Peshawar, Sikh-Muslim marriage, Viceroy's visit to Peshawar, Selling of Jinnah's bungalow in Delhi

Jinnah was determined to merge the North West Frontier Province of three million Pathans with Pakistan at any cost. The Pathans bordering Afghanistan were opposed to the Muslim League and the British government right from the beginning. They developed a close affinity with the neighboring Pathans. The province would be surrounded by Pakistan on its other three fronts. The Pathans were hot headed and fierce warriors. Because of its geographical location, trade and commerce could not develop in the province. Hence theft and looting were the main vocations of the Pathans and they did not consider anything wrong in that. Though they were brave and fearless, they were manipulated and exploited by the selfish and clever political leaders because they were innocent, illiterate and ignorant. They were divided into many groups and clans and their chieftains enjoyed absolute power over them. To them, Islam was what the Mullahs, the Maulvis and the Imams used to interprete. The non-violence was never a creed for the Muslims. Since the *Quran* propagated violence, the Pathans had practiced violence. However, because of the influence of Gandhi, Badshah Khan, known as the Frontier Gandhi, had succeeded in spreading the message of non-violence among them. He made them to support the Congress. They were called *Khudai Khidmatgaars*[1] who wore the red shirts. The Muslim League tried to eliminate the influence of Frontier Gandhi, but failed. The Congress won both the 1937 and the 1946 elections in the province. Badshah Khan's younger brother Dr. Khan Sahib formed the Congress governments.

In such a situation, if the North West Frontier Province was given the right to decide its future, like the provinces of Sindh, Punjab and Bengal, the heart of Pakistan could remain in India. The divided Punjab would cut off the North West Frontier Province completely from India. If the Gurdaspur district in Punjab went to Pakistan after the partition, India would not have any access to the North West Frontier Province and the Kashmir. Jinnah made all these clever calculations.

Jinnah did not want to give the North West Frontier Province the right to decide its future. As a seasoned lawyer, he had worked out a plan. The governor of the province could dismiss the Congress government and order fresh elections. But the Congress had a clear majority in the assembly. Hence it was not possible to dismiss the government. If it was proved that the government had lost the trust of the people and failed to maintain the law and order, the governor could have an excuse to dismiss the Congress government. There was a way out. Though the Muslim League did not have much influence in the province, the leader of the Muslim League in the province, Khan Aurangzeb and Iskandar Mirza could prove useful. Jinnah had used Mirza's services earlier in instigating the *jihad* in the province with the financial assistance of the Nawab of Bhopal. Jinnah now once again decided to utilize the services of these two to engineer communal riots, looting and arson and organise anti-government protests in the province.

A Punjab army officer called Major Khurshid was dismissed from the army on the charge of misconduct. Now he was active in the Muslim League politics. With his vast experience in the army, he could be useful in engineering communal riots and subversive activities. Jinnah decided to send him to the North West Frontier Province to assist Iskandar Mirza and Khan Aurangzeb. Major Khursid, in his first public address at Peshawar said, "The Hindu Congress cannot hold us hostage. We must eliminate these maligned Hindu leaders and the treacherous Muslims, who work as their agents, from our path forever. The Pathans are brave warriors. No one can stop these warriors from taking to arms. You mark my words, Islam would never emerge victorious unless we destroy these enemies."

Major Khurshid knew that if a Pathan was murdered and the blame was shifted to another group, they would resort to mass killings and shed blood. Taking full advantage of their psyche, he engineered mass murders and riots. Soon the entire province was engulfed into communal violence and lawlessness.

Fortunately for Jinnah, the governor of the North West Frontier Province was a bitter opponent of the Congress government. Both the Khan brothers were opposed to the British government. Since the days of the East India Company, Afghanistan did not have a good relation with the British government. The North West Frontier Province was a part of Afghanistan. But the British government wrested its control from Afghanistan many a time. From the point of Pakistan too, the Pathans were more close to Afganaistan, than to the Muslims of Sindh and Punjab. As per the compromise reached between the British government and Afghanistan in the nineteenth century, the Durand Line was accepted as the international border and the North West Frontier Province became a part of India. Jinnah was now scheming to change that.

The time was running out. The work had to be done with a lightning speed. The hired Mullahs and the Maulvis instigated the Pathans. They unleashed the communal campaign of hatred and violence. They spread the fear that Islam was in danger and now the time had come for the people to choose between the temple and the mosque. The fear gripped the people everywhere. The *agent provocateurs* carried out the campaign that Badshah Khan and his brother were the agents of the Hindus and that they were using the poor and the illiterate Pathans as their pawns. In the meantime, an incident occurred which was fully exploited by the Muslim League to its advantage.

In an area called Kohat near Peshawar, a Muslim girl and a Sikh youth eloped and got married. The Muslim League instigated the Pathans that the Sikh youth had abducted the Muslim girl and forcefully married her. The furious Pathans resorted to looting and set the houses of the Hindus and the Sikhs on fire and burnt and destroyed the government property. The police caught hold of the young couple and produced them before a British magistrate. The girl in an affirmed affidavit said before the magistrate that she had voluntarily agreed to marry the Sikh youth and that he was her husband and that she would like to live with him. It was a slap on the orthodox Muslims. The magistrate had no option but to set the couple free. This was something which was unbearable and unacceptable to the Muslim League and their supporters.

The next day, an armed mob entered the house of the Sikh youth. They killed the young man and took away his wife forcefully. The matter did not end there. The armed men marched all over Kohat and raised the religious slogans. They burnt the houses of the Hindus and the Sikhs, killed the men and the children, abducted the women and raped them. The Hindus and the Sikhs could not retaliate as they constituted just five per cent of the population. They fled in order to save their lives, leaving everything behind.

The communal violence spread like a wildfire. Demonstrations were held in Peshawar, Quetta and other cities and the government properties were damaged. The Khan Sahib government got the demonstrators and their leaders arrested and put them in jail. The religious extremists called them *Jihadis.* They succeeded in playing with the mob psychology by exploiting the illiterate Pathans.

This was a golden opportunity for Jinnah. He demanded the dismissal of the Congress government on the ground that it had lost the trust of the people and failed to protect them. It was difficult for Viceroy Lord Mountbatten to accept the demand. He thought merging of the province with Pakistan was the only solution. In a meeting with Nehru, the Viceroy told him that the North West Frontier Province would be cut off from India and that it would be difficult to protect the Hindus there. He also told Jinnah that the province would be a big burden to Pakistan. The province did not contribute a single rupee to the national exchequer, yet the Central government had to spend thirty five million rupees a year on it. The reports of the communal violence and the riots from the province were very disturbing. In order to study the situation personally, Mountbatten decided to visit the province.

The stage was set for the visit of the Viceroy. Jinnah managed to assemble thousands of Pathans before the Viceroy. Lady Mountbatten knowing their ferocious nature, became apprehensive on seeing thousands of armed men. But

Jinnah assuring her said, "The supporters of the Muslim League are not violent people. They are armed with weapons as it is a part of their tradition. The news of their violence reported in the newspapers is planted by the Congress. You don't worry. No Pathan will ever resort to violence without a reason."

Viceroy Mountbatten holding the hand of Lady Mountbatten stood on a tall wall and greeted the crowd. Jinnah proved right. The crowd responded enthusiastically with a huge applause. They raised slogans against the Congress government of Khan Sahib. "Your Excellency," Jinnah addressed the Viceroy triumphantly, "You have witnessed how Khan Sahib has lost the people's trust. You cannot allow the government that lost the people's trust to continue. The government should be dismissed and fresh elections should be held immediately."

An astute statesman Mountbatten did not react immediately. But he had expressed reservation about the Khan Sahib government. He was thinking from a different angle. In the provincial assembly, out of 50 members, 12 were Hindu members who supported the Congress. That meant five per cent Hindus had twenty five per cent representation in the assembly. The country was being partitioned on the basis of religion. The Viceroy felt that this disproportionate representation of the Hindus would disturb the communal balance. Yet, if the government elected only a year ago was dismissed due to the demonstrations on the streets other provinces could make similar demands.

When Nehru came to know about Mountbatten's reservation about Khan Sahib's government in the North West Frontier Province, he strongly protested to him. It was a matter of prestige for the Congress. Mountbatten proposed that since the non-Hindus were a majority in the province, a plebiscite should be held to ascertain the people's choice whether they wanted to join India or Pakistan. Nehru agreed to that to avoid the dismissal of the Khan Sahib government.

When Badshah Khan came to know about the plebiscite, he became furious. If the other provincial assemblies could decide the future of their provinces, why should there be a different norm for his province? It was only a year ago that the Pathans of the province had elected a Congress government by rejecting the Muslim League's demand for Pakistan. Badshah Khan was not willing to accept the demand for plebiscite of the hired goons who incited the violence and instigated the innocent Pathans. He demanded that if a plebiscite had to be held, the people must be given the right to choose an independent Pakhtunistan. But it was too late to make such a demand. Besides, if the demand was conceded, similar choice should also be given to the provinces of Sindh, Punjab and Bengal. And in that eventuality, the princely states would exercise their right to remain independent of India and Pakistan, leading to balkanisation of India into many independent states.

Finally, it was decided to hold a plebiscite in the North West Frontier Province. The Congress accepted this to avoid the dismissal of its government in the province. Badshah Khan, popularly known as Frontier Gandhi, who spent his entire life preaching non-violence, reacted with great anguish, "Now the Congress has thrown us to the wolves." Moulana Azad suggested to Badshah Khan to "join the Muslim League." For the first time in his life, a stout, six feet and three inches tall, Frontier Gandhi had tears in his eyes.

Jinnah had succeeded in his game.

*

Though his health was deteriorating day-by-day, Jinnah was determined to fight on two fronts. On the one hand he wanted to extract the maximum mileage politically and on the other he was making arrangements to safeguard his huge wealth and property. His houses worth millions of rupees, his investments in stock market and his tea gardens in Dehradun—all this would go to the new Indian government. Therefore, he wanted to dispose of them. He was specially attached to the Jinnah House on the Mount Pleasant Road in Bombay. However, instead of being sentimental, a practical Jinnah wanted to sell the House at a high price. A potential buyer offered him 1.8 million rupees for the House. But Jinnah thought that the House should fetch him at least 2 million rupees. Hence the Jinnah House remained unsold. He appointed M/s Fulchand Gulabchand Sanghvi and M/s. Devkaran Nanji & Company as his advisors on other matters. As per their advice, he sold all his shares invested in the stock market. He sold the tea gardens in Dehradun for a million rupees. His Mayfair building on the Gibbs Road in Bombay was also sold.

The bungalow at 10, Aurangzeb Road, Delhi, which he had bought from a Marwari businessman called Lala Chunnumal a few years ago, was sold to another Marwari business man Ramakrishna Dalmia for two lakhs rupees. It was a quirk of fate that Dalmia took the possession of the bungalow before Jinnah left for Pakistan for good. Not only that, he got the entire bungalow washed with the sacred water from the holy river Ganges. As Delhi was situated on the banks of the river Yamuna, he brought the special water tanks filled with the sacred water from the holy river Ganges. Every corner of the bungalow was 'purified' with the sacred water. The flag of the Muslim League hoisted on the bungalow was replaced by the flag of an extremist Hindu organisation associated with the movement that demanded the ban on cow slaughter.

Perhaps Jinnah so busy in Delhi those days, might have had the occasion to pass through the Aurangzeb Road.

NOTE

1. Servants of God.

68

Meeting of the Partition Council, Jinnah-Radcliffe, Jinnah's attempt to hold the first meeting of the Pakistan Constituent Assembly in Delhi, Jinnah declares himself to be the Governor-General, Jinnah in the 'Jinnah House'

The Indian history was changing as fast as the batting of an eye lid. The things were happening as expected. The Sindh provincial assembly voted for joining Pakistan. The assemblies of Punjab and Bengal voted for the partition of their provinces. Out of six lakh voters in the North West Frontier Province, two lakh and eighty thousand voted for joining Pakistan. The Congress already declared that it would not participate in the plebiscite. Badshah Khan and his band *Khudai Khidmatgaars* also boycotted the plebiscite as it did not give them the third option to vote for an independent Pakhtunistan. Thus Pakistan was born. The Partition Council decided on the delineation of the boundaries of Bengal and Punjab.

"Gentlemen, it is indeed difficult to delineate the boundaries," said Mountbatten presenting a picture of the reality, "But there is no escape. I propose to appoint a Boundary Commission whose decisions shall be binding on all of us. There will be no appeal against its decisions. However, you may work out the modalities of delineation of boundaries."

There was nothing anybody could say on the Viceroy's proposal. The issue was whether to consider a village or an entire district as the basis of delineation. The issue was also whether to consider religion or geography or culture. And finally who should head the Boundary Commission? The person had to be somebody acceptable to all the parties. Mountbatten suggested, "Let us choose a person who had never been associated with the Indian politics. Such a person should be neutral and able to do the job without any prejudice."

Some names were suggested. Jinnah suggested a person. "Your Excellency," he said, "if the Congress agrees we can invite Radcliffe to do the job."

The name of Radcliffe suddenly cropped up. Mountbatten knew this British Barrister quite well. He was a non-controversial person. Mountbatten looked at the Congress leaders especially at Jawaharlal. Nehru had no knowledge of

Radcliffe. He looked at his colleagues. A shrewd Mountbatten realised that the Congress leaders were neither enthusiastic nor opposed to Radcliffe.

"I think we should accept Mr. Jinnah's suggestion. Radcliffe is a distinguished barrister. Since he had never been associated with the Indian politics, we can expect him to be neutral."

Jawaharlal looked at his colleagues for a moment and then said, "We accept Radcliffe."

Jinnah gave a rare smile. Cyrill Radcliffe was a fellow barrister of Jinnah in London during the period 1931-34. He was Jinnah's assistant in the Privy Council and he was considered an authority on international law.

The time was running out. And Jinnah worked out yet another strategy to score over his rivals. He secured Pakistan. Having entrusted the work of delineating the boundaries to his former colleague, he could afford to relax a bit. The study of world history attracted him to two personalities—Mustafa Kemal Pasha of Turkey, known as Kemal Ataturk, and Bismark of Germany. It was the inspiration of Kemal Ataturk that made him to give up the permanent residence in London and return to active politics in India. This return contributed to his greater success than what he had imagined. Now if he could only tread on the footsteps of Bismark...

Bismark had announced the establishment of the German Empire from Paris, the capital of the vanquished France. Jinnah found this very fascinating. Had the flag of the German Empire been hoisted from Berlin or Frankfurt, it would not have created any special impression. But it was indeed fascinating to announce the formation of the German Empire from Versailles, near Paris, from the vanquished France. Jinnah wanted to recreate that spectacular image. The Congress and Gandhi who fought for the independence of India for nearly five decades had been defeated. Though Jinnah could secure Pakistan that he wanted, there was no denying the fact that he had succeeded in vanquishing the Hindus who were thrice the number of the Muslims. Now, if he could proclaim the creation of Pakistan from Delhi... Jinnah was thrilled at the prospect of Gandhi's mortification.

Jinnah could fulfill this if Pakistan's Constituent Assembly convened its first meeting in Delhi. The independence was still two months away. The Constituent Assembly of India already started its work. Therefore, he had an excuse to demand the convening the meeting of the Constituent Assembly of Pakistan. If the meeting was held in Delhi it could be possible to hoist the flag of Pakistan on the Parliament House. Only a clever strategist like Jinnah could think that way. He mooted the idea with the Viceroy.

"Your Excellency, it is a matter of great satisfaction that the work of partition is carried out so rapidly and efficiently."

This was something unusual to Mountbatten. Jinnah was not a person to be satisfied ever.

"I am happy to know that you are satisfied."

"I want to suggest something that will make your task more easy," Jinnah said taking a deep breath, "The work of partition is taken care of. The Constituent Assembly of India started its work of drafting a constitution . In the same way, it would be fair and just if the Constituent Assembly of Pakistan also starts its work."

"What is your suggestion? Be clear."

"Delhi is the capital of undivided India. Therefore, it belongs to both the new nations—India and Pakistan. I want you to give us an opportunity to convene the meeting of the Constituent Assembly of Pakistan in Delhi to start its work. This will give us a chance to deliberate on how to go about to make the constitution for Pakistan before it is formed."

The Viceroy accepted the suggestion, though he could not understand Jinnah's intention behind it. Jinnah's suggestion fitted in his overall scheme of things. The Viceroy responded positively.

Encouraged by the Viceroy's response, Jinnah continued, "And Your Excellency, as you know the Congress and Mr. Gandhi always view any suggestion of the Muslim League with a suspicion. If they come to know that I proposed to convene the meeting of the Constituent Assembly of Pakistan in Delhi, they will turn down the proposal."

"Don't worry, Mr. Jinnah," Mountbatten assured him, "I will suggest that to them."

Jinnah thanked his stars. He wanted to take full advantage of the situation.

"I have another request to make," Jinnah said, "As you know, the partition has created many practical problems. It is important that we receive a fair share of the assets on time. Till such time that these problems are sorted out amicably, I want you to be the supreme commander of both the nations, so that India does not bulldoze us."

Jinnah once again trapped Mountbatten by his jugglery of words. He thought Jinnah wanted him to be the Joint Governor General of both the countries. The Governor General would be a constitutional head of both the countries. He thought the suggestion was good, but it needed endorsement by the Congress. "I will think over it," he said. "I will discuss with Jawaharlal."

The Congress unanimously rejected the suggestion of convening the meeting of the Constituent Assembly of Pakistan in Delhi. The Viceroy met separately Jawaharlal Nehru, Sardar Patel and Rajendra Prasad. All of them rejected the suggestion outrightly. Patel vehemently opposed the idea of hoisting the flag of Pakistan in Delhi. If that happened all their efforts till would become futile.

Then the Viceroy discussed with Nehru the question of appointing of a Governor General for India. Nehru welcomed the idea. He requested Mountbatten to continue as the Governor General of India after the independence. He expressed his willingness to accept him as the Governor General even if Pakistan chose someone else as its Governor General.

When Jinnah learnt that his dream of hoisting the flag of Pakistan in Delhi was aborted, he was disappointed. His clever move of proposing it to the Congress through the Viceroy had failed. He felt that had he put the proposal to Gandhi instead of Mountbatten, it could have been accepted. However, he realised that it was not politically wise to stretch the issue any further. He had no other name in his mind except his own for the post of the Governor General. He believed that if he became the Governor General of Pakistan, his stature would be higher than that of even Gandhi, leave alone Nehru. He had the illusion that the British Prime Minister Attlee, the Governor General of India, Mountbatten and the Governor General of Pakistan, Quaid-e-Azam Muhammad Ali Jinnah were on par in terms of status and power.

When Mountbatten told Jinnah that Nehru requested him to continue as the Governor General of India after the independence, Jinnah opened his cards, "It will be good for us if you continue as the Governor General of India," said Jinnah cautiously. "I want both India and Pakistan to have separate Governor Generals. And then you can be a super Governor General over them."

Mountbatten was perplexed for a moment. The Naval Commander, who had been unfazed by the terrible destruction during the war, was unnerved by Jinnah. He was under the impression until now that Jinnah wanted him to be the joint Governor General of both the countries. His suggestion of a super Governor General was very bewildering, indeed.

"Excuse me, Mr. Jinnah. His Majesty's Government will not accept any proposal for a super Governor General. It is ridiculous," said the Viceroy.

"Then you be the Governor General of India. And I would prefer to be the Governor General of Pakistan."

"What are you saying, Mr. Jinnah?" Mountbatten said astonished, "The Governor General has no power. He is only a symbolic constitutional head of the country. The real power is with the Prime Minister. The Governor General has to simply endorse the decisions of the Prime Minister. You can exercise more power as the Prime Minister of Pakistan."

"No," Jinnah disagreed as was his habit, "That will not happen in Pakistan. There the Prime Minister and the Council of Ministers will carry the orders of the Governor General. It is the Governor General and not the Prime Minister who will make the decisions."

"Mr. Jinnah, you are committing a grave mistake. As the Governor General of India, I will be guided by the advice of the Council of Ministers. I will not be able to safeguard the interest of Pakistan. It is a constitutional position. If you accept me as the Governor General of Pakistan along with that of India, I will be able to maintain a balance between the countries."

"Your Excellency, that is impossible. I will become the Governor General of Pakistan at any cost," Jinnah said firmly.

Once Pakistan was created and he became its Governor General, he would not be able to visit India again, especially Bombay—the city that transformed him from the Barrister to the Quaid-e-Azam. Jinnah knew that he would not be able to move freely in that city again. Of all the cities of India, Bombay was his most favourite. Bombay gave him fame, wealth, wife and the innumerable followers. He wanted to see to his heart's content, his dearest city for the last time. He could not sell his palatial bungalow called the 'Jinnah House' in Bombay. He had so many memories of that House and once he left for Pakistan, it would not be possible for him to come and live in that House again. Jinnah took out some time from his very busy political schedule and reached Bombay.

69

Remembering Ruttie in the 'Jinnah House,' trunks—Ruttie's possessions, visit to Ruttie's grave

The sea waves at the Malabar Hills rose in rhythm and covered the coastline with white foam. Jinnah standing on the terrace of his palatial bungalow on the Mount Pleasant Road was observing the waves. He would be able to see these waves of the Arabian Sea at Karachi, but this terrace would not be there. The movement of the vehicles was less in the evening. Some victorias were seen on the road. Jinnah stood there on the terrace watching them for a long time. It was getting dark. Though the evening was very pleasant, Jinnha's heart was saddened. The feeling of sadness was something unusual for him. He knew that this feeling was not new to him, but he had suppressed it all these years. Now that his goal was achieved, a feeling of sadness suddenly seized him.

Jinnah looked at the garden below and stared at the lush green lawns.

"I feel like walking barefoot on these lawns. It would be an insult to the lawns to walk with the footwear."

Oh! Who said that? Jinnah heard somebody saying that. There was nobody around. The servants and Fatima were all downstairs. The voice sounded very familiar. It was not the voice of Fatima or the servants. The evening breeze was pleasantly cool, yet Jinnah was perspiring and wiping the sweat on his forehead with his handkerchief. It was the voice of Ruttie. It was Ruttie who had said that once.

Jinnah turned back and climbed down the stairs. There was a statue in the passage. He stood there and stroke it very gently. Dina had bought the statue from an art exhibition. He knew very little about art, but he now remembered what Dina had explained about it.

Ruttie had gone for ever and Dina never visited him after her marriage. After spending a few days in the Wadia House, the couple went abroad. The father and the daughter wrote letters sometimes. But Jinnah did not write letters like a father to his daughter. The day Dina left the Jinnah House and got married to a Parsee young man, against her father's wish, she became Mrs. Wadia for Jinnah. And whenever he was required to write to her out of compulsion, he addressed her as Mrs. Wadia. His only child remained Mrs. Wadia to him.

In the same way Dinshaw Petit's daughter Ruttie also became Mrs. Mariam Jinnah. Dinshaw Petit never met his beloved daughter again. Jinnah was not aware of the karmic cycle. And he never heard the maxim that 'you reap, as you sow.' But today he was overwhelmed by a feeling of guilt.

He walked into his bedroom on the first floor and looked around. When he came to live in this House with Ruttie after marriage, it was known as the South Court. The walls were replaced but what about the space in between the walls which was a witness to all that had happened within the four walls of the house. The branch of a tree that stretched into his bedroom was a witness to the beginning of an eighteen year old Ruttie's marital life with a forty three year old Jinnah. He gently caressed the walls rather unwittingly. He was amazed to notice that even the hard walls could be so smooth to touch. How could that be?

It was monsoon in Bombay. The sky which looked clear a short while ago was suddenly engulfed with clouds. It turned totally dark. It started pouring with lightning and sounds of thunder. Jinnah looked out through the window.

"Look! What a pleasant weather! Come, let us go out to the beach and drench."

Jinnah, who had never succumbed to his rivals and remained calm even in very testing times, was shaken. Who said that? It was ages since he had heard those words. It was the first monsoon after Ruttie came here as Mrs. Jinnah.

Jinnah remembered how Ruttie had stubbornly insisted on going out in the rain and how he had lectured her on the diseases which spread in the monsoon. Then he was a healthy person. Now even a drizzle could confine him to bed. He suddenly started coughing. After sometime he lit a cigarette. As he inhaled the smoke, he started coughing again. He took the water from the jug kept on the table.

He suddenly realised that he would not be able to sell the house. It was good that he could not sell the house because it did not fetch the price that he had expected. He wanted to sell it for two million rupees. Its value was more than that. It could be twenty or hundred times more than that. How could it be valued in terms of money?

Jinnah walked down the memory lane. The day Ruttie died, he ordered the servant to remove all her clothes, jewels and accessories and put them in the trunks. The servant had kept them in the store room.

"Bhagwan," a troubled Jinnah called out his servant. Understanding the uneasiness of his master, the servant came running.

"Bring whisky and soda," ordered Jinnah.

This was nothing new to Bhagwan. He brought them immediately. Jinnah mixed the drink and sipped it. Bhagwan felt he should withdrawn from there. As he turned back, Jinnah gulped down his throat the full glass and then said,

"Bhagwan, do you remember? The day when your *memsab* died, you had put all her belongings in the trunks and..."

"*Sahib*, I remember. The trunks are safe. I will keep them with the luggage when you leave for Karachi," said Bhagwan.

"Bring all those trunks here right now," Jinnah ordered as if he had not heard anything what Bhagwan had said.

The otherwise faithful and obedient servant did not move. He was stunned and stared at his master.

"Have not you heard me?" Jinnah retorted, "Bring all those trunks here right now," and then filled the glass again.

Bhagwan went out without uttering a word. Jinnah took the glass in hand and walked around. A file of newspaper clippings and some old books were lying in a nearby cupboard. Jinnah stood by the cupboard and looked at the books. His eyes were focused on a title on the back cover of a faded book that read *Grey Wolf*.

Jinnah had purchased that book during his stay in London. It was the biography of Kemal Ataturk of Turkey. He was thrilled when he had read the book. He had told his teenage daughter, "Dina, you must read this book."

"Daddy, you are a *Grey Wolf*—a hungry hunter wolf," she had teased her father.

Jinnah thought that she was not teasing him. Perhaps an innocent girl unwittingly had uttered the truth. Dina was very naughty and mischievous. He wondered, how she would be behaving now?

"*Sahib*, here are the trunks," Jinnah was startled by the words of Bhagwan. He brought the trunks with the help of some servants. He kept the trunks on the floor and stood attentively. "Bhagwan, you can go now. I do not need you now. Go and sleep," said Jinnah. Bhagwan left the room closing the door behind.

Jinnah stood by the trunks and watched them for a long time. He loosened the tie, unbuttoned the coat and removed the heavy pump shoes. He had to sit on the floor to open the trunks. He was not used to sitting cross legged on the carpeted floor. He managed to sit with some difficulty, but he felt pain in his knees. He suddenly remembered Gandhi. While sitting on the floor, Gandhi was always easy and comfortable. How could he sit that way? But every thing was different for Gandhi. He was an enigma to Jinnah throughout his life. Staring at the trunks Jinnah thought that if only he could understand Gandhi, he would not have been so lonely a person today.

"Meow!"

Jinnah was startled. Where did the cat's voice come from? It was ages since the cats had left the house. Ever since Ruttie left the house to stay in a hotel, the cats were either disposed of or dead. There was no one in the house to take care of them. Ruttie had a lot of pet cats. She used to cuddle them so lovingly. Had any of her cats returned and meowed? Jinnah was stunned for a moment. The sound of meowing cats resounded in his ears for quite sometime.

He opened the three trunks one after another. A musty smell emanated from them. He took a deep breath and then started coughing. He lit the cigarette and took a deep puff and crushed the cigarette butt in a nearby ashtray. It was raining heavily outside. One could hear the whistling of the wind due to the stillness of the night.

He emptied the contents of the trunks. He did not have any knowledge of colours and their shades. He could make no distinction between red and pink. Ruttie had a wide range of clothes of different colours and shades—gowns, sarees, dresses and frocks in velvet and silk. He never observed them so closely. He became nostalgic and remembered how beautiful Ruttie looked in those different clothes. And he held the jewels in hand admiring them for a long time. Then he put them down and went on stroking the clothes for quite sometime.

Then he picked up the photo albums. He looked at the photographs taken after marriage. Ruttie looked like a cute girl and he...

He turned around and looked into the mirror. The image seemed to be of a totally different person. Perhaps Ruttie could not have recognized this image of Jinnah. He closed his eyes and sat there for sometime. Both his feet turned numb. He was unable to move them. The clock showed it was four in the morning. He stood up. He emptied the whisky bottle. He lay on his bed, but could not sleep. He stared at the ceiling. He realized that he could never sell the house. He wondered, how nice it would be if he could one day return to live in the house! Could it ever be possible? The deadline given by Dr. Jaal Patel for his survival was about to expire. Even if the Indian government allowed him to stay here for a few days by virtue of being the Governor General of Pakistan, God would not be so kind.

He got up after sometime and finished the morning rituals. The rain stopped. The sun was rising. The sky was clear. The roads were flooded and one could hear the water gurgling down the drains.

The chauffeur Mohammed Hanif was waiting for him. When Jinnah climbed down the stairs, his eyes betrayed the lack of sleep in the night. The chauffeur opened the back door of the car and Jinnah sat inside quietly. The chauffeur was driving the car towards the main gate. He turned back. Jinnah everyday would tell the driver where to go. But today, he did not tell him anything. The driver stopped the car and asked,

"*Sahib*, where to go?" Jinnah looking out through the window was startled. He said, "Take me to the cemetery."

The car descended the slope of the Malabar Hills. It stopped at the entrance of the cemetery. Jinnah was lost in his thoughts. The driver got down and opened the door of the car. He was worried seeing the reddish eyes of Jinnah. Every day he came out of the car before the driver could open the door. Today he was staring blank even after opening the door.

"*Sahib*!"

Jinnah woke up, as if from a trance. He got down quietly. He adjusted the monocle on his right eye and slowly stepped into the cemetery. There were graves all around. Some graves were covered with fresh flowers. Some people were seen offering prayers in front of the graves.

Jinnah stood before the grave of Ruttie. Years ago when Rutties's dead body was lowered into the grave, he was the first one to put the soil on her delicate and pretty body. He was a heart broken man when her dead body was covered with the soil. And now—

Jinnah hardly ever performed a *Namaaz*. It was difficult for him to bend down on his knees and pray. Today, be bent down on his knees in the dust near the grave of Ruttie, unmindful of his crisp suit. He did not know which verse of the *Quran* to recite as he prayed. He was grieved to realise that this was his last visit to Ruttie's grave. He removed with his two hands the stones and the dirt that covered the grave. He forgot for a while that he was one of the supreme leaders of India. As the first Governor General of Pakistan, he would be on par with the Viceroy of India. Jinnah—a legend for the millions of Muslims—did not even remember his adversary Gandhi at that moment. He put his head on the grave and cried incessantly. The pent up emotions since the last night turned into tears.

His driver who followed him was so shocked to see him crying incessantly that he almost forgot to breathe. He stared with his eyes wide open. In spite of witnessing everything, he thought that some magical force had come this way by mistake.

70

Muslim League's last meeting in Delhi, question-answer, second meeting of the Partition Council, India-UN-Pakistan, Jinnah's arrival in Karachi, Governor General's residence—sports, library radio etc., refugee camps, First meeting of the Pakistan Constituent Assembly in Karachi

As the independence day 15th August, 1947 was approaching, instead of rejoicing, the millions of the Hindus and the Muslims were gripped with fear, anxiety and insecurity. The newspapers reported everyday the news of violence and murders in Punjab and Bengal. The news stirred everyone right from the common man to the Viceroy in Delhi. It was the sign of a bad omen. The people feared that even if 15th August passed off peacefully, its aftermath could be a gory bloodshed.

Jinnah did not succeed in convening the first meeting of the Constituent Assembly of Pakistan in Delhi. It was decided to convene the meeting in Karachi on 11th August. Jinnah, by virtue of being the Governor General of Pakistan, was the ex-officio President of the Constituent Assembly. As the date for the meeting was announced, a strange problem faced by the members of the Muslim League surfaced. Some of them were elected from the provinces which would now merge with India. Whom would they now represent in the Constituent Assembly? As the Muslim League decided to boycott the Constituent Assembly of undivided India, they had been alienated. Even if they migrated to Pakistan, they would have no representation in the Constituent Assembly of Pakistan. Since they supported the cause of Pakistan, their position in the Constituent Assembly of India was not secure either. In order to meet all the Muslim members of the Constituent Assembly for the last time and take a stock of the situation before leaving for Pakistan, Jinnah convened a meeting at the Imperial Hotel in Delhi. The meeting turned out to be very hostile. The members whose future was uncertain raised a pertinent question.

"We have supported the demand for Pakistan. Our constituency is now in India. The Hindus look down upon us and consider us traitors. What have the Muslim League and Jinnah thought about our future?"

"In history, there are no permanent friends and enemies. Those who are killing each other today can become friends tomorrow. You must now show your allegiance to the new Indian nation and remain its loyal citizens," advised Jinnah.

But it was easier said than done. Nobody accepted his advice. There was this common question in the meeting.

"Even after the partition, some thirty five million Muslims will be left behind in India. They supported the Muslim League and Pakistan. What steps will the Pakistan government take to make them secure?" Jinnah could not answer. The members lost patience and started shouting.

"Look! Just as thirty five million Muslims will remain in India, twenty million Hindus will remain in Pakistan. It is the duty of both the governments to protect the minorities."

"But if that does not happen?" some members persisted.

"Then both the countries should consider the question of exchanging the population. I personally think the minorities will be safe in both the countries. If not, the minorities in both the countries will suffer a lot. Then we may also have to solve the problem of transferring the population."

They were shaken by the vision of Jinnah. This would lead to untold misery on both the sides.

The militant *Khaksaars* of Punjab armed with weapons forcefully entered the venue of the meeting. In the midst of an uproar, they expressed their anger on Jinnah. They said they would never reconcile to the partition of Punjab and Bengal and Pakistan without a corridor linking it with East Pakistan. "Quaid-e-Azam, you have betrayed the Muslims by accepting a moth eaten Pakistan, you should not have done this" they shouted at him.

"I am fully aware with what I should do. I do not require any advise from you. Whatever I did, I have a support from Muslim league." Jinnah retorted firmly.

"Besides office bearers and members of Legislative Assemblies of Muslim league, there are ten crores of Muslims in the country. All of you are bewildered for capturing the power and as such throwing us in a deep sea. This is not the Pakistan dreamt by Rehmat Ali Choudhary and poet Iqbal. We want that Pakistan." The *Khaksaars* shouted.

And before Jinnah could respond, the agitated militants marched towards Jinnah.

There was a pandemonium. Fearing an untoward incident, some members ran helter-skelter. Jinnah's bodyguards and the armed national guards of the Muslim League rushed towards the militants. There was a scuffle. Every one feared for Jinnah's safety. Fortunately, the security guards of the hotel took the help of the police and brought the situation under control. However, the militants stood their ground, raised slogans calling Jinnah a traitor for a long time.

Any further discussion could precipitate the situation. Realising that the newspapers might sensationalise the news the next day causing anxiety among the Muslims across the country, Jinnah abruptly declared that the meeting had concluded.

*

Mountbatten prepared a report about the problems likely to arise following the partition. While distributing copies of the report to the members of the Partition Council, he said, "I will present this report to the Viceroy's Executive Council, but before that I would like to have your views on the report."

"Excuse me, Your Excellency," Jinnah interrupted, "it is only a temporary Council assisting the Viceroy."

The Viceroy understood. To Jinnah Jawaharlal Nehru's interim government was only a temporary arrangement. To avoid unwanted controversy, he summed-up.

'Let us not call it a cabinet, we may call it an interim Government.'

'If we call a spade diamond or heart, it does not mean necessarily." Jinnah said.

The Viceroy's report stated that Pakistan was a nation that was seceded from India. It meant the new Indian government was the direct successor to the British government. All the international treaties signed by the British government would be binding on the new government in Delhi. India would retain its membership of the United Nations Organisation. Pakistan would have to apply afresh for the membership of the UN. Jinnah was startled as he read the report. Since Pakistan would not benefit directly from the British government, he wanted to ensure that India did not derive any direct benefit either. He wanted the benefits should be shared equally by the two nations.

"Your Excellency, this is a gross injustice. If both India and Pakistan are not the direct successors of the British regime, consider them as the new entities."

"That is not possible Mr. Jinnah. The fact is that India ruled by the British is now being divided into two independent nations," said the Viceroy.

"Really it is not so." Jinnah retorted. "The country named India, ruled by the British is now divided and two new sovereign states named Hindustan and Pakistan have emerged. Pakistan has all the rights over 'India' as Hindustan has".

This logic was vehemently opposed by the members of the Partition Council. The Indian Independence Act which was adopted by the British Parliament has no reference of Hindustan. It has only referred to the Independence of India and creation of a new state of Pakistan. As such the Government in New Delhi becomes automatically the successor of the British Government and Pakistan has to accept the ground reality as a newly born state.

However Jinnah was not prepared to accept this and the Viceroy was determined to reach an understanding. As such he said to Jinnah.

"The new Government of Pakistan can approach to the United Nations and seek the legal opinion in terms of international law."

*

7th August 1947

The Viceroy's special aircraft Dakota was waiting for some VIPs to board at the Safdarjung Airport, Delhi. Quaid-e-Azam Muhammad Ali Jinnah, the Governor General designate of Pakistan, dressed in white *Sherwani* stood with a grim face near the entrance. Fatima, who had been his shadow for the past five decades, stood beside him grim faced. His newly appointed ADC, private secretary, bodyguards and other staff stood in attention. Everyone was carrying either a file, a briefcase or a newspaper. On receiving a signal for boarding the aircraft, the ADC came forward and said,

"Come Sir." The army men in uniform stood on both the sides of the route leading to the aircraft. Jinnah did not move. He looked around the airport. Fatima came near to him and called slowly,

"*Bhaijaan.*"

Jinnah started walking. His staff followed him. Jinnah stopped at the steps of the aircraft and said to Fatima,

"Fati, I think I will never be able to return to Delhi." Before stepping into the aircraft, he looked around and gazed at Delhi taking in as much as he could for the last time. He climbed the steps with a heavy heart and sat in the aircraft. Looking out through the window, he muttered,

"Oh! Everything is over."

During the entire journey of four hours, he did not utter a word. He glanced at the newspapers in between. When Fatima asked him to eat something, he took a couple of morsels. Throughout the journey, his face looked empty and grim.

A huge crowd gathered at the airport in Karachi to welcome the creator of their new independent Islamic country. The cries of *Pakistan Zindabad* and *Quaid-e-Azam Zindabad* reverberated the air. The massive crowd jostled to catch a glimpse of Jinnah. Handing over his leather briefcase to his ADC, he said,

"Now you have to take care of this." Then he greeted the leaders assembled there.

There was no Viceroy's House or Governor General's House in Karachi. The house of the Governor of the Sindh province was converted into the Governor General's house. While climbing the stairs of his new residence Jinnah said to his ADC,

"I never thought that Pakistan would be possible in my lifetime."

He went around his new residence, checked each and every room and gave instructions to the staff. "Look, these two rooms will be for my personal use. Make sure that no one except Fatima comes here. Those two rooms on that side will be only for special guests. That room will be for a Governor or a Chief Minister. And those rooms are exclusively for the important guests like the Shah of Iran or the King of Britain." He noticed the empty book shelves in the library and then asked,

"Where are the books?"

"The British Governor of Sindh took them away with him when he was leaving," came the reply.

"These books were not his personal possessions. They are the property of the Pakistan government. Go and tell him to return them immediately to their lawful owner."

He also noticed some sports equipments missing. On enquiry, an army officer said,

"Sir, the governor of Punjab took them away for his personal use."

"He has no right to take them away. Bring them back from him."

There was no radio in his room. He said,

"I cannot work without a radio. I must keep in touch with the latest news. Make an arrangement to get one immediately."

"Yes Sir, you seem to be tired. Take some rest. The radio will be arranged by tomorrow morning," said the officer in-charge of the house.

"I do not tolerate such absurd excuses to delay the work," Jinnah rebuked him.

While entertaining the visitors, he went on instructing the officers in-charge of the various chores in the house. In the evening when he was relaxed a bit, he went to the terrace of the house and looked at the city in which he was born some seven decades ago. The city was celebrating the independence. The flags of Pakistan fluttered all around. The neon lights were flashing. Suddenly his attention was drawn to a locality. It looked deserted, there was no flash of lights or fluttering of flags.

"Why is that locality so quiet? Why are there no celebrations?" asked Jinnah.

"Quaid-e-Azam, that is a Hindu locality," he got the answer.

He went on staring at the locality. He asked again,

"It is natural, they have nothing to celebrate here." Then he saw an open ground near the governor's house. He saw hundreds of people looking bewildered, their belongings scattered all around and half naked children playing in dirty water. Some stray animals and dogs were seen walking freely in their midst as if they owned the ground. It was jam-packed. There were puddles of water. A stream of dirty water was pouring on to the ground. And the sight of the stray dogs and the vultures poking in the dirty water showed how filthy the ground was.

"What is all this?" asked Jinnah.

"Quaid-e-Azam, this is the camp of the refugees who came from India. They lost everything—the property and the relatives. There are many such camps in Karachi."

Jinnah was stunned. He had seen the hordes of Sikh and Hindu refugees in Delhi. He felt sad at their plight. He could not imagine the creation of Pakistan could lead to this situation. What had happened to the people on both the sides of the border? He wondered. He was a politician. He knew that in politics many unethical things were done. He was shocked to realize how the people who lived together for generations could become so barbaric. He went on staring at the camp for a long time. Suddenly he was overwhelmed by a feeling of guilt. He wiped his eyes with his silky handkerchief. But he stiffened the very next moment. He was surprised. It was strange that he shed the tears over such a small matter.

11th August 1947

The first meeting of the Constituent Assembly of Pakistan was convened in Karachi. The flag of Pakistan fluttered on both the sides of the road leading to the Assembly. The Assembly House was painted in green. The assembly was jam-packed. When the Governor General Quaid-e-Azam entered the house, the members cheered him by giving a standing ovation.

Jinnah was appointed as the Governor General by the British government. Now he would be elected as the President of the Constituent Assembly of an independent and sovereign Pakistan. After a formal proposal and seconding of his name, he was unanimously elected as the President of the Assembly.

At the inaugural speech of the Assembly Jinnah said, "A great responsibility is bestowed upon us. As an independent and sovereign nation, we must set a good example for the world. We have to draft our constitution. We must prove our administrative skills. Our first priority is to maintain law and order. It is our responsibility to the life and property of the people, no matter which religion they profess. We are all free now. We are independent. Pakistan will be a modern democratic state and not a medieval theocratic state. Every citizen of Pakistan will be free to profess his faith. Whether you go to temple or mosque or church or gurudwara,

Pakistan will have nothing to do with it. All citizens will have equal rights. You may belong to any religion or caste or creed, that is your personal matter. I am confident that in due course, the Hindus will cease to be the Hindus and the Muslims will cease to be the Muslims. All are equal partners in the making of the government and in the progress and development of the nation. Let the Muslim League be known as the Pakistan National League hereinafter."

There was a pin drop silence in the hall. No one coughed or sneezed. One could even hear the sound of breathing. Concluding his speech Jinnah said, "Both India and Pakistan cannot live as enemies forever. If one of them is attacked by any outside force, we should unite and give a joint resounding reply to the enemy. We must not forget that blood is thicker than water."

The members listened to him with utter disbelief. They were perplexed. If the Hindus and the Muslims were equal citizens, why was Pakistan created? An astute Liaquat Ali Khan was quick enough to understand the situation. As Jinnah concluded the speech, he was applauded. But it was not as hearty as the one that greeted him at the beginning on his election as the President of the Assembly.

Liaquat Ali Khan did not join the applause. He was worried how the newspapers would report the speech the next day. He felt that if this was Jinnah's idea of Pakistan, then he would be a spent force. The next item on the agenda was approval of the national flag of Pakistan. Before the members could discuss anything further, Liaquat Ali Khan got up and announced the next item in the agenda. It was a very clever move on his part. The members stunned by the speech of Jinnah were excited about the national flag. They approved the national flag without any discussion. Even as the reporters present in the Assembly were making notes and interpreting Jinnah's speech, Liaquat released an official press statement that the Constituent Assembly had approved the national flag of Pakistan. He wanted to avoid the press blowing off and sensationalizing Jinnah's speech. He feared that the Muslims would be shocked by the speech. He wanted to avoid that situation. He succeeded to a large extent in that.

71

Plot to murder Jinnah, Jinnah-Mountbatten—14th August parade, bonquet at the Governor-General's residence, Mountbatten-Fatima conversation, Jinnah's plan to visit Kashmir, rejection by King Hari Singh

Neither any leader in the subcontinent nor the British government could gauge the extent of animosity and hatred the partition had generated among the common people. Faith and understanding were its biggest casualties. The violence unleashed across the country stunned the people. 'We shall make ashamed even Changez Khan and Halaku Khan, the mass murderers in the middle ages with our acts of massacre and genocide'—the call given by Feroz Khan Noon, the leader of Bengal Muslim League some time back had literally come true. The only difference was that this time even Hindus had retaliated in the same fashion.

Pakistan was to observe the Independence Day on 14th August, 1947. The Governor General of Pakistan invited Viceroy Lord Mountbatten to be the chief guest at the Independence Day celebrations. Jinnah would formally take the charge of the new government. In an atmosphere vitiated by violence and rumours of conspiracy came the news of attempts to sabotage the celebrations. The intelligence agencies received the news that Akali Dal leader Master Tara Singh was plotting to murder Jinnah at the Independence Day parade to avenge the killings of the Sikhs in the Muslim dominated areas of Punjab. If he succeeded in the plot, the new nation would plunge into darkness. Jinnah was provided adequate security. There was a sense of anxiety and fear among the top echelons.

The programme for the day included hoisting the flag and a public parade in an open jeep through the streets of Karachi to enable Jinnah to greet the people, followed by Lord Mountbatten, his wife Edwina and daughter Pamela in another open jeep. Other Muslim League leaders would also join the parade. Then both Jinnah and Mountbatten would address the Constituent Assembly in the evening, followed by an official banquet in honour of the guest.

There was a question of protocol at the Constituent Assembly. Jinnah wanted that as the Governor General and the President of the Assembly he should be accorded the highest honour. However, some constitutional experts felt that the power would be transferred only after the midnight on 14th August. Therefore, Lord Mountbatten as the Viceroy of undivided India should receive the highest honour at the meeting of the Constituent Assembly. Jinnah was not willing to reconcile to this. He refused to accept Mountbatten as the Governor General of Pakistan. He was firm that at least in Pakistan his position should be above that of Mountbatten. Mountbatten's private secretary and chief of the staff Lord Ismay arrived two days earlier in Karachi to make arrangements for the meeting of the Constituent Assembly. Then he expressed his displeasure at the talk of according Mountbatten a status lower than that of Jinnah. He immediately briefed the Viceroy about it. The Viceroy got annoyed and told his secretary, "If that is their intention, cancel my meeting. Tell them that you will attend the meeting instead as my representative."

When this message reached Jinnah and the top government officials, they were stunned. The threat of Jinnah's murder was looming large. The news received every hour was very disturbing. The people in both the countries had gone berserk. And the thousands of refugees flocking into major cities every day was creating a grave situation.

The cancellation of Mountbatten's visit could pose more danger to Pakistan. Jinnah wanted to take advantage of Mountbatten's presence to ward off any threat to his life. He thought that instead of taking two different jeeps for the parade, if Mountbatten could ride with him in an open jeep it could serve as a protective shield to him. No matter how tight the security might be, it would not deter an assailant from shooting or throwing a grenade at him with thousands of people on the roads. Jinnah thought that if Mountbatten, his wife and daughter joined him in the open jeep for the parade, it would be difficult for the assailant to target him. In case of any untoward incident, both Pakistan and India would have to bear the brunt of rage of the British government. India along with Pakistan would face the consequences of anarchy and chaos.

He reconciled to the issue of protocol. He agreed to accord equal status to Mountbatten at the meeting of the Constituent Assembly.

Ismay briefed Mountbatten about the threat to Jinnah's life. Mountbatten ordered tight security and directed his intelligence agencies to thwart any such attempt. He assured Jinnah that he would ride with him in an open jeep for the parade. Lady Edwina was not happy about his decision. She feared threat to his life and tried to dissuade him. Mountbatten thought that the fear that he could be the target instead would prevent any assailant from attacking Jinnah.

After taking all the possible precautions, Mountbatten joined Jinnah in the parade.

As the parade passed through the routes as per the programme, it became impossible for the police to control the surging crowds of ecstatic people. Jinnah and Mountbatten stood in the open jeep and received flower bouquets thrown at them and greeted the people.

"Mr. Jinnah," Mountbatten said quietly, "Judging by the people's enthusiasm, it looks you have succeeded in making them realise the dream of Pakistan."

"Your Excellency, there was no other option," Jinnah said triumphantly. "Now these people have understood that the Indian leaders like Gandhi were bent upon destroying the Muslims and that they are still trying to wreak havoc on Pakistan."

"I hope that this distrust ends here and that both the countries now concentrate on progress," said Mountbatten.

"However noble the intention may be, we cannot wish away the truth. The manner in which the Muslims are massacred in India and driven out of the country, it won't be surprising if there is a war between the two countries."

"What are you saying, Mr. Jinnah?" asked a stunned Mountbatten, "I know Jawaharlal Nehru quite well. I am confident that as a Prime Minister he will never allow that to happen."

"Your Excellency, you don't know the undercurrents of reality," Jinnah said confidently, "Jawaharlal is only a showpiece. He is not a practical person. He only knows how to talk eloquently. The real power is in the hands of Sardar Patel—a disciple of Gandhi. You know how cunning Gandhi is. If Patel's intention is good both the countries can live in peace."

"Excuse me, Mr. Jinnah. I do not agree with you. As far as I know Gandhi, his truth and integrity cannot be doubted."

"That is the special quality of Gandhi. There is a venom against the Muslims in everything that he says. But outsiders like you do not understand that. His disciples and rivals understand his venomous messages. I know him pretty well. You will not find a man as manipulative as Gandhi in the world history."

Mountbatten thought that it would not be wise to continue the conversation any further. In his first encounter with Jinnah, he had thought Jinnah was a psychopath. That opinion was now reinforced. And Jinnah was in an advanced stage of that disease.

Everybody heaved a sigh of relief when the parade finally reached the Constituent Assembly after two hours. Nothing untoward happened. When the jeep stopped at the entrance of the Assembly, Jinnah got down and said to Mountbatten,

"Thank God, I brought you safe."

Mountbatten's lips twitched with disdain. He was stunned by the temerity of Jinnah. He said in a firm tone, "Mr. Jinnah, the situation is the other way round. Not you, it is me who brought you safe here."

There was a banquet at the Governor General's House in the evening. The invitees included the ambassadors designate from the foreign countries, the members of the Constituent Assembly, the government officials, the journalists from across the world and the eminent citizens. The main purpose of the banquet was to enable about 1500 guests to come together, get acquainted with one another and exchange good wishes. Mountbatten had instructed that there should be no speeches. However, as soon as the guests settled at the tables, Jinnah took out a written speech and began reading it, deviating from the programme. Mountbatten who sat next to him was astonished. Nobody could start taking the food till he finished the speech. A disappointed Mountbatten looked around. He was surprised to notice that some of the guests did not dress, appropriately for the occasion and even carried the weapons. He never saw the guests dressing in this manner at an official banquet. If these people who call themselves as the eminent citizens of Pakistan did not have the etiquette and modern culture... Then… Mountbatten wondered with a mischievous smile.

Fatima sat to his right and Begum Rana to his left. During the course of conversation, Fatima said to Mountbatten,

"I have heard that the astrologers in India consider the midnight of 14th August inauspicious. Therefore, the government of India is thinking of changing the time. What a strange thing".

"Yes, it is strange," said Mountbatten, "But Jawaharlal does not believe in all that. He is going ahead with the programme."

"These Hindus are indeed strange. They are so superstitious even about such an important occasion," said Fatima.

Mountbatten stared at Fatima for a moment and said in a stern tone,

"Madam, you are forgetting that this banquet was originally scheduled for the noon, but when reminded that it is the month of *Ramzan*, it was rescheduled to the evening."

Fatima pretended to listen to the speech of the Governor General, as if she had not heard Mountbatten.

*

Jinnah had been shouldering the physical and mental burden of the work by the sheer will power. But there was a limit for endurance. Since he had taken the reins of power of Pakisan, both his body and mind refused to oblige him. The doctors advised him to take complete rest for a few days in a peaceful and pleasant place. The aftermath of the partition was so devastating that it did not allow him to rest. He was very unhappy about the manner in which the new government was formed and the ministerial portfolios were allotted. He wanted to entrust the ministry of law to a dalit Hindu called Jogindranath Mandal. He was a staunch supporter of the Muslim League in Bengal. Jinnah knew that some Muslim League candidates aspiring for the ministry wanted to make Pakistan an Islamic state governed by the *Shariat*. This was not acceptable to him. He had his own reasons for wanting to entrust the ministry of law to Jogindranath. He wanted to checkmate the Islamic extremists. He also wanted to send a message that the minorities in Pakistan would get equal opportunities. But Liaquat Ali Khan and other colleagues strongly objected to his choice. All of them wanted Pakistan to be an Islamic state governed by the *Shariat.* The *Ulemas* were also unhappy about Jinnah's choice. What does a Hindu know about the *Hadis* or the *Shariat*? How can we expect him to observe the *Shariat*? Most of the people were unhappy about the speech Jinnah made at the first meeting of the Constituent Assembly. Now the dissent was growing against him.

On the other hand, the princely states were asked to choose between India and Pakistan irrespective of the religion of the people or the geographical location. The right to accession was given to the rulers of the princely states. Jinnah received the support from the Nawab of Bhopal, but it was impossible for Bhopal to merge with Pakistan. Hyderabad was another princely state in India and majority of its people were Hindus. But it was ruled by a Muslim Nawab, Nizam-ul-Mulq. Jinnah had met the Nizam two years ago, but the experience was not pleasant. Though Hyderabad could not merge into Pakistan, it would benefit Pakistan if it remained as an independent state instead of merging with India. The Nizam was actually thinking on those lines. Jinnah was eager to assist him in every possible manner.

More than Hyderabad, Pakistan's stakes were very high in Kashmir. It was ruled by a Hindu King Hari Singh. But majority of the people were Muslims. The Muslim Congress leaders and Sheikh Abdullah, a personal friend of Jawaharlal Nehru, were keen that Kashmir merged with India. Hari Singh, like the Nizam, wanted to Kashmir to remain as an independent state. Jinnah knew that even Mountbatten wanted Kashmir to join Pakistan and not India. Mountbatten travelled to Kashmir to advise Hari Singh accordingly. Hari Singh did not accept his advice. Ramachandra Kak, Hari Singh's Prime Minister, married an English woman. And due to the influence of his wife, he sent a message to Jinnah that Kashmir would merge with Pakistan. When Hari Singh came to know about it, he immediately dismissed Ramachandra Kak and installed Justice Meherchand Mahajan, the Chief Justice of Punjab High Court, as the Prime Minister. Jinnah saw danger in this move. He wanted to take some swift action. He was physically tired and needed rest. He thought camping a few days in Kashmir would serve his purpose.

Jinnah sent his private secretary to the King of Kashmir with a message. He expressed his desire to rest for a few days in Srinagar. He requested the King to make suitable arrangements for his stay.

But the King and his new Prime Minister understood the motive behind. They thought that if Jinnah visited the state at that crucial juncture, it would create more problems and send a wrong signal. This could not be a casual visit of Jinnah. After a careful consideration, Hari Singh sent a polite reply to Jinnah—

"Now you are the Governor General of an independent and sovereign Pakistan. We should be able to provide suitable residence and security cover befitting your status. It is difficult for us to arrange all that at such a short notice. After making the necessary arrangements we will invite you in near future. Then we will be very glad to welcome you."

The reply was polite couched with wisdom. But the message was very clear. The King did not want Jinnah to come to Kashmir. It was the rejection of Jinnah in unambiguous terms. Jinnah could not bear it. He was enraged.

72

Jinnah's plan to take revenge on Kashmir, General Messervy, Autocratic rule of Jinnah in Pakistan, keeping in personal custody files relating to Kashmir, Jamshed Patel-Jinnah dialogue, Jinnah's no to compound wall for his residence

Enraged by the insult, Jinnah began making his political calculations. At the time of the partition of the country, Mountbatten and General Auchinleck, Chief of the Army, had told Jinnah to keep the common army and not to divide it. If the army remained under the unified command of a British General, there would not be any possibility of a war breaking between the two countries. Besides, Delhi would remain as the army Headquarters. That would be advantageous to India. Pakistan would be at the mercy of India, if it had no army of its own. Jinnah understood this. He insisted that the army should be divided before 14th August. The Indian army was under the command of the British Generals until then. Accordingly, British General Messervy was appointed as the Chief of the Army of Pakistan. Thus, Jinnah succeeded in getting a separate army for Pakistan.

Jinnah thought that he had shown a greater foresight in getting a separate army by not accepting the advice of Mountbatten. He could not imagine that he would be using the army so soon to teach a lesson to the King of Kashmir. He summoned General Messervy for a discussion.

"General," Jinnah said, "as per the intelligence reports, the Hindu King of Kashmir is committing atrocities against the local Muslims. Not only that, he is trying to merge his state with India much against the wishes of his people. To stop this, we must take immediate military action. What do you think?"

"By military action, do you mean marching of the army into Kashmir?" asked an astonished General.

"General, you must understand properly that, that is what I mean," Jinnah said in a firm tone. "Just as the Russian army invaded Poland and captured it, Pakistan army should invade Kashmir and capture it. This is my order."

"Order!" General Messervy was stunned for a moment and sat up erect. "Quaid-e-Azam, do you want to know my opinion or are you ordering me as the Governor General?"

Jinnah did not expect this rebuttal from the British General. He kept quiet for a moment. Taking advantage of his silence the General said, "I hope you understand the implications of what you are saying. If we march into an independent Kashmir, it would be called an aggression as per the international law. And if the King of Kashmir seeks the help of the Indian army to counter the aggression, we won't be able to face them. It is obvious, there will be a war between India and Pakistan," warned the General.

"You are mistaken, General. You don't know the history of the Hindus. They are never prepared for war. Their mentality is to shun war. You don't worry."

"You may be right, but in case of a war, there will be the British Generals on both the sides. It will be very ridiculous for the British Generals to fight against each other. I cannot give orders for such a war. If you insist on it, the British officers from both the sides will retire."

Jinnah never anticipated this. If the British officers retire, how can the Pakistan army fight? He needed time to think it over. He immediately relieved the General. While climbing down the stairs, the General muttered to himself,

"He must be in the final stages of delirium."

Taking a serious note of what Jinnah's suggested, the General reported the matter to Prime Minister Liaquat Ali Khan. He knew how rigid Jinnah was once he had decided on anything. The General himself was unable to stop the impending action. It was important that Liaquat Ali Khan stopped the misadventure.

Liaquat himself preferred some firm action on the Kashmir issue, but it was not that easy. He realised that the extreme step that Jinnah was contemplating, if indeed materialized, it would plunge the infant Pakistan into a calamity. India could win the war by virtue of its strength and then the very existence of Pakistan could be endangered.

"Prime Minister," said the General candidly,"It looks the Governor General is serious about the military action. If he insists on that, the British officers will not allow that to happen."

"I understand your difficulty, General," said Liaquat, "But nobody could ever understand Quaid-e-Azam. To tell you the truth, he has become a big problem after the creation of Pakistan. And he is doing nothing to build the nation, except putting hurdles. Yet nobody understands how to get rid of him."

*

After General Messervy's rebuttal, Jinnah began to think of an alternative plan of action. For that to materialize, it was imperative to use the government machinery covertly. He had a secret discussion on this with Liaquat Ali Khan. The road transporting the essential goods to Kashmir passed through the Pakistan border. All the essential goods that Kashmir required were purchased from the markets of either India or Pakistan and transported through the trucks. If these goods did not reach on time, it would create a havoc in Kashmir. The blocking of these essential goods could provide an opportunity to arouse the sentiments of the local Muslims and instigate the Muslims in the army to revolt against King Hari Singh. It was decided to block the trucks carrying the essential goods to Kashmir at the check posts. Accordingly, the orders were issued immediately.

But that was not enough. This was one of the methods to contain the King. It did not show the results immediately. Jinnah did not want to waste time any more. And once King Hari Singh decided to sign the instrument of accession with the Indian government and Kashmir acceded to India, it would be difficult to take military action. Jinnah wanted to take swift action before the King and the Indian government acted. In a few days, the people of Kashmir would face hardships due to the blockage of the supply of essential goods. That would be the right opportunity to take the extreme step.

Liaquat Ali Khan convened a secret meeting of trusted colleagues in Lahore. Colonel Akbar Khan and Major Khurshid Anwar were the chief among them. Both of them were Pathans. Major Anwar had the experience of organising, looting and carrying out other destructive activities against the *Khudai Khidmatgaars* in the North West Frontier Province. Colonel Akbar Khan, who had graduated from the Sandhurst Military Academy, was considered an expert on terrorist and guerilla warfare. As the Governor General, Jinnah already dismissed the Congress government of Dr. Khan Sahib in the Frontier Province. There were skirmishes between the supporters of the Muslims League and its rivals. Now all that ended. The warrior Pathans were idle. Akbar Khan and Khursid Anwar knew how to use them. They could be provoked to carry out the *jihad* by unleashing a propaganda against the Hindu King and the Hindus in Kashmir: that the Muslims were persecuted and massacred and driven out and their mosques destroyed. The Pathans were good in arson and looting.

Under the direct supervision of Liaquat Ali Khan, Colonel Khan and Major Anwar were entrusted the responsibility of sneaking into Kashmir in the midnight and create a reign of terror. Adequate food stocks and weapons were procured from the streets of Quetta and Peshawar and supplied to them. The situation was grave on the border. The blocking of the supply of essential goods to Kashmir has resulted in a serious crisis. The King sent a message that Pakistan was not acting in a friendly manner but creating a hostile situation. He said that he would procure the essential goods for the people through some other sources and deal with the hostility created by Pakistan in Kashmir. Jinnah was impatient, but could not do anything because of the stand taken by General Messervy. He was waiting for the right opportunity. He got the opportunity. General Messervy left for London to procure some army equipments. Taking advantage of his absence, it was decided that the armed Pathans and the tribesmen would enter Kashmir in the midnight and cut off the power supply to major cities like Srinagar, Jammu and Baramullah.

At midnight on 23rd October, 1947 hundreds of the armed Pathans and tribesmen crossed the Pakistan border and infiltrated into Kashmir. They carried huge ammunition with them in trucks and jeeps. They kept marching in the nights, committing atrocities, massacring people and setting the villages on fire on the way. They reached the first army check post in Kashmir. A division of four hundred soldiers was stationed at the check post under the charge of Colonel Narayan Singh, a Hindu. They were well trained in warfare. Considering their track record, the King had posted them at the sensitive border of Pakistan. The Muslim soldiers in the division conspired to revolt against Colonel Narayan Singh. They murdered him and joined the armed tribesmen. Now the raiders could march up to Baramullah without any resistance.

Jinnah was monitoring the progress of the raiders. The festival of *Eid* was due after five days. Jinnah hoped to reach Srinagar to celebrate the festival. He was confident that King Hari Singh's forces would not be able to resist the raiders more than a couple of days. The Pakistani army men followed the raiders in plain clothes. Jinnah was sure that even if the King wanted he would not be able to obtain any assistance from the Indian government. Gurudaspur in Punjab was India's link to Kashmir, but it had no proper road. It was almost certain that the raiders would capture Srinagar on 27th October.

This was a miscalculation. The raiders did not immediately proceed further after capturing Baramullah. They went on a looting spree. They forcefully entered the churches and raped the nuns. That day was very critical for King Hari Singh. He signed the instrument of accession with the Indian government and agreed to merge Kashmir with India. There after, immediately the Indian army was flown to Srinagar airport. Now the raiders were forced to fight the Indian army.

When Jinnah came to know about it, he ordered the army men in plain clothes to rush to the aid of the raiders. The raiders who reached the doorsteps of Srinagar were forced to retreat by the Indian army. And the wish of Jinnah to celebrate the *Eid* in Srinagar remained unfulfilled.

Jinnah kept with him all the files relating to the Kashmir issue. Ismail Chhundarigar, the Home Minister of Pakistan, wanted that the files should pass through him. As the Prime Minister, Liaquat Ali Khan wanted the Home Minister to hand over the files to him with his notes. If required, the files could be sent to the Governor General with the Prime Minister's notes. If the Governor General wanted to change the decision, he could do so only after consulting the Prime Minister by giving the reason thereto.

Thus, there was a power sharing struggle within the government. Jinnah was furious. He was a dejected man. Not did only his Kashmir plan fail, but also Pakistan was accused of being an aggressor. He called for the files relating to Kashmir and instructed his private secretary, "Tell both Liaquat and Chundarigar that I have created Pakistan and the distribution of ministerial portfolios will be done as per my wish."

When the message was conveyed, both of them got annoyed. They did not expect this. There was no denying the fact that Jinnah was responsible for the creation of Pakistan. But no one had any doubt that Pakistan would be a theocratic country governed by the Islmaic law. But what Jinnah wanted was a dictatorship. Both of them were incensed.

An angry and dejected Jinnah sat in an armchair in the lawns of his bungalow. He was dead tired. His body could not take the strain any more. This was not the Pakistan that he had wanted. Thousands of innocent people were butchered on both the sides of the border. Property worth billions of rupees was destroyed. Hordes of refugees were wandering on the roads. And countless women were kidnapped.

Jamshed Patel, the chairman of the Karachi Municipal Corporation, was a personal friend of Jinnah. He came to meet him. The gardener was standing at a distance. He did not stop Patel as every one knew how intimate he was with Jinnah. When Jamshed came close to Jinnah, he found his eyes closed and his hands making some incomprehensible gestures. Jamshed was alarmed. He observed Jinnah muttering some incoherent words.

"Quaid-e-Azam," Jamshed called softly.

"No, go away from here. I do not want to talk to anyone," Jinnah said agitated.

Patel was shocked by Jinnah's behaviour. He had never behaved like this.

"Quaid-e-Azam, I am Jamshed, Jamshed Patel."

A startled Jinnah opened his eyes and turned his face.

"Oh! Jamshed! I am sorry. But...but, my friend, I am really tired. I don't know what to do."

*

The height of the compound wall of the bungalow was rather low. The people in the vehicles passing through could easily see the garden and the porch of the bungalow.

It was necessary to raise the height of the wall for the security of the Governor General. When the persons from the concerned department came to measure the height of the wall, Jinnah asked them,

"Why are you taking the measurement?"

"Sir, it is decided to raise the height of the compound wall of the bungalow."

"Decided!" Jinnah shouted, "I am staying in this bungalow. How could anyone decide without my knowledge?"

"It was decided for the security of the Governor General," the hapless government servants answered politely.

"There is no need for that. Leave the compound wall as it is. This is my order, go and tell the people who made the decision," said Jinnah excited.

But his body was not in a position to tolerate such excitement. He felt dizzy. He had bouts of coughing and then collapsed in a nearby chair.

73

Jehangir Patel-Jinnah-Gandhi, Gandhi's fast in Delhi, assassination of Gandhi, condolence message from Jinnah, riots in Lahore, massacre in train,—Pakistan's empty treasury—Nizam, Special car and aircraft for Jinnah, Jinnah in Dacca—emphasising on Urdu as the national language of Pakistan

Jehangir Patel, a cotton trader in Bombay, was an old friend of Jinnah. During his stay in Bombay, Jinnah had a very cordial relation with some Parsee families. Jehangair Patel had supported the freedom movement of the Congress and had a close relation with Gandhi.

One morning the private secretary to Jinnah received a phone call in the Governor General's Office from Jehangir Patel. Jehangir requested him, "Sir, could I talk to Quaid-e-Azam? I am Jehanagir Patel, his old friend from Bombay."

The secretary hesitated for a moment as he wanted to know from him what he wanted to talk to. But being impressed by his politeness, he informed Jinnah about the call.

Jinnah was surprised. He wondered how an old friend suddenly remembered him. He immediately talked to Jehangir.

Jehangir wanted to come to Karachi to discuss an important matter with Jinnah. He gave no details of the matter. Jinnah gave him an appointment. Jehangir reached Karachi. After listening to what he had to say, Jinnah felt uneasy and annoyed.

It was something unusual.

Gandhi camped in Calcutta and Noakhali to defuse the communal tension in Bengal. He travelled along with his colleagues to the most dangerous places without any security. He wanted to visit the communally volatile Punjab and then reach Karachi. He expressed his desire to visit Pakistan to empathise and console the millions of people who were uprooted by the partition. He would have preferred the government to arrange his visit. But in the hindsight he feared that if the government of India made the arrangement and then Pakistan denied the permission for his visit, it could become a big political issue. Hence, he made a personal request to Jehangir to arrange the visit.

Jinnah contemplated seriously. He doubted Gandhi had some ulterior motive behind this. His experience of working with Gandhi in the Congress for fifteen years from 1915 to 1930 was not a happy one. He thought there might have been some sinister design of the Indian government, particularly of Sardar Patel, behind his goodwill visit. Jinnah rejected Jehangir's request to make the arrangement for Gandhi's visit saying, "Jehangir, tell Gandhi that he should try to stop the atrocities committed against the Muslims in India. Pakistan government is capable of controlling the situation here."

Thus, Gandhi's visit to Pakistan did not materialize.

However, the subsequent development totally changed Jinnah's perception of Gandhi. The Sikh refugees from Punjab reached Delhi and forcefully occupied the houses of the local Muslims. They forcefully entered the mosques and converted them into refugee camps. In some mosques, the weapons were seized. This led to riots endangering the lives of the Muslims. Delhi witnessed a large scale plunder, arson and murders. The government failed to contain the riots.

At this juncture, the eighty year old Gandhi, putting his life at stake, declared that he would go on fast until the riots were stopped and the houses and the mosques of the Muslims were returned and they were guaranteed security. He declared that he would continue the fast till the normalcy was restored in Delhi. When Jinnah heard of this, he was overwhelmed by the thoughts which he never had before.

Only a few days ago, he had rejected Gandhi's request to visit Pakistan. He had attributed a motive behind his visit. Now, it was the same Gandhi who risked his life to protect the Muslims. For the first time in his life, Jinnah realised that Gandhi's intentions were noble. He immediately sent a message to Jahangir Patel—

"Jehangir, you can arrange a programme for Gandhi's visit to Pakistan as per your convenience. The Pakistan government will make necessary arrangements for his stay and security." And then added, "Tell Gandhi to reach Karachi from Bombay by a yacht or an aircraft. We will receive him in Karachi . And we will make arrangements for his itinerary. Tell him specially that it is not safe to enter the Punjab border on foot."

When Jehangir conveyed the message to Gandhi, peace had returned to Delhi. Gandhi gave up the fast. During his fast, Jinnah had conveyed a message to the Indian Muslims through the newspapers where he said, "Gandhi is a true friend of the Indian Muslims. All the Muslims must stand behind him and give him the moral support."

No one knew whether Gandhi was amused by the message. Nevertheless, he was not destined to visit Pakistan and enjoy the hospitality of his lifelong adversary.

*

30th January, 1948

A tired Governor General Muhammad Ali Jinnah was resting in a chair in the lawns of his bungalow. His face showed how exhausted he was. He became restive about the news of Kashmir. He dozed off in the chair. The sun went down the horizon. Suddenly his defense advisor Bernie came running, frightened and breathless and yelling in utter violation of all the norms of discipline.

"Oh! This is a terrible news!"

Jinnah opened his eyes and looked at Bernie inquisitively.

"Why are you so frightened, Mr. Bernie?"

"Quaid-e-Azam! This is a very terrible news! How...how can anybody do this? And that too, a Hindu!"

Jinnah was all ears when he heard the word Hindu. He sat up erect and asked curiously, "A Hindu! What is the matter? What has he done?"

"Sir, just a few minutes ago in Delhi a Hindu fanatic shot dead Mahatma Gandhi on his way to his evening prayers," Bernie shared the news.

The news was unexpected and startling for Jinnah. He jumped from his chair.

"Mr. Bernie, the news must be on the radio. Go, get the radio set here."

The radio was flashing the news of Gandhi's assassination. Bernie brought the radio and conveyed yet another piece of news,

"Sir, the reason for the assassination of Gandhi was more shocking. The assassin says that Gandhi supports the Muslims and he is an agent of Pakistan. And that he murdered him for the sake of India."

The reason given for assassinating Gandhi shocked Jinnah more than the assassination. In the twilight he looked around the compound wall of his bungalow. The people in the vehicles passing by were looking at his lawns. He was annoyed.

"Mr. Bernie, a few days ago, there was a proposal to raise the height of this compound wall ..."

"Yes Sir," said Bernie, "That work is stopped because you objected to it."

"Now you can raise the height of the wall. Do it as fast as you can. If possible do it today," Jinnah said and went inside the bungalow.

Bernie was surprised. Why did he suddenly remember the wall in the midst of such a terrible news of Gandhi's assassination? He could not understand the connection between the two. Why did the Governor General suddenly talk of raising the height of the compound wall? Bernie noticed some change in Jinnah's voice. He saw Jinnah climbing the stairs of the bungalow quickly.

Jinnah lay down on his back in his room. Just as out of fear he had opposed every action of Gandhi during his lifetime, now Gandhi's death created a fear in his mind. The way Gandhi was assassinated, some passer-by on the road outside could take advantage of the low lying compound wall and shoot at him in the lawns.

The radio relayed the condolence messages from all over the world. Jinnah instructed his private secretary to send a condolence message to Delhi on his behalf. The message read,

"There should be no controversy in death. Mr. Gandhi's death is very tragic. He was one of the greatest men produced by the Hindu community. His death is a great loss to Hindustan..."

His secretary instantly raised a doubt about the propriety of sending such a message. He pointed out to Jinnah, "Quaid-e-Azam, how far is it fair to say that Gandhi belonged to only one community? How can we say that he belonged to the Hindus alone?"

Jinnah looked at his secretary for a moment with his jawbones stuck out and his eyes sunk deep. An event that had taken place thirty two years ago flashed vividly before his eyes. A felicitation function had been organised for Gandhi on his triumphant return from South Africa by the Gurjar Sabha in Bombay. A young Jinnah had presided over the function. Jinnah could never forget what Gandhi had said then, "I am glad that brother Jinnah in spite of being a Muslim is enthusiastic about serving the country." If Jinnah was a Muslim to Gandhi, then Gandhi too should remain a Hindu and a Hindu alone to Jinnah.

"No, whatever he may be, to me he was a great Hindu," he said to his secretary.

Only a few days ago, Gandhi had risked his life to protect the Muslims. Jinnah then had called him, "a true friend of Muslims." He forgot that totally. But the event that had taken place some thirty two years ago was still fresh in his mind.

Lahore was engulfed in communal fire. Jinnah was shocked to hear that hundreds of the Hindu refugees carried by a train from Lahore were massacred and the train was sent to India with the mutilated bodies. He decided to go to Lahore and take stock of the situation.

Lahore became a feast for the vultures, dogs and wolves. The Hindus who could not manage to flee were hiding here and there fearing for their lives. Jinnah ordered that they should be protected and settled in camps. He could never imagine such brutal murders and atrocities. Earlier the riots were engineered for political reasons. But now it was a communal frenzy of the people. Jinnah was grieved to see all this. The tales of the Muslim refugees who lost their families and property in India were harrowing. The women were abducted and raped in the midst of carnage. Jinnah ordered the police and the army to stop the abduction of women. The abducted women should be traced and restored to their families.

Jinnah had seen the killings in Calcutta, the riots in the Frontier Province, the mass murders in Naokhali and the communal violence in Bihar and Delhi. But he felt the abduction of women and gang rapes were the worst offences which should not be tolerated. He could still understand the killing innocent people for political reasons, but could never tolerate the atrocities against women.

Jinnah's stay in Lahore got extended indefinitely. The situation was such that he did not want to leave Lahore in flames and return to Karachi. As a result, a lot of files got accumulated in the Governor General's office. The government machinery virtually came to a standstill. Liaquat Ali Khan and his colleagues were unhappy. Pakistan was facing a grave financial crisis. The treasury was almost empty. If some financial aid was not arranged immediately, the country could face a grave situation. The Prime Minister sent an urgent message to the Governor General.

Jinnah did not anticipate the crisis. After a careful consideration, he instructed Liaquat Ali Khan to include Layak Ali, the Prime Minister of the Nizam of Hyderabad in the Pakistan delegation to the United Nations Organisation. Layak Ali was asked to meet Jinnah at Lahore.

Jinnah's relation with the Nizam of Hyderabad was not cordial. But he was personally acquainted with Layak Ali who was a supporter of the Muslim League. He was a staunch communalist and sympathized with the cause of Pakistan. Jinnah was once insulted by the Nizam, but he thought it wise to forget it now. The princely state of Hyderabad, located in the centre of India, was still independent and had not yet merged with India. If Liaquat wanted he could appeal to the Nizam in the name of Islam and obtain financial aid for Pakistan. Therefore, Jinnah decided to lure him by including Layak Ali in the Pakistan delegation to the UN.

This strategy worked. Layak Ali reached Lahore the very next day. And Pakistan received a financial aid to the tune of 200 million rupees from the Nizam. Jinnah himself wanted to lead the Pakistan delegation to the UN and raise the Kashmir issue. But his health did not permit him to travel to New York. Mohammed Zafarullah Khan was made the leader of the delegation. Jinnah instructed him to buy a good bungalow in Washington to serve as a permanent base for Pakistan, a latest model car Cadillac from the General Motors and a special aircraft for the personal use of the Governor General. Jinnah did not bother to think how a country which got into a debt of 200 million rupees could afford such extravaganza. A bungalow in Washington costing one hundred and fifty thousand dollars and a brand new green Cadillac worth six thousand dollars were bought. The aircraft Viking Armstrong that Jinnah used till his death was also procured from the United States of America.

Jinnah had never visited Dacca during his political career spanning five decades. This ancient city of Bengal, only next to Calcutta in riches, had now become the capital of East Pakistan. As the Governor General of Pakistan, he visited Dacca in March. A greater part of Pakistan's territory was in the west. But the Bengalees constituted more than half of the population of Pakistan. There was nothing common between the Bangalees and the Muslims of West Pakistan except the religion. Jinnah was anxious about this dissimilarity. He knew that the people in East Pakistan were skeptical about the political capital of Pakistan being located in the West. A military parade was arranged to welcome Jinnah as his special aircraft landed at the Dacca airport. He looked very tired and worn out. Before starting the march past, the British officer in-charge came close to Jinnah and whispered politely,

"Sir, please stand in this position in your place," he demonstrated the position known as attention in the military parlance.

"Why?" Jinnah asked rudely, "Why should I stand in that position?"

"Because, this is a military parade and we are expected to observe the military discipline."

Jinnah felt belittled for a moment. He had never observed any such military discipline. But here the armed soldiers were standing in columns and on the other side thousands of people were welcoming him with joy. He quietly stood in the position suggested by the officer.

The next day some three lakh Bengalees gathered at a ground in Dacca to listen to the country's first Governor General. They did not know any language other than their mother tongue Bengali. Unfortunately, their supreme leader did not know any language other than English. Jinnah addressed them for an hour in English and the people clapped at times without understanding a word of what he had said. He said, "You must remain vigilant against the enemies opposed to our progress. They may misguide you. No nation can survive without a national language. Urdu and Urdu alone will remain as the national language of Pakistan. I know our enemies have planted some spies in your midst, but with the grace of God we will not allow them to succeed in their design."

Jinnah clearly hinted at India when he referred to "our enemies." He wanted to quell the unrest among the Bengalees over the issue of Urdu being made the national language by fanning the communal animosity towards the Hindus and India. He himself did not know the Urdu language. In fact, even among the seventy million Muslims of Pakistan, only the five million refugees who came from India knew the Urdu language. These refugees, called *Mohajirs*, were treated like aliens by the rest of the Pakistanis. When Jinnah finished his speech, the Gods in heaven perhaps must have laughed at him. The unity that he was trying to forge by fanning the animosity was to break in a few years on the very issue of language. And he had sown the seeds of disharmony.

74

Jinnah's desire to meet Badshah Khan-Qayyum Khan, denial of permission to Liaquat to meet Jinnah, Jinnah's condition—Dr. Riyaz Ali, Sri Prakash—Jinnah House, Jinnah residence in Ziarat, treatment by Dr. Illah Baksh

Jinnah's health was deteriorating. The burden of the Office was telling on him. He would get exhausted after working for a few hours. He organised the office work in such a way that all the files relating to important matters would come to him first before they were sent to the Ministers concerned so that he could pass orders. The Ministers resented this. That the Prime Minister opposed the style of the functioning of the Governor General was an open secret.

Jinnah's mental condition also deteriorated along with his physical condition. Immediately after the partition, he declared that there would be no minorities and majority in Pakistan and that all the people would have equal rights and that they would work together for building the new nation. He also declared that the Hindus would enjoy equal political rights and that the Muslim League would be now rechristened as the Pakistan National League. This was not acceptable to the League. It decided to retain its identity. In order to keep the League alive in India, a meeting of the Indian Muslims was convened at Madras.

Jinnah wanted to meet Badshah Khan to utilize his services for building Pakistan. Jinnah knew that the people in Sindh, Bengal and the North West Frontier Province were poor and did not have any work for a greater part of the year. Jinnah was opposed to Gandhi's popular spinning wheel and the *Khadi* movement. But he could see the movement generating employment and income for the poor. He had ridiculed the spinning wheel for political expediency. Now he wanted to take the help of Badshah Khan to popularize the spinning wheel in Pakistan. He entrusted the task to Qayyum Khan who worked under Badshah Khan as a *Khudai Khidmatgaar*. He had been a Congress member of the provincial assembly of the North West Frontier Province. He left the Congress when Dr. Khan Sahib did not make him a minister in his government. He had contested the election against the Congress and lost. After that he joined the Muslim League. Jinnah told him,

"Badshah Khan has opposed the League throughout his life. But he has a unique place among the Pathans. It will be a great service to the nation if we can forget the opposition and utilize his services in building the nation. I want you to meet Badshah Khan and convey this to him. If he agrees, I will meet him."

Though Qayyum Khan agreed with Jinnah, he did not like the idea of Badshah Khan coming close to Jinnah in this manner. Because of his prejudice against Badshah Khan, Jinnah's desire to meet him never materialized.

Jinnah was unable to cope up with the increasing work in his office. The files were piling up. He was not sending them to the concerned Ministers either. Because of this, the government machinery came to a standstill. Liaquat Ali Khan sought an appointment with him to discuss the problem. He sent a note stating that this had tarnished the image of Pakistan and its progress was hampered.

Jinnah was enraged on reading the note. He told his private secretary, "Go and tell Liaquat that I have created Pakistan. I have secured this country with the help of a clerk and a typewriter. I do not need anybody's advice. I know why he wants to meet me. I have no time to spare for him."

The secretary was stunned. He politely drew his attention to the government procedure, "Quaid-e-Azam, I cannot convey your message directly to the Prime Minister. However, if you wish I can pass your message to his secretary."

"Do what you think is right, but do not disturb me," ordered Jinnah.

The rumors about his health spread thick and fast. The health bulletins that Jinnah's doctor Riyaz Ali issued every day added to the rumor mills. Of late, he was seen less in his office. He was not entertaining any visitors. Jinnah suspected that Liaquat's request for an appointment was an excuse to find out the condition of his health.

Jinnah would sit in the lawns of his bungalow and doze off quite often. It posed a grave problem for his security guards. The height of the compound wall was now raised. Sometimes he would yell at his ADC,

"That plant with red flowers is not growing properly. Why do not you pay attention. Tell the gardener that the trimming of all the plants should look alike."

"Red colour!" The ADC looked surprised and then said, "Sir, they are pink."

"Whatever! The trimming of all the plants should like alike," ordered Jinnah.

The ADC bent his head in agreement.

Jinnah, who was never attracted to any flower or its smell or its beauty, was particular till his last days that every plant should be neat and trimmed properly.

On one occasion when Dr. Riyaz Ali came to examine him, Jinnah said,

"Doctor, why do you examine me every day? Nothing has happened to me. Yes, sometimes I get fever, but that is due to my advancing age. I get tired. I have been working fourteen hours a day for the past fifty years. You go, do not waste your time."

The doctor was taken aback. It was against the professional ethics to leave a patient without examining him. At times, patients lose mental balance. A doctor should do what he thinks appropriate and not listen to the patient.

"I am sorry doctor," said Jinnah. "Sometimes I am unreasonable. You do not feel bad. Come, examine me. But I am sure, I have no disease."

Sri Prakash, India's newly appointed High Commissioner to Pakistan, came to meet Jinnah. Though he was not entertaining any visitors of late, he agreed to meet him. Jinnah had met him many times in India as he was an eminent Congress leader. Jinnah remembered his gentle, courteous and pleasant nature. He was happy to meet a former colleague after the partition. Jinnah reminisced the days spent in Delhi, Lucknow and Bombay. He remembered his bungalow at the Mount Pleasant Road in Bombay and the pains that he had taken to build it. How nice it would be if he could spend a few days in that bungalow !

He was lost in his thoughts when Sri Prakash came to meet him. After the formal greetings, Jinnah enquired about his bungalow known as the 'Jinnah House' in Bombay. He said,

"Sri Prakash, I want that my palatial bungalow is maintained properly."

"Quaid-e-Azam," said Sri Prakash, "Jawaharlal has sent a message for you. It became necessary for the government of India to take the possession of your house in Bombay. The government was keeping quiet all these days. But now there is a public outcry and the newspapers raise the question now and then as to why the government is not taking the possession of the house."

Jinnah was stunned. His face betrayed the shock.

"Sri Prakash, please tell Jawaharlal..." Jinnah's voice quivered, "Not to take the possession of the House. You all know, how much pain I took to build that House. It has beautiful verandahs and serene atmosphere..." Jinnah closed his eyes and was lost in his thoughts.

Sri Prakash was surprised. This behaviour was something unusual.

"And in case the Indian government takes the possession of the house..." Jinnah said opening his eyes overwhelmed by emotion, "then I may be permitted to stay in that house whenever I want. I love Bombay and that house very much."

"Really! Quaid-e-Azam! Do you want to come and stay in Bombay sometimes?" a surprised Sri Prakash asked him.

"Yes, that city gave me so much. I am deeply indebted to that city," said Jinnah.

"Then should I convey this to Jawaharlal?" asked Sri Prakash.

"Yes. Please do," said Jinnah gasping due to exhaustion. Sri Prakash looked at him. Then Jinnah said, "And tell Jawaharlal that if ever the house was rented out to anyone, it should be on the condition that it would be vacated whenever I come to stay there." Jinnah paused for a moment, took a deep breath and then said, "That house be rented out to no ordinary person. Tell Jawaharlal to rent it to a small European family or to an Indian prince. And not to anyone else."

It was ironical that Jinnah who claimed to be the sole representative of a hundred million Muslims of India, was making a condition that his bungalow should not be rented out to a Muslim. The man, called the greatest Indian Muslim after Aurangzeb, was forbidding the entry of a Muslim in his bungalow. It was a quirk of fate.

Jinnah's health was fast deteriorating. He was getting fever almost every day. He was too weak to move around. He continued to drink and smoke. Because of the rainy season his health was seriously affected and he developed a serious breathing problem. Dr. Riyaz Ali felt that if Jinnah was shifted to a dry hill station for three months of the rainy season, he would get some relief from the breathing problem and the intermittent coughing. He advised Prime Minister Liaquat Ali Khan accordingly.

Liaquat was waiting for an excuse. He was upset that Jinnah neither worked nor allowed others to work. Besides, the Council of Ministers, the Maulvis and the Ulemas were unhappy about the statements he was making now and then on the policy matters of the government. His dream of Pakistan was totally different from theirs. If the Hindus and the Sikhs were the equal citizens, Pakistan was to be governed by a modern democratic law and not by the *Shariat*, what was the need for creating Pakistan? This question troubled everyone. Liaquat thought that if Jinnah was sent out of the capital on the pretext of his poor health, the situation would improve and then he would be able to carry out the government business independently. He immediately accepted the doctor's advice. And he chose Ziarat—a hill station seventy kilometers from Quetta. The government bungalow, used as the summer residence by the Governor of the North West Frontier Province, was converted into a temporary residence of the Governor General. Jinnah along with his office staff and sister Fatima reached Ziarat.

However, even the dry and pleasant climate of Ziarat could not improve the health of Jinnah. He found it difficult to talk even normally. Dr. Riyaz Ali's treatment was doing no good. A message was sent to the Prime Minister's Office to relieve Lt. Col. Dr. Illah Baksh of the Indian Medical Service from his duties and send to Ziarat for the treatment of the Governor General. The Chief Secretary of the Pakistan government contacted Dr. Illah Baksh at his residence in Lahore and instructed him to proceed to Ziarat immediately.

On reaching Ziarat, Dr. Bakhsh met Fatima. Jinnah was fast asleep. After getting the necessary information, he went through the patient's file. He discussed the patient's condition with Dr. Riyaz Ali till late night. The next day morning, he was introduced to Jinnah.

"Good morning Your Excellency," the doctor steeped in the military tradition greeted Jinnah.

Jinnah looked up and said to him, "Doctor, you must know that the Britishers were addressed in that manner. It reminds me of slavery. I do not like anybody addressing me in that manner. You can call me 'Quaid-e-Azam' or ' Sir,' at the most."

The doctor looked at him. Jinnah was gasping for breath. His lips were quivering. The doctor removed his shirt to examine him. He was stunned. Jinnah's body had become like a skeleton and so that it could be easily held in the palm of a hand. One could count each and every rib of the body. It looked as if the skin was just hanging on the bones. The doctor wondered how the patient was still alive.

"Doctor, nothing has happened to me," said Jinnah, "It's only some stomach upset. I just need some rest."

The doctor looked at him astonished.

"And listen," Jinnah continued, "The doctors in London examined my stomach and advised me to go for a surgery. But I did not accept their advice. I was examined by a German doctor. He told me to get admitted to his hospital and get the treatment for three weeks. But how can I spare so much time? Then the doctors in Bombay told me that my heart is weak, but the German doctors assured me that I am hale and hearty…

Dr. Baksh listened quietly. That helped him to understand the physical and mental condition of the patient. He immediately started the treatment.

"Quaid-e-Azam, you will have to stop drinking and smoking from today," the doctor advised.

"How is that possible, Doctor? I have been smoking at least fifty cigarettes a day for the past thirty years. In spite of that, I did not have any major ailment," said Jinnah.

The doctor looked at him and then said, "Look, there is no harm if the smoke does not get into the lungs with breathing. If you can ensure that you can smoke one cigarette every day..."

Jinnah did not object to that. But the next day when the doctor saw the four cigarette butts in the ashtray, he reminded the patient.

"But, doctor, you said there was no harm if the smoke did not get into the lungs. I smoked the four cigarettes taking care of that."

The doctor was surprised by the logic of Barrister Jinnah. He realized that he would not be able to treat the patient only by his medical knowledge.

75

Jinnah in Ziarat, buying of waistcoat, Jinnah's message on the first anniversary of independence of Pakistan, Jinnah's serious condition, return to Karachi, the last breath

The beautiful and pleasant atmosphere of Ziarat was enchanting. The intermittent drizzle made the soil moist and spread a wonderful fragrance. The cool and pleasant climate could have been a great joy for a normal person, but Jinnah found it bitterly cold. When it did not rain, the atmosphere became warm.

"Fati," Jinnah asked, "Have you brought my waistcoat?"

She did not find it among his clothes. Instead, she handed him over his sweater.

"No, I want the waistcoat. If it was left behind, send someone to get a new one."

Fatima sent a staff member to the market and got it. Jinnah liked its colour and its woollen texture. He wore it.

After three days the waistcoat was given for a wash. The colour of the waistcoat faded. Jinnah summoned the person who bought the waistcoat,

"Where did you buy this waistcoat from?" He demanded, "Go and tell the shopkeeper that he has cheated."

He went to the shopkeeper and returned after two hours.

"Sir," he said, "the shopkeeper has no stock to exchange it. He said that he would exchange it when he gets a new stock."

"In that case, you should have asked for some discount and collected the money.

Go and tell him that the colour of the waistcoat has faded and, therefore, he should give some discount."

He went to the shop again. It was quite far away. He returned after a few hours and handed over five rupees. Jinnah took the money and said,

"Youngman, you must understand the value of money."

While climbing down the stairs, the young man smiled mischievously and muttered,

"Who will tell him that it is not the shopkeeper who returned the five rupees, but it is me who paid the amount to close the matter?"

Pakistan celebrated the first anniversary of its independence on 14th August. As per the tradition followed in other countries, Pakistan wanted to broadcast a message of the Governor General on the occasion. But Jinnah was not in a position to go to the radio station and record the message. His voice was also weak. Liaquat and his Council of Ministers insisted that the message should be relayed from Karachi. Jinnah agreed, but he did not want to raise a needless speculation regarding his health by appearing in public. He sent his written message to the Director of the Karachi radio station for broadcasting.

When he learnt about it, Prime Minister Liaquat Ali Khan felt offended that the Governor General sent the message directly to the radio station and did not have the courtesy of taking him into confidence. He felt it was a breach of protocol. And yet he thought it prudent not to make an issue of it. As per the information he received, Jinnah was in his last days. But when his message was broadcasted on the radio, Liaquat and his colleagues were stunned.

Jinnah in his message to the nation said, "Today we are celebrating the first anniversary of our independence. We faced the year with fortitude and determination.

I compliment you all and particularly Prime Minister Liaquat Ali Khan for his leadership.

I would like to remind you once again what I had said in my first address to the Constituent Assembly. There is no such thing as the majority and the minorities in Pakistan. All are equal citizens. Just as there are Brahmins, Vaishyas and Shudras among the Hindus, there are Shias, Sunnis and Pathans among the Muslims. There are linguistic majorities among the minorities like the Bengalees, the Punjabis, the Sindhis and the Pathans. These had created hurdles in India's struggle for freedom and Pakistan was created. Now we do not want to create New Pakistan."

This was his last public address. The public career of a young nationalist Jinnah, who had been opposed to the Muslim League and worked closely with the Congress, had come full circle. The clock had come to its full circumference.

Jinnah's intake of food had reduced considerably. He stopped eating altogether after 28th August. He was not able to eat even pork his favourite food. He would turn away his face on seeing the dinner plate. Dr. Illah Baksh was particular that he should eat something. When he tried to offer him some food, Jinnah screamed at him saying,

"Doctor, don't you know that I have taken my food? Why do you offer me the food again and again? Today I have eaten more food than what I used to eat even in my younger days. You can check my stomach."

The doctor was lost in deep thought. The patient did not eat anything for the past four or five days. After sometime, the doctor asked,

"Quaid-e-Azam, today is Friday. I will tell the chef to prepare your favourite dish. Tell me what you would like to eat."

Jinnah opened his eyes. He nodded his head and turned to his sister, "Fati."

"Yes...*Bhaijaan*..." said Fatima.

"Do you know the special dish *laapsi*[1] that our family used to make at Karachi?" Every one in the room was eager to listen.

"Yes, I do, *Bhaijaan.* Whenever *laapsi* was cooked, Ghee was poured and sugar sprinkled ..." Fatima recalled.

"I want to eat *laapsi* today. Can you prepare it? The chef will not be able to prepare it," Jinnah pleaded with Fatima.

The people in the room stared at each other. The doctor was happy that at last Jinnah would eat something.

The doctor was astonished when Jinnah ate the *laapsi* prepared by Fatima. When the hot *laapsi* was brought in a bowl and the ghee and the sugar were mixed, his mouth watered. When the doctor saw him eating to his heart's content the delicacy of his native land Kathiawar, he thought he could perhaps save his life this way.

But that was not to be. It was the last time that Jinnah ate food. After that he stopped eating completely. He did not even look at the various delicacies brought for him every day. The Kathiawari *laapsi* that his mother Mithibai used to make was the last meal that the Governor General of Pakistan had in his life.

It was the first week of September. The doctor gave up the hope of his survival. Most of the time, Jinnah was unconscious and whenever he regained his consciousness, he talked incoherently. It looked as if a skeleton wrapped in clothes lay on the bed as his structure did not resemble a human body of flesh and bones. After consulting Fatima, the doctor decided to shift him back to Karachi. Every possible treatment was given to him in this bungalow at Ziarat during the past three months. And it was prudent that he spent his last days in the Governor General's House in Karachi rather than in this bungalow in a remote and unknown place. Initially, Fatima was against informing Liaquat Ali Khan about Jinnah's return to Karachi. But the doctor felt that it was neither advisable nor practical. However, he ensured that a very few people knew about Jinnah's return to Karachi. Even the staff at the airport did not know who was flying in the special aircraft.

11th September 1948

When Jinnah was taken to the Governor General's House from the Karachi airport, he was totally unconscious. With the exception of his monocle, everything that he insisted on wearing—the suit, the tie and the shoes—was intact. Fatima always sat by his side. Prime Minister Liaquat Ali Khan quietly entered Jinnah's room. There was an agonizing silence in the room. Fatima looked at Liaquat. Her eyes turned reddish and moist. Her lips were quivering. Liaquat observed her and quietly turned his back. Fatima put her hand on the head of her brother, lowered her head and then with a choking voice screamed,

"*Bhaijaan*, if you had not listened to this scoundrel and stayed back in London, we would have been living there happily today. *Bhaijaan*, Liaquat and Begum Rana have made a fool of you. The person who never allowed anybody to manoeuvre him, had become a victim of their ploy." Then Fatima started sobbing.

Whether Jinnah heard or not what Fatima had said nobody knew, but he opened his eyes before she stopped sobbing. The pupils in his sunken eyes stood still. There was a stillness in the atmosphere outside. It was getting darker. Fatima lifted her head and looked at Jinnah. His lips quivered. Fatima put her ears to his lips.

"Fati," she heard as if the voice came from a cave.

"Doctor, come quick," Fatima screamed.

Dr. Illah Baksh along with his colleagues were standing. All of them surrounded Jinnah's bed. Dr. Baksh took Jinnah's hand and tried frantically to locate his pulse, but in vain. Frightened, he put his finger on Jinnah's vein again. The pulse was too weak. He signalled to Dr. Mistry, who handed him an injection. Dr. Baksh tried to inject the syringe into Jinnah's body. There was no flesh between the bones and the skin. The doctor with a great difficulty found a soft point to inject the syringe, but the fluid in the injection could not enter the body, because there was no life in the body. The dead body now lying on the bed which once belonged to Barrister Muhammad Ali Jinabhai Punja Valji Thakkar, village Paneli, District Rajkot, Kathiawar—*alias* the Governor General of Pakistan. As Dr. Illah Bakhsh pulled out the syringe, a chapter in history had come to an end. He covered the body with a blanket. The people standing there lowered their heads. If anybody among the hundred million Muslims had shed tears at his death genuinely it was only Fatima. She clung to her brother's body and sobbed incessantly.

*

Nobody knew the exact period of the reign of King Dhritrashtra, the grandson of King Shantanu. Perhaps it had been four thousand or five or even ten thousand years ago. The crown prince Duryodhan wanted to ascend to the throne of Hastinapur as an heir to his father. But King Dhritrashtra himself was not a rightful heir to the throne. He was a caretaker of the throne that belonged to his brother Pandu. When Pandu's heir Yudhishthir asked for his right eighteen divisions of army were annihilated in the battlefield of Kurukshetra. There was not a single family in *Aryavart*[2] which had not been affected by this gruesome war. The scholars believe that the battlefield of Kurukshetra lies somewhere in the region between Delhi and Karachi. The land that had been strewn with the blood and flesh of the eighteen divisions of army once again witnessed gruesome killings after thousands of years. The *panchmahabhut*—the five elements which include the earth, the water, the wind, the sky and the fire—all turned red with the human blood.

Neither Duryodhan nor Yudhishthir had ever demarcated a boundary on this land. Neither Mountbatten nor Radcliffe nor Jinnah had been able to draw a clear line on this subcontinent. The land was the same—the one and undivided. Only the five holy rivers were soaked in blood[3].

When Jinnah's soul departed from his body at 10.00 p.m. on 11th September,1948, the soul of Duryodhan, the destroyer of the eighteen army divisions, felt that it had at last found a worthy heir thousands of years later. Duryodhan felt happy that a man as capable as himself had met a similar fate. He wholeheartedly welcomed Jinnah's soul.

NOTES

1. A traditional sweet dish cooked in Gujarat.
2. The ancient legendary name of the land known as India today.
3. The characters and episode relate to the story of great Indian Epic 'Mahabharat'.

Bibliography

1.	Gandhiji Ni Dinwari (Gujarati)	Chandulal Dalal
2.	Purnahuti: Parts 1,2,3 and 4 (The Last Phase)	Pyarelal
3.	Ruttie Jinnah	Kanji Dwarkadas
4.	Creator of Pakistan	Hector Bolitho
5.	Roses in December	M. C. Chagla
6.	India Wins Freedom	Maulana Azad
7.	Mahadev Desai's Diaries	Mahadev Desai
8.	Satya Na Prayogo (Autobiography)	M.K.Gandhi
9.	Ketlak Juno Patro (translated into Gujarati)	Jawaharlal Nehru
10.	Mari Jivan Katha (translated into Gujarati)	Jawaharlal Nehru
11.	Sardar Patel	Rajmohan Gandhi.
12.	Jinnah Faces an Assassin	Barrister
13.	India's Fight for Freedom	Kanji Dwarkadas
14.	My Life and Struggle	Badshah Khan
15.	Mohammed Ali Jinnah	S.K.Bandopadhyay
16.	Partition and Independence of India	Manmathnath Das
17.	Jinnah of Pakistan	Stanley Wolpert
18.	Memories of Jinnah	K.H. Khurshid
19.	The Tragic Story of Pakistan	H.V. Sheshadri
20.	Freedom at Midnight	Larry Collins/ Dominique L.
21.	Acharya Kripalani Ni Atmakatha (translated into Gujarati)	Nagindas Parekh
22.	The Life of Mahomet	William Muir
23.	The Transfer of Power in India	V.P.Menon
24.	Mohammed Ali Jinnah	Matlubul Saiyed
25.	Quaid-i-Azam Jinnah	Sharif Al Mujahid
26.	A History of the Freedom Movement	Pakistan Historical Soceity

27.	Sardar Patel No Patra Vyavahar	Compiled by V.Shankar
28.	Struggle of Freedom	Bhartiya Vidya Bhavan
29.	Hind No Komi Trikon	Ashok Mehta/ A. Patwardhan
30.	Mountbatten and Independent India	Lorry Collins/ Dominique L.
31.	Mountbatten and Partition of India	Lorry Collins/ Dominique L.
32.	India Divided	Rajendra Prasad
33.	The Memories of Aga Khan	Aga Khan
34.	India in Transition	Aga Khan
35.	Indian Muslims: Who are They	K.S.Lal
36.	Facts are Facts	Wali Khan
37.	Hindu View of Christianity and Islam	Ram Swarup
38.	Negationism in India	Koenrad Elst
39.	Looking Back	Mehrchand Mehajan
40.	Mr. Jinnah: A Political Study	V.N. Naik
41.	The Sole Spokesman	Ayesha Jalal
42.	Transfer of Power 1942-47 Vols. 1 to 10	British Government
43.	Bharat Vibahjan Ke Gunhagar	Ram Manohar Lohia